GIACOMO JOYCE
ENVOYS OF THE OTHER

edited by

LOUIS ARMAND & CLARE WALLACE

þ
Litteraria Pragensia
Prague 2006

First edition published in the United States by Academica Press, 2002
Second revised and enlarged edition published 2006 by Litteraria
Pragensia Books
Faculty of Philosophy, Charles University
Náměstí Jana Palacha 2, 116 38 Prague 1
Czech Republic
www.litterariapragensia.com

The publication of this book has been supported by research grant
MSM0021620824 "Foundations of the Modern World as Reflected in
Literature and Philosophy" awarded to the Faculty of Philosophy,
Charles University, Prague, by the Czech Ministry of Education.

Cataloguing in Publication Data

Giacomo Joyce: Envoys of the Other, edited by Louis Armand & Clare
Wallace .—2nd ed.

    p. cm.
  ISBN 80-239-5046-0 (pb)
  1. James Joyce. 2. Modernism. 3. Literature.
  I. Armand, Louis. II. Title

Printed in the Czech Republic by PB Tisk

Envoy: Love me, love my umbrella.

Contents

Preface

Of all James Joyce's extant works, *Giacomo Joyce* is the one which has least received what is arguably its due. After the initial critical interest which accompanied its publication had subsided, few Joyce scholars—apart from most notably Vicki Mahaffey and Joseph Valente—explored *Giacomo Joyce* in anything like an extended or comprehensive manner. Other critical encounters with *Giacomo Joyce* have appeared sporadically, but these have largely been dispersed in periodicals and sundry publications. Similarly, a number of important theoretical encounters with Joyce's text, as in the work of Jacques Derrida, have remained on the margins of Joyce scholarship, while at the same time informing, even if elliptically, a significant body of other "poststructuralist" writings whose relevance for *Giacomo Joyce* has not often been acknowledged.

The otherwise erratic availability of scholarship on the text has meant that *Giacomo Joyce* has repeatedly been "discovered," and this has sometimes lead to the reiteration of certain biographical speculations and considerations first raised by Richard Ellmann in 1959, as well as to a tendency on the part of critics to "review" the text, as though groping to find a suitable placement or critical vocabulary for what is made to appear an inexplicable curiosity. As a result, *Giacomo Joyce* has often been treated as predominantly a transitional and marginal work, or as an eccentric stage in the evolution of Joyce's principal *œuvre*.

This book, the first collection of essays devoted entirely to *Giacomo Joyce*, is an attempt to place the critical reception of this text on a less tentative and precarious footing. The selection here is, of course, not exhaustive and some of the work which might have been included has, inevitably, been omitted. However, in compiling the accompanying bibliography, we have attempted, wherever possible, to acknowledge the contribution of those who have written on *Giacomo Joyce*, while at the same time providing an essential resource for future studies of Joyce's text.

One of our objectives has been to treat *Giacomo Joyce* as a work deserving of critical attention in its own right. In assembling a body of scholarship which engages with the text in multiple ways, we hope to initiate a more extensive dialogue and debate on *Giacomo Joyce*, one which goes beyond biographical criticism and seeks to more directly address the complexities of Joyce's text. The contributors to this volume have brought various and divergent theories to their readings of *Giacomo Joyce*. We have not sought to reconcile their differences, but rather, in juxtaposing them, to allow their mutual consonance and discord to emerge in what will hopefully be a provocative and productive manner.

The first edition of this book, published in 2002 by Academica Press in the USA, was made largely unavailable to the reading public and is out of print. We regret that the circumstances of its publication served to counteract our intentions in assembling the present collection as a resource for scholars and students of Joyce. The occasion of this revised edition has, however, allowed us to make a number of corrections to the earlier text and to add two further appendices: a translation of the review of *Giacomo Joyce* published in 1968 by the well-known French theorist Hélène Cixous; and an essay primarily on Jacques Derrida's *The Post Card*, by Gayatri Spivak, which provides supporting context for contributions by Murray McArthur, Joseph Valente, and others in this volume, while also providing a subtle, allusive reading of Joyce's own text via its sublimation and "deconstruction" in Derrida's. Arguably, the "influence" of Joyce here resides not in the exercise of citation and canonicity, but in the effect of a certain marginalisation and unnamability—that aspect of Joyce's work too often supplanted in Joyce's centralisation as a figure of literary historical orthodoxy, but which is necessarily brought into play the moment we confront questions such as "legitimacy" vis-à-vis the status of texts like *Giacomo Joyce*.

Many people have assisted and supported this project. We would particularly like to thank Marjorie Perloff, Ellen Berry, Keith Hopper, Roberta Gefter Wondrich and David Baxter for their generous assistance in locating materials; William Brockman for his assistance in compiling bibliographical data; and Fritz Senn, Giorgio Melchiori, Geert Lernout and Donald Theall for their encouragement and suggestions. We are indebted to John McCourt and Renzo Crivelli for the opportunity to participate in the Trieste James Joyce Summer School in 2000, which proved a source of numerous insights into Joyce's period in Trieste. We are also grateful to Hélène Cixous for permission to publish a translation of "«Giacomo Joyce»: les sanglots ironiques d'Eros" (which originally appeared in *Le Monde*, 17 Août [1968]); to Gayatri Spivak for permission to reprint her essay "Love me, love my ombre, elle" (a version of which previously appeared in *Diacritics* [Winter 1984]: 19-36); to Vicki Mahaffey and Greenwood Press for permission to reprint "Giacomo Joyce" (a version of which first appeared in *A Companion to Joyce Studies*, eds. Zack Bowen and James F. Carens [Westport, CT: Greenwood Press, 1984] 387-420); to the *Joyce Studies Annual* (1990) for permission to reprint Richard Brown's article "Eros and Apposition: *Giacomo Joyce*" (132-141); and to the *James Joyce Quarterly* for permission to reprint Fritz Senn's "Some Further Notes on *Giacomo Joyce*" (*JJQ* 5 [1968] 233-236).

Clare Wallace & Louis Armand
Prague, April 2006

Abbreviations and Reference Style

GJ   *Giacomo Joyce*. Ed. Richard Ellmann. New York: Viking, 1968.

CP   *Collected Poems*. New York: Viking Press, 1957.

D   *Dubliners*. Ed. Robert Scholes with Richard Ellmann. New York: Viking Press, 1967.

E   *Exiles*. New York: Penguin, 1973.

P   *A Portrait of the Artist as a Young Man*. The definitive text corrected from the Dublin Holograph by Chester G. Anderson and ed. Richard Ellmann. New York: Viking Press, 1966.

U   +page number. *Ulysses*. New York: Random House, 1934, reset and corrected 1961.

U   +episode and line number. *Ulysses*. Ed. Hans Walter Gabler et al. New York and London: Garland Publishing, 1984, 1986. In paperback by Garland, Random House, Bodley Head and Penguin between 1986 and 1992.

FW   *Finnegans Wake*. New York: Viking Press, 1958.

CW   *The Critical Writings of James Joyce*. Eds. Ellsworth Mason and Richard Ellmann. New York: Viking Press, 1959.

JJI	Ellmann, Richard. *James Joyce*. Oxford: Oxford University Press, 1959.
JJII	Ellmann, Richard. *James Joyce*. Revised edition. Oxford: Oxford University Press, 1982.
L	*Letters of James Joyce*. Vol. I, ed. Stuart Gilbert. New York: Viking Press, 1957; re-issued with corrections 1966. Vols. II and III, ed. Richard Ellmann. New York: Viking Press, 1966.
Poems	*Poems and Shorter Writings*. Eds. Richard Ellmann, A. Walton Litz and John Whittier-Ferguson. London: Faber, 1991.
SL	*Selected Letters*. Ed. Richard Ellmann. New York: Viking Press, 1975.
JJQ	*James Joyce Quarterly*

Introduction

Through a Glass Darkly: Reflections on the Other Joyce

Why bastard? Wherefore base?
My mind is as generous and my shape as true,
As honest madam's issue? Why brand they us
With base? With baseness? Bastardy? Base, base?
(Shakespeare, *King Lear* I.ii.6-10)

Since its publication in 1968, the critical reception of *Giacomo Joyce* has been defined largely by a concern with biographical placement, stylistic transitions and the vicissitudes of authorial intention. Doubtless this is symptomatic of a certain novelty which this text has offered critics over the last thirty or so years. A novelty which nevertheless more often translates into marginalisation. It is the novelty of a text whose status, within an industry otherwise overly capitalised and overly authorised, remains uncertain if not problematic or, indeed, problematising. In every sense a posthumous text, *Giacomo Joyce* describes an uncanny double, a doppelgänger, a *shemblable*, a bastard self whose illegitimacy as regards the Joycean corpus "proper" has contributed to its being not only Joyce's least critically accessed work, but also, one might say, his least accessible.

One of the premises of this volume is that it takes seriously the claim that *Giacomo Joyce* should be treated on its own terms.

At the same time, however, it is important that the rather unique position of *Giacomo Joyce* with regards to Joyce's other writings should not itself be temporised, or glossed over, in an attempt to engineer a belated succession to the Joycean canon. Despite Richard Ellmann's somewhat whimsical remarks ("When, not long before his death, Joyce said that he would write something very simple and very short, he was thinking perhaps of how he had solidified the small, fragile, transitory perfection of his Triestine pupil into the small, fragile, enduring perfection of *Giacomo Joyce*" [*GJ* xxvi]), there remains no evidence to suggest that Joyce ever actually considered publishing this sixteen page manuscript. Nor, however, is there any way of knowing that, had he lived, some form of revisitation might not have been one of any number of eventualities. There were certainly precedents for Joyce returning to pieces that he had otherwise forgot or discarded. Notable among these are the so-called *Finn's Hotel* vignettes, which Joyce sent in 1923 to Harriet Shaw Weaver to be typed, and then seemed to forget about until *Finnegans Wake* had almost been completed. Be this as it may, one should remain cautious of the special pleading which inevitably accompanies such speculations.

While it may not be a question of claiming an "enduring perfection" for Joyce's seemingly most incidental and fugitive of writings, it does not follow that *Giacomo Joyce* should receive the qualified attention of a secondary text, a mere appendage or appendix to the authorised texts of Joyce. That is to say, as merely a set of autobiographical instructions—something devoid of any textual complexion of its own. On the other hand, it can be argued that it is precisely the "secondary," or supplemental nature of *Giacomo Joyce* which, in light of the textual theories emerging at the time of its publication, lends it a particularly deconstructive force. As a text "on the margin" of the Joycean canon, and itself preoccupied with a certain liminality, it represents not only an other-Joyce, but an othering of Joyce.

In a review published in *Le Monde* in August 1968, entitled *"Giacomo Joyce*: Les sanglots ironiques d'Éros," Hélène Cixous provides one of the earliest readings of the othering of Joyce in the persona of "Giacomo." But while Cixous accepts uncritically Ellmann's biography of the *dark lady* of Joyce's "suppressed" envoy, she nevertheless presents a more ambiguous view of Joyce's treatment of this feminine "other." Projection, transgression, fertilisation—these "tropes" of Eros describe a substitutive reflexivity which extends to the reflexivity of the text itself. A play of doubles—a dialectics of desire crossed through by what Cixous elsewhere describes as a "subject waiting for itself," coming to itself, sending itself.[1] "Joycean eroticism is not merely satisfied with one-sided transgression [...]. It must be said that for Joyce the process of fertilisation is reversible: masculine-feminine, the artist is fertilised himself through the channel of the imaginary."[2] Projection and deferral of the consummative act gives rise to writing, and writing in turn substitutes for the act.

While this more writerly or textualist approach circumvents the biographical fallacy and points in the direction of Joyce's abstractionist concerns elsewhere, Cixous's simultaneous deferral to the assertions of biographical facticity give rise to a set of questions regarding textual authority which need to be addressed. While much has been said about the care with which Joyce cultivated and manipulated his public image, it is important not to forget that this image nevertheless comes to us in a highly interpreted fashion. Just as the Nietzsche familiar to readers of English can be thought of as largely a creature of Walter Kaufmann, so too can Joyce be seen as a creation of Richard Ellmann. From the publication of his 842 page *James Joyce* in 1959, until his death in 1987, Ellmann's official version

---

[1] Hélène Cixous, "Joyce: the (r)use of writing," trans. Judith Still, *Post-structuralist Joyce: Essays from the French,* eds. Derek Attridge and Daniel Ferrer (London: Cambridge University Press, 1984) 15.

[2] Hélène Cixous, "*Giacomo Joyce*: Les Sanglots ironiques d'Éros," rev. of *Giacomo Joyce,* by James Joyce, *Le Monde* 17 Aug. 1968: IV.

of Joyce underwrote almost the entire project of Joycean scholarship.

While several of the essays included in this volume touch upon problems with Ellmann's dating, and with his methodology, the question of his authority as such, and of the complicity of scholars in the affecting of that authority, remain to be addressed. This is above all the case in regard to *Giacomo Joyce*. It is already widely believed that Ellmann "discovered" the sketchbook containing Joyce's unpublished manuscript in 1956, among the possessions of Joyce's brother Stanislaus in Trieste, supposedly then facilitating its acquisition by an "anonymous" collector. The account given by Stelio Crise, and reported at length by Vicki Mahaffey, is less oblique: "When Stanislaus died on June 19, 1955, his widow received no pension, so [Ottocaro] Weiss [a friend of Ellmann] helped her sell off the Trieste library, in return for which she gave him *Giacomo Joyce*."[3]

Three years later Ellmann reproduced large portions of the text in his estate-authorised biography (*JJI* 353-60), and nine years after that he edited the complete text for Viking Press. While it has been suggested that the reason for this delay was to protect the sensibilities of certain other parties, the text of the 1959 biography makes this seem unlikely, and Ellmann himself never chose to explain why he waited twelve years to pursue the full publication of *Giacomo Joyce*. In his twenty-six page introduction to the text, however, he clearly anticipated that this was to be the last of Joyce's published writings. In a sense, *Giacomo Joyce* was to be the last word of Joyce, and in another sense, the last word on Joyce. And to a degree this may have something to do with the text's relative marginalisation. Ellmann the authority on Joyce, the author of Joyce, gives us Joyce's "last published work," buried under a weight of

---

[3] Stelio Crise, "Il Triestino James Joyce," *Scritti*, ed. Elvio Guagnini (Trieste: Einaudi, 1994). Cited in Vicki Mahaffey, "Joyful Desire," *States of Desire: Wilde, Yeats, Joyce and the Irish Experiment* (Oxford: Oxford University Press, 1998) 174.

editorial commentary, exegesis and annotation, in place of an actual work he never quite wrote, perhaps.

There is a sense in which Ellmann no doubt regarded the publication of *Giacomo Joyce* as somehow "completing" it, a completion moreover affected under his own imprimatur, as though he himself were signing Joyce's name to it, in place of Joyce, conveying Joyce's envoy to its proper, final destination. In any case, the publication of *Giacomo Joyce*, as a "posthumous" work, was for all intents and purposes a still birth, an already closed book, and much of what has subsequently been written about it seems to reinforce this view.

It would seem that a significant challenge facing Joyce critics is to effectively extract Joyce's work from this overly determined placement. Hence, in bringing together these particular writings on *Giacomo Joyce*, this volume does not so much seek to consolidate a field or discipline, as to provide a critical context from which future readings of Joyce's text might productively deviate, in turn subjecting the work published here to constructive scrutiny and in so doing scrutinise the terms under which much of the writing on *Giacomo Joyce* has proceeded. It is appropriate, in this respect, that many of the approaches to *Giacomo Joyce* have focused upon questions of otherness. But if Joyce's later writings are any measure of this, it is the otherness of the text itself, as fugitive, subordinated, bastardised, suppressed, which most demands accounting for. And which at the same time, perhaps, provides its most singular critical impetus.

HYPOCRITE LECTEUR

The author of Ulysses, *after having written his own odyssey (itself haunted by a "blindman"), ends his life almost blind, one cornea operation after another. Hence the themes of the iris and glaucoma pervade* Finnegans Wake *("... the shuddersome spectacle of this semidemented zany amid the inspissated grime of his glaucous den making believe to read his usylessly unreadable Blue Book of Eccles,*

> *édition de ténèbres ...").* *The whole Joycean œuvre cultivates seeing eye canes.* (Jacques Derrida, *Mémoires d'aveugle*)[4]

Shem and Shaun, James and Giacomo. In many respects, the Triestine alter ego of the "Dublin Joyce" is itself a doubling of Joyce—silent, exiled, and cunning. What indeed, and who, is this un-authorised Joyce? But here the text is already ahead of us. "Who?" the first word, seems to point above all to that sinister figure of the title script, which Ellmann describes "On the upper left-hand corner of the front cover, the name 'Giacomo Joyce' is inscribed in another hand" (*GJ* xii).

Ellmann's description of the manuscript itself is worth noting. "Joyce wrote it in his best calligraphic hand, without changes, on both sides of eight large sheets, which are loosely held within the nondescript blue-paper covers of a school notebook. The sheets are of heavy paper, oversize, of the sort ordinarily used for pencil sketches rather than for writing assignments. They are faintly reminiscent of those parchment sheets on which in 1909 Joyce wrote out the poems of *Chamber Music* for his wife" (*GJ* xi-xii).

Compared with Joyce's "best calligraphic hand," the other hand in which the name Giacomo Joyce is inscribed on the sketchbook cover appears hesitant, untutored, childish. A halting, uncertain script whose form and placement ought, perhaps, to be considered no less significant than the calculated typography of the fifty textual "fragments" which make up the text of *Giacomo Joyce.* Ellmann, perhaps knowingly, suggests

---

[4] Jacques Derrida, *Memoirs of the Blind: The Self-Portrait and Other Ruins,* trans. Pascale-Anne Brault and Michael Naas (Chicago: University of Chicago Press, 1993) 33.

that the hand-written title was an afterthought, added to the manuscript by someone other than Joyce. He bases this on the claim that "This Italian form of his name was never used by Joyce" (*GJ* xii). Carla Marengo Vaglio, along with a number of other critics, has suggested otherwise, citing numerous instances of Joyce "signing as Jacomo Zois, Jacomo de l'oio (a nobody; a cheat that runs away after having cashed the money for an oil order) and [...] Giacometo."[5]

It is inviting, then, to speculate further on the graphology of this *faux titre*. Perhaps, after all, it is a writing with the left hand, in truth the sinister, mocking counterpart of Joyce's *proper* hand. An *éminence grise*. As Bernard Benstock has suggested: "*Giacomo Joyce*, the title evolving from the written name on the cover of the school notebook in a foreign hand, tentative, halting, unschooled, immature—in other words, 'foreign,' although the possibility might occur to us that since James Joyce is 'celebrating' a clandestine Triestine love affair, he himself might be the masked amanuensis of his own manuscript, a disguised hand, lefthanded."[6]

Perhaps, also, the "cobweb handwriting" of *an other's* hand. "The other. She" (*GJ* 15). The one who, in the first sentence, both composes and discomposes the author-narrator. "Who?" A pair of "quizzing glasses" directed at the withdrawing figure of Joyce, sketching *him* in this other-portrait of the artist. And yet, like the portrait itself, this quizzing gaze is also a prosthesis, an ellipsis in place of seeing. Veiled, pierced, suffering, mortified and mortifying: "a brief beat of the eyelids," "The long eyelids beat and lift: a burning needleprick stings and quivers in the velvet iris" (*GJ* 1), "sloe-eyed" (*GJ* 8), "her full dark suffering eyes" (*GJ* 11), "her black basilisk eyes" (*GJ* 15). *Giacomo Joyce*, then, as a story of the eye. But

---

5   Carla Marengo Vaglio, "Trieste as a Linguistic Melting-Pot," *James Joyce 3: Joyce et l'Italie*, eds. Claude Jacquet and Jean-Michel Rabaté (Paris: Lettres Modernes, 1994) 64.

6   Bernard Benstock, "Paname-Turricum and Tarry Easty: James Joyce's *Città Immediata*," *James Joyce 3: Joyce et l'Italie*, eds. Claude Jacquet and Jean-Michel Rabaté (Paris: Lettres Modernes, 1994) 33.

conspicuously, one drawn, not from, but nevertheless "through" the eyes of the other. A speculative counterpart which, by means of a metonymic sleight of hand, is substituted by a visual prostheses, "to supplement sight and, first of all, to compensate for this transcendental ruin of the eye that threatens and seduces it from the origin."[7] A pair of "quizzing glasses" which frame, in an elliptical fashion, a certain doubling of this imaginary portrait through the suggestion of a literalised iritis. Its subject, "Who?" crossed through by a two-fold objectification between the name of Giacomo, on the one hand, and the pronoun "she," on the other. As Derrida says, "This is the law of the chiasm in the crossing or noncrossing of looks or gazes: fascination by the sight of the other is irreducible to fascination by the eye of the other; indeed, it is incompatible with it. This chiasm does not exclude it but, on the contrary, calls for the haunting of one fascination by another."[8]

The "ghosts" or spectres of Giacomo. "Who?" "They have owls' eyes and owls' wisdom" (*GJ* 8). A subjectless vigilance of the one who knows. Or the object fascination of non-knowledge, of blindness. A "self-created shadow."[9] The negative by means of which the image itself is produced and reproduced. A counter-portrait, as a retelling of the myth of the origin of drawing. Like the story of Butades—a story between truth, love and memory—*Giacomo Joyce* describes a kind of *skiagraphia* or shadow writing, "*édition de ténèbres*" (FW 179.27). Butades draws her lover's portrait by tracing the outline of his shadow cast in profile on a wall, "in order to remember him in his absence." In *Giacomo Joyce*, the question "Who?" on the first page is echoed on the last page by another question, set uncharacteristically within quotation marks, "'Why?' 'Because otherwise *I could not see you*'" (*GJ* 16). Like writing itself, the portrait is a technique of memory, a memorial, a cenotaph, and

---

7 Derrida, *Memoirs of the Blind*, 70.

8 Derrida, *Memoirs of the Blind*, 106.

9 Percy Bysshe Shelley, *The Cenci*, II.2.143. *Shelley's Poetry and Prose*, ed. D. Reiman (New York: Norton, 1977).

so a form of forgetting. At second hand—an art of shadows, of absence, of blindness. "Giacomo Joyce," a figure drawn with the eyes closed? Or self-portrait of the blind? Or, as in *Hamlet*, the shadow of a dream, a dumb show, a shadow-play. Ghost writing.

A PLAY OF MIRRORS

> *(Stephen and Bloom gaze in the mirror. The face of William Shakespeare, beardless, appears there, rigid in facial paralysis, crowned by the reflection of the reindeer antlered hatrack in the hall.)*
> *(U 567)*

Situated temporally and stylistically between *A Portrait of the Artist as a Young Man* and *Ulysses*, there is yet another sense in which *Giacomo Joyce* may be seen as a type of counter-portrait. Or rather, anti-portrait: "Giacomo" as Caliban to the Prospero-like "fabulous artificer" (*U* 270) "invisible, refined out of existence, indifferent, paring his fingernails" in amnesiac detachment (*P* 215). Despite claims by writers like Hélène Cixous about *Giacomo Joyce* being "overwhelming in its verity," an idea has persisted of a type of ill-conceived bastard, an abortive understudy.[10] "*Non hunc sed Barabbam!*" (*GJ* 16). (Barabbas, literally in Hebrew "the son of the father," mocking counterpart of the saturnalian "son of man.")[11] And yet it is difficult to escape the sense that the one mirrors the other. The bastard mirroring the legitimate son-of-the-father ("Old father, old artificer" [*P* 253])—a son nevertheless fitted out in second hand clothes. The borrowed *Metamorphoses* of Dublin mirrored in the discarded *Tristia* of Trieste. A counter-portrait mirroring the *Portrait*, the model mirroring the portrait-artist—"forged" or plagiarised from an already confabulated artificer.

---

10 Cixous, "*Giacomo Joyce*: Les Sanglots ironiques d'Éros," IV.
11 J.G. Frazer, *The Golden Bough*, ed. Robert Fraser (London: Oxford University Press, 1994) 666ff.

But while the prismatic quality of this most "transitional" of Joyce's texts has often if briefly been reflected upon by scholars in search of textual echoes in the other, authoritative works of Joyce, its more affectively transitional nature has been left largely unremarked. Written at the time Joyce was completing the last chapter of *A Portrait of the Artist as a Young Man*, and overlapping at least in part with the composition of *Ulysses* (*GJ* 15), there is the sense in which *Giacomo Joyce* describes a type of chiasm, a two-fold crossing and a crossing-out between two "portraits." Between *A Portrait* and *Ulysses*, *Giacomo Joyce*. Portrait-Giacomo ... Joyce-Ulysses. An ellipsis in which yet another "she," the (m)other, passes away, and in which the son, crossing the sea-mother from Dublin to the continent of exile, returns, a reflection-effect or revenance of himself, summoned by an ambiguous telegraphic instruction (envoy?): "Nother dying come home father" (*U* 42). Cixous:

Between Daedalus and Icarus: *Ulysses*. And: "My will: his will that fronts me. Seas between" (*U* 217). From father unto son, via the mother, always, begun again. This delayed birth constitutes the movement of a work which playfully undermines gestation, the play inscribing itself in the various falls, losses, repeated and unexpected exiles, which are all the more astounding in that the goal seems accessible, is named, puts itself forward, fascinates, is not hidden but rather pointed out (I, the Artist, the Word), is not forbidden but rather promised, and in that the subject, held in suspense, pursues it with [...] the weapons of the self (silence, exile, cunning), marking out its passage with theories, incorporated hypotheses of formalisation: one or two ideas of Aristotle, a pinch of St. Thomas; a chapter on poetics and literary history; several chapters on the problems of autobiography; and, in a pre-Freudian context, an implicit theory of the authorial unconscious, and of the textual unconscious, in a blasphemous analogy with the Arian heresy, showing in the Trinity the three-sided, divinely ordered production that allows the Father to see through the Son's eyes, where the Holy Spirit would be like that chain linking the

Name of the Father to the Name of the Son, the scriptor to writing: the breath of the unconscious on the text.[12]

The spectral son of Dedalus the father: "He proves by algebra that Hamlet's grandson is Shakespeare's grandfather and that he himself is the ghost of his own father" (*U* 18). And between *A Portrait* and *Ulysses*, the cracked glass of a mirror:

> —Look at yourself, he said, you dreadful bard!
>   Stephen bent forward and peered at the mirror held out to him, cleft by a crooked crack. Hair on end. As he and others see me. Who chose this face for me? [*U* 6]

> —The rage of Caliban at not seeing his face in a mirror. [*U* 6]

In any case, one should never take a portrait at face value. As Joyce makes clear, the model, the "subject," is already a spectre, a reflection, a double, a shadow. "Who is the ghost from *limbo patrum*, returning to the world that has forgotten him?" (*U* 188). Mon semblable, mon frère: as Stephen Dedalus says, "A brother is as easily forgotten as an umbrella" (*U* 211). Ombre. Shadow of a shadow. The cracked image cancels itself, blinds itself. Who: the ghost. A portrait "lost in transmission." Its trace nevertheless reserved, *preserved*, for what other service?

> It is a symbol of Irish art. The cracked lookingglass of a servant. [*U* 6]

> *Ulysses* [...] Symbol of the intellectual conscience .... Ireland then? [...] Intellectual symbol of my race. [*GJ* 15]

> I go to encounter for the millionth time the reality of experience and to forge in the smithy of my soul the uncreated conscience of my race. [*P* 253]

---

[12] Cixous, "Joyce: the (r)use of writing," 16.

Describing *Giacomo Joyce* as a "poem in prose," Cixous points towards a transitional effect of the formal structure of the text itself. Hesitating between genres and between textual placements, the counter-portrait of "Giacomo" can also be read as a counter-portrait of writing itself, in a form of aphoristic prose which Lautréamont called *"prosaïques morceaux."* Posed against the Thomistic aesthetics of the last chapter of *A Portrait* and the formal innovations of *Ulysses*, *Giacomo Joyce* affects an anti-aesthetic. From *Bildungsroman* to subjectless and subjective pseudo-drama. *Non serviam!* of an aesthetic heresy miming the fall of Stephen-Giacomo in the ironised, almost satirical form of a fissured and fragmented "paradox lust," anti-epic of the cracked lookingglass of Dedalus-Joyce. Contracted between the one and the other, a radical poetics of apposition: this strangely composed envoy, as beautiful "as the fortuitous encounter of a sewing machine and an umbrella on a dissecting table."[13]

The language of this prose poem ("vêtement verbal d'une émotion" as Cixous describes it) stands in contrast to what Ellmann refers to as "the rather anaemic style [Joyce] reserved for his verse" (*GJ* xviii). And yet, in an uncanny doubling and deferral of this already substitutive text, Joyce "traduced" and transposed whole sections of *Giacomo Joyce* into (or perhaps from?) *Pomes Penyeach*: "Watching the Needleboats at San Sabba," "A Flower Given to my Daughter," "Tutto è Sciolto," "Nightpiece." In an oblique comment on the strange revenance of *Giacomo Joyce*, Ellmann notes that Joyce sent the first of these poems (whose last line reads "Return, no more return") to his brother Stanislaus in a letter which also included a quotation from Horace: *Quid si prisca redit Venus?* ("What if the old love should return?") (*JJI* 358).

Not merely transitional, *Giacomo Joyce* is also translational, "duplicitous" both in the sense of a writing simultaneously between and across genres, and in the projective "presencing" of other texts in which it is constantly deferred and "returning."

---

[13] Lautréamont, *Les Chants de Maldoror*, trans. Guy Wernham (New York: New Directions, 1965) 263.

In textual genetics this effect is ascribed to what Daniel Ferrer and others term *avant-texte*. This does not refer to what might otherwise be thought of simply as preparatory drafts or notes, but rather to a text "in advance of itself," a type of haunting which is also an alterior discourse "within."[14] "My voice, dying in the echo of its words [...]" (*GJ* 14). Maurice Blanchot has similarly described this effect in terms of discursive emplacement and of the "fragment" as an element of metonymic recursion: "the fragment, as fragments, tends to dissolve the totality which it presupposes and which it carries off towards the dissolution from which it does not [...] form, but to which it exposes itself in order, disappearing—and along with it, all identity—to maintain itself as the energy of disappearing: a repetitive energy, the limit that bears upon limitation."[15]

Miming the "disappearances" of Giacomo, *Giacomo Joyce* might be thought of as naming, not a single work bounded by the covers of a book, but rather a matrix of textual fragments, whose traces and tracings through other texts (*Ulysses, Exiles, A Portrait*) describe a type of ghost writing. *Giacomo Joyce* itself is no more or less than the locus of a certain "blinding" of the subject, a disappearance or *détournement* in the portrait of the (in)visible. Which is to say, of the (un)knowable. One is never sure of the precise location of this gnomic text, or of its lines of filiation. A mirror-effect of its "other texts," written and rewritten in *Giacomo Joyce*—it is impossible to know, in fact, which precedes the other. The shadow play of a writing disseminating itself between so many white spaces, a dance of veils. Who or what is it that disappears between them? Is it the blindness of a too-acute prescience? Or an after-effect of spectrality? A "tardy spirit" (*P* 189), an accessory, as it were,

---

14 Daniel Ferrer, "Archéologie du regard dans les avant-textes de «Circé»," *James Joyce «Scribble» 1: genèse des textes*, ed. Claude Jacquet (Paris: Lettres Modernes, 1988).

15 Maurice Blanchot, *The Writing of the Disaster*, trans. Ann Smock (Lincoln: University of Nebraska Press, 1995) 60-61.

after the fact? Perhaps it is only the writing that knows. A counter-portrait that draws forth, or reveals, only the ghost of itself.

GHOSTS IN THE MACHINE

> *Being in memory of him: not necessarily to remember him, no, but to be in his memory, to inhabit his memory, which is henceforth greater than all your finite memory can, in a single instant or a single vocabulary, gather up of cultures, languages, mythologies, religions, philosophies, history of mind and of literatures.*
> (Jacques Derrida, "Deux mots pour Joyce")[16]

It is a curious feature of Joyce criticism that while readings of *Giacomo Joyce* frequently refer to its re-fragmentation and dispersal in other texts, little is made of the implications of this in the question of the text's marginalisation. It is not so much what is read in place of *Giacomo Joyce*, but rather of its *emplacements*, and of the determining "influence" this will have had upon the structural organisation of Joyce's writing in general, as a blueprint or map of a virtual territory not yet realised.

This "matrix effect" in the virtuality of *Giacomo Joyce* could also be thought in terms of hypertext, anticipating the cybernetics of Joyce's later work, which Jean-Michel Rabaté has described as a "perverse semic machine" which "has the ability to distort the classical semiological relation between 'production' and 'information,' by disarticulating the sequence of encoding and decoding,"[17] and which Derrida has referred to

---

16 Jacques Derrida, "Two Words for Joyce," trans. Geoffrey Bennington, *Post-structuralist Joyce: Essays from the French*, eds. Derek Attridge and Daniel Ferrer (Cambridge: Cambridge University Press, 1984) 147.

17 Jean-Michel Rabaté, "Lapsus ex machina," trans. Elizabeth Guild, *Post-structuralist Joyce: Essays from the French*, eds. Derek Attridge and Daniel Ferrer (London: Cambridge University Press, 1984) 79.

as a "hypermnesiac machine."[18] Which is to say, a machine which remembers through a process of sublimated self-substitution and self-erasure. It describes a mnemotechnic which is also a programme, or *pro-grammē*—the virtuality of a writing "in advance" which, like its metonymic envoy, never quite arrives at its destination. A writing which is simultaneously present, manifest, as it were, in the discarded manuscript of Joyce, and which is nevertheless "not yet." A reading and a re-writing elsewhere, of an always other-text.

The possible dates for the composition of *Giacomo Joyce* also suggest a particular historical placement within the development of the European avant-garde and an aesthetics of the machine, or what Donald Theall has called "techno-poetics."[19] Between 1913 and 1914 Picasso's *Tête*, the first of Marcel Duchamp's *boîtes*, Velimir Khlebnikov's *zaum* manifesto, Blaise Cendrars's *Prose du Transsibérian* and Guillaume Apollinaire's *Calligrammes* each signalled an emerging pre-occupation with the technics of simultaneity, collage, formal reduction and the radical juxtaposition of "found" compositional elements. Writing almost contemporaneously, it would be difficult to believe that Joyce was unaware of the technological undercurrents in these works, all of which were informed in one way or another by the ideas of Marinetti and the Italian Futurists, whose *Manifesto* (of which Joyce possessed a copy) had appeared in *Le Figaro* in February 1909, the year Joyce himself established the first cinematograph in Dublin (*JJI* 310). It is inviting, too, to consider that the abandonment of *Giacomo Joyce* (if that is what it was) might in fact have been a calculated element of the work itself, anticipating the "discarded" works of the Dadaists and of Duchamp's abandoned, occulted, vanished, destroyed and yet highly fetishised objects of the 1920s onwards. It is a curious irony that the "abandonment" of *Giacomo Joyce* would then not only have

---

18   Derrida, "Two Words for Joyce," 147-148.

19   Donald F. Theall, *James Joyce's Techno-Poetics* (Toronto: Toronto University Press, 1997).

been encoded within the text itself, but in a sense most properly achieved through its publication in 1968.

Fixing on the "objecthood" of *Giacomo Joyce*, what is most immediately striking is the typographical arrangement of its fifty textual "fragments." Arguably, typographical concretion had first entered the avant-garde vocabulary with the publication of Stéphane Mallarmé's *Un coup de dés* in 1897. Its "simultaneous vision of the page," locating it somewhere between poetry and drawing, provides yet another context for reading Joyce's "sketchbook."[20] The physical juxtaposition of text-objects, like the radical forms of catachresis and parataxis described by Lautréamont, suggest spatio-temporal relations beyond forms of narrative continuity that previously characterised Joyce's work.

Amongst Joyce's contemporaries, such formal innovation was linked to the idea that the modern work of art must reflect the global nature of contemporary consciousness: tele-communications, newspapers, radio, cinema, and so on. To be able to mirror such a multiple form of consciousness, the work of art abandoned linear and discursive structures, in which events are arranged successively, in favour of what Apollinaire, seeking a verbal analogy to cubism, called *simultaneity*—a textual apparatus that "short-circuits the normal process of reading and requires the reader to reassemble the apparently random fragments in a new order that is independent of the flow of time."[21]

Such dis-continuities not only characterise *Giacomo Joyce*, but also the final section of *A Portrait* and the entirety of *Ulysses* and *Finnegans Wake*. Indeed, critics like Arnold Hauser have identified Joyce as exemplary of precisely this type of *simultanéisme*, as a verbal analogy to the technology of film:

---

[20] Octavio Armand, *Refractions*, trans. Carol Maier (New York: Lumen, 1994) 187.

[21] S.I. Lockerbie, Introduction to Guillaume Apollinaire, *Calligrammes*, trans. Anne Hyde Greet (Berkeley: University of California Press, 1991) 3.

> The accent is now on the simultaneity of the contents of consciousness, the immanence of the past in the present, the constant flowing together of the different periods of time, the amorphous fluidity of inner experience, the boundlessness of the stream of time by which the soul is borne along, the relativity of space and time, that is to say, the impossibility of differentiation and defining the media in which the mind moves. In this new conception of time almost all the strands of the texture which form the stuff of modern art converge: the abandonment of plot, the elimination of the hero, the relinquishing of psychology, the 'automatic method of writing' and, above all, the montage technique and the intermingling of temporal and spatial forms of the film.[22]

Hauser argues that Joyce's use of montage achieves a level of aesthetic autonomy, suggesting, as Marshall McLuhan had earlier done, that Joyce's text represented a convergence of media that translate the "real world" into the "reel world" (*FW* 064.25-6).[23] For Jean-François Lyotard, theorising the "postmodern condition," this has had to do with Joyce's concern with the "unpresentable" and the normativity of concepts like unity and coherence. "Joyce allows the unpresentable to become perceptible in his writing itself, in the signifier. The whole range of available narrative and even stylistic operations is put into play without concern for the unity of the whole."[24]

In *Giacomo Joyce* the visual arrangement of the textual fragments and the blank spaces between them might also be seen as a type of filmic notation, montage effect, or "scriptwriting" —the variable repetition of a "perfect signature" of "word, letter, paperspace" (*FW* 115.06-08) in lieu of its

---

[22] Arnold Hauser, *The Social History of Art*, vol. 4 "Naturalism, Impressionism, The Film Age" (London: Routledge and Kegan Paul, 1962) 226.

[23] Stephen Heath, "Ambiviolences: Notes for reading Joyce," trans. Isabelle Mahieu, *Post-structuralist Joyce: Essays from the French*, eds. Derek Attridge and Daniel Ferrer (Cambridge: Cambridge University Press, 1984) 46.

[24] Jean-François Lyotard, *The Postmodern Condition: A Report on Knowledge*, trans. Geoff Bennington and Brian Massumi (Manchester: Manchester University Press, 1991) 80-1.

"unrepresentable" other-subject. The filmic blind (the screening of the "other" or mechanism of difference as the frame which makes the image visible), simultaneously contracts and runs over from this unequal division, in turn describing the visibility of the mechanism itself, breaking apart the whole of which it nevertheless remains a fragmented, metonymic counterpart.

The spectacle of Giacomo: ghostly play of shadows flickering across the white screen of the page: counter-portrait of this counter-portrait: *pièce dans une pièce*. But what perhaps remains most unpresentable of *Giacomo Joyce* is its "unpresentability." The always retrospective present of a writing between amnesia and nostalgia, as one speculating upon the (failed or belated) arrival of a (failed or belated) envoy. Future anterior. "The time is out of joint," as Hamlet says. But it is precisely for this reason that the "avant-texte" of Joyce, "envoy of the other," can be thought as both *en retard* and *in advance* of Joyce. A telegraphic experiment in transition.

But while it has been argued that *Giacomo Joyce* represents a transitional figure of Joyce, and of the Joycean corpus, it must also be considered that this transitionality might not be an after-effect but rather a pre-condition. That this envoy is most timely in being, from the very first, "unpresentable," a testament or documentary of its own sending and substitution. That the consequences of the experiment which is instigated with it, are likewise already comprehended by it. That these gnomic fragments are already the knowing anti-types of almost all that follows, communicating them, as it were, or rather anticipating them, and being anticipated in them. An "experiment" not only in advance of the Joycean project, but already, as it were, "in place of it." That is to say, obviating its repetition as anything other than the internalised haunting of itself. An experiment effacing itself in its too immediate implications and at the same time affecting a communication of all this implies. Ultimately for Joyce, it seems, the poetic economy of this envoy required the expansive edifice of *Ulysses* and *Finnegans Wake* behind which to achieve anything like a sustained formal expression. If this is the case, then there needs to be a re-evaluation of the way in which *Giacomo Joyce* has been approached until now. And if *Giacomo Joyce* constitutes a formal experiment which can manifestly be shown to have "proceeded," then it is not enough to attribute its marginalisation to an effect of oversight. What it suggests, rather, is a type of clairvoyance, a foresight or before-sight of what the "present" in Joyce must always return to.

Louis Armand
Prague, January 2002

Fritz Senn

On Not Coming to Terms with *Giacomo Joyce*

There was a ripple of excitement early in 1968 when a smallish, limited, expensive edition of a book called *Giacomo Joyce* presented itself to the reading public as a second posthumous work by Joyce, after the considerably longer fragment of *Stephen Hero*. There was a new, unknown work and uncharted territory. Actually there was nothing quite new. Richard Ellmann, the editor and annotator, had already offered extracts and commentaries in his biography of 1959, where a "notebook" in private hands he had inspected dealt with Joyce's involvement, mainly imaginary, with a student and was described as "an account of the affair in his best calligraphy under the title of *Giacomo Joyce*" (*JJI* 353). The publication of the whole in elegant book form complete with facsimiles turned it all from a personal affair into a composition, an artefact. It still retains that position in-between.

Ellmann's monumental biography was still, deservedly, the standard hard rock of Joyce scholarship, and his introduction to *Giacomo Joyce* provided a base for almost all further studies. The biographical packaging had its lasting impact. Though the Triestine phases of Joyce's life were among the most sketchy parts of the book, Ellmann had uncovered tantalising local connections and a personal framework. Inevitably the biographical underpinning conditioned readers' attitudes. *Giacomo Joyce* first emerged as a translation of Joyce's life rather than a work of fiction in its own right, as any publication would be judged whose title is almost identical with the author. Given the embedding, to dismiss the highly useful context and approach the precious prose naively as writing demanded a concerted effort. Expectations preceded unbiased readings.

What was that new work? For those scholars who are (or were then) classifying animals and for some readers a first task was to determine its nature or *genus*. These sixteen pages seemed to read like prose poems, or else they might be made up of notes, though at a high level of composition and obviously structured; some passages looked like drafts (and were in fact transplanted for later use). Perhaps the pattern was a narrative string of those "epiphanies" that are surrounded by so much numinosity. Some parts were in the nature of a diary; there is also an air of disjointed confession about them. Possibly Joyce tried his fingers at *exercices de style* or was testing the ground—how close one can get to purple poses unscathed. (Imagine how readers would respond if the author were not known to be Joyce.)

Such problems, neat compartments, are largely self-imposed. *Giacomo Joyce* is, and has every right to be, as all of Joyce's works are, *sui generis*, perhaps even more so. There is no adequate label for it; even to speak of *Giacomo Joyce* neutrally as a "book" feels problematic though factually it has, but it apparently was never intended to become one. With something so hard to pin down, the challenge is all the greater and a new fascinating happy hunting ground has been staked out which is open on all sides. We are faced with a series of stimuli from which to take off.

The title already is not, as Ellmann noted early on, in Joyce's own hand, we are not even sure if it is his own choice. If it is, most likely then Joyce, a foreigner in Trieste, has assumed a native guise as a homely alien and Italianised his first name, or else the name "Giacomo" is a foreign variant of the Dublin writer. "Quizzing-glasses" figure in the fourth sentence already, like a tacit invitation to apply our own. As always we do rise to the occasion. In the meantime even the spaces of uneven lengths that separate the paragraphs have been subjected to investigative scrutiny. With little categorical prompting, some of us naturally resorted to philological cross-referencing or the tracing of sources from life or literature. If we cannot get at the whatness of something at least we can follow the links to what it is not.

Puzzling as *Giacomo Joyce* may remain, it has the one practical advantage to be short and easy to handle as it comes in small, homeopathic doses. It appears, more and more, to feature many Joycean complexities but as yet none of the sheer bulk and extravagances of the major works to follow. Maybe that makes it the first thing to put in the hands of a prospective reader for training purposes.

Giacomo Joyce stands at the crossroads, Living and Writing intersect, more than elsewhere. It is deeply involved in events, longings and fantasies of the Trieste years, with only passing references to Dublin and Ireland. It is the only piece which explicitly refers to the *Portrait* and *Ulysses* which were in actual or conceptual progress at the time. Many passages became integrated into the later works. Strandentwining cables lead to *Portrait, Exiles, Pomes Penyeach,* and *Ulysses,* a fact which made it easy to relegate the prose to what it is physically, a notebook and therefore a quarry for use in future constructions. Joyce was never one to waste anything, no throwaways for him.

"Who?" the notebook begins with existential triviality, and within the biographical context the person around whom the text pivots was to be determined, assuming it was one person. In real life it was not; Amalia Popper, Ellmann's prime candidate, now seems to be just one among others, as scholars have established, especially John McCourt to whose initiative and impulse we now owe so much. The Trieste School (also its Summer School) has put in a lot of archaeological research and filled many gaps in the local background.

An exhibition in the city staged in 1999 brought out quite well how Joyce in a new, Mediterranean, ramshackle, highly international and mixed city, was meeting, at times just observing from a distance, women so different from those he had so far encountered in Dublin, women more self-assured, frankly seductive, fashion-conscious, and intellectual.[1]

The "She" that moves through *Giacomo Joyce* is an individual and at the same time a composite, nothing unusual in Joyce. The shadowy figure of "E.C." in *A Portrait* has some similarity, and the Temptress of the Vilanelle there now also takes on a Triestine tinge. Such blending technique seems to be exemplified in at least one passage: "On all sides distorted reflections of her image started from his memory: the flowergirl in the ragged dress with damp coarse hair and a hoyden's face who had called herself his own girl and begged his handsel, the kitchengirl in the next house who sang over the clatter of her plates, [...] a girl who had laughed gaily to see him stumble when the iron grating in the footpath near Cork Hill had caught the broken sole of his shoe, a girl he had glanced at, attracted by her small ripe mouth as she passed out of Jacob's biscuit factory [...]" (*P* 183). One girl tends to become all girls, one woman like Marion Tweedy Bloom is of many sources and of many facets, including mythological roles. The locally detailed blurs with fictional archetypes. Several young women that came into Joyce's orbit qualify for *Giacomo*, and we are grateful for every scrap of pertinent speculation, yet in some way the prototypes are also wholly irrelevant. In some essential way, there is no Amalia Popper in *Giacomo Joyce*.

Joyce is already at his intricate naming games. The main figure herself has no name (just like the pivotal sister of

---

[1] A personal aside: In September 2000 a group of natives and some Zürich visitors were invited to the house where Amalia Popper had lived, into the room where, most probably, Joyce the language teacher had nervously waited for her and conversed with her. It felt weird to sit in a room that may well not have changed essentially, among furniture that looked similar to what it would have been at the time, and to call up an atmosphere of décor, constraint, erotic tension and embarrassment. A lasting, somehow relevant impression, yet it all may well have been due much more to our imagination than any faded spirit of the place.

Mangan in "Araby"), yet intriguingly enough, a marginal figure is given a factual and next to pointless identity ("Ralli"). Exceptionally Nora and Gogarty are summoned under their real names. Such a private touch might also indicate that Joyce never planned to share his notebook with the world and elevate it to public exposure. He himself is split up into three names, the Giacomo of the title, one "Jim" and a self-addressed "Easy now, Jamesy" (6). That is how Stephen Dedalus will later admonish himself in *Ulysses*, "Easy now" (*U* 3.459); the prominent "Jamesy" will become a meta-textual, no longer direct, address to the author in Molly's unsuspecting "O Jamesy let me up out of this" (*U* 18.1128). Quite overtly in *Giacomo Joyce* Jamesy let himself *into* it.

Giacomo Joyce is also a tribute to Trieste, and any Irish backdrop would be hard to trace from one lonely reference to "walk the streets of Dublin" and a single mention of Ireland. Nor do there seem to be any of the Anglo-Irish inflections in the wording. Triestine dialect is interspersed; streets, churches are called up the way Dublin is referred to elsewhere. Even so it was possible to transfer a highly characteristic vignette of Trieste rawly waking almost *verbatim* to a Paris scene which appears to be equally evocative and locally coloured in the changed setting. Imagination, it seems, generally takes precedence over observed reality.

Since *Giacomo Joyce* is closest to the author himself, at least at a particular stage, it lends itself to an analysis of the author, of his urge towards confessional exhibitionism combined with concealment, as well as of his tortured relations with the other sex—a great opportunity for those scholars who are at heart psychologists *manqués*. Some have produced valuable insights; conjectures on occasion can take us far afield.

Giacomo Joyce, not alone in its onomatopoeia, alliteration and assonances, bears eloquent witness to that Joycean feature that the words and phrases, at the moment when they swing into our attention, display their full force, value, or glory and seem to come into their own, either read silently or heard aloud.

There "whatness," to use Dedalean terminology, becomes radiant, or resonant. This is one reason why *Giacomo Joyce* too is great for recital, an orchestration of distinctive voices and cadences. Words and phrases may even distract from what they stand for, they impinge foremost as verbal events.

Joyce's published works are reminiscences, novels generally are. Things happened some time ago and are now told in retrospect. Fictional events of 1904 became a story in 1922 when Buck Mulligan *came* from the stairhead. Unique in this way, *Giacomo Joyce* is, or pretends to be, present, in the present, the here and now, or seems jotted down with great artifice right afterwards. This happens scenically and grammatically and brings the work close to *Exiles* and the poems.

The style is of a certain period, between *Portrait*, *Pomes Penyeach* and certain early passages in *Ulysses*, with precise details and choice, often monosyllabic adjectives. Those multiple meanings and overtones that would take over once *Ulysses* got under way appear to be (relatively) absent, which will not of course prevent us from finding them. Somehow Joyce's early phase came to a minute climax in *Giacomo Joyce* and perhaps the path was cleared for new arts as yet unknown, but already prefigured.

Giacomo Joyce can stand (almost) on its own, and yet is deeply involved with the life of the author as we can never know, as well as intricately connected with the rest of the canon. It remains multivalent and mysteriously challenging, as the present volume will confirm once more. At least one project has been timidly aired, a collective effort towards a display of the qualities, the complexity and opulence of the work in a hypertext format which alone perhaps can bring out the interconnections and multiple aspects.

Vicki Mahaffey
"Giacomo Joyce"

In the years just before World War I, as James Joyce was putting
the finishing touches on his portrait of the artist as a young man
and beginning to envision the large canvases of *Ulysses*, he was
also compiling a small book of prose sketches of a young lady:
Giacomo Joyce. Although its ostensible setting is Trieste, *Giacomo
Joyce* takes place primarily in the world of Joyce's imagination, a
highly sensual world tinctured with an almost Oriental
eroticism and a dark morbidity. It consists almost entirely of the
artist's shifting perceptions of a lovely young woman, one of
the students to whom he taught English. His responses to her
mysterious, protean elusiveness are complex and often
contradictory; they include desire, amused self-parody, quiet
reverence, fear, satirical disgust, and hurt, but the artist's
perceptions and responses are always the primary focus of each
sketch.

Giacomo pays homage to his lady's delicacy and to her
power to ensnare him by clothing her in fine webs; he touches
her "websoft" gown (*GJ* 7) and admires her "legstretched web
of stocking" (*GJ* 9). In another sketch, he borrows an epithet
from the Litany of the Blessed Virgin to describe her, "virgin
most prudent" (*GJ* 9), but later she appears before him in a

---

* A version of this article first appeared in *A Companion to Joyce Studies*, eds. Zack
Bowen and James F. Carens (Westport, CT: Greenwood Press, 1984) 387-420.

quite different guise. He pictures her leaning against a pillowed wall in suggestive obscurity, an "odalisque-featured" (*GJ* 14) member of the harem, that serves the Oriental sensuality of his wanton imagination. He imagines that she has drunk his thoughts and received his soul, which has dissolved into her womanhood as "a liquid and abundant seed" (*GJ* 14), and a long ellipsis introduces his exultant challenge to any threatening rival: "Take her now who will!" (*GJ* 14). She appears as a variety of natural and fantastical creatures, many of which will reappear in *Ulysses* when Bloom encounters Bella in a different sort of harem. In *Giacomo* the alternately cold and alluring pupil is portrayed as a "filly foal" (*GJ* 7), a body "shimmering with silvery scales" (*GJ* 8), a helpless sparrow (*GJ* 7), a "pampered fowl" (*GJ* 8), a pullet (*GJ* 12), a basilisk (*GJ* 14), and a cold and venomous nightsnake (*GJ* 14). In a different mood, Giacomo compares the lights and shadows of her falsely smiling face to the hues of rancid food. At still other times, her body emerges as an odourless flower, her mind a quagmire, and the green hue of her dress metamorphoses into lush grass, "the hair of graves" (*GJ* 12).

The woman of *Giacomo Joyce* nimbly plays several roles: she acts as virgin, Virgin Mother, lover, corpse, and faithless whore. Like the ghost of May Dedalus in *Ulysses*, she appears to the man she haunts with a grey face and "dank matted hair," and when she kisses Giacomo, "her sighing breath comes through" (*GJ* 14). She is transformed into a series of venomous creatures who poison him; she appears as one of the daughters of Jerusalem who condemn Christ to death by choosing to liberate Barabbas instead of Christ. She emerges as a powerful, protean image who both destroys and inspires the artist-lover who seeks to possess her.

The slender sketchbook, which Joyce never published, has an odd history of having been alternately neglected and widely celebrated. During the summer of 1914, Joyce painstakingly copied his sketches onto oversized sheets of paper that were enclosed between bluish-grey paper covers. When Joyce left

Trieste for Zürich in 1915, the small book, which bore the crudely written inscription "Giacomo Joyce" on the front cover in an unidentified handwriting, was left behind in the care of Joyce's brother Stanislaus (*GJ* xi-xii). Although Joyce may have consulted it during subsequent trips to Trieste, *Giacomo Joyce* remained essentially forgotten among Stanislaus's possessions until 1956, when Richard Ellmann discovered it as he was researching his massive biography of Joyce.

James Joyce, when it appeared in 1959, contained an interesting section on *Giacomo Joyce* in which Ellmann identified Amalia Popper as the pupil who had inspired it. Ellmann quoted a significant portion of it, interweaving its fantasy into the facts of Joyce's life in Trieste (*JJI* 353-60). Virtually nothing more is heard of *Giacomo Joyce* until September 28, 1967, when the front page of *The New York Times* reported, "MS. of a Joyce Autobiographical Love Story Found." This front-page news item, which included two of the vignettes, marked the beginning of a remarkable sales campaign by Viking Press to promote the forthcoming publication of *Giacomo Joyce* in its entirety, to be edited by Ellmann. From comparative obscurity, these sixteen pages were suddenly illuminated by international attention. On January 1, 1968, the limited first edition appeared, complete with introduction, notes, and facsimile pages, all handsomely boxed and highly priced at ten dollars. It was reset and reissued for a regular trade edition that appeared in May, and an Italian translation appeared in October. The book was extensively publicised and widely reviewed throughout 1968.[1]

---

[1] Henry Raymont, "MS. of a Joyce Autobiographical Love Story Found," *New York Times*, 28 Sept. 1967: 1. For other noteworthy reviews, see Lewis Nichols, "American Notebook," *New York Times Book Review*, 8 Oct. 1967: 66; Eliot Fremont-Smith, "New Year's Day—And a New James Joyce," *New York Times*, 1 Jan. 1968: 13; Melvin Maddocks, "Joyce's Poem Unspoken," *Christian Science Monitor*, 18 Jan. 1968: 11; "Sinking Stones," *Time*, 19 Jan. 1968: 93-94; Harry Levin, "Love Letter," *New York Times Book Review*, 21 Jan. 1968: 22; Raymond A. Sokolov, "Joyce's Toccata," *Newsweek*, 22 Jan. 1968: 90; Hugh Kenner, "The English Teacher Who Wrote *Ulysses*," *Book World*, 11 Feb. 1968: 8; Matthew Hodgart, "Portrait of the Artist as a Middle-Aged Adulterer," *New York Review of Books*, 29 Feb. 1968: 3; Anthony Burgess, "Portrait of the Artist in Middle

Once the flurry of excitement over the book's publication had subsided, *Giacomo Joyce* lapsed once again into obscurity. The reasons for its neglect are complex but understandable: many reviewers criticised the excessive, and in some cases misleading, claims that were made about it as a "finished" work of art.[2] It was readily apparent, too that Viking was attempting to market this small sketchbook as an almost sacred "relic," an object deserving veneration, which prompted reviewers to question the disparity between the elaborate format and the modest text.[3] Ultimately, the financial incentive that fuelled the massive sales campaign undermined the promotional claims that were being made for the book's importance as a "missing link" in the evolution of Joyce's art.

To confuse the issues still more, it seemed as if the publishers and the editor may have been attempting to create a mystery around the identity of the lady where none existed, to present her as an unidentified "dark lady" like the lady of Shakespeare's sonnets, in order to enhance the value and interest of this not-so-new Joycean artefact. Although Ellmann

Age," *Nation*, 4 Mar. 1968: 309-10; John Updike, "Questions Concerning *Giacomo*," *New Yorker*, 6 Apr. 1968: 167-74; "A Fragment and Four Furrows," *Times Literary Supplement*, 23 May 1968: 526; Paul Kresh, "A Gulliver Exposed to Lilliputian Arrows," *Saturday Review*, 25 May 1968: 23-24; Robert M. Adams, "A Very Pretty Piece of Protocol, Mr. Ellmann," *JJQ* 5 (Spring 1968): 229-31; Robert Scholes, "*Giacomo* Once Again," *JJQ* 5 (Spring 1968): 231-32; "Notes on Current Books: Literary Studies," *Virginia Quarterly Review* 44 (Spring 1968): lvii; Erwin W. Geissman, "James Joyce," *Catholic World* (June 1968): 139-40; Adaline Glasheen, Review Article, *AWN* 5 (June 1968): 35-47; John Hollander, "The Dark Lady," *Partisan Review* 35 (Summer 1968): 459-62.

2   For example, in Viking's press release, Ellmann was quoted as saying, "*Giacomo Joyce* is a major achievement, both in its own terms and in the creation of modern writing." See the full-page advertisement in the *New York Times Book Review*, 7 Jan. 1968: 13. Lewis Nichols relays Ellmann's assurance that the story is a finished work and not a rough draft, and Raymont also reports a claim by Ellmann that "intrinsically, it is a great work." Eliot Fremont-Smith supports this view in his *New York Times* article, arguing that *Giacomo Joyce* is more than a fragment; "it is a complete work [...] that stands by itself as a daring and deeply affecting evocation of an infatuation transformed into the artist's act of self-discovery, and into art" (13).

3   See, in particular, the reviews of Scholes, Hollander, Updike, and Adams.

had identified the lady of *Giacomo Joyce* in his biography, he did not even mention her in his introduction to the limited first edition of the sketchbook. Many reviewers pointed out this omission, questioned it, and criticised it. Eileen Lanouette Hughes, in an article in *Life* magazine, took advantage of this omission to rebroadcast the identity of Joyce's "mystery lady." She writes,

> Joyce scholar Richard Ellmann, who had read the work in manuscript, gave the lady's name in his 1959 biography of Joyce: Amalia Popper. But he wrote an analytical introduction to *Giacomo Joyce* without mentioning her name again. And so only a few scholars are aware of her name. None but Ellmann ever saw her face.[4]

Hughes's article, based on Ellmann's biography and on interviews with one of Joyce's former students, at least two of Popper's former classmates at the University of Florence, and Michele Risolo, Popper's husband, supplies the detailed information about Amalia Popper that Ellmann's introduction so noticeably lacked.

The widespread criticism and even suspicion of Ellmann for neglecting to mention Amalia Popper in his introduction prompted the chairman of the Executive Committee of Viking Press, Marshall A. Best, to write an explanatory letter to the *Times Literary Supplement* in which he ascribes full responsibility for the omission to Viking.[5] He explains that they believed Amalia Popper (then Mrs. Risolo) to be still alive in Italy, and advised Ellmann to avoid mentioning her as a way of protecting her privacy. As it turned out, though, she had died a few months earlier; consequently, they restored her name to the regular trade edition of *Giacomo Joyce* that appeared in May.

The complicated web of misunderstanding, mysterious omissions, high-pitched sales campaign, extensive publicity,

---

[4] Eileen Lanouette Hughes, "The Mystery Lady of *Giacomo Joyce*," *Life*, 2 Feb. 1968: 36.

[5] Marshall A. Best, *Times Literary Supplement*, 11 July 1968: 737.

and extravagant praise made *Giacomo Joyce* appear to be highly overrated, and as a result, one claim of Ellmann's, that the book is an important link in Joyce's overall creative process, has never been fully explored. The nature and significance of this short sketchbook have remained as elusive as its shy heroine. *Giacomo Joyce* has been characterised in a variety of conflicting ways: Harry Levin called it a love letter, whereas Anthony Burgess classified it more ironically as "an essay in private onanism." Richard Ellmann's claims for its "small, fragile, enduring perfection" were challenged by reviewers who disliked its artificiality. The reviewer for *Time* magazine complained, "This is Joyce at his worst, in his plush, provincial, 'poetic' vein." In contrast to Eliot Fremont-Smith, who hailed it as "a complete work-story, poem, composition, 'study of love,'" Robert M. Adams dismissed it as merely "a sentimental adventure most memorable for the ironic reservation which limited its growth to a foolscap idyll."[6] In her brilliantly suggestive essay on *Giacomo Joyce*, Adaline Glasheen proposed a great debate about the nature of this Joycean artefact, but the debate failed to outlive the conflicting reviews. In the thirty years since the publication of the complete text, Mrs. Glasheen's plea for a serious consideration of its value has been largely ignored.

Giacomo Joyce has resisted simple classifications partly because it is an *étude* on so many different themes—mutability, betrayal, ageing, frustrated desire, the eroticism of sense of sight, the presence of the past—themes that Joyce does not develop fully until *Ulysses*. Furthermore, although *Giacomo Joyce* offers additional data for a graph of Joyce's artistic development, it demands that any such graph be plotted on more than one set of axes. Most critical effort has centred on establishing the biographical co-ordinates: as Richard Ellmann has shown, *Giacomo Joyce* is first of all a record of Joyce's

---

6 Levin, "Love Letter," 22; Burgess, "Portrait," 309; Ellmann, Introduction, *Giacomo Joyce*, xxvi; "Sinking Stones," 94; Fremont-Smith, "New Year's Day," 13; Adams, "A Very Pretty Piece of Protocol," 231.

fantasies about one of his pupils, most probably Amalia Popper.[7] As such, it affords readers a glimpse into Joyce's private desires, but it also draws from these fanciful yearnings and disappointments a more generalised portrait of youth. It illustrates, through verbal pictures, the gradual disintegration of a young man's dream of love, which ends when his idol betrays a preference for another man. Giacomo discovers that his youth was bound up with this dream and concludes his sketchbook with a wry salute to the passing of both.

Viewed against the background of Joyce's other works, *Giacomo Joyce* yields information about Joyce's way of building character through association. *Giacomo Joyce* arrests Joyce in the process of linking characters to mythical and literary analogues from the past. Like the characters in *A Portrait* and in *Ulysses*, Giacomo and his lady are placed in a rich imaginative context, although here the tradition that they join is an eclectic, even idiosyncratic, one. Giacomo's lady becomes one in a constellation of mysterious, independent women characters as seemingly diverse as Beatrice and Hester Prynne, and Giacomo takes his place with the infatuated men whom they eluded or spurned.

The sketches of Giacomo and his lady, although rudely drawn, add two more figures to Joyce's literary gallery. Because the depictions of Giacomo and his beloved influenced the more finished character portraits of *A Portrait* and *Ulysses*, they give insight, not only into the imaginative ancestry of Joyce's characters, but also into the kinship that binds all Joyce's male characters into one man and all his female characters into a single woman. *Giacomo Joyce* marks a pivotal point in Joyce's representations of women and their male counterparts: only in youth do women pose as idols and temptresses, and men as idolaters and apostates; in middle age, Joyce's women turn

---

[7] The most complete account of the evidence linking Amalia Popper to *Giacomo Joyce* is given in Ellmann's response to Helen Barolini's "The Curious Case of Amalia Popper." See the *New York Review of Books*, 20 Nov. 1969: 48-51.

protean, inspiring a complementary uncertainty and compassionate open-mindedness in their male partners.

Giacomo Joyce marks a different point on the curve of Joyce's stylistic development; it even forces us to replot that curve. Stylistically, *Giacomo Joyce* is an experiment with fantasy, an attempt to reproduce the highly coloured eroticism of the world of the imagination, to copy the emotional, kaleidoscopic peep-show of mental adventure. Fantasy experience, unlike experience in the outer world, is necessarily two dimensional, and it consists only in images and sounds. To invent a stylistic equivalent for fantasy with the visual arts, drawing attention to his technique and to the voyeuristic nature of Giacomo's admiration by presenting his book as a sketchbook, by focusing on images of eyes and vision, and by implying that Giacomo's relationship with his beloved reflects that of an artist and his model.

The clues linking *Giacomo Joyce* to the world of the visual arts are many and varied. Joyce copied his prose vignettes onto oversized sheets of paper "of the sort used for pencil sketches."[8] Adaline Glasheen syllogistically concludes, "Joyce was a man who put a picture of Cork into a cork frame. I suggest that he was also a man who put sketches into a sketchbook." Her argument that *Giacomo Joyce* is a metaphorical as well as a literal sketchbook is supported by the way Joyce alludes to it. Instead of identifying it by the title it now carries, he referred to it only as a collection of "sketches." In 1917, for example, when Pound was dunning Joyce for publishable material, Joyce apparently remembered *Giacomo Joyce*, responding that he had only some "prose sketches" locked up in his desk in Trieste (9 Apr. 1917, *L* I:101).

Another implicit reference to *Giacomo Joyce* as a book of sketches appears in the fictionalised context of *Exiles*, which Joyce was beginning at the same time that he was completing

---

8 Glasheen, Review Article, 40. Glasheen's article contains some of the finest work yet done on *Giacomo Joyce*, and I am indebted to her for numerous provocative suggestions.

Giacomo Joyce. Like Stephen and Giacomo, Richard Rowan plays the role of the artist, and Beatrice Justice, like Giacomo's lady, acts as the inspiration of his youth. In *Exiles*, however, the artist's youth has passed, and he has abandoned the worship of his youthful deity. As a result, although Beatrice resembles Giacomo's lady in education and appearance, and even echoes one of the lady's most devastating lines, milked of its venom,[9] she emerges as an older, more pitiful, and less threatening version of her Triestine sister. Richard tells her that he has written something about her, which he compares to an artist's drawings of his model, asking, "If I were a painter and told you I had a book of sketches of you you would not think it so strange, would you?" (*E* 18).

Giacomo Joyce* served Joyce as a sketchbook, but what he sketched in it were fantasies, lush imaginings coloured by fear and desire. The word *fantasy* comes from the ancient Greek "φαντασία," which literally means "a making visible" (*OED*), and throughout his career, Joyce developed an increasingly more complex set of techniques for enhancing the "visibility" of prose fantasy. *Giacomo Joyce* is not an isolated experiment, either in literary history or in Joyce's own career as an artist. It shows him working to perfect a highly imaginative prose imagism in 1914, the same year that imagism in poetry was at its height. In terms of Joyce's own development, it elaborates on the techniques used in his earliest works and adumbrates some feature of his last. Far from being "a spur on the main stem of his development,"[10] *Giacomo Joyce* emerges as an integral part of that development: it makes one in a series of highly visual fantasies that begins with the early epiphanies and climaxes in the "Circe" episode of *Ulysses* and in the extended dream of *Finnegans Wake*.

---

[9] For a discussion of the enigmatic line "otherwise I could not see you" and its re-emergence in *Exiles* (*GJ* 16; *E* 19), see Glasheen, 43-44. For an account of the similarities between Beatrice and Giacomo's lady, see John MacNicholas, *James Joyce's "Exiles": A Textual Companion* (New York: Garland 1979) 13-14.

[10] Adams, "A Very Pretty Piece of Protocol," 231.

Joyce's presentation of fantasy as a form linked to visual art and to music evolved slowly, and he always counterpointed his descriptive lyrical depictions of the inner world with exposés of the outer world, which he presented dramatically. Joyce's earliest-known experiments with dream visions are his epiphanies, which Stanislaus likened to an artist's sketches.[11] As Scholes and Kain point out, Joyce wrote two kinds of epiphanies that differ in form as well as in mood: "lyrical" epiphanies, which are vivid, dreamlike, highly descriptive verbal etchings, and "dramatic" epiphanies, which are written in the form of dramatic scenes, complete with the bracketed settings and parenthetical stage directions.[12] Joyce used these two kinds of epiphanies as a way of differentiating stylistically between the twin worlds of imagination and everyday reality. Like the later prose sketches in *Dubliners*, *A Portrait*, *Giacomo Joyce* and *Ulysses*, the lyrical epiphanies enlist the aid of fantasy and the visual imagination to create an unsettling, often symbolic prose "image." One lyrical epiphany, for example, presents an image of human history as a still gallery of stone kings, whose vision is darkened as they wearily gaze upon pillars of dark vapours that represent the constant upswelling of human error. The image is an elegiac one, an almost unconscious lament for the eternal paralysis of lawgivers in the face of human folly:

> A long curving gallery: from the floor arise pillars of dark vapours. It is peopled by the images of fabulous kings, set in stone. Their hands are folded upon their knees, in token of weariness, and their eyes are darkened for the errors of men go up before them for ever as dark vapours.[13]

---

[11] Stanislaus Joyce, *My Brother's Keeper: James Joyce's Early Years*, ed. Richard Ellmann (New York: Viking, 1958) 124-25.

[12] Robert E. Scholes and Richard M. Kain, eds. *The Workshop of Daedalus* (Evanston: Northwestern University Press, 1965) 3-4. The lyrical epiphanies are now located at Cornell (they were preserved in Stanislaus's commonplace book), and the dramatic epiphanies at Buffalo, although there is some overlap.

[13] Scholes and Kain, eds. *The Workshop of Daedalus*, 39 (see also *P* 249).

In the early stages of composing what would eventually be *A Portrait*, Joyce attempted to balance the twin realities of fantasy and experience by intertwining the two kinds of epiphanies into a single sequence that traced the progression from childhood to youth. He later plundered that sequence, embedding selected vignettes into *Stephen Hero* and, finally, into the richly allusive context of *A Portrait*, which also traced a child's maturation into youth. The sketches of *Giacomo Joyce* and the drama of *Exiles* play a role in the evolution of *Ulysses* similar to the role played by the lyrical and dramatic epiphanies in the evolution of *A Portrait*. Again, Joyce kept separate records of his fantasies and of his thinly disguised autobiographical experiences and gradually interwove the two to trace a new stage in his development, the movement from youth to middle age. Ultimately, he intertwined elements of both *Giacomo Joyce* and *Exiles* into the richer literary, artistic, philosophical, and fictional context of *Ulysses* in order to depict the same erosion of the intense self-confidence of youth into the uncertainty of middle age. Joyce's way of paralleling fantastical sketches with dramatic revelations, when he began balancing the vision of the "outer eye" that observes the external world with the vision of the "inner eye" of fantasy and dream.

As Joyce developed his skill as a painter, director, and orchestrator of words, he made his prose sketches more self-consciously artistic and interwove them carefully into his narrative for maximum effect. In *Dubliners*, for example, the moments when Joyce's language, chameleon-like, takes on the characteristics of other arts are the moments when the cherished fantasies of an individual or a nation are most movingly exposed. Such moments are highly charged with emotion and are easily punctured by irony, and they are hauntingly memorable, partly because they appeal to the senses so directly. Joyce uses vividly conceived, artistic images to appeal to the sense of sight and to still the movement of the narrative for an uncanny moment; he often accompanies such "sketches" with "phantom refrains" of music. One example of the use of a vivid image that represents the violated dreams of the entire country is the image of the harp in "Two Gallants." The harp, the symbol of Ireland, is presented as a weary, indifferent woman, her clothes fallen about her knees and her body exposed to the eyes of strangers. Her master's hands play the plaintive tune of "Silent, O Moyle" upon her strings (*D* 54). The unsung lyrics of the song and the image of the harp recall Ireland's dreams of greatness as well as emphasising the futility of those dreams. And the image of the harp as a violated woman links the plight of the country to the situation of the serving girl in the story, whom Corley plays upon and betrays for a small gold coin.

In "The Dead" Joyce again links the beginning of an ecstatic fantasy of love to a visual, artistic image and to the soft sounds of music. At the end of the Christmas party, Gabriel gazes up at his wife as she stands in shadow at the top of the stairs, leaning on the banisters and listening to the melancholy strains of "The Lass of Aughrim." In her remoteness and stillness, Gretta becomes a mysterious figure for him, and he imagines painting the scene:

> There was grace and mystery in her attitude as if she were a symbol of something. He asked himself what is a woman standing on the stairs in the shadow, listening to distant music, a symbol of. If he were a painter he would paint her in that attitude. Her blue felt hat would show off the bronze of her hair against the darkness and the dark panels of her skirt would show off the light ones. *Distant Music* he would call the picture if he were a painter. [*D* 210]

Gabriel's eyes, gazing at this remote, sad "painting" of his wife, pander to his desires, and he is soon caught up in a fever of memory and fantasy. Here, as in *Giacomo Joyce*, art, music, fantasy, desire and frustration are intimately interconnected; they inspire the imagination with a swell of emotion that is inevitably punctured by the bare, sharp facts of reality.

Giacomo Joyce is comprised of images analogous to those that Joyce uses so effectively in *Dubliners* and *A Portrait*; in its examination of voyeurism, it anticipates the more comprehensive exploration of the importance of vision that Joyce embarks upon in *Ulysses*.[14] The sketches are suffused with eye imagery and with references to sight and blindness. The entire imagined "affair" between the young lady and her instructor that *Giacomo Joyce* celebrates and laments is, like the affair between Bloom and Gerty MacDowell in *Ulysses*, an affair of the eye. When Giacomo first meets the lady, he imagines that his love for her penetrates her eye like the arrow of cupidinous passion. He writes, "The long eyelids beat and lift: a burning needleprick in the velvet iris" (*GJ* 1). An unusual amount of description is lavished on both his eyes and hers. Her dark eyes (and the quizzing glasses she uses to aid them) are the only features in her pale face that Joyce sketches in. The amorous narrator is caught in a dilemma whether to see or not to see: in the quarter of the prostitutes in Padua, when he feels himself drowned by "a dark wave of sense," he chants, "Mine eyes fail in darkness, mine eyes fail / Mine eyes fail in darkness, love" (*GJ* 3).

Watching his pupil toboggan down a hill with her family, Joyce sees a white flash from beneath her short skirt, and he adapts a line from Cowper's "John Gilpin" to express his avidity to see that sight again: "And when she next doth ride abroad / May I be there to see!" (*GJ* 4). Giacomo's voyeurism becomes more furtive when he pictures himself standing outside her window at night watching her reflection as she dresses for a play. Later, when he sees her at the opera, Joyce

---

[14] Joyce's interest in vision and its relation to fantasy and hallucination seems to have been heightened by his experience of painful eye attacks that began in Trieste. In a letter that he wrote to Harriet Weaver in 1924, in which he reminisces about his years in Trieste, Joyce reveals that these attacks caused a series if vivid mental images to arise before him unbidden. He explains, "Whenever I am obliged to lie with my eye closed I see a cinematograph going on and on and it brings back to my memory things I had almost forgotten" (*L* I.216).

intimates that the image of her hair, face and eyes, literally before him for the first part of the night, will remain in his imagination for the rest: "All night I have watched her, all night I shall see her: braided and pinnacled hair and olive oval face and calm soft eyes" (*GJ* 12). When she metamorphoses into a harem concubine, it is her eyes that drink his thoughts and his "seed," but when he meets her after their visionary intercourse, she averts her "black basilisk" eyes that have the power to poison any man they see. Finally, their association ends when she tells him, "Because otherwise I could not see you" (*GJ* 16).[15]

The obsession with sight and the fear of blindness that dominates *Giacomo Joyce* also characterises *Ulysses*, but in *Ulysses* the ability to see clearly from more than one perspective is an ability essential to survival, whereas in the sketchbook, the "inner eye" of fantasy breeds nightmares out of visions of desire. In *Giacomo Joyce* the artist's perspective towards his beloved is continually changing, but these shifts in point of view have no power to alleviate the pain of rejection and betrayal. In *Ulysses* different perspectives help Bloom to apprehend the mutability of life and love and the ineluctability of loss. Joyce once again associates fantasy with vision and visual arts, and with desire, disillusionment, and remoteness in episodes such as "Nausicaa," in which the "art" associated with Gerty and Bloom's sentimental and erotic fantasies is painting. Bloom, however, unlike Giacomo, bears a share of the responsibility for the scenes he has imagined. He refuses to cast himself in the role of worshipful or spurned lover, although Gerty sees him in both roles; instead, his attitude is practical, resigned, and even weary as he thinks, "We'll never meet again. But it was lovely. Goodbye, dear. Thanks. Made me feel so young" (*U* 382. 5-6).

In *Ulysses*, Bloom's fantasy "affairs" parallel Molly's affair with Boylan; external and internal experience, "objective" and "subjective" perception, are presented as closely analogous.

---

[15] See Glasheen's argument that *Giacomo Joyce* is all about the sense of sight page 45.

This becomes clearest in "Circe," when Joyce finally erases the distinction between observed and imagined reality, using a technique that he described to Linati as "visone animata fino allo scoppio" ("vision animated to the bursting point").[16] "Circe" shows that we may "paint" experiences on the canvases of the mind, or we may act them out in our daily lives, but the two kinds of experience are equally real. Joyce highlights the interdependence of the worlds of fantasy and action in "Circe" by successfully fusing the two styles that he experimented with in *Giacomo Joyce* and in *Exiles*: fantastical sketches and drama.

If *A Portrait* captures the pristine, aesthetic simplicity of youth, and if *Ulysses* is primarily an odyssey through the trials of middle age, *Giacomo Joyce* is a more a private lament for the passing of youth that marks a midpoint between the two. Joyce shows in *A Portrait* that the artist's youth is characterised by an inability to reconcile the highly aesthetic and sensual world of the mind with the grimness of everyday reality. Stephen, although he repeatedly alternates between obedience and rebellion, faith and disillusionment, spiritual exaltation and sensual degradation, remains essentially youthful in his failure to integrate inner and outer realities through compassion or humour. He wraps himself in the beauty of thought and language, only to be roughly exposed by circumstance to the outer world of squalor, noise, and sloth. Stephen, "the artist as a young man," experiences time as a pendulum swing between hope and despair, but the older Leopold Bloom, who also has "a touch of the artist about him," sees time as accelerating loss and struggles to preserve his "presence of mind" against encroachments of the past. Stephen's self-confidence, whether expressed as fervent faith or as audacious rebellion, has been replaced by Bloom's compassion, humour, practicality, and doubt; whereas Stephen failed to reconcile inner and outer realities, these realities are, for Bloom, almost inseparable.

---

[16] See the facsimile and transcript of the schema Joyce sent to Carlo Linati on September 21, 1920, in the appendix to Richard Ellmann's *"Ulysses" on the Liffey* (New York: Oxford University Press, 1972; corrected, 1973).

Giacomo Joyce helps to show that the experience of love and betrayal, whether real or imagined, has the power to shatter the complacency of youth and to challenge the self-sufficiency of the pristine world of the mind. It traces the course of secret love from desire to imagined satisfaction, betrayal, and emotional crucifixion. The voyeuristic lover sees his beloved as growing increasingly colder and more distant; he sees her as "unfaithful" to him, and in his hurt, he mentally transforms her from virgin to whore and back again. The lady of *Giacomo Joyce* becomes a snake in the imaginary Eden of his youth; she strikes, and his aesthetic, voyeuristic world of the mind totters and falls. He sees her rejection of him as an imagined crucifixion or poisoning; his lady, like a beautiful young Delilah, turns her Samson over to the Philistines, causing him to lose his vision and some of his strength. Once the betrayal is complete, strains of old music poignantly clarify the significance of what has happened. Sweelinck's variations for the clavichord play upon Giacomo's imagination, telling him that his youth has finally and irrevocably passed:

> Jan Pieters Sweelink [sic]. The quaint name of the old Dutch musician makes all beauty seem quaint and far. I hear his variations for the clavichord on an old air: *Youth has an end.* In the vague mist of old sounds a faint point of light appears. Youth has an end: the end is here. It will never be. What then? Write it, damn you, write it! What else are you good for? [*GJ* 16][17]

---

[17] *Exiles* tells the same tale dramatically, in a more "realistic" way. Richard Rowan is an older version of Stephen—he lives in an aesthetic world, at least until the play's climax. But his love for a woman, Bertha, plummets him into a different world, a world fraught with "restless living wounding doubt" (*E* 112). She *may* have betrayed him (and like Richard, we are never allowed to know whether she did or not), but the possibility of betrayal wounds him with a wound of doubt that will never be healed. Here too, is a fall into experience like the one sketched out in *Giacomo Joyce,* and both explorations of betrayal directly anticipate *Ulysses.*

If Joyce fills his sketches with images of sight to emphasise the frustration of Giacomo's voyeuristic and artistic ambitions as his lady passes out of his sight, he shrouds his lady in accumulating images of death and coldness to signal her symbolic demise and the demise of the youth she represents. In fantasy, his lady changes almost kaleidoscopically before his eyes; she sympathises with him, reviles him, tempts him, and finally abandons him for another, and this "inconstancy" instils in Giacomo an awareness of the entropy of change and the inevitability of death.

The first suggestions of death take the form of forebodings; Giacomo's apprehension that his beloved might die stems from his perception of her as frail, passive, and easily victimised. He first confronts the spectre of her death on a visit to a Jewish cemetery with Pimply Meissel, who is mourning for his dead wife (*GJ* 6). He later portrays her as a helpless victim, a witless sparrow about to be crushed under the wheels of Juggernaut. Still later, he conflates his fear that she will be killed with the fear that her purity will invite sexual molestation, and he mentally casts her as the violated Beatrice Cenci walking proudly to her death. When he learns from the housemaid that his pupil has been taken away for a sudden operation and that her situation is very "grave," he pictures the painful assault of the surgeon's knife as the sexual rape of a "libidinous God."

After the operation, Giacomo's attitude toward his lady changes subtly. She exchanges her role as passive victim for the role of aggressor, and Giacomo, who has imagined himself as the aggressor, becomes her victim. He sees her as increasingly colder and more remote; his fear that she might die is displaced by his fear of her as someone who is "dead." When watching her at the opera, Joyce finds in the green of her gown's embroidery a suggestion of lush grass, which he describes, after Whitman, as "the hair of graves" (*GJ* 12). The treacherous quagmire of her mind engulfs Giacomo's precise words and stifles them; her cold fingers are contrasted with the glowing shame on the pages of *A Portrait* that she has purportedly read.

He asks of her fingers, quiet and cold and pure, "Have they ever erred?" (*GJ* 13). Her body has lost its appeal to at least one of his senses; Giacomo calls it "an odourless flower" (*GJ* 13). When he next encounters her, she is weak, cold, and weary: "On the stairs. A cold hand: shyness, silence: dark langour-flooded eyes [sic]: weariness" (*GJ* 13). Immediately afterward, his "dying" pupil has faded into a ghost in Giacomo's mind, a corpse that kisses him upon the heath. She emerges out of "whirling of wreaths grey vapour" and he marvels, "Her face, how grey and grave!" (*GJ* 14). Like Stephen's dead mother, who appears to him in *Ulysses* in "leper grey," her hair "scant and lank," breathing "upon him softly her breath of wetted ashes" (*U* 579.26, 28; 580.23-24), Joyce's pupil appears to him with "dank matted hair," and when she kisses him, "her sighing breath comes through" (*GJ* 14). In subsequent encounters she is even colder: she greets him "wintrily" and attacks him in the guise of "a cold nightsnake" (*GJ* 15).

Finally, images of death give way to suggestions of interment. Joyce's youthful fancy is buried in a "coffin of music" (*GJ* 16) similar to the one he chose to have illustrated on the cover of *Chamber Music*. On this long black piano lies the emblem that will serve as her epitaph: her protective armour, her red-flowered hat and her furled umbrella. With gloomy irony, he describes them heraldically, as "a casque, gules, and blunt spear on a field, sable" (*GJ* 16).[18] Joyce's pictorial epitaph for his "dead" love serves as an image of her "infidelity" as well as of her demise; Joyce emphasises this by ironically modelling his design on Hawthorne's description of the scarlet letter that marks that common tombstone of Hester Prynne and Arthur Dimmesdale. Hawthorne uses this heraldic description to close *The Scarlet Letter*, explaining that it "might serve for a motto and brief description of our now concluded legend [...] ON A

---

[18] Stephen perceives his own hat and ashplant in a similar way in *Ulysses*. In "Scylla and Charybdis" he thinks of these accessories as "my casque and sword," and later, in "Circe," they are described as lying on the pianola, much as his pupil's hat and umbrella are lying here (*U* 192.16, 503.11).

FIELD, SABLE, THE LETTER A, GULES."[19] Perhaps the round, red hat and the furled umbrella do seem to depict a small *a* against the black of the piano-coffin, an *a* that reminds Giacomo, not only of his pupil's "unfaithfulness" to him, but also, perhaps, of her name: Amalia. He reflects that this emblem represents the essence of his dead love; her umbrella, or protective shield, is part of her. Her silent, ironic farewell to him closes the "affair" and the sketchbook: "Love me, love my umbrella" (*GJ* 16).

Joyce saps his lady of warmth and vitality as she grows more distant from him, but he depicts Giacomo's suffering by sketching him against a biblical background. In particular, he highlights Giacomo's sense of pained betrayal by illustrating him en route to a private Calvary: her indifference and infidelity have crucified his youth. In three separate sketches, he casts himself in the role of the betrayed and suffering Christ (*GJ* 10, 15, 16), with his lady playing an increasingly more sinister supporting part. The first sketch of Giacomo's passion is set on Good Friday, a "raw veiled spring morning" in Paris (*GJ* 10). He enters a vast gargoyled church and listens to *Tenebrae*; echoes from the Vulgate version of John 18:18 harmonise with the reading from Hosea that begins the service. His pale, cold pupil stands beside him, deeply affected by his pain; he writes, "Her soul is sorrowful" (*GJ* 10). His final words to her echo Christ's imprecation to the crowd of women who follow the cross in lamentation, in Luke 23:28: "Weep not for me, O daughters of Jerusalem!" (*GJ* 10).[20]

---

[19] Nathaniel Hawthorne, *The Scarlet Letter*, ed. Sculley Bradley et al. (New York: W. W. Norton, 1978) 186.

[20] The phrase "weep not for me, O daughters if Jerusalem" reappears in a humorous context in *Ulysses*, where Bloom's Circean fantasies of crucifixion are matter-of-fact rather than tragic. Standing amid phoenix flames "in a seamless garment marked I.H.S.," Bloom intones, "Weep not for me, O daughters of Erin" (*U* 498.16-17). The reference to "daughters of Jerusalem" has erotic overtones as well, since the phrase appears in the Song of Solomon (1:5). In "Circe" Zoe quotes this verse verbatim in Hebrew: "*Schorach ani wenowach, benoith Hierushaloim*" (*U* 477.14).

Joyce sees his compassionate lady as one of the Jewesses who sorrowed at the passing of Christ, but the language and setting of the sketch suggest that he has also cast his lady in the roles of the Blessed Virgin Mary and Mary Jane Murray Joyce, his own mother, who died several years earlier. Fritz Senn sees in the phrase "her soul is sorrowful" a reference to the mysteries of the Blessed Virgin, told in the second chaplet of the Rosary, which include the Crucifixion.[21] Giacomo's pupil relives the sorrows of the Virgin Mother, but the scene described in *Giacomo Joyce* also re-enacts another "crucifixion" that Joyce associated with the pain of his mother's death. The Good Friday service described here recalls the *Tenebrae* service that Joyce attended in Paris at Notre Dame on April 10, 1903, a few hours before he learned that his mother was dying. The news, coming as it did on Good Friday, seems to have prompted Joyce to identify his own suffering at his mother's illness with Christ's crucifixion, an identification that must have been strengthened by the coincidence that it was Easter Sunday when he returned home to Dublin like a "ghost from *limbo patrum*" (*U* 188.10).[22] In 1914 Good Friday again fell on April 10, as it had eleven years earlier, and Joyce seems to be glossing the memory of that excruciating Good Friday with the pain that his lovely student was currently causing him. Mixing memory and desire, he amalgamates the figures of his mother, the Virgin Mother, and his virginal Jewish pupil.[23]

---

[21] Fritz Senn, "Some Further Notes on *Giacomo Joyce*," *JJQ* 5 (Spring 1968): 234-35. Amalia Popper's Jewishness enhances her suitability for the role of the Virgin, for as Joyce reminds Marthe Fleischmann, "Jésus Christ a pris son corps humain: dans le ventre d'une femme juive" (*L* II.432).

[22] See *L* II.41.

[23] The imagery of this hauntingly painful Good Friday service runs throughout Joyce's work. Stephen discusses Christ's isolation on Good Friday with Cranly in *Stephen Hero* (*SH* 116), quoting the lesson from Hosea 6:1-6 that begins the Good Friday mass. (He also alludes to this lesson in *Giacomo Joyce*.) Thereafter, Joyce begins to associate the service fairly consistently with the fear of annihilation, with guilt at the loss of innocence, and with a sense of the insignificance of the individual. Echoes of this scene in *Giacomo Joyce* resound in the third chapter of *A Portrait* and in Joyce's bitter poetic elegy to a dead love,

Giacomo's feeling that crucifixion is imminent colours later sketches as well, but his beloved no longer sorrows for him; instead, she has treacherously joined the crowd of those who revile him. He imagines a crowd spreading carpets under his feet, awaiting his passing as Christ, "the son of man" (*GJ* 14): as he walks to his doom he sees his lady in a hallway, and she darts at him "a jet of liquorish venom" (*GJ* 15). Joyce also uses a reference to the Crucifixion to intensify the climax of this brief, fantastical love story. His pupil tells him that she has chosen another, and Giacomo's world is shattered. Amalia Popper, the student around whom these fantasies were woven, became engaged to Michele Risolo during the Easter holiday of 1913, and she married him in August 1914;[24] possibly Giacomo's pupil has just told him that she will shortly be married. He asks "Why?" and she answers enigmatically, "Because otherwise I could not see you" (*GJ* 16). Perhaps she is telling him that she would no longer be permitted to see him unless she were married, but whatever her reason for choosing another, her announcement overwhelms Giacomo with a feeling of annihilation that suggests that the "son of man" has indeed passed or that Lucifer has once again fallen from the heavens: "Sliding—space—ages—foliage of stars—and waning heaven— stillness—and stillness deeper—stillness annihilation—and her voice" (*GJ* 16). Out of the ruin of all space he hears her choosing another man over himself: "*Non hunc sed Barabbam!*" (*GJ* 16). History repeats itself; echoing the earlier decision of her people,

"Nightpiece," from *Pomes Penyeach* (*CP* 55). Joyce again uses the imagery of inefficacious worship, in the notes to *Exiles*, as a way of describing Beatrice's bleak hopelessness (*E* 119). Several years later, however, in the first draft of the "Tristan and Isolde" section of *Finnegans Wake*, Joyce parodies the hopelessness of such desolate imagery as jejune. "Nightpiece" is the romantic, despairing poem that the young lover Tristan whispers dramatically into the ear of Isolde. Joyce parodies the poem by literally surrounding a handwritten transcript of it with ironic and humorous commentary, but the poem and its marginalia do not appear in the final text of *Finnegans Wake*. See *A First Draft Version of "Finnegans Wake*," ed. David Hayman (Austin: University of Texas Press, 1963) 208-11.

24 Michele Risolo, "*Mia moglie e Joyce*," *Il Corriere della sera*, 27 Feb. 1969: 11. See also Ellmann's response to Helen Barolini: 50.

his pupil chooses Barabbas over Christ, and by her so doing, Giacomo imagines that she has crucified his youth.

In another mysterious scene, which is also set in Paris, Joyce uses the imagery of the Fall to illustrate Giacomo's fantasy of falling from fidelity into adultery. In this passage, which strongly resembles a dream, Giacomo's pupil is no longer virginal and saintly, but whorish and satanic. Instead of commiseration with his suffering within the holy confines of a church, she attacks him in the guise of an adulterous temptress, a cold nightsnake whose touch burns:

A soft crumpled peagreen cover drapes the lounge. A narrow Parisian room. The hairdresser lay here but now. I kissed her stocking and the hem of her rustblack dusty skirt. It is the other. She. Gogarty came yesterday to be introduced. *Ulysses* is the reason. Symbol of the intellectual conscience .... Ireland then? And the husband? Pacing the corridor in list shoes or playing chess against himself. Why are we left here? The hairdresser lay here but now, clutching my head between her knobby knees .... Intellectual symbol of my race. Listen! The plunging gloom has fallen. Listen!
—I am not convinced that such activities of the mind or body can be called unhealthy—
She speaks. A weak voice from beyond the cold stars. Voice of wisdom. Say on! O, say again, making me wise! This voice I never heard.
She coils towards me along the crumpled lounge. I cannot move or speak. Coiling approach of starborn flesh. Adultery of wisdom. No. I will go. I will.
—Jim, love!—
Soft sucking lips kiss my left armpit: a coiling kiss on myriad veins. I burn! I crumple like a burning leaf! From my right armpit a fang of flame leaps out. A starry snake has kissed me: a cold nightsnake. I am lost!
—Nora!— [*GJ* 15][25]

[25] The handwriting of this entry suggests that it was added after the faircopy of the rest of the sketchbook was complete, perhaps when Joyce was working on the early drafts of *Ulysses* or writing *Exiles*. (Hodgart suggests that it was written after 1920; see "Portrait of the Artist as a Middle-Aged Adulterer," 3.)

Although the passage suggests several still-unanswered questions—the identity of the hairdresser, the significance of the allusions to Gogarty and to *Ulysses*, and what basis the scene may have had in reality—the imagery of the dream forms a definite pattern that suggests that the sexual "fall" of the dreamer into adultery re-enacts the original Fall in the Garden of Eden. The woman, "the other," plays the role of the tempter, Lucifer, the morning star turned snake who attempts to persuade Joyce, the uncertain victim, to enjoy the forbidden fruit of adulterous knowledge, to accept her assurance that "such activities of the mind or body" are not unhealthy. Joyce, now in the role of Eve, responds eagerly to her temptation: he hails her as the "voice of wisdom" and begs her to "say again, making me wise." But when the starborn, Luciferian snake-woman coils toward him and strikes him with a kiss, he begins to burn, perhaps with desire, perhaps in anticipation of the fires of hell, crying, "I am lost!—Nora!—"[26]

Unlike most of the other scenes in *Giacomo Joyce*, the scenes of Giacomo's "crucifixion" and "fall" are both set in Paris. Joyce's use of Paris as a background for particularly painful

Joyce seems to have added it on the only page with enough blank space to accommodate it; even then, he wrote smaller and left less space as if he were afraid it would not fit. If Joyce did insert the scene at a later time, it would explain why the passage seems to disrupt the sequence of events developed throughout the rest of *Giacomo Joyce*. In this sketch, for example, Giacomo's lady is married, whereas in the rest of the vignettes, she seems to be unattached and living with her family.

[26] Similar associations between the biblical account of the Fall, the genesis of the world as we know it, and the sexual act—a "fall" that is responsible for the genesis of every individual—may be found in both *A Portrait* and *Ulysses*. In *A Portrait* Joyce uses the imagery of the Fall to inform Stephen's attitudes toward his own sexual indulgences; Stephen regards his treacherous penis as a snake, "a torpid snaky life feeding itself out of the tender marrow of his life and fattening on the slime of lust" (*P* 140). He sees it as a rebel that, like Lucifer, sins in an instant, refusing to serve his sovereign will. Later, in "Scylla and Charybdis," Joyce will again use the imagery and some of the words of the "dream" passage to furnish Stephen's reflections about Eve's fall: "Eve. Naked wheatbellied sin. A snake coils her, fang in's kiss" (*U* 199.9).

experiences has a special meaning; Paris becomes a symbolic as well as a geographical locale, partly because of the mythological and personal events that Joyce associates with it. Both his sensitivity to the name *Paris* and his memory of his own experiences there seem to have prompted Joyce to connect the city with the pursuit of sexual satisfaction and the experience of betrayal. The name of the city recalls the legendary man whose adulterous desire for a beautiful woman resulted in the total annihilation of Troy; more personally, Paris had offered to Joyce himself a more licentious alternative to his "virgin" Irish homeland. The education in the ways of the world that London had given Shakespeare was given to Joyce in Paris, where the energies of sin, prostitution, and infidelity opened up before him on a grander scale than ever before. After Joyce's return from Paris in 1903, he seemed to associate sexual indulgence with his guilt at his mother's death, since it was the news that she was dying that put an end to his Parisian bohemianism. All these associations between infidelity and painful guilt, the "fall" into experience and the "crucifixion" that atoned for it, are compressed into these two brief passages in *Giacomo Joyce.*

Joyce illustrates his sense that the "model" for his art, his pupil, has betrayed him by setting selected sketches against the background of biblical scenes of betrayal, by shrouding his model in images of death and interment, and by portraying her in a state of regressive metamorphosis from "a young person of quality" to a variety of gentle animals, to more poisonous reptiles, and finally to an ironic emblem. Joyce gradually diminishes the stature of his beloved as he depersonalises her through his art. He portrays her as a beautifully shaped filly foal, a silvery mermaid or siren, a witless sparrow, and a pampered fowl; after her operation, he compares her "full dark suffering eyes" to the eyes of an antelope and then pictures her in convalescence as a happily chirping bird and a frightened black pullet. Toward the end of his gallery of drawings, as his disappointment at her "inconstancy" grows, Joyce transforms her into a noxious basilisk and a cold snake, and his final picture of her depicts only the first initial of her name. Like E. C. of *A Portrait*, she has dwindled into a mere symbol; Joyce bids farewell, not to a woman, but to the emblem of her "quality," her "infidelity," and her perpetual reserve.

Joyce's way of "sketching" the de-evolution of a beloved model to illustrate his growing disillusionment with her anticipates a technique that Picasso would also use. In 1946 Picasso drew a series of pencil sketches that depict the metamorphosis and gradual dehumanisation of his former mistress, Dora Maar, in contrast to the suggestive ripeness of his new mistress and model, Françoise Gilot. Both Joyce and Picasso were fascinated by the relationship between an artist and his model. Picasso expressed his intuition that the artist's relationship to his model was a peculiarly voyeuristic one in his many sketches and paintings in which the artist watches a young woman sleep. As Leo Steinberg argues, Picasso uses sleep as a symbol of secure autonomy and of interior privacy; the artist may look at his model the way that a man may study the anatomy of a woman, but he remains an exile from her innermost thoughts and feelings.[27] Joyce's prose sketches of his female models reflect a similar awareness that for him, these women remain essentially mysterious, despite his ability to capture their likeness in his art. From its opening question "Who?" *Giacomo Joyce* emphasises the elusiveness of its female subject. The sketchbook is composed of scenes in which a man watches a woman who is, for the most part, unconscious of his close and constant scrutiny; in a sense, Joyce, like Picasso, is himself a "sleepwatcher," composing conscious, visual fantasies around a woman whose dreams are largely unconscious, natural, and impossible to divine.

Joyce's voyeuristic relationship with the model for his sketchbook is metaphorically comparable to relationships between actual painters and their models, but Joyce's art in

---

[27] Leo Steinberg, "Picasso's Sleepwatchers," *Other Criteria: Confrontations with Twentieth Century Art* (London: Oxford, 1972) 102, 105-12. I am grateful to Wendy Steiner for bringing this book to my attention.

Giacomo Joyce is also highly allusive. His worship of the "lady of quality" in *Giacomo Joyce* followed a precedent set by artists as diverse as Dante, Petrarch, Michelangelo, Mangan, and Ibsen. Like them, he devoted his youthful adoration to women who were essentially symbols of artistic and almost divine inspiration. Joyce seemed to pay homage in his fiction to a number of different ideal women, but all of them are strangely similar: the "Woman of Sorcery" of *Shine and Dark*; the "Beneficent one" of the "Portrait" essay; the "dark, full-figured" Emma of *Stephen Hero*; the brown figure of Mangan's sister in "Araby"; Mercedes, surrounded by the rose gardens and sunny trellises of *The Count of Monte Cristo*; the bird-girl on the strand; E.C.; the Triestine Jewess of *Giacomo Joyce*; and the pitiful Beatrice Justice of *Exiles*. These virgin-temptresses represent different incarnations of a single ideal who inspired the artist in his youth.[28]

In *Giacomo Joyce* the "death" of this youthful ideal who had, in so many different forms, served as a model for Joyce's art raises a question of artistic responsibility: does the creation of art from life reverse the Pygmalion effect? Does the artist symbolically "kill" the models that he once loved? These are questions that also haunted Ibsen, who explored them in his last play, *When We Dead Awaken*. In Ibsen's play, the sculptor Rubek's first love and model returns to him insisting that she is "dead," that she has given her life to the youthful works of art she inspired. In his early review of the play, Joyce showed great appreciation for Ibsen's insight into the way that an artist is haunted by his model, asserting: "No other man could have so subtly expressed the nature of the relations between the sculptor and his model, had he even dreamt of them" (*CW* 54).

Joyce begins to illustrate his realisation that his youthful model is "dead" in *Giacomo Joyce* and in *Exiles*, but only in *Ulysses* does he begin to be haunted by the possibility that he

---

[28] On the kinship of Joyce's fictional virgins, see Mark Shechner, "Nausicaa: The Anatomy of a Virgin," *Joyce in Nighttown* (Berkley: University of California Press, 1974) 153-91.

killed her. There, his fear that the artist kills his model is subsumed by Stephen's fear that he has killed his mother, the pure, religious woman upon whom his own ideal woman is based. She appears to him in "Circe," arrayed for the bridal even in death, backed by a choir of virgins and confessors, to warn Stephen of death and retribution. Although oppressed by the fear that he may be responsible for her death, he defies her imprecations to resume his former worship, or Mariolatry. As Ibsen had shown, if the artist returns to his youthful ideal, he will join her—symbolically—in death. While professing to take Rubek up to the mountaintop to the promised heights, Rubek's former model, shadowed by the nun that is her counterpart, leads them both to a frozen, snowy grave.

Giacomo's relationship to his lady is partly patterned on an artist's relationship to his model, partly on a man's worship of the two Marys, the Virgin Mother and Mary Magdalene, and Stephen's ambivalent attitudes toward his mother in *Ulysses* are indebted to all these paradigms. May Dedalus and Giacomo's lady produce similar reactions in Stephen and in Giacomo: both men regard the woman who haunts them as a Jekyll-and-Hyde apparition—a compassionate, pure, maternal figure and a nightmare that attacks and ages them. In particular, the dreamlike fantasy in which Giacomo's lady assaults him in the form of a lamia foreshadows Stephen's hallucination in "Circe" in which he is accosted by his mother's ghost. Gogarty and his fictional counterpart, Buck Mulligan, play bit parts in both scenes. Although Stephen privately charges Mulligan with usurpation and betrayal in *Ulysses*, Mulligan has openly accused him of having killed his own mother; thereafter, Stephen's feelings of guilt over his mother's death always incorporate a reminder of Mulligan's light mockery. As Adaline Glasheen notes, both Giacomo's lady and May Dedalus also appear to possess stores of secret knowledge: Giacomo's plea to the "voice of wisdom" to speak and make him wise parallels Stephen's imprecations to his mother's ghost to tell him "the word known to all men" (*U* 581). Both apparitions attack the men who love them: the nightsnake poisons and scalds Giacomo with her kiss; May Dedalus extends her black withered fingers toward Stephen, and they become the grinning claws of a malignant green crab that clutch his heart. Both men react by ageing suddenly. Giacomo writes, "Youth has an end. The end is here" (*GJ* 16). Stephen's *"features grow drawn and grey and old"* (*U* 582). The nightsnake of *Giacomo Joyce* metamorphoses into the nightmare of *Ulysses*.

In *Ulysses* the relationships that Joyce had formerly defined in artistic terms he now defines in more universal, familial terms; Joyce's interest in the relationship between an artist and his model broadens into an exploration of a man's relationship to his mother and his wife. Stephen, like Giacomo and Ibsen's Rubek, is haunted by a woman whom he fears he has indirectly "killed," but that woman is his mother, not his model. Bloom, also like Giacomo, is haunted by a woman he both loves and desires, a woman who betrays him, but her "inconstancy," her protean mutability, transforms her into an image, not of death, but of life. Perhaps the older man has intuited what Stephen has only articulated, that "death is the highest form of life." In any event, the two most powerful figures of death and life in *Ulysses*, May Dedalus and Molly Bloom, derive some of their attributes from the same precursor: the lady of *Giacomo Joyce*.

The imagined love affair with his student and "model" that Joyce illustrates in *Giacomo Joyce* also resembles an "affair of the heart" that the Irish poet James Clarence Mangan had with "a pupil of his, to whom he gave lessons in German" (*CW* 77, 181). Joyce mentioned this "affair" in his 1902 essay on Mangan and in the lecture he gave five years later at the Università Populare in Trieste. This lecture, delivered in Italian, bore the title "Giacomo Clarenzio Mangan." "Giacomo" Mangan, like Giacomo Joyce, adored a woman who "recalls the spiritual yearnings and the imaginary loves of the Middle Ages" (*CW* 182). He spent his youth in pursuit of an ideal woman whom he once saw incarnated in one of his pupils; an artist in love with his model, he was "in love with death all his life," like his namesake and fellow countryman, Giacomo Joyce.

The lady of *Giacomo Joyce* is partly an incarnation of an ideal, but she is also modelled on the real woman that Ellmann identified in his biography, Amalia Popper. Little has been written about Joyce's association with his pupil. Most of the available information may be found in a few sources: Ellmann's biography of Joyce and his introduction to *Giacomo Joyce*; Hughes's article in *Life* magazine; a newspaper article by Amalia Popper's husband, Michele Risolo; and an exchange between Helen Barolini and Ellmann in the *New York Review of Books*.

The information that Richard Ellmann has provided about Joyce's relationship with Amalia Popper is familiar and accessible, but Risolo's article requires closer scrutiny, since it has rarely been cited by English and American scholars. Risolo published the article ostensibly to stem the tide of letters and inquires that he claims had inundated him ever since the publication of *Giacomo Joyce*. Risolo's initial response to the sudden publicity must have been an obliging one; he agreed to be interviewed by *Life*, and he gave permission to *Le Figaro Littéraire* to publish photographs of his wife as "la femme d'Ulysse."[29] By February 1969 Risolo had evidently had enough publicity; in his article in the *Il Corriere della sera*, he proposes a new candidate for the lady of *Giacomo Joyce*: the governess of the Popper sisters, Ina Bassano, who was later killed in a concentration camp.

Risolo's evidence in support of his argument in unconvincing; he makes no attempt to prove that his wife could not be the subject of Joyce's fantasies, and every argument that he advances in favour of the governess's candidacy would apply equally well to her charge. As Ellmann has pointed out in the *New York Review of Books*, Risolo himself "seeks a woman in the same house." Far from proving his wife's ineligibility for the role of Giacomo's lady, Risolo concedes that some of the

---

29 "La femme d'Ulysse," *Le Figaro Littéraire*, 26 février-3 mars 1968: 18.

more flattering descriptions of the lady are apt, and he recalls that Joyce considered Amalia Popper his best female pupil.[30]

Risolo's article also aimed to correct some of the inaccuracies in Ellmann's account of Joyce's relationship with his pupil. Risolo points to the highly imaginative nature of the sketchbook and chides Ellmann for using it as a basis for reconstructing biographical details. For example, Ellmann hazards the claim that the Poppers lived on the Via San Michele, presumably because in one sketch Giacomo walks along this street at midnight calling his beloved's name (*GJ* 6). According to Risolo, this reference is incorrect, since the Poppers lived on the Via Alice. The professor also insists that his wife never read any of Joyce's works except for *Dubliners*, which she read after 1920, and ten pages of *A Portrait*, which she began in 1932. If Risolo's recollections are accurate, it is unlikely that Joyce ever gave Amalia Popper a chapter of *A Portrait* to read, as Giacomo imagines having done (*GJ* 12), unless he gave it to her without telling her that he had written it, perhaps as a part of an exercise in English. Finally, although Ellmann notes that Signorina Popper asked and received permission to translate *Dubliners* in 1933, he asserts that she never actually did the translation (*JJI* 369n). Risolo reveals that his wife did in fact publish a translation of five stories from *Dubliners*, which included a "biografia essenziale" that she wrote as a preface to the stories.[31]

Joyce gave Amalia Popper English lessons in the breakfast room of the Popper villa for approximately one year, but there is some confusion about which year this was. In the article in *Life*, Hughes states, presumably on Risolo's authority, that Joyce visited the Popper household three times a week from autumn

---

30 A classmate of Amalia Popper's inadvertently suggests yet another way that she resembles the lady of *Giacomo Joyce* when she describes her as *una donna gelida*, "an icy woman" (Hughes, "The Mystery Lady," 40).

31 James Joyce, *Araby*, trans. Amalia Popper Risolo (Trieste: Carlo Moschieri, 1935). The five stories that she translated are "Araby," "A Little Cloud," "Counterparts," "Eveline," and "The Dead." It is tempting to speculate that the mention of the Via San Michele plays on Michele Risolo's given name.

1907 to July 1908. Ellmann, in his introduction to the sketchbook, also writes that according to Amalia's husband, her lessons spanned 1907 and 1908 (*GJ* xiii). In his own article, Risolo insists that the lessons were given between October 1908 and November 1909, but later in the article, Risolo remembers "with precision" that Amalia took her last lesson a few months after Joyce moved into the new flat at 32 Via Barriera Vecchia. The Joyces took up residence in this flat in December 1910, which would place the last lesson in early 1911, not 1909.[32] Whenever the lessons began and ended, it seems relatively certain that they were in progress in late 1909, since Joyce wrote to Stanislaus on November 17, 1909, that he would like Stanislaus to tutor several of his students while he was in Dublin, and the list includes the name "Popper" (*L* II.262).

Joyce's relations with the Popper family were immediately friendly. He assiduously frequented Sunday afternoon gatherings at the Poppers' "16-room hillside villa filled with antique furniture and paintings."[33] Professor Risolo recalls that amid an abundance of cakes, buns, tea, and coffee, the friends of the Popper sisters would form a little "academia musicale." Joyce would often entertain with arias by Verdi or Puccini, ballads, or popular Irish songs; sometimes his sister Eileen would accompany him on the piano.[34] Risolo does not indicate

[32] See Ellmann, "James Joyce's Addresses," in *L* II.lvii. Ellmann also discusses the inconsistencies in Risolo's account in the *New York Review of Books*: 49-50.

[33] Hughes, "The Mystery Lady," 36.

[34] In one sketch, Joyce suggests that his current infatuation for his pupil resembles an earlier passion that he had secretly nursed in Dublin, presumably his obsession with Mary Sheehy, the Emma Cleary of *Stephen Hero* and the E.C. of *A Portrait*. Giacomo writes, "At midnight, after music, all the way up the via San Michele, these words were spoken softly. Easy now, Jamesy! Did you never walk the streets of Dublin at night sobbing another name?" (*GJ* 6). Joyce's sense that he was reliving this early passion of his youth may have been strengthened by the notable similarities between the Sunday gatherings at the Popper villa and the musical evenings at the Sheehy household in Dublin, which Ellmann describes in *James Joyce* (*JJI* 53-53). In Ulysses such *conversazioni* play a part in Bloom's fantasies of a growing intimacy between himself, Stephen, and Molly. Bloom's fantasy of hosting musical gatherings with Molly may well be based on Joyce's memory of the musical afternoons hosted by Leopoldo and Malì

whether these gatherings continued after Amalia began to study Greek and Latin in Florence. She spent the first half of 1910 in Florence, according to her husband, but she must have resumed her lessons, at least temporarily, when she was back in Trieste in late 1910 and early 1911, if Risolo's recollection that she took her last lesson in Joyce's flat at 32 Via Barriera Vecchia is accurate. It is reasonable to suppose that even after November 1911, when Amalia began to be regularly enrolled in courses in Florence, the Sunday afternoon gatherings may have resumed from time to time when she returned for vacations. The most logical time for her association with Joyce to come to an end, then, was not when her lessons with him ceased, but when she announced her engagement to Michele Risolo, whom she married in 1914.

Joyce's odd, wistful fascination for his pupil probably ended when she unintentionally "betrayed" him by marrying Risolo, but Risolo suggests that the Poppers made a profound impression on Joyce's artistic imagination, at least to the point of influencing Joyce's choice of names for Leopold and Molly Bloom. Amalia's father, Leopoldo Popper, was a cultured and successful Jewish businessman. Risolo recalls an occasion when Popper invited Joyce to visit his office, which bore a sign above the door announcing "Brum and Popper." Risolo speculates that Popper's first name, *Leopoldo*, together with his partner's last name, *Brum*, may have suggested the name *Leopold Bloom*. Risolo also relates that in the Popper household, Joyce would have heard Amalia addressed by her nicknames, "Malietta," "Maliù," and "Malì," and he proposes that these nicknames suggested the name *Molly*.

As the artist of a book of literary sketches, Joyce chose for his model, not only the cool, reserved pupil whom her knew and admired, but he also modelled Giacomo's lady on several other female figures who peopled his artistic imagination. Giacomo

Popper. The narrator of "Eumaeus" relates, "It was in fact only a matter of months and artistic *conversaziones* during the festivities of the Christmas season" (*U* 663.39-664.1).

sees his lover as a fleeting incarnation of Joyce's own dead mother, his past loves, the Virgin Mary, a satanic temptress, and a Jewess who reviles Christ, but he also compared her to five much-beloved, ultimately unattainable characters in literary history: Hedda Gabler, Ophelia, Beatrice Portinari, Beatrice Cenci and Hester Prynne. By linking his lover with these great tragic figures, Giacomo casts himself as the male characters who desired them: Ejlert Lövborg, Hamlet, Dante, Orsino, and Arthur Dimmesdale.

At first glance, this group of fictional lovers seems to be an impossibly heterogeneous one, but on closer scrutiny, it becomes clear that Giacomo sees each of these love stories as in some way analogous to his own. In all the stories, the male lover is forced to conceal or disguise his love. All the tales end with the death of one or both of the lovers, but the failure of the characters to fulfil their great desires has in each case been translated into an artistic triumph for the authors who tell their stories. As the author of his own love story, Joyce is able to compare himself, not only to five characters, both great and mean, but also to the artists who created them: Ibsen, Shakespeare, Dante, Shelley, and Hawthorne. By means of these analogies, Joyce is able to transform a "failed" imaginary love into an important stage in his own artistic development.

In one sketch, Giacomo briefly conflates his love with Ibsen's Hedda Gabler. She is riding on horseback early one morning, and her independence and freedom prompt Joyce to call out to here "Hedda! Hedda Gabler!" (*GJ* 8). The comparison is apt; Giacomo's lady resembles Hedda Gabler both physically and temperamentally. Both are described as uniformly pallid, and both are portrayed as essentially cold women who have instinctively and perhaps unconsciously pledged their strongest allegiance to their fathers.[35] Hedda was the secret love of a profligate artist Ejlert Lövborg, with whom the young Joyce sympathised strongly. When a young man in Dublin, Joyce had

---

[35] Richard Nickerson, "Joyce's *Giacomo Joyce*," *Explicator* 28 (December 1969), item 38.

offered to play the part of Lövborg if the struggling Irish Literary Theatre, as the Irish National Theatre was then called, would consent to perform *Hedda Gabler*. Stanislaus writes that the part seemed to be written for Joyce as he was then.[36] Lövborg's story does bear a marked resemblance to Joyce's own: a genius wasting his talent with drink and debauchery is redeemed by a simple, instinctual woman whom he, in a sense, created. In *Hedda Gabler* it is Mrs. Elvsted who "redeems" Lövborg; for Joyce, it was Nora. But Mrs. Elvsted is aware that a woman's shadow always stands between her and Lövborg; the shadow is Hedda Gabler, Lövborg's first love, a cold, envious, courageous, independent, and rebellious woman who uses her power to destroy both Lövborg and herself. Like the lady of *Giacomo Joyce*, she is a beautiful woman who eventually emerges as a seductive temptress—icy, unreliable and deadly.

During the course of his lectures on *Hamlet*, which he delivered to a Triestine audience that presumably included his pupil, Joyce mentally compares his lady to Ophelia, another character who is strongly influenced by her father. In his lecture, Joyce argues that it is Hamlet's "embittered" idealism that causes him to be rude only to Polonius, perhaps because "he can see in the parents of his beloved only grotesque attempts on the part of nature to produce her image" (*GJ* 10). An ellipsis follows, and Joyce drives home his apology for Hamlet with a Shakespearean phrase borrowed most probably from Polonius himself: "Marked you that?"[37] This question seems to be an aside addressed to Joyce's pupil; perhaps he is using his discussion of *Hamlet* as a public way of making a private apology to her for some thoughtless rudeness to her father. In any event, Joyce seems to be using the character of

---

[36] Stanislaus Joyce, *Recollections of James Joyce*, trans. Ellsworth Mason (New York: James Joyce Society, 1950) 21.

[37] When Hamlet declines to sit with his mother at "The Mousetrap" and instead lies down at Ophelia's feet, Polonius says to the King, "O, ho! Do you mark that?" (III.ii.108 in the edition that Joyce owned in Trieste, *The Tragedy of King Hamlet Edited for the Use of Students*, edited A. W. Verity [Cambridge: Cambridge University Press, 1909]).

Hamlet as Stephen will later use it in *Ulysses*, as a mask for himself.

Giacomo's lady bears a slight resemblance to Ophelia in her dutiful obedience to her father and in the simple naturalness that prompts Giacomo to see her, at least initially, as vulnerable and easily victimised, but the links between Joyce and Hamlet are more important than the ties binding Giacomo's lady to Ophelia. In 1912, when he began the series of lectures on *Hamlet*, Joyce, like Hamlet, was thirty years old, complained that he had been exiled from his home,[38] and felt himself to be an embittered idealist. Joyce concluded his Hamlet lectures with a passage from George Brandes's 1898 critical study of Shakespeare, in which Brandes presents Hamlet as a dreamer, a man betrayed by the friends of his youth. He sees him as an enemy of hypocrisy, a "brother" whose contemptuous wit lashes those who "fill the earth with noise and are its masters." His final picture of Hamlet is a melancholy, fantastical, sardonic man who, like Giacomo, is left ruminating on betrayal, death and decay. Joyce's lecture series evidently ended with a description, not only of Hamlet's state of mind, but also of his own, at least in his "Giacomo" mood:

> We too have been betrayed by the friend of our youth: for us, too, have swords been dipped in poison. How well do we know that graveyard mood in which disgust and sorrow for all earthly things seize upon the soul. The breath from open graves has set us, too, dreaming with a skull in our hands.[39]

If Giacomo's "graveyard mood" recalls that of Hamlet, the mood in which he idealises his love into a pure, quietly superior, and distant icon of secret worship recalls Dante's adoration of Beatrice in the *Vita Nuova*, especially as another

---

[38] Verity notes, on page 304, that Hamlet is thirty. Joyce gave his lectures on *Hamlet* at the Università Popolare from November 1912 through February 1913. See William H. Quillian, "Shakespeare in Trieste: Joyce's 1912 *Hamlet* Lectures," *JJQ* 12 (Fall 1974/Winter 1975): 7-63.

[39] Quillian, "Shakespeare in Trieste," 63.

Dante, Dante Gabriel Rossetti, interpreted it. In *Giacomo Joyce* Giacomo's lady walks before him down a corridor, her dark hair slowly uncoiling and falling. Giacomo reflects, "She does not know and walks before me, simple and proud. So did she walk by Dante in simple pride" (*GJ* 11). Giacomo's image of Beatrice proudly passing Dante may have been suggested by one of Rossetti's illustrations in the Italian version of *La Vita Nuova* that Joyce owned in Trieste, entitled "Beatrice nega il saluto a Dante."[40] If Joyce was indeed basing his sketch on Rossetti's, it would be yet another example of his way of conjoining the literary and the artistic in his sketchbook; his vignette recalls, not one, but two Dantes—one a poet, the other both poet and painter.

Rossetti read Dante's *Vita Nuova* as an "autobiography or autopsychology of Dante's youth until about his twenty-seventh year."[41] In addition, he saw it as an autobiography of youth in general, an argument that he supported by contending that the adjective *nuova*, which literally means "new," also carried the connotation of "young," and he argued that both Dante and other early writers often used it in this sense. He concludes by asserting that "the 'Vita Nuova' is a book which only youth could have produced, and which must chiefly remain sacred to the young; to each of whom the figure of Beatrice, less lifelike than lovelike, will seem the friend of his own heart."[42] For Rossetti, Dante's Beatrice represents the first idealised love of every young man, including his own, a view that he expresses in his illustrations of the *Vita Nuova* by using his own beloved, Elizabeth Siddal, as the model for his portraits of Beatrice.[43]

---

[40] *La Vita Nuova di Dante*, con le illustrazione di Dante Gabrielle Rossetti, 2nd ed. (Torino-Roma: Casa Editrice Nationale, 1903) 54.

[41] Dante, *The New Life of Dante Alighieri*, trans. and illustrated, Dante Gabriel Rossetti (New York: Russel, 1901) 25.

[42] Dante, *The New Life of Dante Alighieri*, 26-17.

[43] Elizabeth Siddal, like Dante's Beatrice, was one of the young Rossetti's most powerful artistic inspirations. He was engaged to her when he was translating the *Vita Nuova*. After a long engagement, they were finally married, but their

In *Giacomo Joyce*, Joyce, like Rossetti, illustrates his view that the Beatrice of any artist is the idealised woman who served him as the first great inspiration of his youth. Again like Rossetti, Joyce cast his own ideal woman as Dante's Beatrice and presented the story of his love as the story of his youth. Joyce resembled Rossetti in another way: as one of Rossetti's biographers pointed out, Rossetti turned from Beatrice to Guinevere, from the dead Elizabeth Siddal to Jane Morris. Joyce, too transferred his allegiance from icons of youthful purity to a figure of sensual adultery, recording the death of his first love in a slender book that he left "buried" in Trieste.

Joyce continues to explore the parallel between the cold, remote loved one of his youth and Dante's Beatrice in *Exiles*, in which he gives the name Beatrice to the woman whom Richard Rowan once loved, a woman closely akin to the lady of *Giacomo Joyce*. Dante's Beatrice died in June of her twenty-seventh year; in *Exiles*, which is set in June 1912, Beatrice Justice is also twenty-seven, and Joyce presents her as spiritually rather than physically dead. Only after Beatrice's death did Dante begin to see that she was leading him to a fuller, more comprehensive kind of love, and at that point, when he was in the middle of the road of life, he began his great work, the *Divina Commedia*. Joyce, too, followed his account of the "death" of his youthful Beatrice with his major work, *Ulysses*, which he also began at the mid-point of his life. Joyce saw that the "death" of his youthful infatuation was a step toward his discovery of a fuller, more mature, and compassionate kind of love, one that left

love quickly crumbled into unhappiness and disillusionment, and two years after they were married, Elizabeth Siddal died. For other similarities between the Pre-Raphaelite woman and the women in Joyce's early fiction and poetry, see Archie K. Loss, "The Pre-Raphaelite Woman, the Symbolist *Femme-Enfant*, and the Girl with the Long Flowing Hair in the Earlier Work of Joyce," *Journal of Modern Literature* 3 (February 1973): 1-23.

behind the fluctuations between religious ecstasy and despair and was riddled, instead, by uncertainty and doubt.[44]

Just as Joyce casts himself in the role of two Dantes, Dante Rossetti and Dante Alighieri, he superimposes the outlines of another Beatrice, Shelley's Beatrice Cenci, over the features of his pupil and of Beatrice Portinari. Shelley's Beatrice is beautiful, courageous, proud, and innocent; like Giacomo's lady, she is secretly loved by a man who pretends to be a friend and counsellor but who is actually motivated primarily by lust. In *The Cenci*, Orsino, like Giacomo, is plagued by fantasies of sexual desire and illicit possession. He confesses,

> Her bright form kneels beside me at the altar,
> And follows me to the resort of men,
> And fills my slumber with tumultuous dreams,
> So when I wake my blood seems liquid fire;
>   ... her very name,
> But spoken by a stranger, makes my heart
> Sicken and pant; and thus unprofitably
> I clasp the phantom of unfelt delights,
> Till weak imagination half-possesses
> The self-created shadow.[45]

Like Dante's Beatrice, and like Giacomo's inflamed visions of his proud but guiltless pupil, Beatrice Cenci must die. Violated by her father and stained by his blood, Beatrice asserts her inviolable innocence as she walks to the death decreed for her, her mother and her brother Giacomo. As a last simple gesture, she and her mother bind up each other's hair in preparation for death. Joyce, as he watches his pupil's dark hair fall slowly down her back, imagines that she, too, is walking majestically

---

[44] For an account of Dante's lifelong impact on Joyce's imagination, see Mary T. Reynolds, *Joyce and Dante: The Shaping Imagination* (Princeton NJ: Princeton University Press, 1981).

[45] Percy Bysshe Shelley, *The Cenci*, *The Poetical Works of Percy Bysshe Shelley*, vol. 2, ed. Mrs. Shelley (London: Moxon, 1839), 2:2.133-43.

to her death, and he softly recites to himself a portion of these moving last lines:

> Here, Mother, tie
> My girdle for me, and bind up this hair
> In any simple knot; aye, that does well.
> And yours I see is coming down. How often
> Have we done this for one another! now
> We shall not do it any more. My Lord,
> We are quite ready. Well, 'tis very well.[46]

The Cenci also may have suggested some of the images that Joyce uses to describe his love. For example, Giacomo claims that the dark, suffering eyes of his beloved are "beautiful as the eyes of an antelope" (*GJ* 11), an image that may well be indebted to a metaphor that Orsino uses to describe Beatrice's helplessness. He exclaims, "I were a fool, not less than if a panther / Were stricken by the antelope's eye, / If she escape me" (II.ii). Similarly, Joyce's description of his lover as a cold nightsnake recalls an image in the song Beatrice sings in the last act of the play, "False friend, wilt thou smile or weep." The first stanza of the song, which, according to Padraic Colum, Joyce used to sing beautifully on request,[47] ends with an image of the treachery of love: "There is a snake in thy smile, my dear, / And bitter poison within thy tear."

Joyce pictures his pupil as the Beatrices of Dante and Shelley, as Shakespeare's passive Ophelia, and as Ibsen's fearless Hedda Gabler, but his final vision of her is as Hawthorne's adulteress, Hester Prynne. The sketchbook ends with an ironic allusion to the heraldic emblem emblazoned on

---

[46] Shelley, *The Cenci*, 5:4.159-65. In a copy of Shelley's *Poetical Works* that he owned in Trieste, Joyce wrote an illegible word followed by the date 5/5/1910 after this speech. This date could be a reasonable candidate for the date that the sketch in *Giacomo Joyce* was composed. Michael Gillespie, *James Joyce's Trieste Library: A Catalogue of Materials* (Austin, TX: The Humanities Research Center University of Texas Press, 1989). Joyce's Trieste library is housed in the Humanities Research Center, the University of Texas at Austin.

[47] Ulick O'Connor, ed. *The Joyce We Knew* (Cork: Mercier Press, 1967) 66-67.

the common tombstone of Hester Prynne and her secret lover, the Reverend Arthur Dimmesdale, in *The Scarlet Letter*, which Joyce evokes as a way of burying the remains if his own imagined "affair." Giacomo's lady, like Hester, had seemed to wear the "frozen calmness of a dead woman's features,"[48] but unlike her Puritan sister, she had never worn the *A* of an adulteress before the world; that ignominy only brands her in the world of Joyce's imagination. By linking his beloved with Hester Prynne, Joyce expresses his bitterness at her inconstancy, but he also emphasises his own kinship with her unhappy, furtive lover. As Stanislaus has noted, Joyce was sometimes mistaken for a minister when he was a young man in Dublin because of his mode of dress. He recalls that Joyce "really caught the eye" with his "round wide-brimmed soft hat, which in Dublin is only worn by Protestant ministers."[49] The Stephen Dedalus of the third chapter of *A Portrait* also has much in common with Hawthorne's sensual, highly intellectual Dimmesdale. Both Dedalus and Dimmesdale are tortured by their inability to confess their sins of lust and are stung by the hypocrisy of their "holy" demeanour; both laugh, in bitterness and agony of heart, at the contrast between what they seem and what they are.

Giacomo Joyce has a special place in the Joycean canon, partly because it shows Joyce searching for literary, artistic, and philosophical contexts for the real and imagined experiences that eventually blossom into *Ulysses*. It shows that Joyce consistently began to translate his life into art by creating an intricate context for whatever experience or perception he wanted to communicate. He created this context by noting parallels between an experience of his own and accounts of experiences or perceptions analogous to his, accounts that he

---

48 Hawthorne, *The Scarlet Letter*, 161.

49 Stanislaus Joyce, *Recollections*, 17; cf. *My Brother's Keeper*, 249. In "Oxen of the Sun," someone in the babble of voices notes the resemblance of "Parson Steve" to a Protestant minister, exclaiming, "Jay, look at the drunken minister coming out of the maternity hospital!" (*U* 424.24-25).

found in literature, theology, biography, philosophy, and music. Joyce sought not to find a single analogy for his experience, but to locate a point where the experiences of several different people, characters, or artists intersected with his own. He would then pattern the experience of his character, not only on personal history, but on all the related histories that he had uncovered. The result of this technique is a weblike interrelation of correspondences that has literary, theological, philosophical and personal implications. Art *is* context for Joyce. It is the activity of anchoring isolated and isolating individual experiences to a larger human context, to a harmonious humanising tradition made up of selected works of art, literature and philosophy, and encompassing a variety of time periods, cultures, religions, and points of view.

An analysis of the partially finished likenesses in *Giacomo Joyce* provides special insight into the techniques Joyce characteristically used in his literary portraiture. It shows that Joyce consistently modelled his characters partly on real people—here, himself and Amalia Popper—and partly on a diverse group of figures from the past—some dead, some fictional or even mythical. Stephen Dedalus, Giacomo Joyce, Richard Rowan and Leopold Bloom are all partly caricatures of Joyce and partly portraits that stress the resemblances and differences between himself and other great or notorious men: Christ and Lucifer, Daedalus and Icarus, and Parnell and Byron in *A Portrait*; Christ, Ejlert Lövborg, Hamlet, Dante, Orsino and Arthur Dimmesdale in *Giacomo Joyce*; King Mark of the "Tristan" legend, Wagner, Nietzsche, and Lohengrin in *Exiles*; the senior Hamlet, Elijah, and Odysseus in *Ulysses*—to name only a few.

Joyce's sketchbook also shows that a close kinship binds Joyce's female characters together, just as it does his male ones. Joyce amalgamates Amalia Popper's image with the images of other elusive, essentially "foreign" women from his earlier fiction and from literary history, and at the same time, he presents her as the source of a young artist's inspiration, an enthralling model who incessantly fluctuates between the extremes of virgin and whore. But Giacomo's lady is not only an incarnation of the "double" woman of Joyce's youthful dreams, a woman who is alternately a cold, ethereal ideal and a dangerous concubine who bewitches and poisons him; she is also the subject of Joyce's first experiments with the protean inclusiveness of Bertha Rowan, Molly Bloom and Anna Livia Plurabelle, figures who come to embody the variety of life itself.

The evolution of Giacomo's lady into Molly Bloom, like the displacement of Stephen Dedalus by Leopold Bloom, reflects a profound change of attitude, an acceptance of imperfection and human mutability as part of the larger human comedy. In *Giacomo Joyce*, Joyce uses continually shifting visual perspective to emphasise the lady's inconstancy, which is a kind of betrayal, and the pain of loss that she inflicts makes her symbolic of a greater and more final loss: death. In *Ulysses* Joyce's different stylistic perspectives of his characters still stress their changeability, but this volatility is presented as an attribute of life rather than as a foretaste of death; the effect of a sudden change in point of view is as often humorous as it is unsettling.

The distribution of the characteristics of Giacomo's lady throughout *Ulysses* helps to show how Joyce's conception of women had broadened and changed with maturity, just as his conception of men had changed when he followed his portrait of the young Stephen Dedalus with the much more versatile and humane figure of Leopold Bloom. In *Giacomo Joyce* the lady's image illustrates the young artist's idea of womanhood as an unlikely combination of sanctity and profligacy. Joyce's drawings of this young woman retrace the features of his young artist in *A Portrait of the Artist as a Young Man*; both Giacomo's lady and Stephen Dedalus are cold and remote, and both alternate between two extreme guises, the guise of anaemic purity and the guise of sinful, lecherous depravity. In *Ulysses*, Leopold and Molly Bloom also resemble one another; both are complex characters who play a variety of roles. Joyce illustrates the comprehensiveness of Molly Bloom, not by making her a representative of all women, but by suggesting that all the female characters in the book represent, for Bloom, different aspects of Molly.

The disguises for Molly are manifold: Bloom, in fantasy, regards Gerty MacDowell as a version of his wife when she was younger; Martha, in von Flotow's opera, is a pseudonym adopted by an adventurous woman when she wants to play a new role, which suggests that Bloom's secret infatuation with Martha is a disguise for his desire for Molly. Milly, too, Bloom sees as a younger reincarnation of her mother; her nickname "Marionette," is simply the diminutive if her mother's name. Bella/o Cohen is a kind of sorceress whose many metamorphoses act out the various facets of Bloom's relationship with his wife.

The protean lady of *Giacomo Joyce* becomes one of the prototypes of the many women of *Ulysses*—vital, seductive, magical, treacherous—all of whom are, for Bloom, disguises for Molly: his counterpart, his betrayer and preserver. Joyce distributes the characteristics of Giacomo's lady almost equally among the virgins, whores, mothers, wives, and daughters in *Ulysses*; she bequeaths her "jet of liquorish venom" to THE BAWD of Nighttown (*U* 431.24), her "coffin of music" to the sirens of the Ormond Hotel (*U* 263.26), to Circe's pianola (*U* 561.15, 22), and to Molly's piano (*U* 706.21-22). Her "stretched web of stocking" becomes the "cobweb hose" of the wax model Raymonde that Bloom admires in Mansfield's (*U* 529.27-28), and the excitement occasioned by her "sudden moving knee," which reveals "a white lace edging of an underskirt lifted unduly" (*GJ* 9), is translated into Gerty MacDowell's provocative (and deliberate) self-exposure in "Nausicaa." Bello Cohen inherits the lady's "basilisk stare" (*U* 530.17), Zoe Higgins her "odalisk lips" (*U* 477.12), Mrs. Bellingham her *"quizzing glasses"* (*U* 465.35-466.1; 468.14), and the nursery rhyme that Giacomo recalls to describe his lady on horseback, *"The lady goes apace, apace, apace"* (*GJ* 8), becomes the refrain for Bello as "he" rides Bloom roughly round the brothel (*U* 534.24-

25). The sketch of Giacomo's pupil as a corpse with "dank matted hair" (*GJ* 14) is transferred to the vision of May Dedalus (*U* 579.25-30), and both the description of the young lady as a filly foal and the reference to her "starborn flesh" are used to furnish Bloom's memory of his daughter. Perhaps Bloom's dream of Molly as a Turkish concubine is indebted to the erotic sketch of Giacomo's lady leaning, odalisque-featured, against a pillowed wall (*GJ* 14); Molly does wear opoponax, the perfume that plays a part in the "symphony of smells" that Giacomo analyses while he is watching his lady at the opera (*GJ* 12).[50]

There is additional evidence that Joyce's Triestine pupil was one of the most important models for Molly Bloom. Joyce insisted that Gorman add a note about the model for Molly to his biography. According to Willard Potts, Joyce wrote: "There was also a second major model for Penelope, an Italian, much handsomer than her Dublin rival. Her correspondence during wartime passed through my hands. There was nothing political in it but I wonder what the Austrian censor thought of it. That did not perturb her."[51] In the letter Joyce wrote to Amalia Popper in 1934, authorising her to translate *Dubliners* into Italian, he urged her to remember that he once played the part of her postman.[52]

The delicate sketches of *Giacomo Joyce* record a pivotal phase in the artist's development. They illustrate the intricate connections that Joyce wove between fantasy, erotic desire, and the visual arts, and they help to show how Joyce consistently counterpointed these creations of the artistic imagination with the harsh, brutal drama of worldly experience. Through the arrangement of these prose etchings, Joyce imagistically depicts

---

[50] For echoes of *Giacomo Joyce* in Joyce's other works, see Ellmann's notes to Giacomo Joyce, xxxi-xxxvii, and Fritz Senn, "Some Further Notes," 233-36.

[51] Willard Potts, "Notes on the Gorman Biography," *ICarbS* 4 (Spring-Summer 1981): 86. The notes on Gorman's biography are housed in the Croessmann Collection of James Joyce, Southern Illinois University at Carbbondale.

[52] Joyce wrote, "I would like to forget that I was also your postman!" (Risolo, "*Mia moglie e Joyce*," 13). For the note that Gorman added to the biography at Joyce's request, see Herbert Gorman, *James Joyce* (New York: Rinehart, 1939) 281, n.1.

the artist's betrayal by his model, a model who is herself drawn to resemble several women, both real and fictional. Most importantly, however, Giacomo's lady acts as a mirror image of the artist himself, just as later, in *Ulysses*, Leopold and Molly Bloom will reflect one another in multifaceted ways. Like Giacomo and the Stephen Dedalus he resembles, Giacomo's lady seems to embody the promise of life and love, but eventually, her coldness and haughty disdain prompt her to reject full involvement, and she becomes a horrifying image of the deadness of an artistic figure divorced from life. Joyce emphasises her change of attitude through the contrast between her first word, "yes," and her last word, which is essentially "no," when she tells Giacomo that she has chosen not him but another ("*Non hunc sed Barabbam*") (*GJ* 16). In *Ulysses* Molly's odyssey is in the opposite direction, toward warmth of life and away from the coldness and lovelessness of death. Her first word is "no" ("*Mn*") (*U* 56.25), but her last words are a repeated affirmation of life and love with all their unpredictability and painful uncertainty: "yes I said yes I will Yes" (*U* 783.14).

Murray McArthur

The Image of the Artist: *Giacomo Joyce*, Ezra Pound and Jacques Derrida

Giacomo Joyce, alone among Joyce's texts, had a high Modernist production and a Postmodernist reception. The fifty prose sketches, as Joyce called them, of *Giacomo Joyce* were written in the years immediately before World War I when the major Modernist writers—Joyce, Pound, Eliot especially—were emerging into their mature artistic mandates, almost all in some way through the discipline of the movement called Imagism. Ezra Pound, of course, was the proselytiser and impresario of Imagism during these years, the organiser of the Imagist circle in London and a tireless promoter for an international Imagism. Through his efforts, figures like Joyce, isolated in remote Trieste, were brought into the Imagist or Modernist movement and into the international eye through publication. Pound never secured publication of *Giacomo Joyce,* nor did he ever see the manuscript. He may have been, however, the only person outside Joyce's immediate circle to whom Joyce revealed the existence of these spectrally precise images of himself, this series of verbal snapshots or photographs of the artist himself poised between *A Portrait of the Artist as a Young Man* and *Ulysses.* Unknowingly, Pound may have played an indirect role in the delayed completion of the manuscript, in the inscription of the final sketch; however, his own obsessive concern with his image in his letters to Joyce (Pound wrote Joyce first in 1913, but they did not meet face to face until 1920) must have returned or reflected back to Joyce his own techniques, his principles of selection, for sending his image at a distance.

Unpublished in the lifetime of either the artist or his model Amalia Popper, his student in Trieste, *Giacomo Joyce* is Joyce's unique experiment in the highly encoded duality of the image of the artist that through the history of its Modernist writing and Postmodernist publication became his final sending from a distance. Published in 1968, only after the death of Amalia Risolo *née* Popper, the young woman portrayed in the sketches, the images of *Giacomo Joyce* appeared in the public eye in the year of Postmodernism's or Poststructuralism's emergence and the triumphant and ghostly return of Joyce to Paris. Jacques Derrida, more than anyone, has calculated the terms of this necessarily delayed reception. His epistolary novel or autobiography, the "Envois" of *The Post Card*, receives and recognises the legacy of Joyce's encoded images and rewrites them as a Postmodern return. The technology of the post card, of picture and text, visual and verbal images, which Derrida identifies with literature itself, becomes the vehicle by which Derrida returns Joyce's complex image to him, much as Joyce had, in fact, already done himself. Joyce was always very aware of the complex semiosis of his image, especially as sent from a distance. The first long distance sending of his image was at the end of his very brief first period of Continental exile, his sojourn in Paris from 1 to 18 December in 1902. His mother, anxious about her twenty year old son, arranged for him to come home almost as soon as he had left. Joyce, very glad to come home, as Ellmann reports (*JJII* 114-5), but no doubt anxious about his not quite fledged image as wandering artist and exile, after only two and half weeks abroad perhaps more Icarus than Daedalus in the mythological image he would eventually fashion, sent to Dublin a three-part postal statement of the self-image he wished to circulate. He went to Photo-

Cartes, 28 Boulevard Poissonière, in the heart of right bank Paris to have his photograph taken and affixed to the verso of a *carte postale.* In 1902, the private picture post card was a relatively new technological and postal development, having only been licensed, as Derrida notes in *The Post Card,* in 1894.[1] During this brief voyage out, letters went back and forth between Paris and Dublin; however, Joyce must have understood almost immediately the possibilities for self-disclosure and self-concealment that this new technology offered. The picture post card, with visual image and text, a communication both addressed and open, both private and public, would be the perfect device for placing in restricted and open circulation the dual portrait or image that he would so carefully cultivate for the rest of his life and that would be at the heart of *Giacomo Joyce.*

He sent three of these picture postcards, one to his family and one each to his friends Vincent Cosgrove and John F. Byrne (*JJII* 115-6). Only the last card has survived; however, the story of its survival demonstrates how carefully Joyce had planned this first sending of his image from a distance. The visual image, the photograph taken at Photo-Cartes, was presumably the same on all three. As all the photographs we have of Joyce attest, he had a movie star's or publicist's concern about his photographic image or persona. In photographs of himself, Joyce was both artist and model, both creator and object of creation, and the amazing variety of the photographs indicate that he took great care with each image. Full length or head shot, hatted or not, with glasses or without, with props like a guitar or a book, in profile or full face on, costumed in suit or evening dress or overcoat, Joyce's photographic image metamorphosed through a remarkably protean sequence. In the Photo-Cartes image, Joyce appears full length, costumed in a heavy, full length overcoat, scarved and hatted with the Latin Quarter hat he would later give to Stephen Dedalus, with his

---

[1] Jacques Derrida, *The Post Card: From Socrates to Freud and Beyond,* trans. Alan Bass (Chicago: University of Chicago Press, 1987) 139.

hands behind his back and with his profile turned slightly to the right. The facial expression is enigmatic, though Ellmann calls it "long suffering." With the coat and hat and the hands folded behind his back as if bound or rendered powerless, he looks like either a weary but defiant wanderer or a jaded *flâneur* of the cold Parisian streets in December, the two images he wished to promote.

How the three addressees would read this visual image was influenced, of course, by the written text that appeared beside the photograph on the verso of the postcard. His mother's return letter indicates that he complained to her about the mundane but nagging problems of money and his health and expressed his uncertainty about taking a job teaching English at the Berlitz School in Paris (*L* II 22). Money, health, and the Berlitz Schools would be nagging themes of his life for the next twelve years, and the weariness these problems were already causing him must have been evident to his mother in his coated and scarved resignation. His complaints to her about these problems would end, however, four months later with the most devastating event of his young life: the telegram from his father that he received in Paris on Good Friday, 10 April, 1903, telling him that his mother was dying. The image of this event haunts all of Joyce's writing; however, it is narrated or dramatised only in the private, concealed, and decisively encrypted *Giacomo Joyce*.

The messages to his two friends encoded more publicly the duality that he wished to cultivate in his public image. The friends were carefully chosen. Vincent Cosgrove would become the cynical Lynch of *A Portrait of the Artist as a Young Man* who hears Stephen's aesthetic theory in chapter V, part 1, and Byrne would become the much concerned Cranly who questions Stephen about his mother in chapter V, part 3. Cosgrove would also be Joyce's rival for the affections and favours of Nora Barnacle in the summer of 1904, and he would poison Joyce's mind during Joyce's return to Dublin in the summer of 1909 with false tales of Nora's dalliance with him. Devastated by

Cosgrove's revelations, Joyce would seek out Byrne who, in the kitchen of 7 Eccles Street, disabused Joyce of Cosgrove's lies (*JJII* 278-89). To Byrne, his sympathetic and thoughtful friend, Joyce wished to appear as the artist in exile, the weary but defiant wanderer, and he inscribed a poem of wandering on the postcard, entitled by a direct reference to the allegory of the image: "Second Part—opening which tells of the journeying of the soul":

> All day I hear the noise of water
> > Making moan
> Sad as the sea-bird is, when going
> > Forth alone
> He hears the winds cry to the waters'
> > Monotone.
>
> The grey winds, the cold winds are blowing
> > Where I go;
> I hear the noise of many waters
> > Far below;
> All day, all night I hear them flowing
> > To and fro. (*L* II.20-1)

So Joyce sent from a distance one of his first images of himself as daedalean wanderer, as pelagic sea-bird or winged artificer flying all alone over the dark and wintry ocean. This poem would eventually become number XXXV of *Chamber Music* and the source for his personal and public mythology. To Cosgrove, on the other hand, his cynical and ribald friend, Joyce wished to appear as a Parisian rake, a cynical and sexually experienced man of the world, and he inscribed a description in dog Latin of the *scorta* or prostitutes of Paris. Byrne, unaware of Cosgrove's postcard, proudly showed his to him, saying that no man in Dublin knew Joyce as well as he did. Cosgrove, unable to resist, showed Byrne his image of Joyce. Shocked, Byrne then gave his postcard to Cosgrove in disgust, who, in turn, gave it to Stanislaus Joyce, who preserved this first image and the story of its double or triple sending (*JJII* 115-16).

Joyce always remained intensely aware of the semiotics of photographic publication or circulation in the life of an author, and this awareness had a complicated relation to his disclosing and concealing of the one text he never published, *Giacomo Joyce*. In what would have been the midst of his writing of *Giacomo Joyce* in Trieste eleven years after this first double or triple sending, Joyce received out of the blue a letter from a young American poet soliciting any work Joyce might have for publication. Ezra Pound, acting as William Butler Yeats's secretary and as propagandist and publicist for modern literature, which he was then calling Imagism and would soon call Vorticism, wrote to Joyce on 15 December, 1913 and began an intense postal relation that would result in the sudden emergence into print of the thirty-one year old Irishmen, who had only one slender volume of published poetry to his credit in 1913. They would not meet for more than six years, a meeting, as we shall see, that may have had a decisive effect on the completion of *Giacomo Joyce*. Pound, however, would carry on through the mail a tireless campaign to have all of Joyce's work published. After bringing about the serial publication of *A Portrait* and its publication as a book, after doing all he could for *Exiles*, Pound continued to beg Joyce for more. This pressure produced what we take to be Joyce's only written mention of *Giacomo Joyce*. On 9 April, 1917, Joyce wrote to Pound from Zürich: "As regards stories I have none. I have some prose sketches, as I told you, but they are locked up in my desk in Trieste."[2] Joyce reveals and conceals much in the last sentence. The nomenclature he chooses—"prose sketches"— demonstrates, as Adaline Glasheen brilliantly argued, Joyce's conception of these texts as sketches, verbal-visual artefacts, images, as we shall see, of artist and model. They are also "locked up" in his desk, not merely rendered inaccessible by the war, but sealed, buried, encrypted, and there they will stay, except for one last crucial addition.

[2] Ezra Pound, *Pound/Joyce*, ed. Forrest Read (New York: New Directions, 1967) 105.

Joyce does mention them, however, to Pound, and he has before ("as I told you"). These sketches of his personal and artistic crisis brought about by his erotic infatuation with a younger Jewish woman, Amalia Popper, a student of his at the Berlitz school in Trieste, are an image of himself that he seems both to want and not to want to share with his fellow artist. This ambiguous prohibition, conveniently or inconveniently brought about by the war, is both odd and unique in Joyce's artistic life, especially in his circulation of images of himself and his reception of images of others. Pound and Joyce did not meet for six years, not until June 1920 when they met in Sirmione and Pound persuaded Joyce to leave Trieste for Paris. Joyce's letters to Pound are mostly lost; however, Pound's letters indicate that Joyce continually asked him for photographs, images of himself. On 21 July, 1914, during the summer in which Joyce inscribed *Giacomo Joyce* into its sketch book, Pound wrote: "I haven't a decent photograph at the moment but Arbuthnot has asked me for a sitting and you are welcome to the result when it comes, tho it won't much adorn the landscape."[3] One year later, Joyce was still agitating, and Pound wrote him a carefully written reply that must have stunned the author of *Giacomo Joyce* in its analysis and representation of the image of the modern author:

> Also I solemnly swear that I will someday send you a photograph, at present I am torn between conflicting claims. I have an excessively youthful and deceptive photograph (very rare edition). I have several copies of a photo of a portrait of me, painted by an amiable jew who substituted a good deal of his own face for the gentile parts of my own. I have the seductive and sinister photograph by Coburn which I expected to have photograved in order to sell my next book of bad poems. It is like a cinque, or quattrocento painting. My father-in-law says "A sinister but very brilliant italian." My old landlady said "It is the only photograph that has ever done you justice," and then as she was sidling out of the door, with increasing

---

[3] Pound, *Pound/Joyce*, 31.

embarrassment. "Ah, ah. I. I hope you won't be offended, sir, but it is rather like the good man of Nazareth, isn't it sir?"[4]

Pound was clearly as obsessively aware of the structure and semiotics of the artist's photographic image as Joyce, and the three instances he verbally sketches here and the fourth he draws in the next paragraph uncannily parallel certain crucial aspects of Joyce's portrait of himself and his model in *Giacomo Joyce*.

"Torn between conflicting claims," Pound first mentions a simple photograph of himself as a young man, an image characterised solely by its paired adjectives, "excessively youthful and deceptive." The second has two levels of technological reproduction, a photograph of a painting, a doubling reflected in the projection that the artist made onto the image of the model, as Pound's gentile face was, he claims, judaicised by the Jewish artist. The third, "a seductive and sinister photograph," also characterised by paired and antithetical adjectives, will also be submitted to a second level of technological reproduction, "photograved" (in which a photographic negative is transferred to a metal plate and then etched in); however, the modernity of the process only intensifies the historicity of the image, "like a cinque, or quattrocento painting," which his father-in-law situates in the Italian Renaissance: "A sinister but brilliant Italian." The landlady joins the second and third image, Old and New Testament, as it were, Judeo-Christian, by identifying it as "rather like the good man of Nazareth, isn't it sir?"

As Joyce's Photo-Cartes indicate, he was also intensely aware of the doublings of the artist's verbal and visual images, especially as sent from a distance, whether spatial or temporal. In the next paragraph, Pound seizes on the decisive European precursor in this self-sending from a distance, this imaging of oneself artistically in crisis:

---

[4] Pound, *Pound/Joyce*, 35.

Dante, you remember, at the beginning of the epistle to Can Grande (at least I think it is there) mentions a similar predicament about presenting one's self at a distance. It is my face, no I can not be represented in your mind by that semitic image [*insert*: alone (which I enclose)], it is my face as it may have been years ago, or my face greatly beautified, or as I enclose, my face as immortalised by vorticist sculpture, which I enclose, this bust is monumental, but it will be no use to the police, it is hieratic, phallic, even, if you will consider the profiles not shown in the photograph.

No, I will either, get a new photo, or send you the photogravure in good time.[5]

Dante's *Vita Nuova* provided a crucial model for *Giacomo Joyce*, but the fourth image that Pound does not send, the photograph of the Vorticist sculpture, the "Hieratic Head of Ezra Pound" by Gaudier-Brzeska, provided an unseen, uncanny phantom parallel to the Imagist or Vorticist and "hieratic, phallic even" doubling representation of the artist and his model that Joyce had already written in *Giacomo Joyce*.

The fifty prose sketches of *Giacomo Joyce* are both hieratic and phallic, both sacred and profane, both Byrnean and Cosgrovean, if you will, as well as turning on a judaicising of the artist by the model and on an historicising of the artist in an Italianate and Renaissance context and on a self-imaging of the artist as Christ. The sketches are also, as many commentators have noted, Imagist in two distinct methods of notation. Adapting the double method of his epiphanies written ten years before, the lyric and the dramatic presentations, as Vicki Mahaffey has demonstrated,[6] Joyce wrote two kinds of sketches: very brief, often asyntactic or asyndetonic two level notations—one literal, one figurative—that function in their most condensed form like the haikus that inspired Imagism; longer though still brief narrative snapshots that set the artist

---

5 Pound, *Pound/Joyce*, 35.
6 Vicki Mahaffey, "Giacomo Joyce," *A Companion to Joyce Studies*, eds. Zack Bowen and James F. Carens (Westport, CT: Greenwood Press, 1984) 392.

and/or model in particular though often unclear settings. As in Imagism, the reference or deixis of time, place, or person of the sketches is often ambiguous or suspended in some way, but in other instances the deixis is precise.

The first page of the sketchbook contains four of these sketches or images, two of the first method, two of the second:

> Who? A pale face surrounded by heavy odorous furs. Her movements are shy and nervous. She uses quizzing-glasses.
> *Yes*: a brief syllable. A brief laugh. A brief beat of the eyelids.
>
> Cobweb handwriting, traced long and fine with quiet disdain and resignation: a young person of quality. [*GJ* 1]

The first sketch, set perhaps in the Berlitz classroom in Trieste where Joyce first saw Amalia Popper, opens with an interrogative pronoun or deictic, followed by three notations of her face, gestures, and props. The second part of the sketch is structured the same, with what seems to be her first word spoken to him modified by the three appositional phrases. The second sketch, separated by the blank space from the first, references her high social class in three phrases through the style of her handwriting. So the artist first draws his Beatrice with paired minimalist, lyric notations of her speech and writing, focusing on signs, on the relation between the verbal and the visual in symmetrical phrasing.

The second pair of sketches are dramatic, setting the context inside and outside the classroom. In the first, Joyce, or Giacomo Joyce, the title character as we call him only because someone other than Joyce wrote that name across the manuscript, situates himself and his speech in the classroom:

> I launch forth on an easy wave of tepid speech: Swedenborg, the pseudo-Aeropagite, Miguel de Molinos, Joachim Abbas. The wave is spent. Her classmate, re-twisting her twisted body, purrs in boneless Viennese Italian: *Che coltura!* The long eyelids

beat and lift: a burning needleprick stings and quivers in the
velvet iris. [*GJ* 1]

Speaking of mystics and heretics, Joyce is praised in language
that identifies the body, the classmate's twisted body, with
speech, the "boneless Viennese Italian." He is also seeing and
being seen in the fourth sentence, in a figure of visual
wounding. In the second of the pair, the context seems to be
shifted outside the classroom to what may be a vocative of
audible wounding also in the fourth sentence:

> High heels clack hollow on the resonant stone stairs. Wintry air
> in the castle, gibbeted coats of mail, rude iron scones over the
> windings of the winding turret stairs. Tapping clacking heels, a
> high and hollow noise. There is one below would speak with
> your ladyship. [*GJ* 1]

The deixis of time, place, and person is difficult to establish in
this sketch. A possible reading is that the high heels are those of
a messenger, a school official perhaps, sent up the winding
stone stairs of the school building to call the antecedent of
"Who?" (the "young person of quality") out of the classroom:
"There is one below would speak with your ladyship." The
gothic and wintry details of the castle and the "high and hollow
noise" of the heels, mentioned twice and obviously heard
coming towards the classroom from a distance, give this sketch
an ominous foreshadowing. The young lady will be called
away, almost, but very closely, by death and then, in the end,
by another in a necessary betrayal that will transform Giacomo.

What *Giacomo Joyce* presents, then, is a gallery of images of
the lover-artist and the beloved-model, a sequence still best
described by Adaline Glasheen:

> A painter—his personality refined nearly out of existence—
> loves and paints "a young person of quality." He never paints
> her twice from the same angle, or in the same pose, never twice
> in the same setting, light or costume; he paints her alone and in

crowds, indoors and outdoors; he paints her as herself, or as some famous woman of history; he notes her anatomical parts from jawbone to entrails; sometimes he isolates a part of her and paints it alone.[7]

Glasheen brilliantly insists on the discontinuous painterly or imagistic technique of the fifty sketches; however, she uncannily denies the carefully concealed and revealed principle of selection that governs the fifty sketches. The narrative course of a phantom affair can be followed from its beginning to its end in the sequence of sketches; however, the technique, as most commentators have noted, renders problematic any full narrative coherence or confidence in the reference of time, place, and person. The structure of the sketches is much more Postmodern, in this sense, characterised more like the sequence of adjectives that Margot Norris uses to describe John Bishop's reading of *Finnegans Wake* as "highly postmodern: fragmentary, minimalist, randomising, self-exhausting."[8] The minimalist fragments of *Giacomo*, self-exhausting in the spectral struggle of the non-affair, are not fully randomised, however. As the opening page demonstrates, Joyce throughout paints his model and himself twice from the same angle, pose, and setting, though the second image is usually reversed, inverted, the negative of the first in photographic terms. Single or unique images appear so seldom that they are highly significant. In Modernist terms, the sketches test out the visual principle of parallax, in which the distance to an object is measured by the displacement of the object when viewed from two different viewpoints, the principle that Bloom thinks about so often and that structures so much of *Ulysses*. We are almost always shown things from dual viewpoints in *Giacomo Joyce*. In their minimalist duality, the sketches also demonstrate the law of the Postmodernist signifier: they go in pairs.

[7] Adaline Glasheen, Review Article, *A Wake Newsletter* 5 (June 1968): 41.

[8] Margot Norris, "The Postmodernisation of *Finnegans Wake* Reconsidered," *Rereading the New: A Backward Glance at Modernism*, ed. Kevin J.H. Dettmar (Ann Arbour: University of Michigan Press, 1992) 355.

Four of the sketches, for example, are set outside of Trieste, two in other places in Italy and two in Paris. The two in Paris are the most important sketches, the double crises of this imagistic novella or novelistic photobook. In the first Italian setting outside Trieste, drawn on the second page, the model appears in the countryside, drenched in sunshine her face thrown into shadow by her hat:

> A ricefield near Vercelli under creamy summer haze. The wings of her drooping hat shadow her false smile. Shadows streak her falsely smiling face, smitten by the hot creamy light, grey wheyhued shadows under the jawbones, streaks of eggyolk yellow on the moistened brow, rancid yellow humour lurking within the softened pulp of her eyes. [GJ 2]

This sketch seems to have been produced by the expansion of the first or lyrical method, with the figurative level of what seems to be something like cake batter—"streaks of eggyolk yellow"—and the literal referent of her face, end focusing on her eyes. The effect perhaps is that her face is still unfinished, unbaked, adolescent, though the atmosphere is mostly light, bright, and innocent, an innocence complicated, however, by the shadow of that "falsely." In the other Italian setting outside Trieste, drawn on the third page, the artist appears in the city, plunged in a darkness outside him and within him, both physical and moral:

> Padua far beyond the sea. The silent middle age, night, darkness of history sleep in the *Piazza delle Erbe* under the moon. The city sleeps. Under the arches in the dark streets near the river the whores' eyes spy out for fornicators. *Cinque servizi per cinque franchi.* A dark wave of sense, again and again and again,
>
> > *Mine eyes fail in darkness, mine eyes fail,*
> > *Mine eyes fail in darkness, love.*
>
> Again. No more. Dark love, dark longing. No more. Darkness. [GJ 3]

Between these two Italian scenes comes the only appearance of Giacomo's daughter: "A flower given to my daughter. Frail gift, frail giver, frail blue-veined daughter" (*GJ* 3). This gift is clearly wholly innocent, and the daughter is one of the few characters not subject to the law of parallax. Her innocence perhaps does not require the complication of the parallactic viewpoints. In stark contrast to the bright light of the Vercelli scene and this innocent gift, however, the darkness of the Paduan sketch among the whores emphasises the rancid, corrupt, adult sexuality of Giacomo, his knowledge from the beginning of the moral blindness of his infatuation with this young woman, his awareness of his phallic or Cosgrovean intent which darkens and blinds him but that he must, because this is also his nature, follow to its conclusion.

He must pass through this rite of passage because it is his artistic destiny as well. In this sense, *Giacomo Joyce* is both trivial and profound, both the unpublishable jottings of Joyce's frustrated lust for an unattainable student and the complex of personal and artistic experiences and devices, the terminus or switching points, by which this Master Thinker, in Derrida's terms from *The Post Card*,[9] finished his two masterpieces of this period. As Richard Ellmann first emphasised, the Joyce of this period stood between the conclusion of *A Portrait of the Artist as a Young Man* and the beginning of *Ulysses* (*GJ* xi). The two methods of the image production in *Giacomo* reflect the two dominant styles of these texts, as Ellmann also pointed out, the longer dramatic images reflecting the discursive periods of *Portrait* and the shorter lyric images the fragmentary interior monologues of *Ulysses* (*GJ* xix-xx). Images from *Giacomo* were used in both texts, and both texts are mentioned in *Giacomo*. The lady is given *Portrait* to read and comments on its sexual frankness (*GJ* 12), and *Ulysses* is mentioned as "the reason" (*GJ* 15) in the crucial second Parisian sketch almost certainly added later when *Ulysses* was well underway.[10] In 1911 to 1914, when

---

9 Derrida, *The Post Card*, 207.
10 Mahaffey, "Giacomo Joyce," 417.

the datable events in *Giacomo* take place, Joyce was no longer as young as Stephen and not yet as old as his emerging protagonist. In fact, in 1912, Joyce was thirty years old, midway between the twenty-two year old Stephen Dedalus of *Ulysses* and the thirty-eight year old Leopold Bloom.

The image production of *Giacomo* was essential, I would argue, to the emergence of Joyce's Odyssean Jew. In his artistic and erotic fixation on his young Jewish model, Joyce entered into a process of semiticising or judaicising his image that had both negative and positive effects necessary to this emergence. Vicki Mahaffey and Joseph Valente have most fully analysed the anti-Semitic and misogynist elements of Giacomo's fixation with the Jewish young woman and his overcoming of them.[11] In working through the process of this racial and sexual fixation, Joyce attempted to know and to understand and to possess to some degree her Jewishness and her sexuality, though he can only experience such things visually and verbally from the outside. As many commentators have noted, the relation between the older Giacomo and the young woman pre-stages the relation between Gerty MacDowell and Bloom in "Nausicaa," though we do not enter the young lady's mind as we do Gerty's. Giacomo only sees and hears the young lady from the outside. In an early sketch, on the second page, Giacomo draws in paired modifiers his visual and verbal infatuation with her race and sex and tantalises himself with exogamous possibilities and endogamous realities: "Rounded and ripened: rounded by the lathe of intermarriage and ripened in the forcing-house of the seclusion of her race" (*GJ* 2). What do the two participles modify? Her body? Her speech? Certainly both, but the suspension of reference and the further modification of the prepositional phrases makes her both

---

[11] Vicki Mahaffey, "The Case Against Art: Wunderlich on Joyce," *Critical Inquiry*, 17 (1991): 667-692. Joseph Valente, "Dread Desire: Imperialist Abjection in *Giacomo Joyce*," *James Joyce and the Problem of Justice: Negotiating Sexual and Colonial Difference* (Cambridge: Cambridge University Press, 1995) 67-131.

available and unavailable to him, both open and closed. He can both know her and not know her.

This racial and sexual knowledge or half knowledge is concentrated in the eyes that Giacomo notices first and that fixate him. For Joyce, the eyes of a young woman concentrated the racial and sexual knowledge that he sought and that both possessed and eluded him, especially in the two races that fixated him, the Irish and the Jewish. Thinking of the shadowy E___ C____ during the villanelle episode in *Portrait*, Stephen Dedalus's angry response to her flirtation with a priest generates multiple reflections of her image:

> Rude brutal anger routed the last lingering instant of ecstasy from his soul. It broke up violently her fair image and flung the fragments on all sides. On all sides distorted reflections of her image started from his memory: the flowergirl in the ragged dress [...] the kitchengirl in the next house [...] a girl who had laughed gaily to see him stumble [...] a girl he had glanced at [...] [*P* 239]

The four reflections concentrate their racial and sexual knowledge in a single pair of eyes that draws irresistibly his ambivalent homage: "And yet he felt that, however he might revile and mock her image, his anger was also a form of homage. He had left the classroom in disdain that was not wholly sincere, feeling that perhaps the secret of her race lay behind those dark eyes upon which her long lashes flung a quick shadow." Wounded on the first page of sketches ("a burning needleprick stings and quivers"), the Jewish girl's eyes, behind which lay "the secret of her race," govern the course of the visual and verbal affair of artist and model, including the two basilisk sketches (*GJ* 15) in which she first averts and then turns her murdering eye on him and ends it.

The eyes also lead Giacomo to an historical knowledge, an image of himself as a figure from the Renaissance, appearing twice, of course, once on the upslope of the affair and once after its basiliskic end, both associated with music:

> I play lightly, softly singing, John Dowland's languid song. *Loth to depart*: I too am loth to go. That age is here and now. Here, opening from the darkness of desire, are eyes that dim the breaking East, their shimmer the shimmer of the scum that mantles the cesspool of the court of slobbering James. Here are wines all ambered, dying fallings of sweet airs, the proud pavan, kind gentlewomen wooing from their balconies with sucking mouths, the pox-fouled wenches and young wives that, gaily yielding to their ravishers, clip and clip again. [*GJ* 9]

The "eyes that dim the breaking East" situate Giacomo in the age of Dowland and King James, a Shakespearean age of gay and grim harlotry. In *Portrait*, Stephen imagines himself playing this song on the piano to please E____ C____ (*P* 237-8), and later he has a slightly modified historical vision of "the court of a slobbering Stuart." He has learned, however, that this fantasy of historical license is not how he should think of her: "The images he had summoned gave him no pleasure. They were secret and inflaming but her image was not entangled by them. That was not the way to think of her" (*P* 253). Through the twin crises of *Giacomo*, Joyce himself learned this, and the second musical sketch focuses on his own age and on his own image as an artist:

> Jan Pieters Sweelink. The quaint name of the old Dutch musician makes all beauty seem quaint and far. I hear his variations for the clavichord on an old air: *Youth has an end.* In the vague mist of old sounds a faint point of light appears: the speech of the soul is about to be heard. Youth has an end: the end is here. It will never be. You know that well. What then? Write it, damn you, write it! What else are you good for? [*GJ* 16]

The first musical sketch takes place immediately before the first Parisian crisis (*GJ* 9 and 10); the second takes place immediately after the second (*GJ* 15 and 16). In the first, temporality is reversed, sending the artist back to a fantasy time of easy Elizabethan lechery. In the second, time is focused and concentrated into the present age of the artist and his responsibility to his art. In their focusing on time, the two musical sketches frame the passage through death or the work of mourning and the resurrection or waking that the two Paris episodes stage.

Death haunts *Giacomo Joyce* from the beginning, from the messenger summoning the young lady to someone below on the first page. In the first of the two dressing sketches, Giacomo, looking up from outside, sees ghosts in her mirror: "Moving mists on the hill as I look upward from night and mud. Hanging mists over the damp trees. A light in the upper room. She is dressing to go to the play. There are ghosts in the mirror ..... Candles! Candles!" (*GJ* 6).

In the second, seen from inside, he fantasises about helping her dress and undress, unbuttoning the back of her garment which falls revealingly away:

> It slips its ribbons of moorings at her shoulders and falls slowly: a lithe smooth naked body shimmering with silvery scales. It slips slowly over the slender buttocks of smooth polished silver and over their furrow, a tarnished silver shadow .... Fingers, cold and calm and moving .... A touch, a touch. [*GJ* 7]

Like a mermaid or siren, the young lady is amphibious throughout, double natured, both human and animal in a dazzling sequence of metamorphoses, Jewish and Italian, angel and demon, and alive and dead. Her mortality, her double nature, is the mirror in which he must see her.

In the theatre scene, Giacomo sees this amphibiousness in her green dress:

> All night I have watched her, all night I shall see her: braided and pinnacled hair and olive oval face and calm soft eyes. A green fillet upon her hair and about her body a green-broidered gown: the hue of the illusion of the vegetable glass of nature and of lush grass, the hair of graves. [*GJ* 12]

The crowded theatre sketch, with its masses of odorous human flesh ("a symphony of smells fuses the mass of huddled human forms") and its double vision of the lady's alive-dead body, echoes with its opposite, the scene in the *Cimitero Israelitico*, where the corpses of her race lie massed as in the theatre:

> Corpses of Jews lie about me rotting in the mould of their holy field. Here is the tomb of her people, black stone, silence without hope ..... Pimply Meissel brought me here. He is beyond those trees standing with covered head at the grave of his suicide wife, wondering how the woman who slept in his bed has come to this end ..... The tomb of her people and hers: black stone, silence without hope: and all is ready. Do not die! [*GJ* 6]

Giacomo fears for the fragility of her life before a vengeful and libidinous God, and he twice creates an image of her as a vulnerable and foolish bird, once before her intimate brush with death and once after (*GJ* 7, 11). Immediately before the two sketches of her near death, Giacomo compares her to two doomed literary women, Dante's Beatrice and Shelley's Beatrice Cenci, one dead at the hand of God and one at the hand of man (*GJ* 11). The near death of Giacomo's Beatrice is both provoked by natural causes and carried through by human hands. In the first sketch, the housemaid tells him that she has been taken to the hospital. In the second, immediately following, he imagines the surgical wound and sees her suffering eyes: "Operated. The surgeon's knife has probed in her entrails and withdrawn, leaving the raw jagged gash of its passage on her belly. I see her full dark suffering eyes, beautiful as the eyes of an antelope. O cruel wound! Libidinous God!" (*GJ* 11).

On the page opposite appears the first Parisian sketch. The sketch has three movements, organised around two sets of ellipsis. In the first, Joyce crosses the Seine to the Île de Cité on a particular day which he sets in the context of the dense historicity of the Parisian island:

> In the raw veiled spring morning faint odours float of morning Paris: aniseed, damp sawdust, hot dough of bread: and as I cross the Pont Saint Michel the steel-blue waking waters chill my heart. They creep and lap about the island whereon men have lived since the stone age ..... [*GJ* 10]

On Good Friday, April 10, 1903, during his second sojourn in Paris, Joyce attended the service at Notre Dame Cathedral, and several hours later received the news that shattered his life, the telegram from his father summoning him home because his mother was dying. In the second movement, set in the sacred space of Notre Dame, he experiences the service again in a second, contemporary enactment:

> Tawny gloom in the vast gargoyled church. It is cold as on that morning: *quia frigus erat.* Upon the steps of the far high altar, naked as the body of the Lord, the ministers lie prostrate in weak prayer. The voice of an unseen reader rises, intoning the lesson from Hosea: *Haec dicit Dominus: in tribulatione sua mane consurgent ad me. Venite et revertamur ad Dominimum* .... [*GJ* 10]

With the memory of the pain the announcement of his mother's impending death caused him and that still causes him, Joyce takes on the image of Christ: the Passion becomes his, and the lady becomes one of the Jewish women weeping for Christ:

> She stands beside me, pale and chill, clothed with the shadows of the sindark nave, her thin elbow at my arm. Her flesh recalls the thrill of that raw mist-veiled morning, hurrying torches, cruel eyes. Her soul is sorrowful, trembles and would weep. Weep not for me, O daughter of Jerusalem! [*GJ* 10]

In 1914, as Vicki Mahaffey has pointed out, Good Friday occurred on 10 April for the first time since 1903.[12] The repetition of the date, its parallax, as it were, rhymed in some way the pain that Joyce remembered and that he was currently

---

12 Mahaffey, "Giacomo Joyce," 399.

suffering. The two events become one and identical, in Joyce's self-imaging, with the Passion of Christ.

We usually understand the pain that the lady caused him as his agitation over Amalia Popper's rejection of him and her engagement to Michele Risolo at Easter 1913,[13] a rejection enacted in the two basilisk sketches and rhymed with Christ's Passion in her selection of another: *"Non hunc sed Barabbam!"* (*GJ* 16). The two basilisk sketches were inscribed on the next to last page of the sketchbook, the only ones written in the original hand on that page. Some time later Joyce added the second Paris sketch, which is in a different hand and written smaller to fit the lengthy sketch, the longest and strangest of the fifty, on the page. Scholars since Ellmann have dated the original inscription of the sketches at the summer of 1914.[14] Joyce, then, either added the second Paris sketch sometime in the year after this date, before he went to Zürich in June of 1915, or he added it more than five years later, during the ten months he spent in Trieste, from October 1919 to July 1920, after his four years in Zürich (*JJII* 389, 469, 482). As his letter to Pound of 9 April, 1917 from Zürich indicates, the manuscript of the sketches was "locked up in my desk" in Trieste throughout.

The reference to *Ulysses* in the sketch—"*Ulysses* is the reason"—argues for the later dating. Joyce wrote to Pound in June of 1915 when he left Trieste for Zürich that he had only progressed as far as the first pages of "Proteus," and he considered the novel "a continuation of *A Portrait of the Artist as a Young Man* after three years' interval blended with many of the persons of *Dubliners*" (*JJII* 383). He did not yet have a conception of the scale and importance that he would have four years later when he returned. By then he had progressed as far as the thirteenth chapter, which would have put him very much in mind of his "locked up" manuscript. He finished this chapter, "Nausicaa," that other tale of a visual and verbal erotic

---

[13] Vicki Mahaffey, "Fascism and Silence: The Coded History of Amalia Popper," *JJQ* 32.3-4 (1995): 503.

[14] Richard Ellmann, Introduction (*GJ* xv), and Mahaffey, "Giacomo Joyce," 388.

relation between an older man and a young woman, on 2 February, 1920. Paris would also be very much in his mind. During this period, Pound was continually advocating by letter for a meeting at last between the two artists and for Joyce's removal to somewhere other than Trieste, preferably Paris.[15] The meeting finally occurred at Sirmione on 8 June, but only after Joyce's elaborate and significant procrastination. The thought of meeting Pound seemed to cause him considerable agitation and even fear. He started out several times and turned back, citing his paralysing fear of thunderstorms.[16] Meeting Pound, he perhaps knew, would inevitably draw him out of provincial Trieste and into the Parisian orbit, which shortly happened when Joyce and family, under cover of only passing through on the way to Ireland, arrived in Paris on 9 July, not to leave for twenty years. Joyce seemed very much to want and not to want to situate himself in Paris again. Paris was a location of intense ambivalence for Joyce during this period. In other words, then, the complex of events—the recognition of the significance of *Ulysses*, the return to Trieste, the writing of "Nausicaa," the lure and memory of Paris, and something else—could have caused Joyce to seek out the manuscript he had "locked up," buried, encrypted in his desk more than five years earlier and add the second Paris sketch.

Whether he made the addition in 1914-15 or 1919-20, the manuscript and his image of himself was obviously incomplete without the second Paris sketch. An irresistible artistic need—the something else—made him dig up the sketchbook to make the completing strokes on a manuscript that he would then lock up or bury again, never to publish and never to mention in public again, as far as we know. In the first Paris sketch, he had encoded his most sacred and painful and profound memory. The death of his mother rendered permanent the loss of everything that he believed he had to renounce in order to become an artist, the loss of his family, his church, and his

---

[15] Pound, *Pound/Joyce*, 162-79.
[16] Pound, *Pound/Joyce*, 175.

country. He would be an exile forever, the pelagic wanderer of his Byrnean postcard. The loss must have been like his own death, and the Good Friday setting made it a crucifixion. That he encoded the lady of *Giacomo Joyce* into this sketch, the scene of his most sacred personal memory, indicates the profound impact she had on his self-image. This death in the register of the sacred, however, this crucifixion, had to be matched and overcome by an awakening, a resurrection, in the profane. There would, in fact, have to be an overcoming of the profane. Joyce would have to wake from this self-created nightmare and return to his real life. So, five years after the inscription of the forty-nine sketches, I would argue, contemplating leaving Trieste forever and returning to Paris, he was compelled to write the second Paris sketch and complete the parallax.

The sketch itself seems to be written in the compulsive encodings of dreamwork, both banal and strange, with a deixis that is both precise and blurred. The scene is a Parisian room, perhaps a hotel room, but a bare room with only a lounge with a peagreen cover, a profane space very different from the stripped but magnificent interior of Notre Dame on Good Friday. As in the first Paris sketch, the scene unfolds around two sets of ellipsis, though the narrative or dramatic sequence does not break into a clear tripartition. In the first two sections, the identity of the dramatis personae are both clear and unclear:

> A soft crumpled peagreen cover drapes the lounge. A narrow Parisian room. The hairdresser lay here but now. I kissed her stocking and the hem of her rustblack dusty skirt. It is the other. She. Gogarty came yesterday to be introduced. *Ulysses* is the reason. Symbol of the intellectual conscience .... Ireland then? And the husband? Pacing the corridor in list shoes or playing chess against himself. Why are we left here? The hairdresser lay here but now, clutching my head between her knobby knees ....
> [*GJ* 15]

The identity of the hairdresser cannot, it seems, be deciphered. Clearly, this later Giacomo has had some sort of sexual encounter with her, and the pronouns seem to make a double reference to both the hairdresser and a more significant she, the lady of the other forty nine sketches: "It is the other. She. Gogarty came yesterday to be introduced. *Ulysses* is the reason." For obvious class reasons, the hairdresser and the young lady cannot be the same person, but the logic of the dream and the pronouns conflates them. Gogarty, it seems, has come to be introduced to her. The original of Buck Mulligan in *Ulysses*, Oliver St. John Gogarty was identified in the novel and in Joyce's life as a betrayer, classed by Byrne in the scene at 7 Eccles Street in 1909 with Cosgrove as a co-conspirator in the plot to destroy Joyce through sexual jealousy (*JJII* 281). His presence and the presence of what seems to be the husband of the young lady, a dream version perhaps of Michele Risolo, pacing in the corridor or playing chess, presumably while the hairdresser/lady and Giacomo have sex, clouds and corrupts the turbid sexual and dream-like atmosphere.

The dream logic seems to project some sort of future or present alternative reality, depending on whether this sketch was written in 1914-15 or 1919-20, in which the author of *Ulysses* and the lady of *Giacomo Joyce* carry to its adult and squalid conclusion their erotic relationship, a sexual liaison in a sleazy Paris hotel room, with perhaps an identity of convenience for the lady as a hairdresser, a certainly leering Gogarty, and an open contempt for a compliant husband. On the opposing page, Joyce had inscribed two scenes of seduction, one lyric sketch set upon a gothic heath in which he may or may not actually kiss her in the real of the fictive or the actual world (*GJ* 13) and a second longer sketch set in the clearly fantasised space of a harem ("She leans back against the pillowed wall: odalisque-featured in the luxurious obscurity") in which his soul possesses her sexually: "my soul, itself dissolving, has streamed and poured and flooded a liquid and abundant seed ...... Take her now who will! ...." (*GJ* 13). The casual flippancy of his response to this phantom deflowering indicates, as Valente and Mahaffey have most fully shown,[17] how Joyce degrades his model to the status of an object, a fantasy houri in a Mid-Eastern brothel, a sexual and racial degradation of the model that corrupts most the artist himself. In the second Paris sketch, Joyce continues the logic of this degradation of his own image to its conclusion and overcoming. In the sketch, the lady speaks, exonerating their actions and making possible his awakening:

> Intellectual symbol of my race. Listen! The plunging gloom has fallen. Listen!
> —I am not convinced that such activities of the mind or body can be called unhealthy—
> She speaks. A weak voice from beyond the cold stars. Voice of wisdom. Say on! O, say again, making me wise! This voice I never heard. [*GJ* 15]

As Valente argues, the lady now becomes fully human to him, a voice that he must at last attend to.[18] With paradoxical logic, this emergence of the fully human and adult subject results in a final metamorphosis in which the lady becomes a vengeful and predatory nightsnake that scorches Joyce with *her* desire and forces him to wake from the dream of *Giacomo Joyce*:

> She coils towards me along the crumpled lounge. I cannot move or speak. Coiling approach of starborn flesh. Adultery of wisdom. No. I will go. I will.
> —Jim, love!—
> Soft sucking lips kiss my left armpit: a coiling kiss on myriad veins. I burn! I crumple like a burning leaf! From my right armpit a fang of flame leaps out. A starry snake has kissed me: a cold nightsnake. I am lost!
> —Nora!— [*GJ* 15]

---

[17] Mahaffey, "The Case Against Art," 667-692. Valente, "Dread Desire," 67-131.
[18] Valente, "Dread Desire," 119.

Calling Nora's name, Joyce wakes, a resurrection into his real life. This awakening answers the crucifixion of the first Paris sketch, and it is also the second ending of *Giacomo Joyce*, the counterpart to the fetishised and encrypted first ending that he had written perhaps five years earlier. With the addition of this sketch, the parallactic structure of *Giacomo Joyce* was complete.

With the writing of his name and his wife's name, Joyce also almost certainly sealed the fate of *Giacomo Joyce*. The sketchbook could not be published in his lifetime, nor in the lifetime of his model. Conceived and written during those few years before World War I when Modernism emerged fully matured, when Joyce, Eliot, Pound and others were creating their Modernist images, *Giacomo Joyce* would wait fifty four years for publication in 1968. A high Modernist document, the switching point between not only *Portrait* and *Ulysses*, but also anticipating *Finnegans Wake*, *Giacomo* would not move from the private to the public domain until the year of the emergence of Poststructuralism and Postmodernism, the year of *les evenements* of May and the intellectual and political transformations in Paris. In a remarkably Joycean coincidence, 1968 was also the year in which the ghost of Joyce triumphantly returned to Paris to inaugurate what Geert Lernout calls "this new Joycean era,"[19] twenty-eight years after he fled the city in 1940 for Zürich and his death. In 1968, *L'Arc* published a special edition entitled "Retour à Joyce," Hélène Cixous published her monumental doctoral dissertation on Joyce, and the Joycean and Poststructuralist era in Paris was underway, in which Joyce was celebrated as *the* writer of the Post, the writer who through *Ulysses* and especially *Finnegans Wake* pre-established the literary and linguistic cosmos of the contemporary world. *Giacomo Joyce*, translated into French in 1973,[20] played its modest part in the reception and influence of Joyce in this era. The principal beneficiary or legatee of that influence was

[19] Geert Lernout, *The French Joyce* (Ann Arbor: University of Michigan Press, 1990) 28-39.

[20] Lernout, *The French Joyce*, 38.

Jacques Derrida, and this legacy most strongly asserts itself in the "Envois" of *The Post Card*.

I have enumerated elsewhere Derrida's explicit and concealed debts to this delayed sending by Joyce, his sending of his image from a distance.[21] A private love offering as well, the "Envois," whose addressee or model is both known and unknown, revealed and hidden in code, hesitates between the private and the public, between self-disclosure and concealment. It is also generically uncertain, both novel and autobiography, both continuous and discontinuous, both open and closed. The text reflects on writing and speech, cemeteries (including the crucial scene at Joyce's gravesite in Zürich)[22] fidelity and infidelity, self-address, the self-sending of suicide, and the life and death of artist and model. *Giacomo Joyce*, as Derrida explicitly asserts, is one of the names of Babel, the play of seven and five across languages, imaged in the Matthew Paris engraving of "*Socrates* and Plato" that Derrida, the singular plural author who we designate by this name, obsessively reads.[23]

As the obsessional or delirious play with the engraving makes clear, the "Envois" are, above all, concerned with the dualities, the doubleness of the author-artist's visual and verbal image, its parallax in Joyce's term. The verbal text is always to be read beside the told out of the engraving of the bearded, hatted, cloaked twins of the five and the seven, the latter writing and erasing with two hands. The writer of the "Envois" asserts throughout that "our story is also a twin progeniture, a procession of Sosie/sosie, Atreus/Thyestes, Shem/Shaun, S/p, p/p, (*penmen/postmen*),"[24] derived from Joyce at every point. The obsessive concern of the writer-artist with the duality of his image and of the relation of his verbal and visual images drives

---

21 Murray McArthur, "The Example of Joyce: Derrida Reading Joyce," *JJQ* 32 (1995): 227-41.
22 Derrida, *The Post Card*, 148-52.
23 Derrida, *The Post Card*, 238-9.
24 Derrida, *The Post Card*, 142.

the relentless motifs of self-imaging, especially the motif of the photomaton, the booth for taking photos that are placed in great public switching points like train stations or airports, automated versions of the Photo-Cartes where Joyce had his cards made in 1902. In the card of 11 June, 1977, Derrida inserts his photo image into the engraving: "The 'photomaton' that I pasted under the *grattoir* on S.'s table comes from Paddington. When I have nothing to do in a public place, I photograph myself and with few exceptions burn myself."[25] In the card of September 9, he invites his multiple addressee to take a photomaton with him and try to find that vanishing point where their two glances intersect:

> If you came back alone we could once again abuse the photomaton in the station. As always we would not succeed in looking at each other, turned symmetrically the one toward the other hoping that the machine's eye finally will surprise, in order to fix it, the point of intersection, the unique one, of the two glances. The one will look at the other who will look elsewhere, and it will remain like that in a wallet.[26]

This multiple addressee is "the 'verso' of everything I write (my desire, speech, presence, proximity, law, my heart and soul, everything that I love and that you know before me)."[27] Who is this twin, this double, this verso, whose identity Derrida carefully reveals and conceals?

Among the multiple or composite identities of the addressee, I have argued elsewhere, one is "James (the two, the three), Jacques, Giacomo Joyce,"[28] whose ghost, as Derrida put it in "Two Words for Joyce," "is always coming on board" every time he writes.[29] In other words, Joyce's image, his highly encoded legacy, generates and dictates all of Derrida's and our

---

25 Derrida, *The Post Card*, 37.
26 Derrida, *The Post Card*, 79.
27 Derrida, *The Post Card*, 197.
28 Derrida, *The Post Card*, 238.
29 Derrida, *The Post Card*, 149.

writing. As Derrida puts it in the crucial card set at Joyce's grave site, "he has read all of us—and plundered us, that one."[30] His spectral image or ghost joins Derrida's in the photomaton booth in the intersecting gaze. His ghost, seated in Michael Hebald's funerary statue at the tomb in Zürich, overlays the seated Socrates in Matthew Paris's engraving like a photographic negative. In the play of reversals that Derrida uses throughout as an image or emblem of writing itself, and that appear in the grave site card in the reversal of positions between Lacan and Derrida that Barbara Johnson identifies,[31] Joyce and Derrida are the twins, the pair, the dual image of writing itself, the reversible five and seven, each writing at the other's dictate, as, so Derrida's argument runs about his new Joycean age, we all do.

In the first ending of *Giacomo Joyce*, Joyce prepared the funerary monument or crypt for this relation, an affair that, Derrida insists, we all have with Joyce. He ended his exercise in parallax with a pair of fetishised and heraldic objects laid at the tomb of the affair:

> Unreadiness. A bare apartment. Torbid daylight. A long black piano: coffin of music. Poised on its edge a woman's black hat, red-flowered, and umbrella, furled. Her arms: a casque, gules, and blunt spear on a field, sable.
>
> Envoy: Love me, love my umbrella. [*GJ* 16]

The single of a pair of objects, one shoe, one glove, is the classical fetish, both affirming and denying castration and death. Paired single objects, the hat and the umbrella share, nonetheless, the structure of the pair. Vicki Mahaffey first speculated that they might represent the signifier, the letter "a," for Amalia, and Joseph Valente countered that they might spell "p" for Popper as well.[32] I would argue they could as easily

---

30 Derrida, *The Post Card*, 148.
31 Derrida, *The Post Card*, 15-20.
32 Mahaffey, "Giacomo Joyce," 398. Valente, 130.

signify "a" and "j," for Amalia and James. Whatever the range of possible interpretations, the pair of heraldic objects encrypt the principle of selection, the parallax, that opened and now closes this text. Derrida seized, in his turn, on this encrypted ending to encrypt his own text:

> James (the two, the three), Jacques, Giacomo Joyce—your *contrefacture* is a marvel, the counterpart to the *invoice: "Envoy: love me love my umbrella"*
>
> [...]
>
> I forgot. Giacomo also has seven letters. Love my *ombre, elle*—not me. "Do you love me?" And you, tell me.[33]

So the high Modernist exercise in parallactic imaging became the Postmodernist pair.[34] Whatever "love me, love my umbrella," may mean (and I argued elsewhere that it also means "love me, love my code"), one of its meanings is "love me, love my images." So the affair begins and ends.

[33] Derrida, *The Post Card*, 238-9.

[34] The *locus classicus* for the Postmodern pair is Derrida's polylogue on Van Gogh's pair of shoes in "Restitutions of the Truth in Painting," *The Truth in Painting,* trans. Geoff Bennington and Ian McLeod (Chicago: University of Chicago Press, 1987).

Michel Delville

Epiphanies and Prose Lyrics: James Joyce and the Poetics of the Fragment

James Joyce's first meeting with William Butler Yeats took place in early October 1902 in the smoking room of a Dublin restaurant. According to Yeats's own account of the interview, Joyce, then a twenty-year-old undergraduate, claimed to have "thrown over metrical form" and succeeded in creating "a form so fluent that it would respond to the motions of the spirit" (*JJII* 102). That Joyce declined to call his prose sketches *prose poems* is hardly surprising, considering his well-known reluctance to be assimilated into any specific literary tradition. The term "prose poem" (which, in English literature, had so far been applied, somewhat loosely, to a variety of neo-Ossianic eclogues and Wildean *contes-poèmes*) probably appeared far too restrictive to the young man whom Richard Ellmann describes as already confident enough in his talents as a prose writer "to feel he might outdo George Moore, Hardy, and Turgenev, if not Tolstoy" (*JJII* 83). Be that as it may, Joyce's description of the "epiphany," despite its claims to novelty, reads like a quasi-verbatim rerun of Charles Baudelaire's famous definition of the genre as "the miracle of a poetic prose, musical though rhythmless and rhymeless, flexible yet rugged enough to identify with the lyrical impulses of the soul, the ebbs and flows of reverie, the pangs of conscience" (*Poems* 25). A second, even more striking similarity between the Baudelairean prose poem and the Joycean epiphany lies in the capacity of both genres not only to render the fluidity of mental states, but also to give shape to an essentially modern and urban reality. Like Baudelaire's *flâneur*, Stephen *Dedalus* likes to wander through the streets of his native city, gleaning moments of poetic inspiration from seemingly unimpressive and random events:

> He was passing through Eccles St one evening, one misty evening [...] when a trivial incident set him composing some ardent verses which he entitled a "Vilanelle of the Temptress." A young lady was standing on the steps of one of those brown brick houses which seem the very incarnation of Irish paralysis. A young gentleman was leaning on the rusty railings of the area. Stephen as he passed on his quest heard the following fragment of colloquy out of which he received an impression keen enough to afflict his sensitiveness very severely.
>
> The Young Lady—(drawling discreetly) ... O, yes ... I
>   was ... at the ... cha ... pel ...
> The Young Gentleman—(inaudibly) ... I ... (again
>   inaudibly) ... I ...
> The Young Lady—(softly) ... O ... but you're ... ve
>   ... ry ... wick ... ed ...
>
> This triviality made him think of collecting many such moments together in a book of epiphanies. By an epiphany he meant a sudden spiritual manifestation, whether in the vulgarity of speech or of gesture or in a memorable phase of the mind itself. He believed that it was for the man of letters to record these epiphanies with extreme care, seeing that they themselves are the most delicate and evanescent of moments. [*SH* 211]

Most of the forty surviving epiphanies were later adapted and used in Joyce's more extended works of fiction.[1] Many critics

---

[1] Morris Beja has found fourteen clear uses of the original epiphanies in *Stephen Hero*, eleven in *A Portrait*, four in *Ulysses*, and one in *Finnegans Wake*. See

have therefore tended to consider them as merely preparatory material for Joyce's "ambitious" works. However, the neatly and carefully written manuscripts Joyce left behind him—all of which seem to date from between 1902 and 1904—leave no reason to believe that he did not originally consider them as literary achievements in their own right.[2] Joyce even played for a time with the idea of gathering them in a volume and, in a letter sent to his brother Stanislaus in 1903, referred to them as a single work simply entitled "Epiphany" (*L* II.28). In a brief, self-mocking remembrance, Stephen's reincarnation in *Ulysses* later dismissed the project as the product of an arrogant and immature mind: "Remember your epiphanies on green oval leaves, deeply deep, copies to be sent if you died to all the great libraries of the world, including Alexandria? Someone was to read them there after a few thousand years, a mahamanvantara. Pico della Mirandola like" (*U* 41).

Stephen Dedalus's definition of the epiphany in *Stephen Hero* (the earlier version of *A Portrait of the Artist as a Young Man*) as "a sudden spiritual manifestation, whether in the vulgarity of speech or of gesture or in a memorable phase of the mind itself" points to the existence of two distinct epiphanic modes reflected

"Epiphany and the Epiphanies," *A Companion to Joyce Studies*, eds. Zack Bowen and James F. Carens (Westport, CT: Greenwood, 1984) 712-713.

2   Twenty-two manuscripts of epiphanies—carefully written on separate sheets of ruled paper by Joyce himself—are housed at the Poetry Collection at the State University of New York at Buffalo. The twenty-five remaining ones (seven of which are duplicates from Buffalo) are at Cornell University. All but one of these are copies made by Stanislaus Joyce; the remaining one (concerning Oliver Gogarty) is a rough draft in Joyce's hand. The numbers ranging from 1 to 71 written on the back of the twenty-two holograph manuscripts currently held at Buffalo suggest that the entire collection ran into the seventies or more. The Buffalo manuscripts were first published and edited by A.O. Silverman in 1956. In 1965, Robert Scholes and Richard Kain published an annotated edition of all the surviving epiphanies, which they ordered into a sequence following the numbers on the versos, in Part I of *The Workshop of Daedalus*. The most recent edition of the manuscripts was compiled by Richard Ellmann and A. Walton Litz in 1991. For a detailed account of the composition of the epiphanies and of the adaptation made by Joyce for his novels, see Ellmann *JJII* 83-85 and Beja, "Epiphany and the Epiphanies," 709-13, respectively.

in the extant manuscripts themselves: the one consists in a brief dramatic dialogue, the other in a short descriptive or narrative sketch. While the "dramatic" epiphanies (which include Stephen's description of an overheard conversation in the above-quoted passage) arising from "the vulgarity of speech or gesture" are evidently preparatory, the "lyric" epiphanies are in the form of short but relatively self-contained vignettes, often inspired by a dream.[3]

Joyce's early fascination with dreams, which he shared with a number of other Dublin poets such as George Russell and W. B. Yeats, suggests that at least one of the original impulses behind his short prose sketches was quite independent from his project to incorporate them into a larger narrative. Richard Ellmann is undoubtedly right in suggesting that, although Freud's *Traumdeutung* appeared in late 1899 (that is, shortly before Joyce wrote his first dream-epiphanies), Joyce's interest in dreams was pre-Freudian "in that it look[ed] for revelation, not scientific explanation" (*JJII* 85).[4] This is not to say, however, that Joyce was not interested in the secret or latent meaning of the oneiric mind.[5] As his brother Stanislaus wrote, retrospectively, in *My Brother's Keeper*, "there is no hint [...] that [Joyce] considered dreams anything but an uncontrolled rehash of our waking thoughts, though he may have hoped they would reveal things our controlled thoughts unconsciously conceal."[6] Considering the revelatory quality Stephen consistently ascribes to the epiphany, it seems very unlikely indeed that Joyce should have been interested solely in its potential for

---

3   Robert E. Scholes and Richard M. Kain, eds. *The Workshop of Daedalus* (Evanston: Northwestern University Press, 1965) 3-4.

4   According to most critics, the forty extant epiphanies were composed in the years between 1900 and 1904. See Ellmann *JJII* 83; Scholes and Kain, *The Workshop of Daedalus*, 5; Beja, "Epiphany and the Epiphanies," 709; Vicki Mahaffey, "Giacomo Joyce," *A Companion to Joyce Studies*, eds. Zack Bowen and James F. Carens (Westport CT: Greenwood, 1984) 190.

5   As Ellmann himself points out, Joyce interpreted one of his dream-epiphanies as being about Ibsen (*JJII* 85).

6   Stanislaus Joyce, *My Brother's Keeper: James Joyce's Early Years*, ed. Richard Ellmann (New York: Viking, 1958) 127.

reproducing the basic rhythms of the unconscious. Just like the "dramatic" epiphanies, the dream-narratives were supposed to deliver one or several "evanescent" moments of insight—the writer's task was to perceive and disclose their symbolic relevance in the outside world.

Epiphany #30 demonstrates quite clearly this dialogical process between the waking and the unconscious mind. Joyce's dream-vision illustrates his conflicting feelings towards his mother country, as well as his fear of spiritual imprisonment. More generally, it outlines the theme of the relationship of the artist to his family, culture and race which was to preoccupy Joyce throughout the composition of *Stephen Hero* and *A Portrait of the Artist as a Young Man*:[7]

> The spell of arms and voices—the white arms of roads, their promise of close embraces and the black arms of tall ships that stand against the moon, their tales of distant nations. They are held out to say: We are alone,—come. And the voices say with them, We are your people. And the air is thick with their company as they call to me their kinsman, making ready to go, shaking the wings of their exultant and terrible youth. [*Poems* 190]

If one refers to Yeats's description of the epiphanies as "a beautiful though immature and eccentric harmony of little prose descriptions and meditations" (*JJII* 102), there is good reason to believe that all or most of the pieces Joyce submitted to him belonged to the so-called "narrative" or "lyric" species. Considering Joyce's own emphasis on the malleable fluency of prose, the dream-narrative evidently corresponds to the Baudelairean ideal of a form freed from the constraints of metrical verse, one which is capable of reproducing the "actual"

---

[7] "[The Spell of Arms and Voices]" appears in the final section of *A Portrait of the Artist as a Young Man* (275), in the form of a journal entry written down ten days before Stephen's resolution to "forge in the smithy of [his] soul the uncreated conscience of [his] race" (*P* 276).

movement of consciousness and accommodating the capricious narrative logic of the dream mind.

While some dream-epiphanies, like "[The Spell of Arms of Voices]," are certainly imagined and visionary, others seem rooted in the observation of an everyday incident:

> Dull clouds have covered the sky. Where three roads meet before a swampy beach a big dog is recumbent. From time to time he lifts his muzzle in the air and utters a prolonged sorrowful howl. People stop to look at him and pass on; some remain, arrested, it may be, by that lamentation in which they seem to hear the utterance of their own sorrow that had once its voice but is now voiceless, a servant of laborious days. Rain begins to fall. (Epiphany #8 [*Poems* 168])

Virtually nothing distinguishes this piece from even a fairly "realist" passage excerpted from one of Joyce's works of fiction. In "[The Big Dog]"—which Joyce himself interpreted to be about his brother Stanislaus[8]—the "dream-like" quality of the vignette arises mainly from the absence of contextual elements. Since Joyce's "dreamscape" appears isolated and independent from a larger narrative or dramatic whole, the type of reading it imposes on the reader is one which encourages what Jonathan Culler has called "the expectation of totality or coherence."[9] In the same way as William Carlos Williams's "This Is Just to Say" turns from a note left on a kitchen table into a self-contained poem as soon as it is set down on the page *as* a poem, the intimidating margins of silence which frame Joyce's epiphanies (which were neatly and carefully calligraphed on separate sheets) invite a reading which urges us to assume their inherent totality at the same time as it insists on their incomplete and fragmentary nature.[10]

---

[8] Joyce, *My Brother's Keeper*, 136.

[9] Jonathan Culler, *Structuralist Poetics: Structuralism, Linguistics and the Study of Literature* (London: Routledge and Kegan Paul, 1975) 170.

[10] For an extensive discussion of the fragment as both the expression of a lost totality and the desire for its recuperation within the realm of subjective

"Poems which succeed as fragments or as instances of incomplete totality," Culler writes, "depend for their success on the fact that our drive towards totality enables us to recognise their gaps and discontinuities and to give them a thematic value."[11] As a result of Joyce's emphasis on the "lyric" quality of the piece, to the detriment of its narrative progress, the reader has to rely almost exclusively on the (potentially) revelatory nature of the epiphany in order to construe it as a self-contained whole. In "[The Big Dog]," this particular interpretative strategy is consolidated by the intervention of an authorial voice, commenting, albeit tentatively, on the reaction of the passers-by, and endowing the dreamscape with symbolic value. More generally, the semi-allegorical significance of the dream scene is best understood in the context of Stephen's project to transmute both the content of the subconscious mind and the raw material of "trivial" everyday experience (here reunited in a single dreamt "incident") into a spiritual "manifestation"; a moment of revelation or "inscape" at which the commonplace object delivers a sense of "sudden radiance," which here occurs when the passers-by begin to see in the howling dog an emblem of their own sorrowful lives.[12]

discourse, see, in particular, Philippe Lacoue-Labarthe and Jean-Luc Nancy, *The Literary Absolute: The Theory of Literature in German Romanticism* (1978; Albany: SUNY Press, 1988) 69-78 and Pascal Quignard, *Une gêne technique à l'égard des fragments* (St Clément-la-Rivière: Fata Morgana, 1986) 42-62.

[11] "Poems which succeed as fragments or as instances of incomplete totality," Culler writes, "depend for their success on the fact that our drive towards totality enables us to recognise their gaps and discontinuities and to give them a thematic value" (*Structuralist Poetics*, 171).

[12] Note that the term "epiphany," in Joyce's writings, variously refers to: (1) the "sudden manifestation" itself; (2) the written record of the moment of revelation; (3) the verbal strategy used by the artist in order to find meaning in the seemingly insignificant.

GIACOMO JOYCE: FRAGMENTS OF A LOVER'S DISCOURSE

> *I have the illusion to suppose that by breaking up my discourse I cease to discourse in terms of the imaginary about myself, attenuating the risk of transcendence; but since the fragment (haiku, maxim, pensée, journal entry) is finally a rhetorical genre and since rhetoric is that layer of language which best presents itself to interpretation, by supposing I disperse myself I merely return, quite docilely, to the bed of the imaginary.*
>
> (Roland Barthes, *Roland Barthes by Roland Barthes*)

By translating the liturgical meaning of the term "epiphany" into secular (though still Platonic and essentialist) terms, the young Joyce purported to redefine nothing less than the role of the modern artist, who would henceforth seeks to grasp, record and transcend the trivial, prosaic incidents and realities of everyday life into moments of extraordinary aesthetic and spiritual significance. In Joyce's writings, however, the stress is often not so much on the moment of insight as such as on the process of apprehension of the object by the individual consciousness. The "apprehensive faculty" of the artist is described by Stephen as "the gropings of a spiritual eye which seeks to adjust its vision to an exact focus" (*SH* 189). "The moment the focus is reached," Stephen adds, "the object is epiphanised"—only then can the aesthete hope to recognise the thing in itself, "its soul, its whatness" (*SH* 190).

This double process of aestheticisation and interpretation of the real also lies at the heart of *Giacomo Joyce*, a series of prose sketches Joyce wrote in Trieste between late 1911 and 1914, shortly before the publication of *A Portrait of the Artist as a Young Man* and at a time when he had already started to work on *Ulysses*. The manuscript comprises fifty fragments of variable length—ranging from a single line to a little more than one page—painstakingly transcribed onto eight oversized sheets of heavy sketching paper enclosed between the blue paper covers of a school notebook. When Joyce moved to Zürich in 1915, the sketchbook, which bore the name "Giacomo

Joyce" on the front cover in an unidentified handwriting, was left behind in the care of Joyce's brother Stanislaus.[13] The small book remained unknown until 1956, when Richard Ellmann discovered it among Stanislaus's possessions. Although Ellmann's biography, published in 1959, featured a discussion of *Giacomo Joyce* (including a significant portion of it), the book first appeared in its entirety in an annotated edition issued by Viking Press in 1968.

Joyce never attempted to have his manuscript published, and the fragments were ultimately "recycled" to form pages of his longer works of fiction: both *A Portrait* and *Ulysses* contain direct or paraphrased borrowings from *Giacomo Joyce*. The amount of painstaking care which went into the calligraphy of the manuscript, however, leaves no room for doubt concerning its original status as an independent work. Furthermore, *Giacomo Joyce*, unlike Stephen's project of a "book of epiphanies" (*SH* 211), is not merely a florilegium of precious but disparate moments of revelation. It is a collection of lyric and narrative fragments all related to a single subject: Joyce's infatuation with one of his female students in Trieste, whom Ellmann identifies as Amalia Popper, the daughter of a Triestine Jewish businessman.[14] The explicitly autobiographical

---

[13] Ellmann's comments on the title of the manuscript are rather misleading. In his biography of Joyce, he acknowledges that the name was inscribed "in another, unknown hand," but almost immediately adds that Joyce "was content to keep what he had written under this heading," for the title must have expressed "his sense of *dépaysement* as a Triestine Dubliner pining for requital in two languages" (*JJII* 342). Ellmann's account, however, gives us no reason to believe that the name was written before Joyce's departure for Zürich and, therefore, casts some doubts upon the validity of his interpretation. (Note that the "unknown hand" which wrote the name "Giacomo Joyce" on the sketchbook cover was more than probably Italian, as suggested by the hesitant calligraphy of the letters "j" and "y," which are nonexistent in the Italian alphabet.) For the purpose of clarity and consistency, I shall nevertheless apply the name "Giacomo" to the "poetic persona" of the poem.

[14] For a detailed account of the life of Amalia Popper and a thought-provoking examination of the social and political realities surrounding her alleged relationship with Joyce, see Vicki Mahaffey's article "Fascism and Silence: The Coded History of Amalia Popper," *JJQ* 32.3-4 (1995).

character of the poem and the scabrousness of the subject eventually prevented Joyce from publishing the work in its original form. Nevertheless, other considerations of an aesthetic nature may have led Joyce to disown a work whose inherent poetics were irreconcilable with his current aesthetic development as a novelist. In other words, Joyce's prose lyrics may have been, as I will argue, aesthetically embarrassing, as well as biographically compromising. My second purpose is to re-examine the position of *Giacomo Joyce*, within or outside the Joyce canon, in the context of Joyce's ongoing experimentations with both lyric and narrative form. In order to do so, I propose to look first at a number of rhetorical and phenomenological strategies as they operate in Joyce's use of the fragment, as well as in his changing conception of the lyric self. The generic negotiations at work in *Giacomo Joyce* will also be given special attention as they account for the text's ambivalent status as what Henriette Lazaridis Power calls a "maggot,"[15] a formally and thematically unstable quirk whose hybrid poetics test the validity of our assumptions concerning Joyce's chief preoccupations as a poet and a novelist.

> Who? A pale face surrounded by heavy odorous furs. Her movements are shy and nervous. She uses quizzing-glasses.
> *Yes*: a brief syllable. A brief laugh. A brief beat of the eyelids.
> [*GJ* 1]

The opening lines of *Giacomo* are representative of the phenomenological premises of Joyce's fragments, which often originate in the brief but scrupulous observation of a specific part of the student's body. This particular aspect of Joyce's prose lyrics makes them akin to the epiphanies, whose heuristic potential also results from the artist's apprehension of a given object or incident in its irreducible spatial and temporal

---

[15] The generic negotiations at work in *Giacomo Joyce* will also be given special attention as they account for the text's ambivalent status as what Henriette Lazaridis Power calls a "maggot," in "Incorporating *Giacomo Joyce*" *JJQ* 28 (1991): 623.

particularity. According to Stephen, the first stage of the epiphanisation of the real indeed consists in "divid[ing] the entire universe into two parts, the object, and the void which is not the object." The general presentation of the fragments—a series of short blocks of prose surrounded by white space—is particularly well-suited to Stephen's desire to grasp the radical "integrity" of things for the sake of aesthetic illumination or Thomist *claritas* (*SH* 212).

There is no dearth of books and articles on the literary and philosophical origins of the Joycean epiphany. As Ashton Nichols and other critics have shown, its revelatory value originates in the nineteenth century, notably in Wordsworth's "spots of time," Coleridge's "flashes," Shelley's "best and happiest moments" and Keats's "fine isolated verisimilitude," all of which similarly revealed the mind's ability to perceive the hidden meaning of ordinary events and situations. Another possible influence, that of Ignatius of Loyola, has, to my knowledge, escaped the attention of critics. Saint Ignatius of Loyola, to whom Giacomo appeals for help at the end of the thirteenth fragment (*GJ* 5), occupied a privileged position in Joyce's Jesuit education. One of his *Spiritual Exercises*, the "composition of place," which is mentioned in the third chapter of *A Portrait*,[16] recommends meditating upon a physical object as a prelude to the contemplation of a spiritual truth. More than anything else, Loyola's insistence on the essential role played by the imagination in the self's attempts to recognise the heuristic potential of the physical world probably appealed to the young Joyce.

However that may be, Joyce's concern with the self-contained wholeness of the beheld object is as much characteristic of *Giacomo* as it is an essential element of Imagist poetry, a movement in which Joyce was briefly involved and whose heyday roughly coincides with the composition of the

[16] Ignatius Loyola, *Exercices Spirituels* (1548; Paris: Seuil, 1982) 137.

Giacomo manuscript.[17] The Imagists' belief in economy of language and brevity of treatment, as well as their penchant for short, single images or objects presented for "direct apprehension," may indeed have inspired some of Joyce's shorter fragments, which—had they been presented in a versified form—would have fitted perfectly in an Imagist anthology:

> A flower given by her to my daughter. Frail gift, frail giver, frail blue-veined child. [*GJ* 3]

> Great bows on her slim bronze shoes: spurs of a pampered fowl. [*GJ* 8]

> My words in her mind: cold polished stones sinking through a quagmire. [*GJ* 13]

The last two haiku-like fragments also bear a striking resemblance to Ezra Pound's "In a Station of the Metro" ("The apparition of these faces in the crowd; / Petals on a wet, black bough" [1913]), which also results from the juxtaposition of two images unconnected by any kind of comment or explanation. The unmediated apprehension, "hard and clear, never blurred or indefinite," of images or objects which *Giacomo* shares with Imagist poetry is made possible by the asyndetic dynamics of the collection through which each single "image" acquires

---

[17] Imagism flourished between 1912 and 1917, from Ezra Pound's first printed reference to the Imagist "school" in the appendix to *Ripostes*, to Amy Lowell's unofficial dismantling of the movement. The first Imagist anthology (*Des Imagistes: An Anthology*; 1914), edited by Pound, featured Joyce's "I Hear an Army," which was later included in *Chamber Music*. Note that "I Hear an Army," which Pound included in his anthology on the grounds of its uncompromising "objectivity," is a far less "Imagist" poem than the fragments of *Giacomo Joyce*, even by Pound's own standards. The brevity of treatment which characterises Joyce's fragments also echoes the brief juxtaposed "flashes of inspiration," surrounded by blankness and silence, of Italian Hermeticism, whose chief exponent, Giuseppe Ungaretti, published his first collection, *L'allegria*, in 1914.

irreducible autonomy and is framed in a particular lyric moment.

The fragments quoted above clearly indicate that the very brevity of Joyce's prose lyrics functions as a constitutive part of Giacomo's discourse, which seeks to disclose the essential significance of a series of ephemeral impressions. The elusive, fragmented nature of Giacomo's observations illustrates a principle Roland Barthes was later to describe as one of the major manifestations of the pleasure of the text. Discussing his own taste for discontinuous writing, a tendency apparent in such works as *A Lover's Discourse* and *Roland Barthes*, Barthes explains that his mode of writing was "never lengthy, always proceeding by fragments, miniatures, paragraphs with titles, or articles." One implication of this, he continues, is that the fragment breaks up with what he calls "the smooth finish, the composition, discourse constructed to give a final meaning to what one says."[18] In the preface to *A Lover's Discourse* (revealingly entitled, in French, *Fragments d'un discours amoureux*), Barthes adds that "no logic links the figures (i.e. the incidents or schema in the book), determines their contiguity: the figures are nonsyntagmatic, nonnarrative, they are Erinyes; they stir, collide, subside, return, vanish with no more order than the flight of mosquitoes."[19]

The resistance of Barthes's writings to narrative and logical linearity is symptomatic of his longing for a mode of discourse which he calls the "novelistic" ("le romanesque"). The "novelistic," Barthes insists, is a form distinct from the novel, in that it is no longer structured by coherent psychological characters and plot structures. "A mode of notation, investment, interest in daily reality, in people, in everything that happens in life,"[20] the novelistic—which Barthes defines

---

[18] Roland Barthes, *The Grain of the Voice: Interviews 1962-1980*, trans. Linda Coverdale (New York: Hill and Wang, 1985) 209.

[19] Roland Barthes, *A Lover's Discourse: Fragments*, trans. Richard Howard (New York: Hill and Wang, 1978) 7.

[20] Barthes, *Grain*, 222.

elsewhere as "simply that space where subtle, mobile desires can circulate"[21]—is concerned with the raw material of common, everyday experience uncontaminated by the pressure of narrative. For Barthes, the *actual* transformation of this novelistic material into a novel—a form of writing he sees as dominated by the "superego of continuity"[22]—is bound to lead to an impoverishment of the text's semantic and psychological open-endedness. In *Roland Barthes par Roland Barthes*, Barthes applies the principle of the novelistic fragment to the art of autobiography and comments that this process of disordering and discontinuing ("that science of apportionment, division, discontinuity, what I referred to somewhat ironically as 'arthrology'")[23] inevitably entails a dispersal of the speaking or writing subject into a "circle of fragments." The possibility of finding psychological coherence in Barthes's fragments is precluded by the lack of narrative continuity in the discourse itself:

> To write by fragments: the fragments are then so many stones on the perimeter of a circle: I spread myself around: my whole little universe in crumbs; at the centre, what?[24]

Barthes's conception of the fragment as disjunctive and anticlosural device—one which resists any extended narrative or syntagmatic development and ultimately results in the decentring of the writing self—proves particularly useful in the context of an analysis of the basic dynamics of Giacomo's discourse. The opening question ("Who?") already indicates the real "subject-matter" of Joyce's fragments, for *Giacomo Joyce* is almost entirely dedicated to the narrator's ever-changing perceptions of his pupil, whom he perceives now as a charming specimen of fragile adolescent beauty: "Frail gift. Frail giver,

---

[21] Roland Barthes, *Le Bruissement de la langue: Essais critiques IV* (Paris: Seuil, 1984) 394.

[22] Barthes, *Grain*, 132.

[23] Barthes, *Grain*, 132.

[24] Roland Barthes, *Roland Barthes par Roland Barthes* (Paris: Seuil, 1975) 92-93.

frail blue-veined child" (*GJ* 3); "A cold frail hand: shyness, silence" (*GJ* 13); now as a source of deadly threat: "She answers my sudden greeting by turning and averting her black basilisk eyes." / "A starry snake has kissed me: a cold nightsnake. I am lost!" (*GJ* 15). Giacomo's responses to the young woman follow contradictory patterns of admiration and contempt, submission and domination, desire and disgust. More often than not, they gravitate around a double diptych in which the student is alternately represented as (*GJ* 1) a virgin and a whore; (*GJ* 2) a woman and a child. In this respect, the constant juxtapositions of images of pallor and vividness, candour and sensuousness are facilitated by the inherently paratactic relationships between and within the fragments. Sometimes the juxtaposition occurs within a single sentence, as in "a pale face surrounded by heavy odorous furs" (*GJ* 1). Typically, Giacomo's doubly obsessive attraction to his pupil's virginity and the carnal act are channelled into a vision of endangered virginity and potential prostitution, as in the following juxtaposition of the pupil's assiduousness and the corrupted exuberance of the city's demi-monde:

> She listens: virgin most prudent.
> [...]
> Here are wines all ambered, dying fallings of sweet airs, the proud pavan, kind gentlewomen wooing from their balconies with sucking mouths, the pox-fouled wenches and young wives that, gaily yielding to their ravishers, clip and clip again. [*GJ* 9]

The image of the "sucking mouths," which represents the menace of unbound sexuality, echoes another fragment in which the student's "long lewdly leering lips" are compared with "dark-blooded molluscs" (*GJ* 5). Giacomo's imaginary projections reach a masochistic climax when he envisions the possibility of his committing adultery with his pupil now married and turned into a "cold nightsnake" (*GJ* 15). At the very last moment, the dream vision is short-circuited by a desperate cry to Nora Barnacle:

> Soft sucking lips kiss my left armpit: a coiling kiss on myriad
> veins. I burn! I crumple like a burning leaf! From my right
> armpit a fang of flame leaps out. A starry snake has kissed me:
> a cold nightsnake. I am lost!
> —Nora!— [*GJ* 15]

The shifting nature of Giacomo's desire, which, simultaneously
or alternately directed towards two different objects, oscillates
between attraction and repulsion, is also apparent in his
variations on the woman-child diptych. In the following
fragment, for instance, the pale, frail child's aseptic innocence
("Her body has no smell: an odourless flower." [GJ 13]) is
threatened, not only by marriage—and the loss of virginity
followed by the possibility of adultery—but also by mortality
itself:

> She walks before me along the corridor and as she walks a dark
> coil of her hair slowly uncoils and falls. Slowly uncoiling,
> falling hair. She does not know and walks before me, simple
> and proud. So did she walk by Dante in simple pride and so,
> stainless of blood and violation, the daughter of Cenci, Beatrice,
> to her death:
>
> > .... *Tie*
> > *My girdle for me and bind up this hair*
> > *In any simple knot.* [GJ 11]

The image of Beatrice proudly passing Dante and the reference
to another Beatrice, that of Shelley's *The Cenci* (the final
quotation is from her death speech), introduce the themes,
respectively, of love for a young girl and incest. They reflect
Giacomo's incapacity to express his feelings otherwise than by
means of the related strategies of projection, juxtaposition and
narrative. Giacomo's comparison of the student with a series of
famous female figures in literary history (he also casts her as
Shakespeare's Ophelia, Ibsen's Hedda Gabler and even
Hawthorne's Hester Prynne) is also symptomatic of his repeated attempts to turn the desired object into an unattainable

icon of secret worship.[25] By linking the young woman with these tragic literary figures, Giacomo implicitly casts himself as the male characters who worshipped them and were forced to conceal or disguise their love: Dante, Orsino, Hamlet, Ejlert Lövborg and Arthur Dimmesdale. More generally, these literary allusions blur the borderlines of the student's bodily and textual identity while asserting it in a new paradoxical shape which mirrors Giacomo's own anxieties. As Vicki Mahaffey has pointed out, however, Giacomo's projections can also be seen as a reflection of Joyce's own aesthetic ambitions at the time of writing the *Giacomo* manuscript. "As the author of his own love story," she argues, "Joyce is able to compare himself, not only to five characters, both great and mean, but also to the artists who created them." Joyce is therefore able to "transform a 'failed' imaginary love affair into an important stage in his own artistic development."[26] In the same way as the "trivial incident" related above will wait to be transmuted by the young Stephen into some "ardent verses," the young lady only exists in the world of Giacomo's imagination, where she stands as a "writerly" text opening itself up to all kinds of metamorphoses and interpretations. Like Stephen's epiphanies, the "novelistic" fragments of *Giacomo* show that the young Joyce consistently sought to translate his own experience into art by allowing his imaginative powers to interfere with his vision of the external world. The result of this method is a succession of heavily aestheticised sexual fantasies, increasingly divorced from the "real," observed reality which nourishes Giacomo's insatiable voyeurism.

On a formal and stylistic level, the conflicting nature of Giacomo's textual constructions is often mirrored in the juxtaposition of antipodal tones and modes of representation. Surreal visions or "dreamscapes," impressionistic sketches (Giacomo's lady often appears shrouded in faint or shadowy

---

[25] For a detailed discussion of the major themes, motifs and literary origins of Joyce's manuscript, see Vicki Mahaffey's "Giacomo Joyce," 387-420.

[26] Mahaffey, "Giacomo Joyce," 407.

light) coexist alongside more realistic passages, sometimes verging on the unsavoury and the morbid. In the context of Joyce's career as a poet and a novelist, the stylistic and modal ambivalence of the prose lyrics of *Giacomo Joyce* appears to constitute a transitional stage between the restrained sophistication of his early verse lyrics in *Chamber Music* and the epico-burlesque prosaism of *Ulysses*:

> A ricefield near Vercelli under creamy summer haze. The wings of her drooping hat shadow her false smile. Shadows streak her falsely smiling face, smitten by the hot creamy light, grey wheyhued shadows under the jawbones, streaks of eggyolk yellow on the moistened brow, rancid yellow humour lurking within the softened pulp of the eyes. [*GJ* 2]

> Loggione. The sodden walls ooze a steamy damp. A symphony of smells fuses the mass of huddled human forms: sour reeks of armpits, nozzled oranges, melting breast ointments, mastick water, the breath of suppers of sulphurous garlic, foul phosphorescent farts, opoponax, the frank sweat of marriageable and married womankind, the soapy stink of men ...... All night I have watched her, all night I shall see her: braided and pinnacled hair and olive face and calm soft eyes. A green fillet upon her hair and about her body a green-broidered gown: the hue of the illusion of the vegetable glass of nature and lush grass, the hair of graves. [*GJ* 12]

The first fragment is typical of Giacomo's ambivalent responses to the student's mysterious beauty, in that the description of the girl's serene pallor, emphasised by a subdued but pervasive light, irresistibly slips into a recognition of the potential for treason and corruption hidden beneath the varnish of virginal innocence. Typically, also, the young aesthete associates his distasteful vision of the *loggione* (gallery) in the second fragment with the threat of marriage, which appears to him as a condition of sordid, domestic vulgarity. Giacomo's admiration for the girl's meticulous submissiveness (her "meek supple tendonous neck" [*GJ* 3], "braided and pinnacled hair and calm soft eyes" [*GJ* 2]) alternates with a tone of mockery and contemptuous disdain for her carefree immaturity and her cold indifference to his attempts at seducing her:

> Once more in a chair by the window, happy words on her tongue, happy laughter. A bird twittering after storm, happy that its little foolish life has fluttered out of reach of the clutching fingers of an epileptic lord and giver of life, twittering happily, twittering and chirping happily. [*GJ* 11]

> My words in her mind: cold polished stones sinking through a quagmire. [*GJ* 13]

Here, Giacomo's infatuation (which constantly alternates between patterns of admiration and contempt, domination and submission) turns into a significantly embittered version of the neo-Elizabethan celebration of courtly love of *Chamber Music*. Yet, if Joyce's fragments take place primarily in Giacomo's imagination, the pupil's cold remoteness, she greets him "wintrily [...] darting at [him] for an instant out of her sluggish sidelong eyes a jet of liquorish venom" (*GJ* 15), can be usefully related to the real circumstances of Joyce's life in Trieste. Giacomo's sense of social inferiority climaxes in the above-quoted *loggione* scene, in which the English teacher—sitting amid the smelly "mass of huddled human forms" of the gallery—contemplates his pupil's fragile beauty, inaccessibly nestled in the velvet luxury of the stalls. In order to compensate for his position of inferiority, Giacomo rewrites some of his unproductive encounters into scenarios of imaginary posses-sion:

> She raises her arms in an effort to hook at the nape of her neck a gown of black veiling. She cannot: no, she cannot. She moves backwards towards me mutely. I raise my arms to help her: her arms fall. I hold the websoft edges of her gown and drawing them out to hook them I see through the opening of the black veil her lithe little body sheathed in an orange shift. It slips its ribbons of moorings at her shoulders and falls slowly: a lithe

> smooth naked body shimmering with silvery scales. It slips slowly over the slender buttocks of smooth polished silver and over their furrow, a tarnished silver shadow .... Fingers, cold and calm and moving .... A touch, a touch. [*GJ* 7]

As the fragments quoted above have shown, Giacomo's love story remains an affair of the eye which can only lead to various forms of imaginary—and primarily aesthetic—gratification. Giacomo's attempts to transform the pupil into a textual construction lacking wholeness and identity go hand in hand with his incapacity to acknowledge and describe her other than in terms of the clothes she is wearing or the parts of her body on which his attention momentarily focuses. The object of his desire appears successively, not as a person, but as "a pale face," "a brief beat of the eyelids" (*GJ* 1), "a skirt caught back by her sudden moving knee; a white lace edging of an underskirt lifted unduly; a leg-stretched web of stocking" (*GJ* 9), "slowly uncoiling falling hair" (*GJ* 11), "quiet and cold and pure fingers," or "a cold frail hand" and "dark langour-flooded eyes" (*GJ* 13). The frequent use of the indefinite pronoun further impersonalises the young woman and confirms her status as a mere source of inspiration for Giacomo's visual fantasies.

Through the paratactic and synechdochial strategies at work in the fragments, the narrative of Giacomo's unacceptable desires—"the pages, foul and fair, on which my shame shall glow for ever" (*GJ* 13)—is shattered into pieces and the poem itself is converted into a puzzle which can only be metonymically reconstructed. Typographically speaking, the synecdochial dismemberment and the subsequent objectification of the student is emphasised by the already reified *en bloc* composition of the prose fragments. In the same way that each block of prose is perceived by the reader as a frozen vision of restrained beauty, the young lady herself is ultimately ascribed the static, disembodied grace of a work of art.[27] Ironically enough, the poem ends with a heraldic transcription of the pupil's hat and umbrella, and a final, disenchanted comment on the further reification of the desired object:

> Unreadiness. A bare apartment. Torbid daylight. A long black piano: coffin of music. Poised on its edge a woman's hat, red-flowered, and umbrella, furled. Her arms: a casque, gules, and blunt spear on a field, sable.
>
> Envoy: Love me, love my umbrella. [*GJ* 16][28]

GENRES AND MODES: JOYCE'S CONFLICTING POETICS

In the light of Giacomo's ever-changing perceptions, *Giacomo Joyce*, which Ellmann describes as "Joyce's attempts at the education of a dark lady" (*GJ* xi), would, instead, be more aptly characterised as a fragmented and tortured hymn to the meandering of a narcissistic self racked by the all-powerful strategies of its imagination.[29] However, the synecdochial

---

[27] A striking parallel can be drawn between Giacomo's sketches and the following "lyrical" epiphany, in which the artist as a young voyeur also attempts to turn his model into a work of art. As is the case in the opening fragment of *Giacomo Joyce*, the aesthete's observations almost immediately give rise to an act of interpretation:

> She stands, her book held lightly at her breast, reading the lesson. Against the dark stuff of her dress her face, mild-featured with downcast eyes, rises softly outlined in light; and from a folded cap, set carelessly forward, a tassel falls along her brown ringletted hair [...].
> What is the lesson that she reads—of apes, of strange inventions, or the legends of martyrs? Who knows how deeply meditative, how reminiscent is this comeliness of Raffaello? (Epiphany #39 [*Poems* 199])

[28] As Vicki Mahaffey has pointed out, the final heraldic description of Giacomo's lady was probably modelled on the closing lines of Hawthorne's *The Scarlet Letter* ("Giacomo," 398).

[29] In his introduction to *Giacomo Joyce*, Ellmann apparently contradicts his own earlier version of Joyce's "affair" with Amalia Popper, which he described a few

strategies at work in Joyce's vicarious celebration of the student's remote sensuousness do not serve merely to reflect the complexity of Giacomo's emotional turmoil. By placing the emphasis on the perceiving consciousness and its attempts to fictionalise the real, the fragmented form of Joyce's prose lyrics also entails a *mise en abyme* of the fragmentariness and decentredness of the lyric self, whose conflicting feelings—just like the student's body—are scattered amongst a number of discrete, metonymically-linked "lyric units." As a result of these multiple (self-)manipulations, Giacomo's discourse disintegrates into a succession of euphemised moments and temporary resolutions, so that what begins as a fairly coherent and credible first-person lyric narrative (the "I-persona," after all, is named Jim and has a wife named Nora) becomes just another exercise in the transformation or "epiphanisation" of the raw material of personal experience into art. The issue of the fictionalisation of autobiographical material is raised several times in *Giacomo Joyce*, notably by the student herself (or is she merely being cast as a mouthpiece for Giacomo's lack of self-confidence as a writer?), who, after having "touched the pages, foul and fair, on which [his] shame shall glow for ever" (*GJ* 13), expresses her misgivings about the moral and intellectual integrity of Giacomo-Joyce's writings. Typically, the student's voice is interrupted by Giacomo's attempts to regain ironic control over his material:

> She says that, had *The Portrait of the Artist* been frank only for frankness' sake, she would have asked why I had given it to her to read. O you would, would you? A lady of letters. [*GJ* 12]

In the context of his own development as an artist, Joyce's ambivalent relationship with the lyric mode in *Giacomo Joyce* raises the issue of the relationship between the fragments and the longer narrative productions into which they were later in-

years earlier as a "silent, secret wooing" (*JJII* 347) which always took place in the presence of another person.

corporated. In this respect, the fragmentary and paratactic dynamics of *Giacomo Joyce* can be linked with Joyce's increasingly radical critique of the unified wholeness and linear dynamics of the traditional nineteenth-century novel. As Vicki Mahaffey has remarked, the structural premises of Joyce's shorter works—his poems and epiphanies, *Giacomo Joyce*, and *Exiles*—give us an outline of the basic design of all of their longer and better known counterparts. What Joyce's prose and verse lyrics share with his more extended works of fiction, she writes, is "the strategy of producing a longer and more complicated text by stringing together a series of formally self-contained units." Therefore, she continues, "the minor works make it much more apparent that Joyce's technique—even in the longer texts—is in large part an imagist one, adapted from poetry to narrative and massively elaborated in the process."[30] In this respect, an interesting parallel can be drawn between Joyce's "novelistic" prose lyrics and the definition of the prose poem put forward by Des Esseintes, the protagonist of Huysmans's *À Rebours* (1884). Des Esseintes, who sees the prose poem as "the concrete pith, the osmazome of literature, the essential oil of art," defines the genre as a concentrated and supremely writerly avatar of the novel: "Then the words chosen would be so unpermutable as to substitute for all the others; the adjective, placed in such an ingenious and so definitive a way that it could not be legally divested of its position, would open such perspectives that the reader could dream for weeks on end about its meaning, at the same time fixed and multiple, could take note of the present, reconstruct the past; could guess the future of the characters' souls, revealed by the light of that unique epithet."[31]

Despite its strong Decadent overtones (the emphasis on stylistic refinement and semantic ingeniousness, in particular),

---

[30] Vicki Mahaffey, "Joyce's Shorter Works," *The Cambridge Companion to James Joyce*, ed. Derek Attridge (Cambridge: Cambridge University Press, 1990) 186.

[31] Joris Karl Huysmans, *À Rebours/Against Nature*, trans. Margaret Mauldon, ed. and intro. Nicholas White (1884; Oxford: Clarendon, 1996) 320.

Des Esseintes's definition suggests that Huysmans, like Joyce, saw in the prose poem the possibility of turning the concentrated brevity and semantic ambiguity of poetic language into a means of expanding and complexifying the creation of plot and character. In this perspective, also, the prose lyrics of *Giacomo Joyce* enact the principle of contamination between narrative linearity and poetic closure, poetic ambiguity and novelistic verisimilitude which characterises Joyce's work and the development of a modern tradition of the prose poem. The specific nature of the "elaboration" of the isolated lyric moments of *Giacomo Joyce* and the epiphanies into larger narrative units lies outside the scope of the present essay. Suffice it to say, at this stage, that what in *Giacomo* remains primarily a means of articulating (albeit in a self-consciously manipulative fashion) the sudden bursts of the lyric self subsists in Joyce's fiction within a larger referential system obeying its own internal logic and in which the self tends to be engulfed in the more impersonal arts of irony, satire, allusion, parody and pastiche. When Joyce left Trieste in 1915, leaving behind him the *Giacomo* manuscript, the fragment and the aesthetics of the first person prose lyric had already been put aside to give way to the luxuriant anonymity of the third person encyclopaedic parody of *Ulysses*.[32]

In order to further situate Giacomo's prose fragments in the development of Joyce's poetics, we must turn to Stephen, who, towards the end of *A Portrait of the Artist as a Young Man*, develops his own theory of literary genres. According to Stephen, "art necessarily divides itself into three forms progressing from one to the next "the lyric form, in which the artist presents an image "in immediate relation to himself"; the

---

[32] It would be tempting to see the sudden appearance of Molly Bloom's interior monologue at the end of *Ulysses* as something of a resurgence of the lyric repressed. Joyce, however, did not conceive of Molly's monologue as a lyrical piece in the strict sense. In a letter to Harriet Weaver, he commented that he had "rejected the usual interpretation of [Molly Bloom] as a human apparition" and had tried to depict nothing less than "the earth which is prehuman and presumably posthuman" (*L* I.160).

epical form, in which the image is "in mediate relation to himself and others"; the dramatic form, in which the image is "in immediate relation to others" (*P* 231-32):

> The lyric form is in fact the simplest verbal gesture of an instant of emotion, a rhythmical cry such as ages ago cheered on the man who pulled at the oar or dragged stones up a slope. He who utters it is more conscious of the instant of emotion than of he himself as feeling emotion. The simplest epical form is seen emerging out of lyric literature when the artist prolongs and broods upon himself as the centre of an epical event and this form progresses till the centre of emotional gravity is equidistant from the artist himself and from others. The narrative is no longer personal. The personality of the artist passes into the narration itself, flowing round and round the persons and the action like a vital sea. This progress you will see easily in that old English ballad Turpin Hero which begins in the first person and ends in the third person. The dramatic form is reached when the vitality which has flowed and eddied round each person with such vital force that he or she assumes a proper and intangible esthetic life. The personality of the artist, at first a cry or a cadence or a mood and then a fluid and lambent narrative, finally refines itself out of existence, impersonalises itself, so to speak. The esthetic image in the dramatic form is life purified in and reprojected from the human imagination. The mystery of esthetic like that of material creation is accomplished. The artist, like the God of the creation, remains within or behind or beyond or above his handiwork, invisible, refined out of existence, indifferent, paring his fingernails. [*P* 232-33]

As Gérard Genette has remarked, Stephen's theory is, in fact, a somewhat simplified version of August Wilhelm Schlegel's dialectical trinity (1801), according to which the "pure objectivity" of the epic and the "pure subjectivity" of the lyric should be interwoven into a single "dramatic" sequence. A few years later, Schelling reworked Schlegel's triad into a diachronic sequence much like Stephen's "progression" from the lyric to the dramatic. According to Schelling, art begins as a subjective utterance and has to raise itself to epic objectivity before it reaches the state of dramatic "identification," which he defines as "the synthesis of the universal and the particular."[33] Clearly, Stephen subscribes to Schelling's notion of the dramatic mode as the supreme form of art. For Stephen, however, the dramatic mode is not so much a synthesis of its lyric and epic counterparts as the ultimate stage of a process of emancipation of the work of art from its subjective premises. The superiority of the dramatic form therefore lies in its capacity to "refine" the raw material of personal experience and turn it into a work of impersonal, "intangible" finesse. In this sense, Stephen's theory reflects his commitment to a form of art that reveals the world in all its meaning, as well as his conception of the artist as a semi-angelic figure standing apart from the multitude (or what Joyce himself called the "rabblement"). Finally, Stephen's ideal of the dramatic mode is one in which the artist appears as a highly self-conscious craftsman—a condition antipodal to that of the lyric self described above as "more conscious of the instant of emotion than of he himself as feeling emotion."[34]

Significantly enough, the word epiphany which occurs at the most crucial point of the discourse on aesthetics in *Stephen Hero* has disappeared altogether from Stephen's theories in the *Portrait*. This is hardly surprising since Stephen's "lyric" metaphor of the epiphany—which still laid the emphasis on the artist's personal apprehension, unmediated by irony and dramatic distance, of the "whatness" of a given object or incident—would have been inconsistent with Stephen's own "impersonal" theory (in the *Portrait*) of the progressive separation of the artist from the lyric impulse. In view of the development of Joyce's *œuvre* as a whole, one may reasonably

---

[33] Gérard Genette, *Introduction à l'architexte* (Paris: Seuil, 1979) 124.

[34] Paradoxically, the ballad *Turpin Hero*, "which begins in the first person and ends in the third person," is the antithesis of Joyce's novels which start with the third person and end with a shift to the first person. The paratactical style and arrangement of the diary entries at the end of *A Portrait* is reminiscent of the fragments of *Giacomo*. (Is this an implicit statement on Stephen's immaturity and his incapacity to achieve as yet the "dramatic" mode?)

argue that Stephen is, at least to some extent, a fictional mouthpiece of the author's younger self and of his aesthetic convictions at the time. As suggested above, the lyric mode was gradually abandoned by Joyce in the years that followed the publication of Stephen's three-form theory of genres. In the context of Stephen's "three forms progressing from one to the next," it seems probable that Joyce's decision not to publish *Giacomo* was prompted by aesthetic as well as personal reasons. In the same way as Stephen's theory of the epiphany was replaced, in *A Portrait*, by another theory concerning the development of the poet away from the raw lyric impulse towards dramatic objectivity, Giacomo's lyric effusions—for all their paradoxical attempts to enact the *failure* of the constitution of the lyric self—were soon discarded in favour of the more controlled and detached mode of *Ulysses*, whose parodic and ironic tenor indeed seems to correspond to Stephen's ideal of the artist-as-god, "refined out of existence, indifferent, paring his fingernails."

Thus, one way of approaching *Giacomo Joyce* is as an example of the type of lyric epiphanies the Stephen of *Stephen Hero* and, indeed, the young Joyce would have written and, by the time of *Ulysses*, abandoned. In this respect, also, *Giacomo Joyce* and the prose lyric, which stand at the junction of a lyric discourse already on the wane and the genesis of the "dramatic" novel, mark a turning point in Joyce's career. The very title of the manuscript, itself a dichotomy, carries the implications of a struggle between the lyrico-poetic writing of Joyce's early work—with its focus on the expression of transitory moods or momentary illuminations—and the ambitions of the mature novelist. Yet, if Joyce progressively moved away from lyric brevity towards the impersonality of the monumental "dramatic" novel, the fragments of *Giacomo* nevertheless testify to the existence of an alternative undercurrent in Joyce's poetics, one in which the lyric epiphany no longer seems to mediate between the mind and its object but is displaced onto the split consciousness of the speaker. Joyce's later return to poetry with *Pomes Penyeach*, a collection of thirteen formally conventional and overtly sentimental poems in verse published in 1927—despite Ezra Pound's claim that the poems were not worth printing and belonged "in the Bible or in the family album with the portraits" (*JJII* 591)—confirms that his *œuvre* was never really immune to a return of the lyric repressed. Similarly, the rather unexpected appearance of a poem from *Pomes Penyeach*, "Nightpiece," in an early draft of the parody romance of "Tristan and Isolde" in *Finnegans Wake* points to the ambivalent nature of Joyce's relationship with his own "poetic" works.[35] Joyce, whose interest in poetry was always inseparable from his enthusiasm for music, never completely forsook the pre-ironic musicality of his early lyrics. Towards the end of the *Giacomo* manuscript, Joyce—who, a few months before his departure for Italy, had failed to raise enough money to tour England as a singer and a lute player (*JJII* 154-55)—writes what seems to be a rather bitter and disillusioned adieu to the frustrated ambitions of his youth, as well as a comment on the superiority of musical lyric over its literary counterpart:

> Jan Pieters Sweelink. The quaint name of the old Dutch musician makes all beauty seem quaint and far. I hear his variations for the clavichord on an old air: *Youth has an end*. In the vague mist of old sounds a faint point of light appears: the speech of the soul is about to be heard. Youth has an end: the end is here. It will never be. You know that well. What then? Write it, damn you, write it! What else are you good for? [*GJ* 16]

In the course of his career as a novelist, Joyce tried to satisfy his penchant for the musical aspects of the lyric through the medium of prose. This tendency reaches a climax in *Finnegans Wake*, which Joyce—countering accusations of unnecessary obscurity—kept defending on the grounds that it was "pure

---

[35] *A First Draft Version of* Finnegans Wake, transcribed David Hayman (London: Faber and Faber, 1963) 210-11

music" and that the fact that it was "pleasing to the ear" was one of the book's justifications (*JJII* 702-03). In this perspective, the simple and nostalgic songs of *Chamber Music* and the sophisticated multilingual experiments of *Finnegans Wake* are not as diametrically opposed to each other as they may seem.

If Stephen's theory of genres provisionally sounds the knell of Giacomo's lyric impulses, it nonetheless offers a number of insights into the inherently heterogeneric quality of any literary work. Stephen's translation of the traditional triad into modal rather than strictly generic features, in particular, presents the lyric, the epic and the dramatic not as mutually exclusive categories, but as different degrees of "genericness" coexisting within the same work, as exemplified in the absorption and the subsequent dissolution of the personal mode into its narrative extension in *Turpin Hero*. It would therefore be tempting to see the "novelistic" prose lyrics of *Giacomo Joyce*, as most critics have done, as so many lyric "snatches" destined to be recycled in the increasingly complex narrative structures of Joyce's later works of fiction. As the preceding pages have shown, however, *Giacomo Joyce* should not be considered solely as a "missing link" in the development of Joyce's career as a novelist. By resisting the pressures of narrative linearity and poetic closure, Joyce's fragments also emerge as a new, hybrid form of lyric discourse which seeks to embrace the complex and discontinuous nature of experience and memory and, eventually, offers itself up to the ludic authority of the reader's desire. In this respect, the essentially paratactic relationships between and within the prose blocks of *Giacomo* are once again reminiscent of Baudelaire's project of a "writerly" text *avant la lettre*—a literary work which, like the prose poems of *Paris Spleen*, is "both head and tail, alternately and reciprocally"[36] and in which both the writer and the reader are free to participate in the construction and the dispersal of subjectivity, longing for no other form of narrative coherence than that of

---

[36] Charles Baudelaire, *The Poems in Prose (Paris Spleen)*, ed. and trans. Francis Scarfe (1869; London: Anvil Press, 1989) 23.

the movements of the mind itself. Joyce's desire to reproduce the actual movement of the perceiving consciousness, as well as his careful balancing and counterpointing of subjective and objective experience, prefigure a number of creative and phenomenological strategies which were to dominate the entire history of the contemporary prose poem.

Kevin Nolan

Feydeau's Republic

Modèles. Mécanisés extérieurement. Intacts, vierges intérieurment.
(Robert Bresson)

To rehearse once more a knowable sequence, we see him in Trieste after 1904, an almost public man. Three years after Bloomsday he gives English lessons to the daughter of Leopoldo Popper, for some indefinite period. Between November, 1912 and February, 1913 he delivers his lectures on the "Ameletto di G. Shakespeare" at the Università Populare. He is all the while refining the views of his puppet, the "classical" Stephen Dedalus, who can be heard in the National Library of Dublin in 1904 expounding a view of Shakespeare which may not be that of his author and where, for the benefit of the assembled, the blazonry of self-creation and the mythology of the Man of Letters come together: "Like John of Gaunt his name is dear to him, as dear as the coat of arms he toadied for, on a bend sable a spear or steeled argent, honorificcabilitudinitatibus, dearer than his glory of greatest shakescene in the country" (*U* 210).

Then after the Hamlet lectures and on the eve of war, he casts the narrative we know as *Giacomo Joyce*, to which he adds, six or more years later, one additional scene around which in both gesture and implication the text now pivots, between the heroic *confiteor* of its author and a more secretive awareness of the opacity of experience to any language, even the most directly confessional.

All this comes after, in *Stephen Hero*, the conventional acceptation of lyric as "the art whereby the artist sets forth his image in immediate relation to himself." Despite the tantalising remark in the ur-Portrait that sees "A philosophy of reconcilement (possible)," the final 1916 text still relies upon the monadic *stasis* of the "aesthetic image," "luminously apprehended as self-bounded and self-contained upon the immeasurable background of a space and time which is not it [...]." From which proceeds the nominalist confusion of clarity with singularity, "quidditas." Always the mediation of art ("the human disposition of sensible or intelligible matter for an aesthetic end") is an *image*, yet only of a certain kind: the Parisian notes on aesthetics from 1903 assert that "a photograph is not a human disposition of sensible matter. Therefore it is not a work of art." The problem then is also the starting point, the lyric self as the primary condition, in which, as Stephen avers, "the artist presents his image in immediate relation to himself." Only the dramatic in this schema permits the presentation of "his image in immediate relation to others."

That little has apparently changed in Stephen's Republic in those thirteen years is important evidence of changefulness impending. Behind the defensive closure of the image, Dedal neoplatonism is already succumbing to Plato's own critique of imagery as *eikasia*, just as *Dubliners* demonstrates the temporal limitations of the *point of view*. From this, perhaps, it is only a matter of time before the infiltration of new kinetic conditions of dramatic life, even perhaps the abandonment of the doctrine of the image itself, together with the focal subjectivism it is meant to defend.

The frame series of forty-nine interlinked exposures (plus envoy) in *Giacomo Joyce* suggests both a closer accommodation to the photographic principle of mechanical imagination and a more precise awareness of the contradictions which that medium intensifies, everything entailed by the notion of a fixed point of view *publicly intelligible*. If the abstraction of early twentieth century Modernism suggests a defensive incorporation of the photographic in order to claim the advantage for language or paint (collage, say, or the Imagiste polaroid, "an intellectual and emotional complex in an instant of time" etc.) then Joyce by 1914 was already moving beyond the antinomy of verbal versus visual saturation, (the pathos of distance), to an intertwining of the two. How to incorporate "a dramatic awareness of others" shorn of parlour pictorialism though, the "sixty miles an hour pathos of some cinematograph" as he calls it in a letter of 1909? Or how to demonstrate a cardinal awareness of form (as distance, exteriority) without the lyric formalism of mere viewpoint supervening as the guarantor of artificial intelligence?

To be clear, it is the *photographic* and not the painterly image which occasions this. The formulaic unoriginality of the photograph, which everywhere dramatises absence, exposes the inadequacy of the language it also solicits. To paraphrase Wittgenstein, *the photograph does not belong to the world; rather, it is a limit of the world.*[1] If, after a certain date, everything exists *in potentia* as a photograph, then even that writing which resolutely disclaims pictorial method, (the unidentified verbal object, the performative convulsion, Dada etc.) may also be in thrall to the regime of the lens. For when has any new form ever been heard without wanting to be seen?

Certainly in *Giacomo Joyce* the pathos of being visible and overlooked is rendered with an almost monochromatic intensity. The stark retinal display of every movement runs up against the dense aurality of each phrasal revision, and the feelings this closely patterned texture evokes stand out all the more

---

[1] Ludwig Wittgenstein, *Tractatus Logico-Philosophicus*, trans D.F. Pears and B.F McGuinness. (London: Oxford University Press, 1961, p.117):

> 5.632 The subject does not belong to the world: rather, it is a limit of the world.
> 5.633 Where *in* the world is a metaphysical subject to be found?
> You will say that this is exactly like the case of the eye and the visual field. But really you do *not* see the eye.
> And nothing *in the visual field* allows you to infer that it is seen by an eye.

powerfully for moving beyond the scenic and hypervisual towards what I believe to be the central issue of the text, the *pathos of apperception itself,* that is, a gradual recognition of the exile of meaning within forms of subjectivity knowingly exposed to the terms of their own self-estrangement. Such pathos hinges on the moment of withdrawal: for Stephen Dedalus this is the whole lyrical matter of life. For Hegel, it is the central pathology of all irony:

> nothing is treated in and for itself and as valuable in itself, but only as produced by the subjectivity of the ego. But in that case the ego can remain lord and master of everything, and in no sphere of morals, law, things human and divine, profane and sacred, is there anything that would first have to be laid down by the ego, and that therefore could not equally well be destroyed by it. Consequently everything genuinely and independently real becomes only a show, not true and genuine on its own account or through itself, but a mere appearance due to the ego in whose power and caprice and at whose free disposal it remains [...]. I live as an artist when all my actions and all my expressions in general [...] remain for me a mere show and assumes a shape which is wholly in my power. In that case I am not really in earnest with this content, or generally, with its expression and actualisation. For genuine earnestness enters only by means of a substantial interest, something of intrinsic worth like truth, ethical life etc.[2]

For Hegel, the artist-ironist commits the fundamental error of conflating his entire self with powers of creation or negation. In *Giacomo Joyce* a dawning awareness of this displays the limitations of irony as method, and suggests a closer relation, not of the visual and the linguistic, united by an ethics of visibility which transcends them, so much as an ethics of *recognition* which is the central matter of Joyce's later art.

---

[2] G.W.F. Hegel, *Aesthetics,* trans. T.M. Knox (Oxford: Oxford University Press, 1975) I.64-5. See also Hegel's later discussion on the character of Hamlet for an important reflection on the meaning of "show."

In the course of his scenic vignettes, Giacomo places himself in most of the familiar stations of the starcrossed lover, from abasement to euphoria. Yet throughout the travail of his infatuation we see changes of state but no change in *view*. To the ironical constancy of "his" desire, immune from alteration, everything exists so as to be perceived, even when veiled in deception, impercipience and counter-assertion. Giacomo is the primary perceiving condition; she on the other hand is the *contreblason* to the heraldic sequence of his passion: as snake, bird, fowl, oriental princess, she is all metaphor. He is not so much a narrative persona as a lyric subject, discontinuous and episodic, an ego abandoned to the mutations of "destiny" inside this veiled scenario of stolen sideways glances.

That he is a kind of affective instrument rather than agent, Giacomo himself seems to be aware. As orator he launches forth "on an easy wave of tepid speech." No uncreated conscience here to redeem, or nightmare to awake from in setting keel to breakers, these rehearsals of presence pass through all the main organs of rhetoric, from public oratory to half-remembered parentheticals, never ceding awareness of the total visibility and painful self-exposure of every thought and deed. If (as in the Linati schema) one textual aim was *visione animata fino alla scoppia* then here we begin to see really consistently how this limit might be reached, as well as how and why this particular framing method had, eventually, to be superseded:

> I expound Shakespeare to docile Trieste. Hamlet, quoth I, who is most courteous to gentle and simple is rude only to Polonius. Perhaps, an embittered idealist, he can see in the parents of his beloved only grotesque attempts on the part of nature to produce her image .... [*GJ* 10]

Does "I" forget Hamlet's rancour with Gertrude and obscenity to Ophelia because in the next frame he sees himself as gentle and simple too, or because he feels violently wronged and thereby ennobled in suffering? In the following scene he chances upon Amalia in the guise of Ophelia herself, "loosed" in the corridor where she walks before him, just as Ophelia appears before Hamlet in the lobby scene of Act II, Scene 2, the scene of Hamlet on which Joyce made the most extensive notes in the Shakespeare *Quaderno* of 1913. Already then, ideality is crumbling before irresolution. What should he do, must he do, *might* he do? Is Amalia an Ophelia to come? Or if she here is cast in the form of Beatrice, she is a "Beatrice" already tinted and overcast by ironies which no reversion to Dante may expunge. "She," in fact, is already shadowed by *La Béatrice* of Baudelaire:

> Contemplons à loisir cette caricature
> Et cette ombre d'Hamlet imitant sa posture
> Le regard indécis et les cheveux au vent
> N'est-ce pas grand pitié de voir ce bon vivant
> Ce gueux, cet histrion en vacances, ce drôle ......

From here the way is clear for the later Laforguean disfigurement of Hamlet as contemplative Pierrot, or his subsequent incarnation in Yeats and Eliot as the emblem of impotent alienation. To the lover, in his own eyes always "The Lover," the oscillations of spleen and ideal show all too clearly how the will to power works by transference of libidinal investment away from persons to a language patently theatrical, and back again :

> I rush out of the tobacco-shop and call her name. She turns and halts to hear my jumbled words of lessons, hours, lessons, hours: and slowly her pale cheeks are flushed with a kindling opal light. Nay, nay, be not afraid. [*GJ* 4]

How would this play to an observer? One not quite convinced by Giacomo's own declarations, a Proustian sceptic, say? The problem is that Giacomo is that sceptic, and his quizzical doubts swerve between the Scylla and Charybdis which Schulte-Sasse sees as the permanent option of literary romanticism, "between the ethical imperative to grasp one's identity and the equally ethical obligation to endorse alterity."[3] The question is pressing and not merely to Giacomo, for though this may indeed be a lyrical problem, it is framed even here on epic terms and entails Ulyssean perspectives.

That the encounters of *Giacomo Joyce* are often dramatised as acts of vision is part of this question. Each scene hovers between the lyric mode (conceived as an epiphanic, Keatsian solicitation of the ineluctable) and a more epic phenomenology, comically understood as the impossible mastery of circumstance. Once again, the risk is that of the ironist, of instrumentalising selfhood so that no particular action bears any specific meaning. Or, the self that sees and even foresuffers all is rendered powerless through "insight." Yet success would lie in a reconciling paradox: that the capacity to be a self and be moved as a self is also the capacity for loss of self, the overcoming of theatricality. To reach that point would mean exposing the nihilistic potential of any encounter, the reduction of all exchange to the egology of mastery. And this would imply something like a human comedy; the return to a community of ethical possibility or "agonistic respect," in which the literary itself figures merely as one moment among others. Was Joyce ready for this, by 1914?

I would argue that this movement is only imperfectly comprehended by the frame narrative of *Giacomo Joyce*. Reflexion multiplies self-reference, whose principal device is neither the "prose poem" or imagist narrative-sequence but the *secular confessional*. In the nineteenth century evolving of romantic autobiography it is possible to watch this form gradually unravel as the interior audits of conscience foreground a far stagier process of self-understanding, at which failure is guaranteed for many and the auditioner is never quite sure if he or she is *right for the part*. The travails of mortified obsession, anatomised in *Werther* and *La Nouvelle Héloise* are surely raised to the heights of

---

[3] Jochen Schulte-Sasse, "Romanticism's Paradoxical Articulation of Desire," *Theory as Practice: A Critical Anthology of Early German Romantic Writings*, ed. and trans., Haynes Horne, Andreas Michel, Elizabeth Mittman, et al. (Minneapolis: University of Minnesota Press, 1997) 36.

bathos in Hazlitt's *Liber Amoris, or The New Pygmalion* (1823), in nearly every scene of which the persecutory splitting of the lover is diffracted through a screen of grandiose diabolism.

> Demoniacal possessions. I see the young witch in another's lap, twining her serpent arms around him, her eye glancing and her cheeks on fire.

Almost a century before *Giacomo Joyce* we recognise the techniques of metamorphic pantomime, and see how powerless these are to alter the static nature of the desires they display. Mere change of form does not entail change of essence, and this impasse only intensifies the frenzied transformations the beloved is obliged to undergo.

> I saw her pale, cold form glide silent by me, dead to shame as to pity. Still I seem to clasp this piece of witchcraft to my bosom; this lifeless image, which was all that was left of my love, was the only thing to which my sad heart clung. Were she dead, should I not wish to gaze once more upon her pallid features.[4]

Already the frame of the *Künstlerroman* has begun to fracture under the counterpressure of ideality and abjection, now insupportable either by stoic self-mastery or the superinducements of exterior form. Flaubertian irony was of course the self-administered diagnostic of a modernist naturalism that wished to anatomise this phase of the male *education sentimentale*, although the lyric detours through gothic derangement in Hoffman or Poe suggest alternative routes of phantasmal allegory, a route which Baudelaire avowedly preserves and Eliot clung to as the form of anti-naturalism most suited to a redemptive transvaluation of the secular absolute.

But for Joyce the epiphanic credo had already rejected this second pathway. His true Penelope was Flaubert and thus the ironies implied by Hazlitt's *Pygmalion* figure in more harshly

---

[4] William Hazlitt, *Liber Amoris or The New Pygmalion*, ed. Jonathan Wordsworth (Oxford: Woodstock Books, 1993) 183.

structural terms. Given that the statue could not come alive, that mere will could not animate the indifference of matter and persons alike, what were the terms of any encounter in which the ironies of "personal desire" would not instantly degenerate into sheer farcicality? Psychological obsession may well be the *materia prima* of "personal tragedy" in the 1840s, but also conditions the melancholy of *film noir* a century later, in which the drama of appetite is reduced once more to the dialectic of nihilism. Since death is the price of absolute desire then each want is everything and nothing to its possessor, and thus the proximity of monomania and physical abasement always borders on the absurd.[5]

Stephen Dedalus plainly recognises this (from the perspective of 1921) back in 1904 when during his disquisition in the National Library on Kildare Street he alludes directly to the impasse:

> Read the skies. Autontimerumenos. Bous Stephanoumenos. Where's your configuration? [*U* 210]

Here the allusion is (via Menander) to Baudelaire's *L'Heautontimoroumenos*, also a touchstone for Eliot.

> Je suis la plaie et le couteau!
> Je suis la soufflet et la joue!
> Je suis les membres et la roue,
> Et la victime et le bourreau!

As hyperbole and metabole vie for mastery within the same hallucinatory frame, Baudelaire's self-tormentor is no longer able to contain the density of antithetical self-disgust. But if the *L'Heautontimoroumenos* supplies one important aspect of the psychomachia of Giacomo, Baudelaire himself is only framing in retrospect the Romantic transformation of irony from the *drama of*

---

5 This is perhaps why the greatest noir director is not Lang or Siodmak but Wilder.

conscience to the *secular confessional*, crucial to which, once again is the bivalent structure of ironical self consciousness, the separation of freedom and determination. The Kantian philosophy imposed a cardinal separation between a free, noumenal realm of things in themselves and a phenomenal world of causally determined human experience.[6] The self becomes polarised between its empirical and transcendental moments, making for the kind of persecutory division within the *self* which had formerly been an agonistic moment between *persons*. Human finitude becomes a dialectic of subjectivity and interpretation, and irony supplies the tension of normativity. But (as Hegel contested) irony is powerless before any specific object or person. The Dedalean reduction of the drama of otherness to the problem of self-alterity, a problem which by Stephen's own admission is *lyrical* rather than novelistic, needs to be overcome rather than merely admitted to. Otherwise irony merely eternalises the negative freedom of endless self interpretation, or reinstates the controlling perspective of narrative omniscience, however much this is disguised as a reflex of consciousness itself.

In which case, *Giacomo Joyce* may be seen as a kind of conversion-narrative, a movement away, as Valente argues, "from the aesthetic of transcendence announced by Stephen in *A Portrait*, a vision of the artist dwelling both within and beyond his work, to the aesthetics of finitude intimated by Stephen in *Ulysses*, a vision of the artist materially inscribed in his own work, unable to master fully 'the wisdom he has written or ... the laws he has revealed.'"[7]

---

[6] In his very compelling article, "*Epiphanoumenon*," *JJQ* 31.2 (Winter 1994): 55-64, David Weir proposes an equivalence between the Dedalean epiphany and the Kantian *noumenon*, arguing for a direct instrumentality of cognitive intuition over the restrictions of the phenomenal standpoint. The successive refinements of Joyce's view of Stephen over the years, suggests Weir, then show the naive limitations of Dedalus's intellectual self-confidence, transforming hubris into ironical self-torment on Baudelairean lines.

[7] Joseph Valente, *James Joyce and the Problem of Justice: Negotiating Sexual and Colonial Difference* (Cambridge, Cambridge University Press: 1995) 69.

What laws? How is this anti-mastery structured? What we see firstly is the *Liber Amorosus* turned to a kind of *progression d'effets*, en route from tragedy to antipathos. The *kammerspiel* of erotic alienation is projected beyond the 19th century bourgeois interior into new spaces of exile, panoramically avid for some restitutive antagonism yet frozen into repetition by embarrassment, the obstats of hilarious neurotic crisis. Is this predicament knowingly courted and controlled, or does it arise from an overdetermination of motive, the Aristotelian conflation of intention and action leading to self-blindness? The text, with its many ocular images, hints at both of these at once, yet since this is already the method of Flaubert then the forms of overstatement here, the text's "melodrama," might better be taken as stages in the passage through irony, entailing the production of newly absurd reflexes, "in excess," as Eliot averred of Hamlet "of the facts as they appear." *Giacomo Joyce* is, in great part, a melodrama of projective disappointments only because it is, first of all, a comedy of mistaken appearances:

> The housemaid tells me that they had to take her away at once to the hospital, *poveretta*, that she suffered so much, so much, *poveretta*, that it is very grave ...... I walk away from her empty house, I feel that I am about to cry. Ah no! It will not be like that, in a moment, without a word, without a look. No, no! Surely hell's luck will not fail me! [*GJ* 11]

In the new comic pathology of action and its chemistry of unintended consequences Joyce was searching for, dramatic irony is not enough. Ego and desire are remorselessly conflated in *Giacomo Joyce*, but the self is imaged in flagrant *contraposto* to the way it would be seen if only "it" were doing the framing. And so the *mise en abîme* of spectacle itself becomes internalised and then replayed through the figures of usurpation, exile, betrayal. We could call this situation "cinematic" but it is only later, in *Ulysses*, that the limited point of view is electrified by alternative perspectives into forms which are the equivalent of cinema's fluid displacements and reconnections of language and action. It is true that the monocularity of a text like *Eveline* already indicates one possible move in this direction, but the method of ironic distancing this entails leaves the diagnostic privileges of the bystander unexamined and therefore cannot fully project what I earlier referred to as the pathos of apperception, now seen to be the controlling force of irony. The *same self* is both in the world and also a limitation of it: irony thus implies a transcendental perspective, as the reifications of experience are "seen" from a superior vantage. That is the theatrical moment within Romantic irony: one is at the same time both agent and spectator, yet since the spectator cannot act on what he sees, the consequences of ironical limitation are merely formal. All are captive in the same spectacle.

This is the crisis of self-reference which for the male Modernist generation of the 1880s was incarnated by the "Hamlet question": not *esse or non esse* so much as *esse est percipi*, with Kenner's Denmark Street a labyrinth of auditors, spies and numberless usurpations (as Kenner rightly points out, Hamlet is the only myth in *Ulysses* which the characters themselves acknowledge). The familiarity of this situation indicates the pervasiveness of spectacle in modern life, and cannot be overcome by irony alone. Only the transvaluation of spectacle (theoria) itself might go beyond a generalised theatricality in which symptom and diagnosis are versions of the same thing. If hyper comedy or sadomasochistic degradation are simply understood as techniques for the demarcation of subjectivity, or, worse, the restoration of "perspective" they do nothing to upstage the voyeurism which gives rise to them.

What Joyce had begun to realise by this stage was that the comedy of manners furnished only an imperfect genealogy of self-irony. If it were to be understood, then its future trajectory lay through the gates of outright farce rather than mere parody, as "Circe" demonstrates, six years later, to an unrivalled degree. *Through*, and not within, though, for farce to Joyce is an instrument rather than a condition. Through it he was able to view the limitations of the Flaubertian method, and also see his own return to dramatic naturalism in 1915 as a too-literal demonstration of what the exile of meaning might mean if restricted to drama alone. From now on, it is an awareness of the use-value of farce that gives density to the later Joycean *œuvre*. Henceforward, the agent seeking to locate "his" desires as though these were original emblems of conduct, divorcing the vulgarity of their attainment from the heroism of their projection, is also the motive force that constantly miscasts their energies onto newly dissociated parts *not* of the self alone, but of the collective.

But if farce is the instrument, its prime matter is the emblematic structure of conduct, the social formalism of behaviour. How does the procedure of *Giacomo Joyce* differ technically from any more conventional textual narcissism of the Nabokovian kind, in which the via dolorosa of petty obsession is overdetermined by theoretical ironies of which its characters remain unaware? The narrative self is still a substantial form, but since self-activity is hardly exempt from irony and cannot be original, the drama is circular and unresolved, play within play within play. So much, so premodern; but Joyce suggests that it is already too late for ironical vertigo along these lines, and anything more corrosive, the "infinite unmastered negativity" which Hegel deplored, would simply inflate the theatricality of action without risking a true reversal of perspective, not from humour to tragedy (for in both, kings may be both subject and abject) but from comedy to farce, in which the hypertrophy of motive implicates the *bystander* too. This is its superior lucidity of farce, for there is found precisely that surplus of motive that polarises the question of spectacle and breaks down the bystander's disingenuous objectivity.

"Irony produces no effect in the farce" argued Søren Kierkegaard anticipating Brecht, in his *Gjentagelsen*. "The farce itself is all naïveté, and the spectator therefore must be self active as an individual. For the naïveté of the farce is so illusory that it is impossible for the cultured person to enjoy it naively."[8]

Structurally crucial to this movement away from the comedy of manners are the failure of forgiveness and reciprocity.

> My words in her mind: cold polished stones sinking through a quagmire. [*GJ* 13]

That the text is the rehearsal for a farce that never quite plays out is itself part of its serious rhetorical demonstration, already observed by Kierkegaard, that "the accidental comes right after the ideal." Spleen and adoration are no longer allegorical contraries but simple metonyms of force. The retarding of conciliation goes beyond a nineteenth century preoccupation with spectacle and even its twentieth century correlate, the formalism of the "gaze" (howsoever gendered), both of which merely postpone the ethical question the text everywhere implies: if not this person, then which? Or, as Giacomo frames the question more succinctly in its first moment: "Who?"

It seems appropriate that the scenes of the classic "fall" into adulterous liaison should take place in Paris, yet the encounter in the "Parisian room" displaces anagnorisis into open question forms and oblique hints at a future ethics:

> It is the other. She. Gogarty came yesterday to be introduced. *Ulysses* is the reason. Symbol of the intellectual conscience .... Ireland then? [*GJ* 15]

Vicki Mahaffey is right to claim that "Joyce's use of Paris as a background for particularly painful experiences has a special meaning,"[9] but we may also recall that the transformation of pain into reconciliation through comedy became Joyce's chief preoccupation after this time, and that this crucial moment of

---

[8] Søren Kierkegaard, *Gjentagelsen*, published in English as "Farce is Far More Serious," trans. Louis Mackey, *Yale French Studies* 14 (Winter 1954-55): 3-9.

[9] Vicki Mahaffey, "Giacomo Joyce," *A Companion to Joyce Studies*, ed. Zack Bowen and James F Carens (Westport, CT: Greenwood, 1984) 401.

Giacomo's dalliance with Amalia Popper, now cast as a spectral, punitive *cocotte*, takes place in the city which in 1908 saw the first appearance of Georges Feydeau's most celebrated avatar of the femme fatale, Amelie Poche (in *Occupe Toi d'Amelie*). There is more than local relevance here. I suggest that the farce exists as an internal critique of the bourgeois family romance: it is also a critique of spectacle insofar as it hypertrophies it. Qua farce, though, *Giacomo Joyce* is self stunting by deliberate calculation. Spectacle to an Aristotelian like Joyce is, after all, the least important moment of social theatre, but it was an important step away from psychologism. Even so, Joyce's solution is halfway. We cannot take the trials of Giacomo seriously because we are not, quite, meant to. Each blind encounter solicits a sympathetic involvement it knows it cannot requite, yet it will take more than a wry foreknowledge of the perils of spectatorship to eliminate the romantic psychology of dispossession and its allied pathos. Thus a self-stunting riot of counterappraisal floods the text with an excess of animus it cannot place, foregrounding the temptation towards an ethical formalism everywhere satirised in the *Wake*, and polarised (triestised?) by the question in the tale of Honuphrius (*FW* 573:32) : "Has he hegemony and shall she submit."

> This, lay readers and gentlemen, is perhaps the commonest of all cases arising out of umbrella history in connection with the wood industries in our courts of litigation.

Giacomo is not yet prepared for the steady irruption of estrangement that *Ulysses* and the *Wake* normalise. What a *nonhistorical* demonstration might have looked like in 1914, beginning with the noumenal object rather than the phenomenal self, is evident in another paranarrative concerning an umbrella and the powers of closure, transformed over the space of three pages from "A cause and no curve, a cause and loud enough, a cause and extra a loud" to "The lesson to learn is that it does show it, that it shows" to the restful punctum

AN UMBRELLA

> Coloring high means that the strange reason is in front not
> more in front behind. Not mere in front in peace of the dots.[10]

Tender Buttons is Gertrude Stein's reply to the philosopher's commonplace that intuitions without concepts are blind. Here reasons are not attendant on persons or things but appear to exist on the same plane of qualification, by no means more diminished ("mere") for taking place among readymade grammatical tokens. An umbrella is also a framework yet if, concerning the ambiguous relationships posited here, we ask again *"who has hegemony,"* then *Tender Buttons* will retort: "What is the use of a violent kind of delightfulness if there is no pleasure in not getting tired of it." In Joyce the vividness of the object world may well demonstrate the limitations of the personal standpoint, but this is merely one method among many, in the constant move to determine "the presence of the others" with all the ergative ironies attendant on that verb. Stein also incorporates the emblem form, though in the transfer of pathos from persons to *quidditas*, she too reaches a perspectival limit, not within the terms of the lyric or ironic selfhood, but in causality itself.

At the close of *Giacomo Joyce* we see the emblematic method once again at work in the field of the subjective. Since the subjective here is nothing more than a series of devices, tragic action and comic spectacle are stages in the same circular process. One example is the penultimate frame.

> Unreadiness. A bare apartment. Torbid. Daylight. A long black
> piano: coffin of music. Poised on its edge, a woman's hat, red-
> flowered and umbrella furled. Her arms: a casque, gules, and
> blunt spear on a field, sable. [*GJ* 16]

Mahaffey, proposing that "Joyce's pictorial epitaph for his 'dead' love serves as an image of her 'infidelity' as well as of her

---

[10] Gertrude Stein, *Tender Buttons, Gertrude Stein: Writings and Lectures, 1911-1945*, ed. Patricia Meyerowitz (London: Owen, 1967) 161-165.

demise," suggests that the allusion is to the close of Hawthorne's *The Scarlet Letter*[11] which on its own admission makes not quite good sense, since Amalia has not committed adultery, does not have a daughter and is not yet dead. A more plausible attribution is the concluding stanza of Andrew Marvell's poem *The Unfortunate Lover*.

> This is the only *Banneret*
> That ever Love created yet:
> Who though, by the Malignant Starrs,
> Forced to live in Storms and Warrs;
> Yet dying leaves a Perfume here,
> And Musick within every Ear:
> And he in Story only rules,
> In a Field *Sable* a Lover *Gules*.[12]

Here then we see a slender redistribution of justice; not Amalia is downcast by this symbolism, but Giacomo the unfortunate lover, who sees his fortunes cast within the frame not merely of some pregiven dramatic narrative, but a cold sequence of heraldic clichés that barely distinguish him from any other unlucky aspirant. Far from Prince Hamlet, he is the echo of a citation of an allusion.

Yet the mechanics of the *mise en abîme* are hardly a Joycean deformation but an allusive property of language itself (consciousness if you prefer). Beings and objects become mythic emblems not by writerly fiat but through overdeterminations they do not absolutely control, and history itself, with all its rumpled blazonry, is one of these. Joyce, knowing that he could not escape it, called this moment "politics" and saw it not as a

---

[11] Mahaffey, "Giacomo Joyce," 398.

[12] Stanza 8 of Andrew Marvell, "The Unfortunate Lover," *The Poems and Letters of Andrew Marvell*, ed. H M Margoliouth (Oxford: Oxford University Press, 1971) 29. Marvell's poem possibly recalls Hamlet II.ii, where the arms of the "rugged Pyrrhus," formerly sable, are also now "total gules." William Quillian's text of Joyce's Shakespeare notebook, in *Hamlet and the New Poetics; James Joyce* (Westport, CT: Greenwood, 1983) gives nine citations of reading allied to Act II sc. ii of Hamlet (134).

mode of seeing into history, but of evading it, even as he sought by contrary methodology some alternative exit from the ineluctable, as he put it in 1903, "A philosophy of reconcilement (possible)."

Envoy: Love me, love my umbrella. [*GJ* 16]

Does the hold of *Giacomo Joyce* depend on the circumstances of its relinquishment, or its figuring a knowable sequence between the worlds of Amalia Popper and Annalivia Plurabella? (*Love me*) What is ever abandoned in Joyce, what bridge is ever truly burned? I have claimed the allure to be elsewhere, in what it tells us of a crucial change in Joyce's *poetics of action*, a renewed understanding of the comedy of melancholy, played out through this micro-drama of emblematic part selves and half-understood rituals of misunderstanding and wanton self-regard. What is comical in *Giacomo Joyce* is precisely what its protagonist would see as tragical, "the passing of youth," since the comedy of history is a passing also, played through the constant undercutting of ironical perspectives that renew, then successively obscure, new fields of vision. In the fifty short heraldic stanzas of Giacomo's Republic, the instrumentality of farce exhausts itself through the reparative symbolism it now puts aside: any other justice would be merely lyrical.

Joseph Valente

(M)othering Himself: Abjection and Cross-Gender Identification in *Giacomo Joyce*

Unpublished in the author's lifetime, *Giacomo Joyce* was probably unintended for publication at any time, not only because it is so fragmentary, a mere sketchbook of the artist,[1] or because it is so intimate, a lover's diary wherein Joyce confesses in a less than foreign language, but because it is so ideologically uncensored, constituting, as Vicki Mahaffey has amply demonstrated, a gallery of invidious portraitures (of women, Jews, Near Eastern peoples, Italians, etc.) which Joyce would dramatically revise and rework in his later writing,[2] thanks in large part to the ethico-political understanding he achieved in living this interlude and composing this artefact. The one provision Joyce did make for the audience of history was to go back to this self-indulgent production and enclose, by way of the wry title and a single, profoundly leavening interpolation, the beginnings of a critical reassessment. The technical innovations that Joyce introduced as a function of this effort simultaneously define *Giacomo Joyce* as a transitional stage in his development as an artist and a somewhat tortured reaction to a

---

[1] Vicki Mahaffey, "Giacomo Joyce," *Companion to Joyce Studies*, eds. Zack Bowen and James F. Carens (Westport CT: Greenwood, 1984) 391.

[2] Vicki Mahaffey, "The Case against Art: Wunderlich on Joyce," *Critical Inquiry* 17 (1991): 672-4.

moment of political as well as emotional delirium, an attempt to expose and situate his dalliance with some of the deadliest impulses of modern European culture.

Appended at some indeterminable point, in an anonymous hand, the title *Giacomo Joyce* shifts the referential burden of the sketchbook from the model rendered, the unidentified Amalia Popper, to the rendering mind.[3] It asks the reader to consider the source, if you will, of these aesthetic images and ethico-political judgments—James Joyce, to be sure, with all of the literary weight that name carries, but James Joyce as an imaginary or would-be Casanova.[4] His early method of characterisation, fashioning fictive protagonists out of diminished and diluted versions of himself, is here recalled and reversed. Joyce casts a recognisably factual image of himself in a fictive or at least fantastical light as a way of ironising his own sentiments and perceptions without pretending to contemplate them altogether objectively and without renouncing his connection with or responsibility for them. With this title, Joyce situates himself, by way of the allusion to Casanova, in a tradition of securing a masculine identity and authority via the romantic mastery of women. By the Victorian period, that vision of masculinity had been supplemented by a corresponding norm of self-mastery, self-possession, and self-containment, according to which the male gender ideal, manhood or manliness, could serve as a virtual synonym for

[3] Peter Costello disputes the claim that Amalia Popper was the model for *Giacomo Joyce,* noting that "the dates" connecting the notebook to Joyce's familiarity with Amalia "don't fit." But no one has said that *Giacomo* constitutes a *simultaneous translation* of Joyce's experience, the only claim to which Costello's contention is relevant. Costello's other tack is to cite Helen Barolini as effectively confuting Ellmann's identification of Amalia as the *Giacomo* girl. But in "Fascism and Silence: the Coded History of Amalia Popper," *JJQ* 32.3-4 (1995): 501-22, Vicki Mahaffey effectively confutes Barolini on both factual and motivational grounds, restoring Amalia as the only viable candidate. Finally, Costello ignores the envoy to *Giacomo Joyce,* which clearly ascribes the initials, A.P., to his paramour. Peter Costello, *James Joyce: The Years of Growth* (New York: Pantheon, 1992) 308.

[4] Mahaffey, "The Case against Art," 672.

full and stable self-identity *as such*.[5] Joyce's notebook is concerned, on one level, with enacting both dimensions of triumphal masculinity to which his title lays claim. At the same time, however, as an allusion to someone other than the author, whom it nonetheless continues to name, the title stages the undoing of self-containment and self-consistency, both as it pertains to Joyce, whose primary mode of existence, so far as the title goes, is 'in translation,' and also as it pertains to normative masculinity, which the title reduces to a scripted persona or cultural mask.

No less significant, for our purposes, is Joyce's addition of the long scene in "the narrow Parisian room" (*GJ* 15) after the fair copy of the sketchbook was completed and probably over six years later.[6] The factual and phantasmatic material Joyce contrived to squeeze into the only available space in the manuscript reflects his subsequent change of attitude and is associated, as he explicitly notes, with his great anti-hierarchical epic, *Ulysses*. It would seem that Joyce retrospectively incorporates his distanced, ironical perspective on the experience *Giacomo* represents as a part of that experience, interrupting the chronological sequence of recorded impressions shortly before the resolution in order to disclose another, unsuspected teleology. In this move, we see foreshadowed the recursive narrative method of *Finnegans Wake*, in which the competing interpretations surrounding the dream letter (the *Wake* itself) recirculate as effects or variations of the letter itself and so disrupt that unitary progression of events upon which all authoritative world views finally rest.

More specifically, this belated and anachronistic interpolation links a reappraisal of Joyce's relationship with his

---

5 See Joseph Valente, "'Neither Fish nor Flesh'; or how 'Cyclops' Stages the Double-Bind of Irish Manhood," in *Semicolonial Joyce*, eds. Derek Attridge and Marjorie Howes (Cambridge: Cambridge University Press, 2000) 96-98.
6 Mahaffey, "Giacomo Joyce," 417. As evidence of this passage's belated inclusion, Mahaffey adduces not only the immediate historical reference to *Ulysses* but the character of the handwriting, cramped so as to be squeezed into the only available space in the notebook.

student to an analogous questioning of his relationship with Ireland, especially his quixotic role as the spiritual—intellectual saviour of his people:

> It is the other. She. Gogarty came yesterday to be introduced. *Ulysses* is the reason. Symbol of the intellectual conscience .... Ireland then? And the husband? [...] Why are we left here? .... Intellectual symbol of my race. Listen! [...] She speaks [...]. Voice of wisdom [...] voice I never heard. [*GJ* 15]

Furthermore, by staging these twinned reappraisals as an indirect response to the fanfare surrounding *Ulysses*, Joyce highlights and transvaluates the numerous sentiments expressed in *Giacomo Joyce* which are retailed, modified, decisively ironised, and even defeated in his later work. He sets up a metaleptic reversal of present and future contexts, the surrounding discourse of *Giacomo* being transformed into an allusive field by the name "*Ulysses*," which it everywhere anticipates. The overall impact of this prospective re-vision, this pre-post-erous gesture, is a sort of double textuality: the poisonous writing of Joyce's narcissistic desire for Amalia is supplemented by his antidotal re-reading, which takes some account of her positive otherness, acknowledges, however obscurely, her separate perspective, agency and value, and, in the process, alters the internal design of the work so as to bring out the systematic stifling and gradual emergence of her voice. The rhetorical violence of *Giacomo Joyce* is by no means effaced in this manner, but it is theatricalised by reference to a future in which Joyce wrote in deliberate opposition to this sort of sexual, racial, and cultural imperialism. The text thus settles down rather uncomfortably between the contradictory postures it adopts and the more complete political evolution it predicts.

The double valence of *Giacomo Joyce* bears the imprint of Joyce's borderline cultural status, his occupation of a no man's land between a majority, aggressively imperialistic culture, whose language he spoke, literature he read, and liberal individualistic ethos he affected, and a minority, aggressively irredentist culture he called his own, and also between positions of relative empowerment and disempowerment with regard to European culture in general, as defined by a complex of gender and class determinations. If, as Homi Bhabha has written, the enunciative position of the colonial estate is one of "hybridity,"[7] where the positions of authority are themselves part of a process of ambivalent identification, then the enunciative condition of a metropolitan colonialism such as Joyce's might be termed radically hybrid, i.e. neither marginal nor normative as ordinarily conceived, but on the margin between the margin and the mainstream. This *radically* marginal status animated Joyce with impulses and identifications associated with both an authorised, normative subjectivity and a subordinated, pathologised other, allowing the prejudicial attitudes cited above to act as an instrument for sorting out his warring identifications and clarifying his claims to social entitlement. But this dual experience also came to render those states of centrality and marginality peculiarly negotiable, permeable, and symbiotic for Joyce, conditioning his critical insight into the hierarchical and discriminatory arrangement of modern sociocultural practice. That is to say, paradoxically, that Joyce's initial susceptibility to the prevailing strains of modernist bigotry (sexism, racism, Orientalism, intellectual elitism, etc.) was part of a larger economy of experience that produced his eventual challenge to the underlying structures of such discourse.[8]

At perhaps no other point in his life, however, was Joyce so liable to lapse into the discourse of patriarchal imperialism as in his relationship with his Triestine student, Amalia Popper. The comparative social authority he enjoyed as a mature, Gentile, Western, pseudo-Aryan, northern European pedagogue

---

[7] Homi Bhabha, "Signs Taken for Wonders," *Critical Inquiry* 12 (1985): 153-4.

[8] Mahaffey, "The Case against Art," 671. Mahaffey argues that Joyce's understanding of sexism and racism grew out of his inadvertent complicity in both. I would say that Joyce's understanding of racism and sexism inadvertently grew out of his complicity in both.

confronting a young, Jewish, Orientalised, southern European female student was further reinforced by his role as a *de facto* agent of the strongest empire on earth, toward which he nonetheless remained, ethnically and confessionally, a subaltern. As a newly minted *"maestro inglese"* (*GJ* 5), subjective and objective genitive, Joyce found himself suddenly deputised to advance the sprawling hegemony of British culture to an already colonised people whom he characterises, without apparent irony, as "a multitude of prostrate bugs [that] await a national deliverance" (*GJ* 8). The latter phrase effects a double objectification that labours to render Joyce's own subdominant ethnicity less obviously relevant. Embracing both Italians and Jews in its implicit field of reference, the phrase takes the act of stereotyping, the elision or disregard of individual differences, to a supra-racial level, yielding a new and still more indiscriminate other. Inasmuch as discourse is no less performative than descriptive, the phrase simultaneously illustrates Joyce's double empowerment as an officially recognised "subject who knows." Deemed a *"maestro inglese"* by Amalia's father, in a classic patriarchal transfer of power, Joyce is in a position to define as well as instruct his charge, to define her in the course of his instruction and to instruct her on the basis of his definition. In this overdetermined political context, even Amalia's evident superiority in class or economic terms does not act as a simple counterforce in her relationship with Joyce, at least not directly, but combines with his own acute professional frustration at this point in time to challenge his rather ambiguously sanctioned *amour propre* and, in so doing, to intensify his will to possess her—intellectually, emotionally, aesthetically, and sexually.[9]

---

[9] Mahaffey, "The Case against Art," 673. Mahaffey makes a good case for the rather more direct effects of Joyce's economic weakness.

II

As Joyce's sketchbook graphically displays, the relatively empowered and therefore normative subject is susceptible of a truly violent ambivalence toward his culturally demarcated other.[10] Even while disdaining them, he desires attributes of the other for their socially charged difference, the appropriation of which by the subject, whether as knowledge, pleasure, or enrichment, consolidates his own privileged mode of self-identity and the assumed inferiority of his other. Owing to the reciprocal constitution of the respective positions, however, the subject fears, dreads, or shrinks from the contact with the other that such appropriation entails, finding in the significant difference to be possessed a source of potential contamination, inundation, castration. The subject's dread of contamination and castration feeds the desire to subsume the other outright, which desire works to contain the dread in a dream of absolute mental and physical possession, the self finally completed and reintegrated by the other. Conversely, the subject's desire to take hold of the other feeds the dread of being contaminated thereby, which acts in turn to check the desire by insisting on the alternative ideal of rational self-possession, the self finally completed *over against* the other. Each of these forms of sovereignty is purchased with some portion of the other that sustains it. The transcendence of self-possession entails a certain withdrawal of social power, a loss of reach; the enjoyment of other-appropriation entails a certain self-abandon, a loss of grip. What drives imperialist activity, in the broad sense of the term, is precisely its internally corrosive structure. The power of

---

[10] For a political theory of Kristevan abjection that analyses this dynamic, see Joseph Valente, *James Joyce and the Problem of Justice: Negotiating Sexual and Colonial Difference* (Cambridge: Cambridge University Press) 75-81. For the concept of the abject, see Julia Kristeva, *Powers of Horror* (New York: Columbia University Press, 1982) 1-18. I use the phrase "normative subject" to speak to the privilege certain subjects enjoy of seeing the social norms created more or less in their image, i.e. of participating directly or indirectly in the construction of norms which they themselves happen to embody.

the authorised subject is not only supported by but alienated in the powerlessness of the other, and it is owing to the paradoxical structure of this interchange that the former is so frequently cast in patriarchal/imperialist literature as a potentially tragic figure, weak in his very greatness, while the latter comes off as an enigma, dangerous in her vulnerability.[11]

The initial focus of Joyce's desire and dread of Amalia Popper is not her body as such but the gendered marks and attributes of her social station, which place her above and beneath him simultaneously.

> Who? A pale face surrounded by heavy odorous furs [...] she uses quizzing glasses. [*GJ* 1]

> Cobweb writing, traced long and fine with quiet disdain and resignation: a young person of quality. [*GJ* 1]

> High heels clack hollow on the resonant stone stairs. Wintry air in the castle [...]. Tapping, clacking heels, a high and hollow noise. [*GJ* 1]

These hollow or surface trappings of social prestige are contrasted with Joyce's display of intellectual substance; to the genteel materiality of her written signifiers, he opposes his spoken mastery of elite signifieds.

> I launch forth on an easy wave of tepid speech: Swedenborg, the pseudo-Areopagite, Miguel De Molinos, Joachim Abbas [...]. Her classmate, retwisting her twisted body, purrs in boneless Viennese Italian *Che coltura!* [*GJ* 1]

If there is what Abdul JanMohammad calls a "manichean allegory" taking shape here—i.e. "a field of diverse oppositions between [...] good and evil, superiority and inferiority,

---

[11] I have elected to map gender difference onto the elite-subaltern split in my pronominal usage in recognition of the gendering of colonial/racial hierarchies and owing to the immediate subjects of analysis, Joyce and Amalia Popper.

intelligence and emotion, rationality and sensuality, self and other, subject and object"[12]—then as yet its basic terms are *lirae* versus *logos*, class versus culture. That is to say, not only the classic masculinist antinomy of spirit/matter, but spiritualism/materialism, an opposition which, in addition to carrying more distinctly anti-Jewish overtones, moves to discount in advance Amalia's economic ascendancy. Later in the piece, Joyce not only extends this conventional anti-Semitic caricature to Amalia's family, but identifies their supposed venality with the practice of simony, in which just a hint of displaced sexuality can be detected—"The sellers offer on their altars the first fruits: green-fleck lemons, jewelled cherries, shameful peaches with torn leaves. The carriage passes through the lane of canvas stalls, its wheel spokes spinning in the glare. Make way! Her father and his son sit in the carriage. They have owls eyes and owls wisdom" (*GJ* 8). In keeping with this rhetorical tenor, the intonations of sexual desire remain sublimated early on, one gaze penetrating another: "The long eyelids beat and lift: a burning needle prick stings and quivers in the velvet iris" (*GJ* 1). But these intonations remain nonetheless profound. If, as Lacan has proposed, the exercise of the gaze can figure the possession of the phallus by returning the (male) spectator to a sense of imaginary, pre-Oedipal wholeness, the eye as I, then the answering gaze on the part of the feminine other, her resistance to being consigned to the role of appropriable artefact, can both figure and trigger the anxiety of castration, a state of affairs mythologised in the power of Medusa.[13] Instead of ignoring or eliding his student's scopic self-assertion, Joyce's representation here makes a great show of taking it into account and subduing it in an statement of phallic authority that is all the more confident and forcible for accommodating the illusion of a certain gendered reciprocity.

[12] Abdul R. JanMohamed, "The Economy of Manichean Allegory," *Critical Inquiry* 12 (1985): 62-5.

[13] For the significance of the Medusa myth, see Hélène Cixous, "The Laugh of the Medusa," *Signs* 1 (1976): 875-99.

The equation changes demonstrably once Joyce's erotic Oriental fantasy begins to surface with the first of several harem images, this one representing concubinage not as an institution of or within Amalia's racial sect, but as the very form of that sect's existence, a metaphor for the condition of the Jews in modern Europe: "Rounded and ripened: rounded by the lathe of intermarriage and ripened in the forcing-house of the seclusion of her race" (*GJ* 2). Relying on what were, or were becoming, fairly stereotypical associations of Jewishness—secretness, exclusiveness, dark sensuality, passivity, erotic mystery and danger—Joyce sets up an implicit ratio, that Jewish culture is to the larger European society as the harem culture is to the larger (Near) Eastern society whence the Jews themselves originally came. In one stroke the analogy sexualises and contextualises the group isolation of the Jews in terms of their genesis in and exile from an exotic "other" world. What is more, because the leading motifs of both male supremacism and Orientalism are distilled in the idea of the harem, Joyce's emblematic use of this motif here and throughout the sketchbook have the effect of situating the Jew along the common border of these discourses as their joint creation. Amalia Popper is not just a Jewish woman in *Giacomo Joyce*. Compact of the sexual mystique of racial sequestration, she represents the Jew as woman and the woman as Orientalised: i.e. as the tacit, supine element inviting Western/male incursion, as the mystery demanding Western/male solution, as the treasure tempting Western/male seizure, as the secret provoking Western/male curiosity, as the fertility tempting Western/male potency, as the instinctive other seducing Western/male consciousness. In so doing, Amalia no less importantly facilitates Joyce's disavowal of those feminine or feminised associations that attached to Irishness over the latter half of the nineteenth century.[14] On a racial as well as

---

14 For a discussion of Joyce and Irish feminisation, see Valente, *James Joyce and the Problem of Justice*, 38-48. Throughout this essay, without exception, I use the word "disavowal" in the Freudian sense, meaning to deny something with "one

sexual basis, Joyce fashions his student as a legitimating foil to his manhood. [15]

From precisely this juncture in the sketchbook through its pivotal event, Amalia's surgery and recovery, Giacomo personifies the life of the mind, percipient agency, and Amalia the fascination of the flesh, perceptual and aesthetic effect, the corpus. Even as his libidinal investments grow more insistent and perverse, they continue to emanate from a disembodied voice and gaze (a transcendent eye/I) located at some indeterminable aesthetic distance, which Joyce re-marks by the high cultural allusions in which he swaddles Amalia's image: Beatrice Cenci, Beatrice Portinari, Hester Prynne, Hedda Gabler, Ophelia, etc. Amalia, for her part, is reduced to a state of inarticulate animality. Her voice, like her gaze, is essentially pre-empted and she is represented as capable of little more than parroting other people's ideas or "sighing" and "twittering" like a bird. In fact she utters not a single coherent thought of her own until after the pivotal crisis of the narrative, her surgery. The initial contrast of feminised material signifiers with masculinised cultural signifieds is extended through the notebook as a contrast of material sound and spiritual sense. Thus, Joyce's spectatorship not only consolidates his self-concept by opposition to the feminine spectacle that it dominates, but works to privilege, even apotheosise, that self-concept as well.

current of the mental processes" while remaining "fully aware" of that reality with another current. Sigmund Freud, *Sexuality and the Psychology of Love* (New York: Macmillan, 1963) 208.

[15] Joyce was, of course, familiar with Otto Weininger's notorious racial-sexual taxonomy, *Sex and Character* (1906), identifying all Jews with women; and the frequent recourse he had to this schema in conversation, particularly the manner in which he rallied Ottocaro Weiss for his racially "feminine" characteristics, suggests that his interest in Weininger's model was in good part defensive, at least initially. For Joyce's conversance with Weininger's theories, see Richard Brown, *James Joyce and Sexuality* (Cambridge: Cambridge University Press, 1985) 101. For Joyce's teasing of Weiss, see Richard Ellmann, *James Joyce* (New York: Oxford University Press, 1982) 464.

Secured behind the veil of his fetishising viewpoint, disavowing the castration that Amalia is taken to display, Joyce is able, in this period of professional desperation, to affirm his aesthetic mastery as a displaced mode of sexual virility.[16] For that very reason, however, the sense of his erotic will to power cannot but pervade his representation of Amalia, and in its effects the aesthetic and the voyeuristic are confounded once more. *Giacomo Joyce* becomes the whirlpool in which commingle Joyce's fabled command of word and image commingles with his enthrallment to them, in which the very seal of his self-styled masculinity passes ironically into its own undoing.

Joyce's fantasy of preparing Amalia for an evening out not only instantiates, but can be seen to allegorise, this compromise formation:

> She *raises* her *arms* in an effort to *hook* at the nape of her neck a *gown* of *black veiling*. She cannot: no, she cannot. She *moves* backwards towards me mutely. I *raise* my *arms* to help her: her arms *fall*. I hold the websoft edges of her *gown* and drawing them out to *hook* them I see through the opening of the *black veil* her *lithe* body sheathed in an orange shift. It *slips* its ribbons of moorings at her shoulders and *falls slowly*: a *lithe* smooth naked body shimmering with silvery scales. It *slips slowly over* the slender buttocks of *smooth* polished silver and over their furrow, a tarnished *silver shadow* .... Fingers cold and calm and moving .... A touch, a touch. [*GJ* 7]

Inasmuch as evening dress, in particular, involves preparing a distanced, harmonised view of one's self and one's body for a projected audience or community, it makes for a compelling allegory of the aesthetics of sublimation that Joyce has been attaching to achieved masculinity. It is therefore significant that Joyce's fantasy of aiding Amalia in this endeavour should

---

[16] Joyce had been unable to get *Dubliners* published through nearly the entire period covered in *Giacomo Joyce*. In terms of public recognition, he was as yet more of a language teacher and amateur journalist than a literary artist.

occasion his single most thoroughgoing conflation of artistic and pornographic energies in the notebook.

The action traverses a set of binary oppositions whose symbolic charge or value is strictly pertinent to these respective forms of discourse: it progresses from the top to the bottom ("nape of neck" to "slender buttocks"), from covering to exposure, mediation to invasion (from attaching the black veiling to peering through the black veil), from visual to tactile impression ("a touch, a touch"), and from the cultural sublimation of the evening gown to the sexuality of her "smooth naked body" and the animality of its "shimmering [...] silvery scales." The verbal repetitions that punctuate the passage, however, serve to bind these polarities together *in both directions*, showing them to be but different spirals of the same winding thread. The first series of repetitions, comprising the terms "raise [...] arms," "hook," "gown," and "black veil," identify the movement to conceal and adorn the body with that which uncovers and in a sense violates it. Joyce's intent to secure the veil, to finish the creation, as they say in *haute couture*, dovetails with his willingness to exploit the "opening" in that veil, to unwrap his "soft merchandise," as they say in the *demimonde*. Conversely, the second series of repetitions, comprising the terms "lithe," "smooth," "slip," "slowly," and "silver," correlate the exposure and the reinvestiture of Amalia's bottom as mutually imperative moments in the voyeuristic experience.

This sort of compromise formation is typical of Orientalist and sexist discourse alike. But the ambivalence staged thereby must be transferred, within the representation itself, onto the figure of the other, as a part of her ontological make-up. For this reason, objectification is a crucially imprecise metaphor for the imperialist (racist/sexist) construction and treatment of the subaltern. Such textual forms, and *Giacomo Joyce* is no exception in this regard, frame the other as neither subject nor object, but as what Julia Kristeva calls the *abject*, i.e. as incompletely or insufficiently emergent from the material stratum of existence.

All of this is to say that imperialist rhetoric typically casts its other(s) as (a) virtual subjects, so that they seem to solicit supervision and control, if only for the purpose of realising their imputed potential, specifically the potential of the Other to be the Same, to be just like the colonising subject and so accountable to his rules of measure.[17] Here we can place the empire's self-appointed civilising mission in which Joyce undeniably implicated himself with the writing of *Giacomo*, his "sentimental education of a dark lady," to paraphrase Ellmann's unwittingly biting *précis* (*GJ* xi). Difference, the imperialist hope runs, can always be settled or annulled on terms dictated by the authorised subject in the name or interest of the ventriloquised other. Virtual objects, and so irreducibly inferior, unable to be the Same, yet responsible for this constitutional disposition owing to the ecstasy of self-abandon with which they are identified. Here we can place the stultifying fetishism of the other's distinctive attributes, i.e. the debasing projection upon those attributes of the wishes, anxieties, and distastes of the authorised observer. In Joyce's case, this symptom threatened his competence as a professional educator; and in certain colonial contexts, it regularly led to a more dramatic social and professional default popularly called "going native." Difference, the imperialist fear goes, might always be settled at the expense of the normative subject (his coherence, integrity, or self-awareness) on the other's terms or terms identified with the other. In the frame under discussion, Joyce finds himself prompted by Amalia's virtual reality qua subject to take control of her acculturation, asserting his superiority over her; while at the same time he finds himself drawn by her materiality qua object, her difference from the phallic and racial norm, to his own dissipation, an impulse that somehow redounds to her degradation rather than his.

The characteristics marking the supposed insufficient emergence of the other vary from one hierarchical situation to another, but the descriptive categories covering them obey a

---

[17] Homi Bhabha, "Of Mimicry and Man," *October* 28 (1984): 131.

certain regularity, in keeping with the Manichean allegory outlined above: sensuality, sentimentality, irrepressible sexuality, promiscuity, changeability, unpredictability, childishness, bestiality, herd mentality, an unreadiness for self-discipline or self-restraint, hence for personal or political freedom[18]—all framed as a lack or failure of cantered consistency and self-ownership. As noted above, over the course of the 19th century, thanks to the writings of Carlyle, Thomas Arnold, Kingsley, Hughes, etc. such self-containment increasingly came to be identified with the ideal of manhood, which Joyce here claims for himself by contrast with the equivocality and indeterminacy ascribed to his student.

Directly following the harem image that initiates Joyce's erotic fantasy comes the first verbal incarnation of his dream girl. There is a physical murkiness or mushiness about Amalia:

> A rice field near Vercelli under creamy summer haze. The wings of her drooping hat shadow her false smile. Shadows streak her falsely smiling face, smitten by the hot creamy light, grey wheyhued shadows under the jawbones, streaks of egg yolk yellow on the moistened brow, rancid yellow humour lurking within the softened pulp of the eyes. [GJ 2]

The frame offers a quite literal illustration of an incomplete emergence from the material stratum of existence, a state of *pre-composition*. Her facial features, traditionally the expressive signifier of psychospiritual interiority lack any coherence or definition; they appear ready at any moment to melt back into a primordial ooze. More subtly, by once again turning verbal repetition to rhetorical effect—creamy, false(ly), streak(s), shadow(s), yellow—Joyce moves the impressionistic catalogue seamlessly from elements of the external environment to facial features emblematic of Amalia's character. In this manner, he evokes a confusion of subjective and objective space, implying the lack, in her case, of any decidable hiatus between them and

---

[18] JanMohamed, "The Economy of Manichean Allegory," 65-8.

thus a failure of that rudimentary ownness or transcendence proper to a human mode of being.

By the end of *Giacomo*, Amalia's physical sedimentation is taken to be homologous with a viscous quality of mind that promises to benefit from and threatens to engulf the penetrating rigor of Joyce's own thought: "My words in her mind: cold polished stones sinking through a quagmire" (*GJ* 13). A few frames later, however, his fear of engulfment by Amalia is swallowed up by his dream of infiltrating and appropriating her outright, all under the banner of Oriental sensuality:

> She leans back against the pillowed wall: odalisque-featured in the luxurious obscurity. Her eyes have drunk my thoughts: and into the warm moist yielding welcoming darkness of her womanhood my soul, itself dissolving, has streamed and poured and flooded a liquid and abundant seed ......Take her now who will! .... [*GJ* 14]

If the psychospiritual stakes in this passage (my thoughts, my soul) disguise the phallic content of Joyce's desire, however flimsily, they positively expose the displacement of castration anxiety that the desire entails. The sexual relation imagined here guards against the very loss of (self) mastery that it figures. Even as Amalia receives his *logos*, she remains all vessel, all body, the symbolic equivalent of generative matter: humid, opaque, recumbent, inchoate. Even as Joyce releases his spirit into the morass of her being, he somehow regains his coign of transcendence, his purchase on the alterity in which he is engrossed. Indeed, the act itself purports to assure an eternalised proprietorship over her. His parting shot claims that now he has (or has "had") her no matter what, or who, the sequel. At the same time, by employing a psycho-spiritual vocabulary, Joyce continues to trope and so legitimate his claim to virile control as a civilising—edifying mission.

Drawing once again upon nineteenth-century Orientalist discourse, the harem motif here connects the stereotype of

Oriental sensuality with that of Oriental despotism. Giacomo's own sense of erotic enslavement, caught in the compulsive cycle of a racially tinctured attraction and repulsion, is transferred to Amalia as the legacy of that guilty racial condition. By casting her father as "the Grand Turk [of the] harem" (*GJ* 4), Joyce can portray himself as not only a free agent but a potential liberator, the master not only of himself and his student but of her racially feminised patriarch as well. He implicitly appeals to a classic topos of European imperialism, a defence of forays into non-Western communities on the grounds that they supplant archaic patriarchal regimes with more enlightened modes of governance. Gayatri Spivak's capsule summary of this justification, "white men are saving brown women from brown men," elegantly captures its fusion of racial and sexual energies.[19] (Joyce's invocation, after meeting Mr. Popper, of Loyola, the founder of an aggressive missionary order, seems ironically apposite in this regard, especially since it aligns Joyce's own countrymen, by way of their famously devout Catholicism and missionary zeal, with expansionist Europe, thereby disavowing their colonial subdominance.)

Joyce takes his affective ambivalence toward his student, an effect of the orientalist/patriarchal Imaginary, and naturalises it as a racial and gendered property of his model, a function of her incomplete transcendence of the material realm. Take the voyeuristic encounter anatomised earlier. By picturing Amalia's body as "shimmering with silvery scales," Joyce lends her the appearance, or at least the metonymic value, of a mermaid, a mythic archetype of precisely this halfway estate, split between the human and the animal, air and water, the surface and the depths, and so, symbolically, between subject and object worlds—reason and instinct, mind and body, consciousness and unconsciousness. This incident is exemplary in that Joyce's erotic meditations upon Amalia's manipulated image

---

[19] Gayatri Spivak, "Can the Subaltern Speak?" *Marxism and the Interpretation of Culture*, eds. Cary Nelson Lawrence Grossberg (Urbana: University of Illinois Press, 1988) 297.

repeatedly give way to similitudes of her to various forms of animal life. In a single move, each such delineation of Amalia not only asserts her racial inferiority, the nature of that inferiority, and the menace it accordingly poses to his dignity, but expresses the dread that prospect arouses as distaste or even revulsion. One more frame in particular underlines this point, linking Amalia's imperfect purchase on her own bodily reality to both Joyce's voyeuristic indulgence and her own bestial status—"A skirt caught back by her sudden moving knee; a white lace edging of an underskirt lifted unduly; a leg-stretched web of stocking. *Si pol?*" (*GJ* 9)

Taken *en masse*, these representations tend to consolidate Joyce's self-image by opposition to the mercurial Amalia, who traverses a veritable bestiary in just sixteen pages. She is likened, in whole or in part, to a filly foal, molluscs, a mermaid, a sparrow, a pampered fowl, an antelope, a bird, a poet, a basilisk, and a night snake. Meanwhile, Joyce identifies himself as the "subject who knows," a stable independent mentality holding to the underlying secret of material flux epitomised in the slippery figure of Amalia, and this self-representation accords a certain masculinised consistency to the different roles that he himself traverses—poet, teacher, master, lover, observer, conqueror, liberator, seducer etc.[20] Her physical changeability is transcribed in the moral register as feminine faithlessness and Jewish treachery, much as the murkiness of her physiognomy (anchored, incidentally, by a "false smile") is later troped as a murkiness of thought, and by comparison Joyce's rigorous intellectual stability lays claim to something like moral integrity

[20] A Lacanian coinage that has passed into wider circulation, the "subject who knows" is a fantasy-subject held to be in full control of the Symbolic field: e.g. God, the master, the psychoanalyst, etc. The ordinary subject erects the "subject who knows" as a point of transference or even identification, so that some sense of stable meaning can be assured. It would seem that the figure of the artist performed this function for Joyce in *Giacomo* and elsewhere. Certainly, Stephen's assertion—"A man of genius makes no mistakes. His errors are volitional and are the portals of discovery" (*U* 9.228-9)—is a classic elaboration of the "subject who knows."

Through this analogical structure, Joyce enlists his cherished motif of betrayal in the labour of a Freudian projection: he translates a crisis of self-division born of his own sexual and racial attitudes into a wrong inflicted upon him by Amalia in keeping with her gendered and racially marked failings. In response to this wrong, he takes up yet another, especially significant role, Christ figure.

III

Joyce's assumption of the role of the Crucified represents a *parade virile* that would have been quite recognisable following the decisive shift in the pre-eminent late-Victorian discourse of manhood, 'muscular Christianity,' from a 'muscular' ideal comprising strength, courage and mastery, including self-mastery, to a more 'Christian' model comprising gentleness, generosity, and sacrifice, including self-sacrifice. Thomas Hughes followed his smash novel *Tom Brown's Schooldays*, the defining work of the earlier, rough and tumble phase, with *The Manliness of Christ*, which dramatically qualified his previous position by promoting the Passion as the exemplary performance of manhood.[21] The significance of the shift in Joyce's own self-presentation can be gauged from the fact that it marks the onset of a crucial bifurcation in his assessment of Amalia and in the ideological valence of the notebook as a whole. On one layer, everything proceeds pretty much as it has. The presumptively untrue lover answers Joyce's suffering by indulging her stereotyped proclivity for the sentimental.

> In the raw veiled spring morning [mourning] Paris...as I cross the Pont Saint Michel the steel-blue waking waters chill my heart ..... Tawny gloom in the vast gargoyled church. It is cold

---

21 For the late Victorian ideal of manhood and Joyce's engagement with it, see Valente, "'Neither Fish nor Flesh'; or how 'Cyclops' Stages the Double-Bind of Irish Manhood," 96-127.

> as on that morning: *quia frigus erat*. Upon the steps of the far
> high altar, naked as the body of the Lord, the ministers lie
> prostrate in weak prayer .... She stands beside me, pale and
> chill, clothed with the shadows of the sin-dark nave, her thin
> elbow at my arm. Her flesh recalls the thrill of that raw mist-
> veil morning, hurrying torches, cruel eyes. Her soul is
> sorrowful, trembles and would weep. Weep not for me, O
> daughter of Jerusalem! [*GJ* 10]

And like the sentimentalist of George Meredith and Stephen
Dedalus, she proves unwilling, in Joyce's eyes, to take
responsibility for the thing done or felt. Her sympathy is
withdrawn in deference to the Jewish mob, the weakness of
sentimentality passing easily into the weakness of social
conformity:

> They spread under my feet carpets for the Son of Man. They
> await my passing. She stands in the yellow shadow of the hall
> [...] and as I halt and wonder and look about me she greets me
> wintrily and passes up the staircase darting at me for an instant
> out of her sluggish sidelong eyes a jet of liquorish venom.
> [*GJ* 15]

The weeping "daughter of Jerusalem" plays once more the
"virgin most prudent," at least that is the way Joyce chooses to
interpret his student's decision to part. In the last instalment of
this mytheme, not just Amalia's opinion but her point of view,
indeed her very presence, have been absorbed into a mass
decree: "*Non hunc sed Barabbam!*" (*GJ* 16). At this moment, racial
and sexual markers, which have cooperated throughout
Giacomo Joyce in the construction of Amalia as the abject, simply
collapse together, effacing all sense of a separate identity.
Abjection approaches annihilation, and it is worth noting that
in the two remaining frames of the notebook Amalia appears
strictly as a reified absence.

There is a lot more going on here than meets the eye,
however. Amalia's image is consigned to the nether reaches of
abjection in this particular narrative sequence because this is the

symbolic juncture at which Joyce encountered his own powerful sense of abjection. The first instalment, frame 28 (*GJ* 10), refers not only to the day of Christ's death but to the Good Friday service which Joyce attended the day he was notified of his mother's impending demise.[22] Taken in this light, the messianic Joyce can be seen as doubly crucified by an imperfectly resolved grief for his mother, herself a Christ figure, and by his imperfectly requited desire for his student; and we can see Amalia as being fixed in a correspondingly double posture of consolation: a Madonna grieving for her son's affliction and a daughter lamenting the plight of her champion. This profound imbrication of the remembered and the imagined event, of past bereavement and present lack, mother love and other longing, uncovers a subterranean layer, a more intimate set of stakes, to Joyce's psychic investment in Amalia. It has its unconscious roots and derives its obsessive vitality from the finally irreconcilable break between Joyce and his mother over his spiritual direction during the period of her fatal illness.[23]

The crucifixion fantasy is central in this respect. "Pale and chill," "clothed in shadows," her elbow "thin," "at his arm," Amalia's body plainly calls to Joyce's mind the wasting flesh of his mother, even as her touch communicates the jagged "thrill" associated with the day Joyce learned of his mother's doom. But Amalia's sorrowful soul suggests that matters are being put to rights, that the emotional alignment binding Joyce to his mother in guilt and regret is or seems to be undergoing something of a reversal. Amalia stands in for the mother not as immolated female victim, her dominant image in Joyce's recollection, but

---

[22] Mahaffey, "Giacomo Joyce," 398-9. Mahaffey explains that the news of Joyce's mother's illness, "coming as it did on Good Friday [1903] seems to have prompted Joyce to identify his own suffering [...] with Christ's crucifixion [...] In 1914, Good Friday again fell on April 10th, as it had eleven years earlier, and Joyce seems to be glossing the memory of that excruciating Good Friday with the pain that his lovely student was currently causing him."

[23] For a psychoanalytic reading if Joyce's maternal abjection in relation to *Giacomo Joyce*, see Valente, *James Joyce and the Problem of Justice*, 81-97.

as specifically unburdened of those sacrificial afflictions, nurturing a son whose own suffering can appear, for that very reason, manly in its redemptiveness. The editorial principle determining the pattern of Joyce's allusion to the Biblical *figura* is designed in large part to underscore its empowering potential. First, the frame dwells upon the "chill" of each relevant Good Friday morning, suggesting a like atmosphere of rigor for the naked Christ and his ministers and the emotionally naked Joyce, whose heart is chilled in reaction. Second, the frame downplays the new messiah's tribulation in favour of the grief he elicits from his "maternal" student. Third, the frame closes with Joyce's grand gesture toward alleviating that sorrow: his manly admonition "weep not for me" is his only citation of Christ's actual speech, a telling choice in contrast with say, "why hast thou forsaken me?" With each of these decisions, Joyce declines the pathos of the abnegatory gesture he has made, opting instead for a more heroic, self-actuating gloss on his ordeal. Concordantly, Amalia is represented as expressing not only pity and solace for Joyce's suffering but also an appreciation of his sublimity, a sorrow for her loss as well as his pain. In this fashion, her spectatorial part in the Golgotha scenario contributes to its function as a vehicle of Joyce's continuing struggle to firm and defend the shifting borders of manhood, even as the maternal complexion of her role facilitates his more regressive fantasies of death as a return to the charmed pre-Oedipal dyad, a dying into the womb.[24]

By adopting the position of the sacrificial parent figure and externalising that of the bereaved child, Joyce evinces his strong continued identification with his mother while casting Amalia

---

[24] Joyce's fantasies of being the literary messiah of the Irish people were likewise tied up with the fantasy of burial in the womb, confirming the connection in Joyce's own subconscious between crucifixion and abjection. In 1909, he had written to Nora: "O take me into your soul of souls and then I will become indeed the poet of my race. I feel this, Nora, as I write it. My body soon will penetrate yours, o that my soul could too! O that I could nestle in your womb like a child born of your flesh and blood, be fed by your blood, sleep in the warm secret gloom of your body" (*L* II.248).

as his own surrogate or stand-in. Notice how the previously cited crucifixion passage pivots upon the double syntax of Amalia's corporeal memory: "She stands beside me, pale and chill, clothed with the shadows of the sin-dark nave, her thin elbow at my arm. Her flesh recalls the thrill of that raw mist-veiled morning, hurrying torches, cruel eyes. Her soul is sorrowful, trembles and would weep" (*GJ* 10). If Amalia's flesh "recalls" that fateful day to Joyce's mind, simulating in its chill pallor the wasting body of his mother, Amalia's flesh also "recalls" that day itself, harbouring the memory as Joyce's experiential double. That is to say, the complex gender and generational valences infusing this episode converge upon the verb "recalls," so that girl's Madonna-like bereavement doubles as filial commiseration, indicated by the phrase 'daughter of Jerusalem,' and her position in Joyce's family romance becomes to that extent reversible with Joyce's own. Now, there is clearly an element of wish fulfilment in this aspect of the fantasy as well. Amalia does not just relive, in her mourning of Joyce—Christ, Joyce's mourning of his mother. Rather, in a division of symbolic labour that is but the flip side of Joyce's abjection of her, she registers as his proxy a depth of sentiment that he felt and yet found inhibiting.[25] She thus gives an idealised rendition of Joyce in mourning. Just as Amalia figures Joyce's mother relieved of her pain in his imaginary sacrifice, so she symbolically "channels" his statement of the grief, affection and regret motivating that sacrifice. Joyce's fractured reconciliation with his deceased mother is thereby completed, as it were, from the other side.

---

[25] Different acquaintances of Joyce on the continent found him inhibited in the statement of emotion. August Suter wrote that "Joyce was ashamed of showing that he was capable of love; he hid his feelings." Nino Frank commented on "his coolness, his reserve." August Suter, "Some Reminiscences of James Joyce," Nino Frank, "The Shadow that had Lost its Man," in *Portraits of the Artist in Exile*, ed. Willard Potts (Seattle: University of Washington Press, 1979) 63, 86.

IV

In Joyce's crucifixion fantasy, he effects a reconciliation with his mother via a conspicuous display of manhood, thereby establishing psychic remove from and proximity to the feminine in a single gesture. In supplying the emotional component of the reconciliation in Joyce's place, Amalia plays an indispensable part in this symbolic manoeuvre. Her trembling, her weeping enable Joyce's approach to this primordial affective condition precisely by preserving him at a certain distance from it, a distance troped as gender *difference*. That is to say, in this crucifixion fantasy, Joyce not only externalises the role of the bereaved, he converts the role into something of a *parade feminine* or womanly display, substituting for the defensive reticence of his own regret a daughter's more demonstrative grief.

Stephen's Shakespeare theory, which Joyce actually espoused, testifies to just this psychodynamic, establishing the girl child ("Marina [...] Miranda [...] Perdita" [*U* 9.421]) as the consummate agency of reconciliation for the exiled or alienated hero:

> What softens the heart of a man, shipwrecked in storms dire,
> Tried, like another Ulysses, Pericles, prince of Tyre?
> [...]
> —A child, a girl placed in his arms, Marina. [*U* 9.402-6]

> What is lost was given back to him: his daughter's child. *My dearest wife*, Pericles says, *was like this maid*. Will any man love the daughter if he has not loved the mother? [*U* 9.422-4]

Stephen, of course, postulates a creative analogy between Shakespeare's drama and the drama of Shakespeare's life. Here, Pericles' response to the discovery of his daughter, his sense of renewal after the "loss" of his wife, supposedly bodies forth in displaced form Shakespeare's own experience upon the birth of his granddaughter, his sense of reconciliation both to Anne's supposed infidelity and to his youthful "undoing" at her hands. But a like analogy can be drawn between Stephen's biographical theory and his own turbulent biography.[26] The sexual trauma and betrayal dividing Shakespeare's husbands and wives, the sense of reconciliation binding his fathers and daughters, these are legible displacements of Stephen's powerful obsession with sexual trauma, betrayal, and reconciliation cantering upon his mother. (More subtle is the proleptic intimation of this displacement: Stephen's substitution of the fox's buried grandmother for his mother in the "Nestor" riddle anticipates Shakespeare's supposed substitution of Pericles' daughter for his own granddaughter.) Behind both the Shakespeare theory and its role in the narrative of Stephen's desire stands James Joyce himself, in whom the displaced and the displacement coincide. The tertiary analogy of both the theory and the narrative to Joyce's life experience emerges quietly in the ambiguity surrounding the use of the terms "daughter" and "mother" in the last cited passage. Stephen's use of the non-possessive article "the" allows the sentence to be read, "Will any man love the [his] daughter if he has not loved the [his] mother?" so that the father—daughter tie can be seen as redressing in some way the mother—son schism, a possibility which, in this biographically saturated context, must be referred to the psychic topology of the author. The "spirit of reconciliation" that Stephen uncovers in Shakespeare's later works indirectly expresses the sense of reconciliation Joyce himself achieved by way of a partial identification with daughter figures like Amalia, or the subjective position of daughterhood itself, where the indulgence in grief or the longing for mother love need not signal emasculation.

It is in these terms perhaps, that we can understand why Joyce identified so much more closely with his daughter, Lucia, than with his son and first-born, Giorgio, and from there assess

---

[26] Stephen himself makes this connection in a number of ways. For example, he outfits Shakespeare "in the cast-off mail of a court buck" (*U* 9.164-5) even as he himself wears the cast-off boots of stately Buck Mulligan.

the impact Lucia had upon his textual construction of Amalia. Prevailing opinion has pegged Joyce's identification with Lucia as an empathetic response to her worsening derangement, and there is no doubt that Joyce came to regard her mental condition as a skewed correlative of his own.[27] So powerfully did Joyce come to identify with Lucia that his friend Paul Léon determined, "Mr. Joyce trusts one person alone, and that person is Lucia. Anything she says or writes is the thing by which he is guided" (*JJII* 682). For his part, Carl Jung thought Joyce's "own Anima, i.e. his unconscious psyche, was so solidly identified with her, that to have her certified would have been as much as an admission that he himself had a latent psychosis" (*JJII* 679). Joyce's wavering opinions tended to corroborate Jung's diagnosis. When Joyce could bring himself to acknowledge the severity of Lucia's disturbance, he would see it as a metonymic effect of his genius: "Whatever spark of gift I possess has been translated to Lucia and has kindled a fire in her brain" (*JJII* 650). When he could not bear to acknowledge its severity, he would see her mental being in metaphorical likeness to his own. He insisted, "she is no madder than her father," and ascribed her breakdown to factors more properly associated with his brand of creative endeavour: "The poor child is not a raving lunatic, just a poor child who tried to do too much, to understand too much. Her dependence on me is now absolute" (*JJII* 676). But in the chiasmic interplay of his absolute dependence on her ("trusts one person alone") and her "dependence…absolute on [him]," we can discern a restoration of the dynamics of the maternal dyad, a pattern fundamental indeed to Joyce's "Anima [or] unconscious psyche" and clearly anterior to the onset of Lucia's symptoms. *Joyce did not identify with Lucia on account of her illness; rather he could identify so readily with her illness partly on account of his long-standing sense of mystic participation with her.* I want to suggest that Joyce's identification with Lucia originally attached to the *structure* of the father-

---

[27] See in particular Ellmann's account of their relationship in *JJII* 645-739.

daughter relationship insofar as it transposes the gender and generational terms of the mother-son relationship.

Of primary significance in this regard, as in most things with Joyce, is the question of the name. Having had the name Lucia in mind during Nora's first pregnancy, Joyce decided to name his one daughter after the patron saint of vision, after light itself in effect, properties which Joyce had been surrendering progressively from early childhood and stood in danger of losing permanently.[28] His naming of Lucia, accordingly, was an attempt to restore or secure by way of the signifier a lost attribute of the self. As such, the naming can be seen to replicate, metaphorically speaking, the constitutive gesture of subjectivity, the attempt to re-place or re-present in the symbolic chain the imaginary plenitude of *amor matris*, what comes to be figured retrospectively as the lost (m)other portion of the self. The overriding importance of Lucia's gender status to this particular psychodynamic cannot be overstated. It helps to explain why Joyce put not only the name Lucia but the traditional prerogative of patronymic identification on hold for two years,[29] and why he invested his daughter, rather than his son, with the name of the father in its more complete form. For Joyce—and here we may be close to the psychoanalytic key of his entire career—the Name of the Father, the fundamental law of language and desire, functions primarily as a vehicle for reopening negotiations with the trace of the Mother, the interfold of personal identity and difference.[30] In aesthetico-

---

28 See Ellmann, *JJII* 262. Brenda Maddox, *Nora* (Boston: Houghton Mifflin, 1988) 82.

29 Maddox, *Nora*, 82.

30 The mother in Joyce has often been conceived along the lines of the Real in Lacan's early writings, the irrepressible, unrepresentable origin/exterior of the Symbolic. Karen Lawrence calls the maternal a "fiction before identity or law"; Maud Ellmann declares "[her] namelessness engraves itself upon the flesh before the father ever carved his signature." But the presence of the mother in *Giacomo Joyce* helps us to see that she more like the Real in Lacan's later writings, the impossible co-implication of interior and exterior, before and after, self and other, at once posed and denied in the Symbolic, "inscribing," in Shari Benstock's words, "an undecidable limit of textuality." See Karen Lawrence,

political terms, this negotiation then passes into the possibility of conceiving an 'envoy of otherness,' an epiphany that otherness forms a constitutive ingredient of the authorial self who would nonetheless seek to keep it at bay through a symptomatic act of imaginative projection.

This cross-gender imperative takes a still more developed form with respect to Joyce's fictive elaboration of his self-identity. By Ellmann's account, Joyce's decision to rewrite his autobiographical novel, *Stephen Hero*, as a "gestation of the soul" in *A Portrait* occurred *only* and *immediately* after Lucia's birth (*JJII* 296-7), even though the earlier version was well underway and clearly in need of formal correction by the time Giorgio was conceived. Now, for Joyce to pattern the development of his alter ego after the embryonic growth of his newborn daughter represents an extraordinary act of identification, not with a person or even an image, but with a certain locus in the intersubjective network of the family, a "feminine" signifier or shadow-term under whose aegis the narrative confrontations with the maternal-filial nexus could unfold. For Joyce to author himself in accordance with the metaphor of gestation, to mother himself, so to speak, it was necessary for him to project himself into the subject position of a girl child, to daughter himself. It is the purely structural nature of Joyce's identification with Lucia, his identification with the daughter position *as such* that allowed Amalia Popper to fit so easily into the role of surrogate child *as* surrogate for Joyce himself.

Joyce earmarks Amalia as a daughter figure early on in *Giacomo* by transforming her seemingly chance encounter with Lucia (in her *only* appearance) into a moment of symbolic communion, a ritual interchange of identity: "A flower given by

"Joyce and Feminism," *The Cambridge Companion to James Joyce,* 248; Maud Ellmann, "Polytropic Man," in *James Joyce: New Perspectives*, ed. Colin McCabe (Brighton: Harvester, 1987) 96; Shari Benstock, *Textualizing the Feminine* (Norman: University of Oklahoma Press, 1992) 186. For modernity's tendency to equate the feminine with unrepresentability, see Alice Jardine, *Gynesis* (Ithaca: Cornell University Press, 1985) 31-49.

her to my daughter. Frail gift, frail giver, frail blue-veined child" (*GJ* 3). What is most striking about this transaction, however, is that Joyce does not pose a performative, functional, or imagistic equivalence between Amalia and Lucia so much as he aligns them in a structural analogy mediated by "a flower," the emphatic alliterative and syntactic priority of which makes it the defining rhetorical figure (or "flower") of their interrelation: "flower given...Frail gift, frail giver, frail...child." The flower, of course, is the ancient emblem of femininity and, more specifically, of the female genitalia. Accordingly, the "frail" quality of the flower, of Lucia, and of Amalia cannot but recall Hamlet's famous declaration, "Frailty, thy name is woman." Congruent with this sense of irresistible change, the flower itself marks an imminent stage of fecundity (the falling of the bloom heralding the appearance of the fruit) and so serves to symbolise a nearly mature or incompletely ripe stage of female sexuality. In both of its dominant significations, then, the flower token conjoins Amalia and Lucia as incestuously regarded daughters. As the officially designated "giver" of the token, however, Amalia simultaneously performs the maternal function of symbolically bequeathing her femininity and her incipient sexuality to Lucia, passing them on, as it were, through the act of being *literally* de-flowered. That is to say, a scene evidently designed to amalgamate Amalia with Joyce's child finds her slipping back into the maternal position, or rather shimmering back and forth between the two. From this, a couple of crucial inferences may be drawn: 1) The underlying stakes of Joyce's identification with Lucia do in fact lie in its reconfiguration of the mother-son tie. 2) Amalia was capable of halving the generational distance between mother and child in Joyce's imagination—unlike Lucia, still strictly a child, or Nora, who, having graduated to the place of mother, seems to have forfeited her childlike aura in Joyce's eyes.

Thus situated to afford a combined site of identification and abjection, Amalia is constructed as the displaced figure of Joyce's own liminal femininity and feminised liminality.

Whereas Stephen Dedalus represents Joyce's alter ego, a fictionalised version of authorial consciousness, another self, Amalia proves to be Joyce's sub-alter(n) ego, a fictionalised variant of authorial unconsciousness, an other-self.

The sub-alter(n) ego represents a fictive externalisation of what Jane Gallop has called "the other within,"[31] a point of rhetorical access to the differential constitution of the subject in its innermost properties. As such, the sub-alter(n) ego does not consist in a simple projection outward of some censored affect or aspect of the self upon some more or less fictionalised other. This rhetorical move tends to moralise the socially coded differences between the dominant (masculine) subject and its designated (feminine) other as a means of fetishising or vilifying that other and thus ensuring the normativity of the dominant subject, i.e. his capacity both to dictate and to embody the cultural norm. The designated other comes to define the upper and nether limits of the human condition which the dominant subject alone exemplifies. Nor does the sub-alter(n) ego consist in a simple appropriation of the other to the self or the secularisation of the self in the other. This rhetorical move assumes the ideal homogeneity of self and other as a means of pre-empting the other outright and thus extending the dominance of the normative subject across the entire social field. The other comes to be defined entirely by the lights of the normative subject, as his double or extension. Instead, the sub-alter(n) ego combines these colonising tendencies in such a way as to expose their underlying interdependence, thereby allowing each to counteract and transvalue the other.

In a context governed by the normative subject's projection of censored material upon the subaltern, a countervailing movement in which the subject regards the subaltern as his double or extension has the virtue of safeguarding the formal possibility of a certain psychic identification with her, however

---

[31] Jane Gallop, "Reading the Mother Tongue: Psychoanalytic Feminist Criticism," *Critical Inquiry* 13.2 (1987): 320.

reflexive it might be, and so of a certain limited will to reciprocity as well. On the other side, in a context governed by the subject's appropriation of the other as his enlarging mirror, the projection of censored material upon her serves to mark, however fetishistically, her difference from the self, and thus has the virtue of safeguarding an otherwise imperilled awareness of the independence of her perspective, the heterogeneity of her world. By bodying forth the profound entanglement of these colonising tendencies, the way they both feed and constrict one another, the sub-alter(n) ego opens up a prospective recognition that the other is necessarily both inseparable from and irreducible to the self, a recognition, that is, both of the subjectivity of the other and the alterity of the self and of the correlation between them, the mutuality of being distinct and being decentred. In this recognition, one might say, resides the demand for a fair or just representation of the other.

The implications of the sub-alter(n) ego can be usefully fleshed out by recourse to the heuristic of Lacanian psychoanalysis. In these terms, the sub-alter(n) ego figures an inversion of the ambivalence attendant to what Lacan calls the mirror stage of consciousness, in which the emerging subject assumes a totalised body image as a way of re-placing the lost plenitude of the mother-child dyad. To this end, the ego fashions itself after another and then struggles to incorporate that other's image or position as his own exclusive property. That is to say, the ego proper enters into being through a drama of imitation-cum-rivalry. The sub-alter(n) ego, conversely, comprises a drama of rivalry-cum-recognition, in which the subject defines himself over against the image of the other he seeks to dominate, only to find its alterity inwrought with his own make-up. With the sub-alter(n) ego, the effort to attain or maintain an illusory sense of wholeness by assuming control of another, an effort characteristic of Giacomo's gaze to this point in the text, issues in the inverse perception of both a primordial lack and a primordial interconnection. Needing a certain socially coded and ranked difference from the other to be himself, the dominant subject can, under certain circumstances, grow conscious of that difference, that otherness, as constitutive of his own identity and yet beyond it.

Such a perception is, of course, actively discouraged within the prevailing psychological and ideological framework of modern, patriarchal society. The splitting of the ego that occurs during the mirror stage carries over into the Symbolic order by way of the gender antagonism at the heart of its fundamental law, the law of the phallus. Accordingly, the psychic formation that stages a reversal of this antagonism, revealing the differential constitution of all achieved (implicitly masculine) identity, points the way toward a new ethical dispensation based upon the contradictory implication of all socially encoded differences in one another and hence the need for some measure of "agonistic respect"[32] amongst them. Instead of a constitutive break opposing sameness and difference, upon which all hierarchical modes of organisation rely, the hybrid after effect of this break, the sub-alter(n) ego, compromises this opposition; and it thereby facilitates a metonymic form of psychic identification, in which the fundamental differences of ego and other can be seen to rest upon their equally fundamental articulation—an identification in otherness.

V

We can begin to unpack the significance of the Joycean sub-alter(n) ego by tracking the textual reverberations of the Good Friday fantasy. Taken as a screed on the perfidy of the grieving sentimentalist, the latter instalments of this crucifixion mytheme (*GJ* 15 and 16) would seem to project onto Amalia the author's mistrust of his own motive in sentimentalising someone. His mother, whose domestic martyrdom may well have been embittered if not hastened by his faithlessness—both

---

[32] I borrow the phrase from William E. Connolly, *Identity/Difference* (Ithaca: Cornell University Press, 1991).

to her and to her allegorical extension, Mother Church. The portrait of Stephen in *Ulysses* does tend to corroborate Joyce's anxiety over who or what killed his mother, while the parodic rendering of Simon Dedalus' ostentatious grief at his abused wife's grave in the "Hades" episode attests to Joyce's shrewd indignation at guilty displays of mawkishness. In allegorising Amalia's supposed treachery in Biblical terms, however, and pegging it to her gender and, ultimately, her racial status— "*Non hunc sed Barabbam*" (*GJ* 16)—Joyce effectively establishes a certain psychic distance from his own affect. To borrow from Stephen Tifft's definition of trauma, Joyce manages "to convert a betrayal (exposure) of his conflicted desires to a betrayal by the other."[33]

At the same time, because this conversion or displacement proceeds by way of an exchange of roles, wherein Amalia figures as Joyce's double or surrogate, the very act of establishing a psychic distance from her releases an immediate and equally powerful identificatory impulse, with which his perception of her otherness is to remain interfused. This movement displays the workings of the sub-alter(n) ego, where the proximity of the alien and the estrangement of the selfsame can come into play and intersect. This countervailing trend to the abjection of Amalia likewise proceeds, shadowed and shadowing in turn, to the end of the sketchbook. Its effect on the narrative progression, or perhaps it would be truer to say syncopation, of *Giacomo Joyce* commences with the passages immediately following the Good Friday scenario, the interlude surrounding the central "event" of *Giacomo*, Amalia's ailment, operation, and recovery.

On page 11, Joyce identifies Amalia with the superimposed figures of the two Italian Beatrices: Portinari, whose unbending sanctity in *Vita Nuova* is the object of Dante's sexualised adoration, and Cenci, whose indomitable innocence in Shelley's drama is the object of "an incestuous passion, aggravated by

---

[33] Stephen Tifft, "The Playboy Riots," *Nationalisms and Sexualities*, ed. Andrew Parker et al. (New York: Routledge, 1992) 321.

every circumstance of cruelty and violence" (preface to *The Cenci*), leading ultimately to her execution in the name and in the defence of a corrupt legal and religious authority:

> She walks before me along the corridor and as she walks a dark coil of her hair slowly uncoils and falls. Slowly uncoiling, falling hair. She does not know and walks before me, simple and proud. So did she walk by Dante in simple pride and so, stainless of blood and violation, the daughter of Cenci, Beatrice, to her death:
>
> ....*Tie*
> *My girdle for me and bind up this hair*
> *In any simple knot.* [GJ 11]

The combined force of these associations places Amalia, for the very first time, in the role of the Crucified, with all of the resonance that such martyrdom carries in the Joyce family romance. The closing, italicised phrase, in fact, is a direct quotation from Beatrice Cenci's death speech. But what is of overriding importance here is that in conflating these figures, Joyce registers an understanding of the intimate relation that exists between his idealisation and his desecration of Amalia. He presents them as two phases of the same fetishistic cycle. He even seems to suggest that his obsessive regard of and for Amalia sentences her to a kind of death, death by reification, appropriating her properly discrete being ("simple and proud") to the ambivalent structure of his erotic delirium, with neither her explicit consent ("she does not know") nor her tacit encouragement ("stainless of blood and violation"). It is not *just* that Joyce has found himself espousing the sexual ethics of Dante Aligheri and Francesco Cenci concurrently, but rather that he has discovered in his Dantesque worship the vital pith of Cencian injustice, the imposition of one's desire upon another. Insofar as Joyce continues to apprehend Amalia as an instance of The Woman,[34] a fantasy figure consolidating man in

---

[34] Jacqueline Rose defines the Lacanian concept of The Woman as follows: "the place onto which lack is projected and through which it is simultaneously

the economy of his desire, she must remain decidedly other yet not quite distinct, harbouring her specific socially defined difference *strictly* in relation to him. That Joyce here seizes upon the murderous implications of this arrangement signals an incipient reversal of the way sameness and difference have been articulated heretofore, a direct consequence of his access to and use of a sub-alter(n) ego. In addition to constructing Amalia as *his* other, a rhetorical tendency in which he undeniably persists, Joyce seems prepared to identify with Amalia in *her* separateness. In addition to constructing Amalia's socially relevant differences as something to be mastered, possessed, and disdained by turns, Joyce is just beginning to construct these differences as defining a mutually held 'no man's' land that problematises any claim to mastery whatever, including the self-mastery proper to late Victorian manliness.

Joyce further encodes his developing insight by aligning his voyeuristic persona in the sketchbook with the character in *The Cenci* who most clearly incarnates the complicity between veneration and violence, self-regard and other-obsession, the double-dealing Orsino. Vicki Mahaffey has proposed that a salient · property uniting Amalia's disparate literary correspondences in *Giacomo* is that all are worshiped and/or pursued more or less secretively, just as Amalia is by Joyce.[35] When it comes to Beatrice Cenci, Mahaffey points out, Orsino is the covert suitor, and he characterises his amorous fantasies in secularising terms that Joyce could not but apply to his own: "I clasp the phantom of unfelt delights. The weak imagination half possesses the self-created shadow" (III.i.141-3). In addition, Orsino, like Joyce to this point in the notebook, manifests some anxiety at the vivisective power of his beloved's return look: "Yet I fear/Her subtle mind, her awe-inspiring gaze, / Whose beams anatomise me nerve by nerve / And lay me bare, and make me blush to see / My hidden thoughts" (I.iii.83-7). As the

disavowed—woman is a symptom for the man." *Feminine Sexuality*, eds. Juliet Mitchell and Jacqueline Rose (New York: Norton, 1985) 48.

35 Mahaffey, "Giacomo Joyce," 407.

last clause indicates, Beatrice's scopic challenge accomplishes more than the Medusa's, more, that is, than simply interrupting the imaginary plenitude of the phallic I/eye.[36] In answering his secularising gaze in kind, she reveals to him his image in her eye, as it were, provoking him to reflect upon the predatory nature of his desire: "Beatrice unveiled me to myself, / And made me shrink from what I could not shun" (II.ii.115-16). Orsino's muted elusive presence in *Giacomo* is itself a testament to the effect Amalia had begun to have in stimulating Joyce to similarly self-accusatory reflection.

Indeed, the true relevance of Orsino's character as a model or a metaphor for Giacomo resides in the treacherousness of his amorous passion, a truly radical treacherousness which does not just belie the homage he pays to Beatrice but also exposes the ideological assumption that his homage mystifies: the equation of value, particularly feminine value, with (male) property. Without forswearing or even seeming to contravene his esteem for Beatrice, Orsino schemes to acquire her dowry, considers Beatrice the "profit" to be drawn from his machinations, and, once these machinations come a cropper, sacrifices her to the exigencies of self-interest: "a name and country new and a new life, fashioned on the old desires" (I.v.89-90). The phrase "a new life" translates in Orsino's native tongue as *vita nuova* and thus sets this lover of Beatrice and the other one, Dante, in an ironic juxtaposition, which Joyce then internalises and reworks, using it specifically to note the element of betrayal he detects in his own passion for Amalia. There is in the first instance, of course, the betrayal of Amalia herself, which like all betrayals in Joyce takes the form of a crucifixion analogue or fantasy. Joyce's betrayal involves a subtle variation on Orsino's perfidy: he extorts Amalia's (feminine) value as securing or confirming the property of (his own) maleness. But there is a second betrayal at work as well: a betrayal of the integrity of his own avowed feelings and perceptions, bad faith if you like, the internal corrosiveness

---

[36] Cixous, "The Laugh of the Medusa," 875-99.

intrinsic to unconscious ambivalence. In this regard, it is worth noting that the other primary victim of Orsino's treachery in *The Cenci* is a namesake of the Joycean persona here: Beatrice's brother, Giacomo. Through this citational web, Joyce contrives to criticise quietly the representational violence he has done Amalia, and to do so from his recently adopted standpoint of psychic identification with her, here expressed in terms of sibling fellowship, a mode of affiliation that can be read as a way of re-figuring his conflation of Amalia qua surrogate child with Amalia qua surrogate self.

It is hardly fortuitous that Joyce immediately follows this frame with an impressionistic rendering of Amalia's actual or presumed brush with death during this period. The concurrence is especially telling since certain metonymic connections between Amalia's malady, calling for an emergency appendectomy, and Mrs. Joyce's liver cancer might well have been of sufficient strength and proximity to trigger Joyce's latent anxiety over both his mother's death and the crucifixion fantasy just rehearsed. On this score, we should not overlook the anatomical proximity of Amalia's area of complaint to that of May Joyce. Nor should we overlook Joyce's conflation of that area of complaint with the maternal womb— "The surgeon's knife has probed in her entrails and withdrawn, leaving the raw jagged gash of its passage on her belly [...]. O cruel wound! Libidinous God!" (*GJ* 11) Joyce's closing imprecation of a desiring if divine father clearly positions Amalia at the maternal vertex of an Oedipal triangle, where her troubles represent a threat of separation analogous to that posed by his mother's terminal illness. At the same time, Joyce's closing imprecation of a divine Father sacrificing his beloved child positions Amalia in the messianic role already performed, with manly éclat, by Joyce himself (*GJ* 10, 16). Amalia's ability to split the distance between the status of mother and daughter, to shimmer along both sides of the parental-filial divide, acquires a cross-gender function as well. In which her figuration of the liminal femininity at work in Joyce's masculine self-identity allows her to symbolically occupy a privileged, even iconic site of that identity.

Viewed by itself, Joyce's initial thought at the prospect of Amalia's passing seems a romantic cliché. He worries that she has departed from him "in a moment, without a word, without a look" (*GJ* 11). Viewed in context, however, this initial reaction proves rather more intriguing. As I have stated more than once, Giacomo's masculinist imperialism, in its alternate modes of Pygmalionesque aestheticism and domineering lust, founds and naturalises itself by denying (that) Amalia (possesses) her own voice and perspective, i.e. treating her as still immanent to the bodily-material stratum of life. That Joyce should now find himself longing for her distinctive address and thus her distinctive purchase on the world not only tends to oppugn his past treatment of her, crediting her with a degree of transcendence he has hitherto denied, but lends an ironic credence to his recent fantastic apprehension that his attraction for Amalia has been in certain respects fatal, that she too was his victim.

Visiting the convalescent Amalia, Joyce takes the measure of the "look" he feared he would never see again. At first blush, his representation of her gaze signals no change in his attitude, but resumes his earlier practice of mastering Amalia's presence, and his own self-doubts, by reducing her to a condition of mute and passive animality whose meaningfulness and value are entirely at his disposal. ("I see her whole, dark, suffering eyes, beautiful as the eyes of an antelope" *GJ* 11). Amalia's gaze suffers Joyce's phallic gaze much as the bird girl suffers Stephen's in *A Portrait*. But this silent exchange also contains a crucial allusion to *The Cenci* which provides a subtext linking this passage to the progress of the preceding frames and riveting the connection between the figurative doom of Amalia-Beatrice and Amalia's literal collapse in the first two frames on page 11.

Hard upon his analysis of Beatrice's "awe-inspiring gaze," whose "beams anatomise [him] nerve by nerve/And lay [him] bare," Orsino disavows (denies/concedes) its critical potency and the castration anxiety it arouses by likening himself to "a Panther [...] panic-stricken by the Antelope's eye" (I.iii.89-90). Now given the citational pattern already in place, Joyce's use of the phrase, "the eyes of an antelope" in this context would seem to signify his implicit recognition (awareness and respect) of the potential incisiveness of a gaze which nonetheless continues to strike him as vulnerable, tractable, and quiescent. Joyce thus remarks his own tendency to disavow Amalia's moral agency, and in the very act of doing so, he begins to slough the tendency as well. Instead of seeking to master Amalia's gaze through an act of mental and spiritual penetration, as he does at the outset of *Giacomo Joyce* (*GJ* 1), Joyce sufficiently masters his own masculine anxiety, for the moment anyway, to admit (concede and receive) the analogous moral penetration of her gaze. In the same elusive motion, he also discloses his persistent reluctance to do so, thus confessing to his own share of vulnerability. The binocularity of his symbolic identification with Amalia affiliates it that much more closely with the anti-phallogocentric construct that I call the sub-alter(n) ego. For it is along that psychic margin, where the mutuality of being distinct and being decentred insists, that Joyce's still tacit recognition of the sovereign subjectivity of Amalia can awaken a sense of his otherness to himself and to his own designs.

As the abbreviated closing movement of *Giacomo Joyce* unfolds, the rehabilitation of Amalia's point of view comes to serve as an increasingly decisive counterforce to her continued abjection. Over the same span, and correlatively, cracks begin to appear in the masculinist stronghold of Giacomo's Imaginary: his faith in and will to self-possession and self-enclosure, aesthetic mastery and transcendence, and ethno-sexual superiority and domination are all progressively if haltingly eroded. Joyce did not come to grips with the underlying conditions and implications of this development until some years later, however, and the interpolated passage I discussed at the outset of this essay was his means of inscribing not only his revised aesthetic and political judgment in the text but his related understanding of how they came about. The interpolated passage (*GJ* 15) supplies a retrospective gloss on the entire notebook that directly alters the text itself and so must be taken into account *ahead of time*. Giacomo's attitude toward Amalia unfolds under the sign of the "will have been" and demands a kind of double reading on that basis. At the same time, the interpolated passage serves both Joyce and his readers as a vehicle for placing the more intimate stakes of his desire for Amalia back into the historical and specifically colonial context that gave this attitudes their distinctive shape.

VI

The leavening influence of this textual revision is in fact so profound and so manifold that to avoid oversaturation the frame must be subdivided and the irradiating effects of the respective passages treated in sequence. The frame begins:

> A soft crumpled peagreen cover drapes the lounge. A narrow Parisian room. The hairdresser lay here but now. I kissed her stocking and the hem of her rustblack dusty skirt. It is the other. She. Gogarty came yesterday to be introduced. *Ulysses* is the reason. Symbol of the intellectual conscience...Ireland then? And the husband? [Michele Risolo] [...] Why are we left here? [...] Intellectual symbol of my race. [*GJ* 15]

This dream interlude is momentous in connecting an implied reassessment of Joyce's colonising aggression toward Amalia to an analogous reassessment of his intellectual stance toward Ireland, specifically that internally imperialistic mission of soul-making summarised in the phrase, "to forge the uncreated conscience of my race" (*P* 252), which is unmistakably recalled here. In the dream context, the hairdresser blends into Amalia, who in turns stands forth as Joyce's symbol of the Irish intellectual conscience. The casting could not be more precisely and devastatingly ironic. For the kind of Manichean allegory that keys Giacomo's representation of Amalia was immediately familiar to Joyce because it corresponded in such great detail with the British iconography of the Irish during the mid and late Victorian period.

The comparatively raw, politically motivated ethno-anthropological discourses of the nineteenth century produced several sexual taxonomies of the races in which the Celts, like the Jews, were classified as essentially feminine and grouped with the Oriental races on that basis. In fact, Otto Weininger's pseudoscientific feminising of the Jews, which so intrigued Joyce,[37] picked up on an ideological tradition popularised by Ernest Renan's pseudoscientific feminising of the Celts.[38] No less august an expert than the historian Lord Acton likened the Irish to the "Hindoos" in their passivity, their indolence, their luxuriousness, and their absence of real historical agency, all stereotypically feminine attributes associated with the material-bodily stratum;[39] while Matthew Arnold located the femininity of the Celts in their supposed sentimentality, their emotional instability, and their undependability.[40] Finally, in the heated atmosphere of the Land War and the Plan of Campaign, the London newspaper and penny weeklies, many of which made their way to the Sister Isle, regularly depicted the Irish as ignorant, bestial, and inherently treacherous. (Madden makes explicit reference to these caricatures in one such publication, *Punch*, during his argument with Stephen over patriotism in *Stephen Hero* [65].)[41] So by identifying Amalia with the Irish race, after having assigned her each of the above traits at one

---

37 Brown, *James Joyce and Sexuality*, 101.

38 David Cairns and Shaun Richards, *Writing Ireland* (Manchester: Manchester University Press, 1988) 46.

39 Liz Curtis, *Nothing But the Same Old Story* (London: Information on Ireland, 1984) 57.

40 Matthew Arnold, *Lectures and Essays in Criticism* (Ann Arbor: University of Michigan Press, 1962) 347. On this basis, Arnold held the Irish incapable of self-government, calling them "ineffectual in politics" (346).

41 L.P. Curtis, *Apes and Angels* (Washington, DC: Smithsonian, 1971).

point or another in the text, Joyce figures his previous indulgence in sexist/anti-Semitic rhetoric as a mediated betrayal of the subdominant position and minority heritage of his own people.

This sort of negative identification in otherness with Amalia seems to have been helped along by Joyce's feeling that they shared, in their different ways, the condition of exile. Ellmann reports that during this period Joyce gradually "began to recognise his place in Europe to be as ambiguous as theirs [the Jews']" (*JJII* 230). Manganiello confirms that while on the continent Joyce gradually came to see the similarity of his position to that of the Jews primarily as regards the state of exile.[42] On the other hand, Joyce fixes on the term "exile" in good part to differentiate the course he had adopted from the mass Irish emigration of the nineteenth century, a phenomenon whose parallel with the Jewish diaspora had been a familiar topos since the days of the potato famine. This is important in understanding the passage in question, for by situating Amalia between past abuse and present redress, literal Jewishness and symbolic Irishness, Joyce suggests that the elitism or supremacism he had entertained is the flip side of colonial self-disgust: either sensibility manifests his internalisation of the phobic bodily antinomies that ground sovereign subjectivity (the clean versus the defiled body, the whole versus the castrated body, the masculine and the feminine body, the sublime versus the submerged body, etc.) as they have been filtered through the symbolic grid of European and specifically British imperialism. Joyce unmasks this very form of colonial mimesis in the more virulent strains of Irish jingoism, rejecting, in his words, "the old pap of racial hatred" (*SL* 110-11). But in *Giacomo*, Joyce discovers (displays and witnesses) his susceptibility to a subtler variant of the same pathological mimesis. Because his Manichean construction of Amalia resonates so distinctively of the English depiction of the Irish,

---

[42] Dominic Manganiello, *Joyce's Politics* (London: Routledge and Kegan Paul, 1980) 52.

Joyce is given to understand how vital a stake he continued to have in hegemonic performances from which he otherwise suffered, how deeply his sense of sovereignty was implicated in them, and so how responsible for and complicit in these practices he remained, his own victimisation notwithstanding. Indeed, the structure of the interpolated passage implicitly acknowledges that in treating Amalia in an Orientalising and misogynist manner, he had basically "identified with the aggressor," the masculine Anglo-Saxon coloniser, in the unconscious desire to exorcise the Orientalised and feminised associations of his own Irishness.[43] Once detected, this purpose reflects rather badly on Joyce's doggedly adversarial disposition toward his homeland. What he had believed a noble, even heroic, effort to save Irish culture by criticising it he could now see as tainted by a certain "West Britonish" collaboration. Under these circumstances, for Joyce to identify with Amalia is a step toward resisting his interpellation to metropolitan subjectivity, toward renouncing the master's values and the values of mastery, and toward reasserting the marginality of his social inscription.

By introducing these doubts about his past micro and macro political practice as an indirect response to the fanfare surrounding *Ulysses*, Joyce simultaneously underlines and transcribes all of those sentiments expressed in *Giacomo Joyce* which are to be subsequently retailed, recontextualised, and decisively ironised in the later work. Two examples of this technique seem especially pertinent to our argument. Joyce's previously cited use of the phrase "prostrate bugs" (*GJ* 8) to describe the Triestine Jews is subject to a highly mediated qualification by this reference to *Ulysses* which brings into the textual play an analogous association of Jews and bugs made by the reprehensibly hyper-masculine, chauvinistic "Citizen" of the "Cyclops" episode: "Those are nice things," says the Citizen, "coming over here to Ireland filling the country with

---

43 For identification with the aggressor, see Ashis Nandy, *The Intimate Enemy* (Oxford: Oxford University Press, 1983).

bugs" (*U* 12.1141-2). Since the violently anti-Semitic Citizen is both an ostentatious Irish nationalist and a secret traitor to the cause, the implication here would seem to be that the exclusionary sensibility that Joyce forswears in alluding to this satirical butt signifies a sham or perfidious commitment to colonial liberation. The second example reinforces this perception. On page 9, Joyce makes the snide remark, "They [the Triestine Jews] love their country when they are quite sure which country it is" (*GJ* 9), the substance of which he later attributes to J.J. O'Molloy in reference to Bloom during the same anti-Semitic interlude in "Cyclops." O'Molloy imagines that he is standing up for a natural conception of Irishness, but he more generally exemplifies what Joyce took to be the singularly Irish proclivity for duplicitous charade. Attempting to trade hard-luck tales for handouts from cronies employed by the Castle, whose patriotism, therefore, is likewise spurious, O'Molloy can properly be characterised as a parasite's parasite. Once again, promoting exclusionary identity-politics in the name of colonial integrity correlates with a certain undermining of that integrity. This connection is ratified, finally, by the presence in this frame of Oliver St. John Gogarty. His persona in *Ulysses*, Buck Mulligan, adopts a strongly masculinist and anti-Semitic posture, which, like that of the Citizen, issues in a pejorative feminisation of Jewishness. He adopts, in short, an invidiously essentialist view of racial and gendered subjectivity, and he too does so as an assertion of his own manhood. All the while Mulligan indulges in such self-serving forms of mummery that he earns the semi-official designation, Ireland's "gay betrayer" (*U* 1.405). His practice thus shows how naturalising distinctions among races of people are themselves a peculiarly malicious factor in the perpetual masquerade which they feign to refute. With this cluster of citations, Joyce simultaneously announces, displays, and renounces the sort of unadmitted, unholy alliance he has joined in abjecting the culturally defined subaltern(s) and, by inference, his own colonial origins. He thereby enacts in the (inter)text of the interpolated passage a shift in orientation from ego, conceived as the primary structure of selfhood, to sub-alter(n) ego conceived as the zone of primordial (self-) difference or relationality. Correlatively, he enacts a shift from a binary construction of gender, which identifies masculinity, racial and otherwise, with self-possession, to a relational construction, in which alterity is primary to any sexed position.

The result of Joyce's more intensely self-conscious shift in subject position is a more intensively self-conscious identification in otherness with Amalia and the correspondingly overt accommodation of her viewpoint. The interpolated frame continues:

> Listen! The plunging gloom has fallen. Listen!
> —I am not convinced that such activities of the mind or body can be called unhealthy—She speaks. A weak voice from beyond the cold stars. Say on! Oh, say again, making me wise. This voice I never heard. [*GJ* 15]

The wisdom that "this voice"—the voice "of the other. She"—has to impart would seem to consist in the objection it raises to the phobic and pathologising take on nonetheless fetishised "activities" which characterises so much of *Giacomo Joyce* and contributes so much to the silencing of Amalia's voice. The passage thus intimates a fundamental reversal in the pedagogical relationship of the protagonists.[44] But what is even more important is the way that it maps onto and throws in relief the play of voice(s) that gives the notebook its comprehensive ethico-political structure: the counterpoint of Joyce's suppressive monologue before Amalia's operation (pages 1 to 11) with the emergent dialogue between them thereafter (11 through 16). Having deprived Amalia of her voice through the long first movement, Joyce here makes a

---

[44] Mahaffey, "Giacomo Joyce," 397. Mahaffey notes, "After the operation [...] she exchanges her role as passive victim for the role of aggressor, and Giacomo, who has imagined himself the aggressor, becomes her victim."

concentrated effort to discern it: "listen! [...] Listen! [...] She speaks [...] Say on! Oh, say again." In recalling a similar attempt during that past—"bend and hear" (*GJ* 7)—this effort indicates that the problem of silence lay not with the speaker but with the auditor, who at first could only pick up the "thin breath of a sparrow" (*GJ* 7) and even now only hears her as a "weak voice from beyond the [...] stars" (*GJ* 15). At the same time, given their prescriptive form, these phrases can be taken as commanding the reader, Joyce himself, or anyone else to rehear the case of Giacomo with an ear to discovering the voice of Amalia. In a sense, it is this very mandate, directing the author/reader back into the text in a certain way, that renders this politically charged play of voice(s) apprehensible in the first place and so might be seen as realising or inducing it as such. Joyce certainly insinuates as much when, standing virtually at the end of the dialogical second movement, he declares, "This voice I never heard" (*GJ* 15).

Undertaking the retrospective search prescribed in the text, one learns that Amalia's voice first finds representation during the post-convalescent period, which is to say directly after Joyce shows some awareness of the autonomous moral force of her gaze. As one might expect, given the constitutive nature of the fantasy at issue, the ethical adjustments Joyce makes in response to this crisis, while decisive, are by no means simple or absolute. His initial impression of a recuperated and giddily relieved Amalia is for our purposes nearly indistinguishable from his past caricatures. He represents her as, well, a birdbrain. ("Once more in her chair by the window, happy words on her tongue, happy laughter. A bird twittering after storm, happy that its foolish life has fluttered out of reach of an epileptic lord and giver of life, twittering happily, twittering and chirping happily" *GJ* 11). Joyce moves from silencing Amalia outright to granting her the faculty of speech only to deny her, at least implicitly, the power of genuine articulation and, quite explicitly, the aptitude to say something weighty or even sensible. But then he turns around in the very next frame and negates this impression by recording her observation on being recruited as a reader of his autobiographical fiction, "*The Portrait of the Artist*" [sic]. Now, just by sounding Amalia out on his work, Joyce necessarily induces some nascent respect for her taste, intellect, or critical acumen, albeit a respect deeply bound up with his own need to be admired both as a man and as an artist. But the comment with which he credits her indicates just how fraught his gesture really is: "She says that, had *The Portrait of the Artist* been frank only for frankness' sake, she would have asked why I had given it to her to read" (*GJ* 12). Amalia astutely taps into the eroticised self-exposure Joyce's offering effects. Since the text in question is not only autobiographical but intimate and, for the time, scandalous, Joyce can be seen as engineering a complex, asymmetrical, but nonetheless dramatic reversal of scopic roles: he adopts the position of aesthetic *exhibitionist* in addition to that of voyeuristic author; Amalia *inherits* the role of voyeuristic reader and critic while remaining an involuntary aesthetic *exhibition*. That Joyce should engineer an interchange of this type evinces what I have called his metonymic identification with Amalia, the secularising element of which depends upon and combines with an element of genuine recognition. He enlists her as his symbolic double and ideal reader, an enlarging mirror for his ego, precisely by submitting his image to the already acknowledged difference of her desire and her judgment.

Joyce's attitude in the aftermath of his offering (gift/tutorial assignment) corroborates its fundamental duplicity. On the one hand he contemplates his words penetrating and occupying Amalia's brain, in the manner of a phallic, colonising force. Indeed, it is at this stage that he introduces the previously cited frame beginning "My words in her mind" (*GJ* 13). At the same time, he senses having transferred to her a recursive if not exactly reciprocal power in the bargain. He finds his self-representation alienated in her gaze as she was in his, subject to her curiosity, inspection, intrusion, and interpretive recreation as she was to his. "Those quiet cold fingers," he writes, "have touched the pages, foul and fair, on which my shame should glow" (*GJ* 13). Even the hazard of sexual contamination seems to be running in the other direction at this point. But what makes this experience so astringent for Joyce is his increasingly *radical* sense of her difference, i.e. his positive incertitude as to the exact parameters of that difference or even whether there are exact parameters.[45] Witness his stereotypical and yet self-conscious marmorealising and aestheticising of Amalia's hands: "quiet and cold and pure fingers. Have they never erred?" (*GJ* 13) By figuring Amalia as a marble or alabaster statue and then questioning the moralised gender assumptions on which his own metonymy is based, Joyce registers an understanding of (sexual) difference, and so his own masculinity) as an open-ended iteration of cultural codes rather than a brute instantiation of biological law. Such an understanding is the condition of possibility for any identification in otherness to occur.

Likewise, and for much the same reason, Amalia's specifically aesthetic scrutiny and judgment pique Joyce in both senses of the term. They irk him, provoking resentment, and they arouse and stimulate him, provoking respect. His retort to her observation is snidely sexist, turning gender difference into an occasion for dismissing an insight he finds embarrassing: "oh you would, would you? A lady of letters" (*GJ* 12). But it is also tinctured with faint surprise and teacherly pride in her literary perspicacity. If "*lady* of letters" exposes a gynophobic condescension, "lady of *letters*" conveys professional regard. That regard, in turn, cannot but unsettle the gynophobic condescension, putting pressure on his received notions of ladyship.

That there might also be a personal, cross-gender identification at work in the phrase "lady of letters" was

---

[45] Barbara Johnson, *The Critical Difference* (Baltimore: Johns Hopkins University Press, 1980) 146. "If we could be sure of the difference between the determinable and the indeterminable, the indeterminable would be subsumed within the determinable."

corroborated retroactively by Joyce's dogged scheme to install Lucia as his lady of letters or *lettrines* further along in his career. Joyce encouraged his daughter to devise filigreed inaugural letters, *lettrines*, for use in a collection whose eponymous title, *The Joyce Book* (*JJII* 641) allowed father and daughter to be subsumed together under the name of the Father. Having deemed her work "exquisite," he subsequently commissioned her *lettrines* for a manuscript version of *Pomes Penyeach*, which he had deposited in the Bibliothèque Nationale and the British Museum (*JJII* 658-9). Ultimately, he used her *lettrines* in manuscripts of two episodes of *Finnegans Wake*: "The Mime, Mick, Nick and the Maggies" and "Storiella as She is Syung."[46] Given the central narrative and thematic significance of letters in the *Wake*, both as characters and as missives, in particular the letters of the schizoid daughter, Issy, and given further the prominent role of elaborate calligraphy in underscoring this significance (e.g. *The Book of Kells*), a textualist reading attentive to the bibliographical codes of the *Wake* can trace a *literal* convergence of father and daughter on its pages and in its authorial function.[47]

The ethical and political implications of this transaction with Amalia are exceptionally rich. The imperialistic (racist/sexist) thrust of Joyce's gaze in the sketchbook shapes the defensiveness of his reaction to this further reversal of pedagogic roles and leaves him vulnerable to feeling annulled by Amalia's probing, readerly scrutiny. Homi Bhabha has analysed this phenomenon under the category of colonial

---

[46] Only once did Joyce propose using Lucia's *lettrines* to illustrate a work not his own, Chaucer's *ABC*, and even this incident betrays the paternal identification motivating his efforts. He wrote to Sylvia Beach, "I spent a wobbly half hour on the top of your ladder today looking for the *father of English literature* but could not find him. Can you lend me a complete Chaucer for a few days. *Mine is locked up*" (my italics) (*JJII* 658-9).

[47] For an analysis of bibliographical codes and their importance, particularly in Modernist literature, see Jerome J. McGann, *The Textual Condition*, (Princeton NJ: Princeton University Press, 1991).

mimicry.[48] The coloniser justifies his appropriation of the other in terms of realising her as a virtual subject, educating or edifying her as Joyce does Amalia. But because she only remains appropriable insofar as she is *also* a virtual object, irredeemably inferior, her adaptation or capture of the coloniser's belief and value structure, her appreciation of his tastes and interests, her facility with his language, her mastery of his criteria of judgment, all with a subtle yet profound inflection, call into question both their elite status and their universal validity and thus challenge both the superiority and the coherence of his social identity. Abjection as dread *desire*, the will to impose the self on the other, leads the coloniser to a perception of his own underlying hybridity, which abjection as *dread* desire, the will to secure the self over against the other, aims to avert.

But as a metropolitan colonial, a racially feminised male, an impoverished and declassed intellectual, a *"maestro inglese"*(*GJ* 5) who was underling to both the *inglese* and, in some sense, to his own protégé, Joyce's inhabited a much more complex affective and political than the one Bhabha explicates. His relation to the normative male subject position *itself* is deeply compromised in *Giacomo*, so that at a certain point maintaining the coherence of his social identity comes into conflict with the whole matrix of hierarchical distinctions and sign values that undergirds his equally self-defining pretension to elite status. For Joyce to defend the peculiar conformation of his social identity, inscribed as it is along and athwart the coloniser/colonised, dominant/subaltern divide, would seem impossible. For he was simultaneously required to reject the elite standards and received logic of value in order to avoid allying himself with imperialist oppression and to continue relying on those standards and that logic in order to mark himself off from some more purely subaltern status. It is this aggravated condition of colonial hybridity, a double or multiple syntax, that Joyce's imperialist abjection of Amalia has to this

---

[48] Bhabha, "Of Mimicry and Man," 125-33; and "Signs Taken for Wonders," 162.

point served to disguise or deny, by emphasising the socially entitled elements of his own profile. So as Joyce begins to take stock of and responsibility for this abjection, he loses not only the security of assumed privilege, but the privilege of assumed security. He has to confront the ethico-political undecidability that attaches to his subject position as a result of its incompatibility with more recognisably hegemonic and subaltern stations.

As one might expect, the effects of this lived dislocation are immediately evident in Joyce's reaction to the emergence of Amalia's perspective. On the one hand, while he allows her previously stifled voice a hearing, he does not perform this liberation joyfully or even dispassionately, but as though he were unleashing an irresistible menace to his authorial identity. Having moved so far toward identification with Amalia, Joyce appears to encounter the limits of this odyssey, beyond which he will lose the moorings of subjectivity altogether. On the other hand, even as he represents the emergence of Amalia's voice as undoing his own self-conception, he insists upon exposing himself to it and effecting its release in the text, and the duress involved only underscores the depths of his investment in the performance. This contorted attitude reflects the radical marginality of Joyce's social inscription—between dominance and subdominance—and the warring allegiances that it elicits. At once a dominant and a subdominant subject, Joyce is torn between his attachment to and his reaction against the racial and sexual ideologies of his time and the conflicting profiles these interconnected regimes offered of his own character and his own standing in the world. In his dealings with Amalia, Joyce structures this conflict in terms of means and ends. He undertakes the *act* of liberating the voice of Amalia while he shrinks from the *fact* of its liberation. He perversely finds proof of his masculine authority and validation of his elite artistic identity in summoning forth the subaltern voice that challenges or at least qualifies that authority and threatens to dislodge that identity. In this light, Joyce's messianic self-imaginings in *Giacomo* and elsewhere seem less an indulgence or a delusion of grandeur than a strategic compulsion, a way of valorising a contradiction he could not dispel: that the affirmation of his subject position was inextricably bound up with his dissolution.

Joyce figures the dissolution of his identity in the concluding frame of *Giacomo* as a *petite mort*. Just as his suppression of Amalia's voice culminates in her dalliance with death, his liberation of her voice precipitates a series of apparently lethal transmissions from different points on her person. First, her hair and dress are seen to mirror "the hue of the illusion of the vegetable glass of nature and of lush grass, the hair of graves" (*GJ* 12). Next, in a typically Joycean series of puns, her face appears "grey and grave" surmounted by "dank matted hair" (14). Then, her kiss communicates the "vapour of death" in a "sighing breath" (14). Finally, as her fatal charm concentrates itself in her gaze, the transmission takes on a phallic quality, signifying a turnabout in the gender masquerade. Joyce ascribes a baneful potency to her "black basilisk eyes. *E col suo vedere attosca l'uomo quando lo vede*" (15), and in a convergence of this narrative sequence and the crucifixion theme, Amalia turns an ejaculating gaze upon the messianic Joyce, "darting [...] out of her sluggish sidelong eyes a jet of liquorish venom" (15). At this point, Joyce's intent to realise Amalia's potential to be like him comes to an ironic fruition in the desubstantialisation and destabilisation of gender norms. Capping and crystallising this sequence is the interpolated passage, the concluding segment of which reads as follows:

> She coils toward me along the crumpled lounge. I cannot move or speak. Coiling approach of starborn flesh. Adultery of wisdom. No. I will go. I will.—Jim, love!—Soft sucking lips kiss my left armpit: a coiling kiss on myriad veins. I burn! I crumple like a burning leaf. From my right armpit a fang of flame leaps out. A starry snake has kissed me: a cold nightsnake. I am lost!—Nora!— [*GJ* 15]

The reversals we have seen in scopic power, pedagogical authority and sexual roles here pass directly into a reversal in vocal or representational prerogative. Joyce is silenced ("I cannot [...] speak") before Amalia's "adultery of wisdom," which has already been metonymically linked with her faculty of speech: "voice of wisdom, say on! O, say again making me wise. This voice I never heard" (*GJ* 15). In this oneiric mixture of memory and imagination, Joyce incurs the sort of aesthetic and sexual objectification he had inflicted, testing it, so to speak, on his own body. What Amalia actually says, "Jim, love!" connects this voice transplant with the most sweeping of the reversals mounted in *Giacomo Joyce*, a reversal in sexual and amorous agency. In keeping with the recovery of her voice, Amalia becomes an aggressive, pleasure-seeking subject; in keeping with the loss of his, Joyce becomes the passive, suffering, and embodied object ("I cannot move").

Joyce gives this reversal of erotic energy a markedly gendered figuration. Amalia's action unfolds throughout the scene in terms of patently phallic imagery—"She coils toward me [...]. Coiling approach of starborn flesh [...]. A coiling kiss [...] a fang of flame [...]. A starry snake has kissed me." (*GJ* 15) Her erogenous target, Joyce's armpit, is notable for being a relatively gynomorphic part of the anatomy, bearing the rounded, hollow, recessive shape associated with the female body in general and the womb in particular. Joyce figures the armpit as a penetrable part of the anatomy as well—her "fang of flame" goes in one and out the other. By pegging normative masculine and feminine sexual attributes to the possession and privation of voice respectively and then reversing them on that basis, Joyce supplants an essentialist with a constructivist mode of gender dimorphism and, more than that, he treats sexual difference as primarily grounded in power relations, as inextricable from sexual dominance.

At the same time, however, Joyce's picture of Amalia at this moment finds something unnatural, even monstrous, in her new stature, betraying his continued investment in that "male system of representation" that he has been willing to violate. The reptilian aspect in which he envisions Amalia combines with the sinister thrust of her own imagined gaze to evoke the figure of the Medusa, the mythic archetype of the phallic woman as castrating bitch, and Amalia's searingly painful method of seduction works to confirm and carry forward the allusion. Under these circumstances, Joyce's appeal to Nora as a protectress can be seen as counterposing the fantasy of the phallic mother, the ultimate guarantor of male satisfaction, to the phallic woman, the expropriator of male privilege, in an almost instinctive recurrence to the old gender typologies. Thus, it becomes clear that while Joyce's powerful ambivalence toward Amalia has been relieved and enriched over the course of the notebook, it has not dwindled away so much as changed dimension. Instead of entertaining a conflict-ridden racial and sexual fantasy of a luxurious, enigmatic, and compliant Amalia, Joyce is torn between the persistence of this fantasy and his daunting recognition of her effective autonomy, agency, and acuity, all of which he has difficulty conceiving without a decidedly masculinised inflection and a decidedly feminising effect on himself. The resulting conflict concentrates itself in the portrayal of Amalia as a grotesque, properly defined as an aesthetic representation which, being constituted in contradiction, defies the effective categories of intelligibility.[49]

Bella/Bello in *Ulysses* is another such grotesque, and her/his connection to Amalia is more than casual. What we have in *Giacomo* is a kind of (non)dress rehearsal for Bloom's masochistic, cross-generational, transsexual encounter in "Circe." Like his Odyssean protagonist, Joyce experiences the interchange of sexual positionality, the loss of manhood, as an imminent threat of personal extinction. Indeed, the whole litany of mortal images I have been reciting is neatly condensed in this gender-reversal passage: the words "starborn" and "starry"

---

[49] Geoffrey Galt Harpham, *On the Grotesque* (Princeton NJ: Princeton University Press, 1982).

recall Amalia's weakened voice from "beyond the cold stars," the "coiling kiss" recalls Amalia's "sighing" kiss and its "vapour" of death, and the "starry snake" with its "fang of flame" recalls Amalia's "basilisk eyes" with their "jet of liquorish venom." Joyce supplements this chain of associations at the end with the simple pronouncement, "I am lost," the contextual nuances of which interrelate the dislocation of masculine identity with outright annihilation.

The affirmation of Joyce's specific social identity enters in precisely with the insistent reiteration of this *petite mort*. He declares himself in all of his radical marginality through a Nietzschean willingness to undergo repeatedly the imagined touch of death in order to encounter finally and authentically the alien voice of Amalia, an effort motivated by his gathering sense of the mutually implicated otherness of their racial and colonial status. The end game of *Giacomo* sees the author exposing himself to the profound difference of Amalia's being, not with the aim of mastering her otherness in order to consolidate his sense of self-identity (a classic abjection pattern), but rather as a way of expressing the distinctive centrality of such difference, such otherness, to his own subject position, as a way of expressing, in short, his solidarity with the abjected. The sexual reversal in the interpolated passage not only dramatises this solidarity, but associates it with the possession of vatic percipience and, by extension, with Joyce's aesthetic *metier*. Joyce confronts the *deprivation* of his I/eye ("I am lost"), i.e. castration/death, in order to be at one with the sociosexual other against whom he has been defining himself, "the voice I never heard." But the ordeal actually winds up *enriching* him with the indispensable gift of wisdom ("making me wise"). Loss, we might say, is Joyce's gain, which is doubtless why he felt it was Shakespeare's as well (*U* 9.476); the pain of solidarity brings the gain of wisdom.

In the frames immediately following this interpolation, Joyce proceeds to underscore the intercourse between writing, as he conceives the practice, and his prospective extinction before the eye and voice of the other. Reflecting upon the end of the flirtation, Joyce tells himself, "It will never be. You know that well. What then? Write it, damn you, write it! What else are you good for?" (*GJ* 16) What Joyce goes on to write points up how far the reversal of scopic and vocative privilege has gone in this relationship and how important such voluntary forfeiture or transfer of masculine authority is coming to be in Joyce's creative scheme, an importance highlighted in his oft-discussed writing of masochism.[50] If the affair itself reflects Joyce's scopic interest, its ending reflects Amalia's:

> "Why [did it end? Must you marry]?"
> "Because otherwise I could not see you." [*GJ* 16]

In Joyce's impressionistic rendition of this ending of the affair, his very prose swoons into a silence that awaits the emergence of Amalia's word: "Sliding—space—ages—foliage of stars—and waning heaven—stillness—and stillness deeper—stillness of annihilation—and her voice" (*GJ* 16). Joyce selects what is perhaps the most personal and idiosyncratic of stylistic approaches, free association, and then trains it to the self-effacing purpose of maximum receptivity, a manoeuvre which epitomises the trend of the notebook as a whole. He is in the process of redefining his writing as a highly specialised and individualised mode of audition, not so much blank recording as simultaneous translation, in which the irreducible distance from and the inexpiable obligation to the other command joint recognition.

---

[50] For the place of masochism in Joyce, see Valente, *James Joyce and the Problem of Justice* 129; Frances Restuccia, *James Joyce and the Law of the Father* (New Haven: Yale University Press, 1989) 131.

ENVOY

In this light, Joyce's final representation of Amalia by way of her personal effects can still be read as an objectifying strategy consonant with the sexist and racist tenor of much of the notebook, but it can also be seen as a strategy of authorial self-effacement consonant with the newfound desire to allow Amalia to speak for herself. Because in a literal as well as a symbolic sense, the independence of Amalia's voice coincides with her independence from Joyce, an heraldic rebus of her family name[61] is left to stand, dreamlike, for genuine utterance on her part:

> A long black piano: coffin of music. Poised on its edge a woman's hat, red-flowered, and umbrella, furled. Her arms: a casque, gules, and blunt spear on a field, sable. [*GJ* 16]

Arranged one way, the hat and the umbrella can be seen to form an "a," as Vicki Mahaffey has argued, but arranged differently, they can also be taken to form a "p."[51] In keeping with Joyce's tendency to embrace both poles of any either/or proposition, the coat of arms here would seem to form a composite or "cubist" portrait of Amalia's name, emphasising her comparative autonomy at this point in the notebook.

Joyce's last image of Amalia, her umbrella, deliberately identified with her person, provides additional ammunition for this interpretation—"Envoy: love me, love my umbrella" (*GJ* 16). As suggested at the at the end of his story, "A Mother," the umbrella, has interchangeably phallic and judicial resonances for Joyce. In that case it marked the phallo-centric structure of judgment itself, the arbitration of any formal symmetry, beginning with gender, on terms set by, expressive of, or favourable to one side of the equation. The visual, phallic symbolism surrounding Burke's closed, "poised," "finally balanced moral umbrella" obscures and pre-empts the

---

[51] Mahaffey, "Giacomo Joyce," 398.

feminine, gynomorphic associations of the umbrella, particularly when opened, the "elle" of the umbrella if you will. Joyce's envoy seems designed to undo this pre-emption and restore the decision-making authority symbolised by the umbrella to the representative female figure, Amalia. To love her, the envoy suggests, is to love the irreducible distinctness and the effective force of her judgment, even when her judgment is to leave. It is truly an envoy of otherness; a passage dedicated to her otherness' otherness of place, feeling, perspective and of the otherness to himself, his enabling lack of self-possession or mastery, that she has helped him to reveal, acknowledge and even embrace.

Clare Wallace

"Ghosts in the Mirror": Perception and the Visual in *Giacomo Joyce*

From the time of its appearance, opinions have varied with regard to the significance of *Giacomo Joyce* and its relation to Joyce's life and *œuvre*. Long buried in Trieste, *Giacomo Joyce* was first disinterred by Richard Ellmann, who included quite considerable portions of the text in his 1959 biography of Joyce (*JJI* 353-360). In 1968, the full text was published with an introduction by Ellmann stating that, "It seems probable that *Giacomo Joyce* will be the last of James Joyce's published writings" (*GJ* xi). The discovery of an unpublished Joyce manuscript was, undoubtedly, a great *coup* for both Richard Ellmann and Viking Press and, predictably enough, precipitated a marketing campaign which, briefly, made the sixteen-page text the focus of international attention. As Vicki Mahaffey notes, Viking's attempts to sell the book "as an almost sacred 'relic,' an object deserving veneration" produced excessive and, in some instances, counterproductive responses from reviewers.[1] *Giacomo Joyce* was a revenant aspect of Joyce's work many found far from credible as "complete" or worthy of such sanctification. Indeed, Ellmann, Fritz Senn and others have shown how *Giacomo Joyce* was extensively dispersed by Joyce,

---

[1] Vicki Mahaffey, "Giacomo Joyce," *A Companion to Joyce Studies*, eds. Zack Bowen and James F. Carens (Westport CT: Greenwood Press, 1984) 89.

who used portions of it for other, better known Dublin-centred, projects.[2] Recycled and expanded fragments of this already fragmentary piece are to be found in *A Portrait of the Artist as a Young Man, Exiles* and *Ulysses,* and it seems fair to assume that Joyce never intended to have *Giacomo Joyce* published. Nevertheless, as the last and posthumous addition to Joyce's corpus, *Giacomo Joyce* is a "ghost in the mirror" (*GJ* 6) which haunts our understandings of that work and thus deserves our attention. Or, as Joseph Valente puts it; "*Giacomo Joyce* is *the* remainder in Joyce studies, the 'literature' we Biddy Dorans have only recently begun to 'look at' and scarcely begun to appreciate."[3]

Giacomo Joyce is a text which might be described as evocative, poetic, romantic or ironic. It resonates with the flow and ebb of desire. Unsurprisingly, it is also a work which resists simple narrative-orientated explication in spite of the many attempts that have been made to resolve "the story" it tells. The "relic," *Giacomo Joyce,* has all too often been viewed as the bones of a dead, yet paradoxically eternal, love affair. Or alternately as a piece of the "real" Joyce, somehow less mediated than the Joyce who is to be found in his other works. Yet one must proceed with some sceptical caution here, for while *Giacomo Joyce* might provide another perspective on Joyce it may equally offer a *trompe l'œil.* In multiple ways perception and perspective are intrinsic concerns of *Giacomo Joyce;* sight, insight, vision and blindness are of particular importance to interpreting this telegraphic Joycean "remainder" and the desire(s) it relates.

References to the visual aspects of *Giacomo Joyce* have arisen repeatedly in descriptions of the text, beginning with Joyce himself who refers to it elliptically in a letter to Ezra Pound as

---

2 Richard Ellmann, introduction, *Giacomo Joyce,* by James Joyce (London: Faber and Faber, 1968) xi-xxvi and Fritz Senn "Some Further Notes on *Giacomo Joyce*" in *JJQ* 5 (1968): 233-236.

3 Joseph Valente, *James Joyce and the Problem of Justice: Negotiating Sexual and Colonial Difference* (Cambridge: Cambridge University Press, 1995) 68.

"some prose sketches."[4] Fixing upon the idea of the sketch, Adaline Glasheen, in an early and influential essay on *Giacomo Joyce*, focuses upon its painterly technique[5] and considerations of the text since then have often returned to its preoccupation with the visual and the implications of that preoccupation.[6] The various critical perceptions of *Giacomo Joyce*, which have emerged since 1968, could be said to follow a number of trajectories, the first of which come filtered through Richard Ellmann's biography, *James Joyce*, and subsequently his introduction to *Giacomo Joyce* itself. Significantly, Ellmann describes the text as a "love poem which is never recited" (*GJ* xi). It is Ellmann who suggests the identity of Joyce's inspiration as being Amalia Popper (a Jewish Triestinian who was one of Joyce's former students), and this speculation has propagated other critical responses to *Giacomo Joyce* which have foregrounded Amalia Popper as a key to reading desire in this work.

In particular, the interpretations put forward by Vicki Mahaffey in various articles and books between 1984 and 1998, increasingly concentrate on Popper as symbolically significant. Mahaffey has meticulously documented the initial reception of *Giacomo Joyce* and the "quest" to identify the lady about whom the text was apparently written. In the article "Fascism and Silence: The Coded History of Amalia Popper," she unravels the story of the Popper family and, later, the Risolo family. Mahaffey delves into some of the many contradictions between the images of Amalia Popper/Risolo (as Mahaffey puts it, a Jew,

---

4   Ezra Pound, *Pound/Joyce*, ed. Forrest Read (New York: New Directions, 1967) 105.

5   Adaline Glasheen, Review Article, *A Wake Newsletter* (June 1968): 41.

6   Of those especially concerned with the political implications of the visual in *Giacomo Joyce*, Vicki Mahaffey and Joseph Valente are to be noted. However, in addition, the fascination with images of women conjured up in the text may be seen in the exhibition, *Le Donne di Giacomo* which took place in Trieste in 1999, curated by Eric Schneider and published as *Le Donne di Giacomo*, eds. Renzo Crivelli and John McCourt (Trieste: Hammerle Editori, 1999).   See also www.artecultura.it/joyce/indexi.htm.

a scholar, a teacher, a translator), Popper/Risolo's infamous reticence about the entire matter of her lessons with Joyce as well as her translation of several of the stories from *Dubliners*, and her husband Michele Risolo's accounts of the relationship with Joyce.[7] In spite of the extensive critical exegesis devoted to Amalia Popper/Risolo, she fails to come to life as the enigmatic and fascinating "mystery lady" of *Giacomo Joyce* and what remains most strikingly about this shadowy (real life) figure is her reticence. In *States of Desire: Wilde, Yeats, Joyce and the Irish Experiment*, Mahaffey develops the analysis of *Giacomo Joyce* further, from an "affair of the eye" to a "contest of the eyes" in which Joyce is the victor, for although

> The story of *Giacomo Joyce* presents Joyce as Popper's suffering victim, [...] its *mode of representation* makes her utterly subject to his representation of her. In short *Giacomo Joyce* has sexist and anti-Semitic overtones that are essential to an understanding of the operations of prejudice and the power of art; in it, Joyce found himself to be inconsequential and undesirable in the eyes of an attractive Jewish woman and responded by instinctively and shamefully defending himself by appealing to the traditional privilege of a man, a Gentile and a writer to help him contain her power.[8]

She argues that these uncensored impulses led to Joyce's suppression of the text. His concomitant understanding of his "complicity" in both sexism and racism apparently then led him to a more "controversial and complex treatment of women and Jews in *Ulysses*."[9]

Joseph Valente also offers a treatment of *Giacomo Joyce* that is similarly attentive to perception and representation, albeit in a more forcefully political manner. In *James Joyce and the Problem*

[7] Mahaffey, "Fascism and Silence: The Coded History of Amalia Popper," *JJQ* 32.3-4 (1995): 501.

[8] Mahaffey, *States of Desire: Wilde, Yeats, Joyce and the Irish Experiment* (Oxford and New York: Oxford University Press, 1998) 151. In particular see chapter four, "Joyful Desire Giacomo Joyce and Finnegans Wake."

[9] Mahaffey, *States of Desire*, 149.

of Justice: Negotiating Sexual and Colonial Difference, he deploys a mixture of post-colonial and psychoanalytic theory to explicate the text. In particular, Valente remarks upon its the "ideologically uncensored" nature which in his opinion, "Vicki Mahaffey has amply demonstrated [as] a gallery of invidious portraitures (of women, Jews, Near Eastern peoples, Italians, etc.) [...]."[10] His critique incorporates a concept of "imperialist abjection," and a detailed exploration of *Giacomo Joyce* as a site of such abjection. He envisions Joyce (as Irish, a British subject, poor and male) caught between a desire to objectify the other as personified by Amalia Popper (Continental, Jewish, wealthy and female), and a wish to ethically and, perhaps, ethnically transcend such desire. For Valente, the dilemma of the text is in its ethical ambivalence:

> The technical innovations that Joyce introduced as a function of this effort simultaneously define *Giacomo Joyce* as a transitional stage in his development as an artist and a somewhat tortured reaction to a moment of political as well as emotional delirium, an attempt to expose and situate his dalliance with some of the deadliest impulses of modern European culture. [...] Joyce translated *Giacomo Joyce* from a rudely formed work to a willfully multivalent text for a specific ethico-political reason, the desire to do justice.[11]

Both these readings of *Giacomo Joyce* foreground the politically transgressive (and, indeed, objectionable) aspects of the text and perceive it as a site of ethical struggle. Both are also extensively dependent upon a closely biographical interpretation of *Giacomo Joyce* in which the "Who?" of the text is assumed to be Amalia Popper. However, another trajectory in Joyce criticism problematises some of these biographical premises. Some facts cannot be denied: *Giacomo Joyce* is indeed remarkable in the context of Joyce's prose writings in that it alone is "set" on the continent; all locational references and

---

10 Valente, *James Joyce and the Problem of Justice,* 67.
11 Valente, *James Joyce and the Problem of Justice,* 67.

allusions are continental and are free of direct associations with Ireland. The events recorded in the text are quite often historically verifiable and have their origins in his experiences while working as an English teacher in Trieste. Similarly, the "hero" of the piece may be closely identified with Joyce himself, or perhaps more accurately, aligned with Joyce's fictions of himself.

The identity of Giacomo's "dark lady" however, has been widely debated since the text's initial appearance. While Ellmann asserts that this figure is likely to have been modelled on Amalia Popper, whom Joyce tutored in the years 1907 and 1908, Helen Barolini, Stelio Crise, Peter Costello, John McCourt and Renzo Crivelli are among some of those who have offered dissenting perspectives.[12] It has been shown that not only are Ellmann's dates slightly inaccurate (Joyce seems to have tutored Amalia Popper between 1908 and 1909) but that there are other contenders for the focus of Joyce's amorous preoccupation, in particular Annie Marie Schleimer with whom Joyce was acquainted earlier and who was not Jewish.[13] As Renzo Crivelli has noted, Joyce tutored Schleimer between 1905 and 1906 and apparently even proposed marriage. Schleimer, unlike Popper, had a fascination with umbrellas and had had an operation for appendicitis.[14]

Such discord with regard to biographical details might initially seem trivial, but it gains enormous significance when biographical criticism is taken as the sole basis for an ethical

---

[12] Helen Barolini, "The Curious Case of Amalia Popper," *New York Review of Books* 20 Nov. 1969: 44-48. Stelio Crise, "Il triestino James Joyce," *Il ritorno di Joyce* proceedings of the Joyce Centenary celebrations, Trieste, 1982. Peter Costello, *James Joyce: The Years of Growth, 1882-1915* (New York: Pantheon Books, 1992). John McCourt, "The Importance of Being Giacomo," *Joyce Studies Annual* 11 (2000): 4-26. Renzo Crivelli, *Itinerari Triestini James Joyce Triestine Itineraries*, trans. John McCourt (Trieste: MGS Press, 1996) and "*Giacomo Joyce*: A Portrait of the Artist as an Imaginary Casanova," UCD Joyce Summer School, Dublin, 20 July 1995.

[13] See Crivelli, "*Giacomo Joyce*: A Portrait of the Artist as an Imaginary Casanova," and *Itinerari Triestini James Joyce Triestine Itineraries*, 58, 60.

[14] Crivelli, "*Giacomo Joyce*: A Portrait of the Artist as an Imaginary Casanova."

analysis of the text, in order to speculate upon the author's motivations and aesthetic or ethical "progress." If we are to consider *Giacomo Joyce* as a "sketchbook," composed over an extended period, then it may be reasonable to assume that he may have used more than one "model." Evidently, the question of desire in *Giacomo Joyce* may be approached from many points of view and eludes simple resolution. As Murray McArthur suggests, we may ultimately have to accept the text as "a private love offering, whose addressee is both known and unknown, hidden in code [...] *Giacomo Joyce* is generically uncertain, both autobiographical and fictional, both continuous and discontinuous, both open and closed."[15] It is, above all, a codified envoy, and this is epitomised, for McArthur, by the image of the umbrella at its conclusion, which might be also said to operate as an "optical code."

OPTICAL CODES IN *GIACOMO JOYCE*

Perception and the ambivalence of "seeing" are at the crux of *Giacomo Joyce*. One means of approaching the way in which perception functions structurally in the text might be to consider it as a type of textual "zootrope." The zootrope is a nineteenth century proto-cinematic optical device consisting of a revolving drum within which a stationary series of images or models (usually of animals or birds) is arranged either parallel with the inner wall or drawn on its surface. The wall of the drum is pierced regularly with slits and when the drum is set in motion the viewer peers through these slits as they pass before the eyes. The result is the illusion that this succession of stationary images or models blends into a single "moving image."[16] In *Giacomo Joyce*, Joyce creates an illusory continuity

---

[15] Murray McArthur, "The Example of Joyce: Derrida Reading Joyce," *JJQ* 32 (1995): 237.

[16] Rosalind Krauss, "The Im/Pulse to See," *Vision and Visuality*, ed. Hal Foster (New York: New Press, 1988) 54-60.

through his assemblage of fragments, each of which may be seen to function like the slits in the barrel of the zootrope, allowing the viewer-reader an intermittent, yet apparently complete, visual apprehension. The subject of each fragment is comparable to those images or models which depict different stages of movement on or within the walls of a zootrope, and similarly may be perceived as both discrete *and* continuous. Furthermore, *Giacomo Joyce* is remarkable for the effect of "double vision" that it involves which may also be comparable to the mechanism of the zootrope. On one level the reader is drawn into an illusion—unravelling a fantasy love story—into, as Rosalind Krauss puts it, "the imaginary identification or closure within the illusion," while being constantly reminded of the mechanism of the fragment through which one peers at that illusion. [17]

Just as the zootrope, when set in motion, pulses to the rhythm of movement within its imaginary space, so *Giacomo Joyce* resonates with the pulse of visual desire. This desire structures the text and generates its introspection. *Giacomo Joyce* is structurally and thematically recursive insofar as it not only recycles (literary) "models" (Beatrice Portinari, Beatrice Cenci, Hester Prynne, Hedda Gabler and so on) but also, as an "affair of the eye," where the eye is turned back upon "I" in the text, calling this "I" into question. *Giacomo Joyce* as an "uncertain text" of desire, as well as a text of "uncertain desire," is propelled by the quasi-dialectical relationship between desire and alterity within its imaginary space.

The optical encoding of this relationship reconnects with the "double vision" solicited by both the zootropic device, and the fragmentary structure of the text, and might be said to demonstrate some aspects of the Lacanian concept of the gaze. The theory of the gaze, as an extension of Lacan's theory of the "mirror stage," proposes that perception is organised around the key principle that "one can only see something by imagining that it is looking at one." As Sheldon Brivic suggests

---

[17] Krauss, "The Im/Pulse to See," 58.

one's perceptions, even of landscapes and still lifes, must be motivated by being drawn toward its objects by desire, and desire is always based on an imagined response [...]. What the eye sees is a field in which the eye itself is an invisible centre, and this field is seen by focusing on a particular point. At the same time, the subject maps himself in the picture [...]. Near the centre of the visual field is a blind spot or hole, a reflection of my pupil, and behind this blind spot is situated the gaze [...]. The centre that covers the gap corresponds to what Lacan calls the *objet petit a*, with the lower case *a* standing for *autre*.[18]

The aperture effect, by which the zootrope "captures" the subject's (optical) desire in its imaginary/invisible centre, is effected in *Giacomo Joyce* not only through the fragment, but also through the obsessive concern with eyes and seeing in the text. Within each frame or fragment of text, the gaze of the subject "I" is directed towards the visual lures of the other. However, from another perspective, *Giacomo Joyce* itself acts as a lure, drawing the eye repeatedly towards its invisible centre, inviting projected meanings and encouraging misrecognition.

To begin with, the text as a visual object—the spaces or gaps between the segments of writing—function to produce a highly visual rendering of the processes of desire, of hesitations, deferrals, approaches and retreats, all of which are faltering, sometimes even convulsive, movements. Via the fragmentary, the absence of a completed, total or ideal work is suggested by what Maurice Blanchot terms a "logic of totality."[19] Yet, as is in evidence in the device of the zootrope, the totality presupposed by the fragment is already dissolved by the existence of the fragment itself. The fragment, therefore, draws attention to the spaces, the absences *within* the text (and the problem of any

18 Sheldon Brivic, "The Gaze," *The Veil of Signs: Joyce, Lacan, and Perception* (Illinois: University of Illinois Press, 1991) 96-97.
19 Maurice Blanchot, *The Step Not Beyond/Le Pas Au-Dela*, trans. and intro. Lycette Nelson (Albany: State University of New York, 1992) 42.

reliable chronology or visual continuum), as well as to the absences *of* text.

Within *Giacomo Joyce*, from the first frame of text, perception is ambivalent and insufficient. The question: "Who?" opens this work, to a quest for identity, but this query is arrested or suspended by the absence of an answer.[20] What follows, rather, is a metonymic shift which emphasises the visual:

> A pale face surrounded by heavy odorous furs. Her movements are shy and nervous. She uses quizzing glasses. [*GJ* 1]

The "Who?" remains indeterminate, while this tropic shift or displacement involves a fragment, a metaphor suggestive of female genitalia, "heavy odorous furs," which symbolise (in psychoanalytic terms) a central lack—the absence of the phallus—expressed in the anxiety of the threat of castration. The indeterminacy of identity encoded in this veiled threat, engendered in "she" (the feminine), introduces the subject and the apparent object of the subject's desire. The "she" here operates already as a type of "blind spot" towards which the subject's gaze is drawn. "She" functions not merely as an object of desire (and, therefore in terms of the gaze, as "a reflection of the pupil" near the centre of the visual field) but, possibly, also ironically as a myopic pupil/student ("She uses quizzing glasses").

However, the passive-active, masculine-feminine, subject-object dichotomy is almost immediately destabilised, and the transmutation of these opposites revolves the zootropic fantasy of the text. "She" acts as the scopic field, or imaginary space, into which the subject is irresistibly lured. "She," as object of desire, is apparently passive; "her movements are shy and nervous" (*GJ* 1). The feminine ideal, situated via lack in passivity, however, is a relation that is disrupted from the very beginning of the text by her use of "quizzing glasses" (*GJ* 1). It

---

[20] For a more detailed discussion of the will to knowledge in *Giacomo Joyce* see Louis Armand "Resistances: Articulating Desire in *Giacomo Joyce*."

is the subject who is caught in this quizzing regard. Within the field of the gaze, the "I" oscillates to the pulse of desire, being both attracted and repelled, attempting mastery and simultaneously fearing the object of its own desire. She, "a pale face," "a young person of quality" (*GJ* 1), then is what, in Lacanian terminology, might be referred to as the illusion or mask of the other, the *objet a*, as fictive counterpart of an hypothesised *Autre.* While the subject is desirous of this "she," as mask of the other, it cannot know her either intellectually or carnally and, by implication, cannot know itself. The frustration of a masculinised will to knowledge reintroduces the question of identity, of what apparently belongs to the "I" and returns to the "blind spot" at the centre of (self)perception. The other as represented by the mask, "she," is not the subject's specular other but an entirely other. The subject is suspended in the desire of the other, to know and be known (or to see and been seen), for affirmation of its own identity, and can only grasp tentatively at this phantom which is always fragmentary and always only a remainder. As is the case with the text's typography, the fragment suggests a totality or total identity that dissolves before it is even formed.

The quizzing gaze of the otherly "she" is followed directly by the subject's desired affirmation:

Yes: a brief syllable. A brief laugh. A brief beat of the eyelids.
[*GJ* 1]

The italicised "yes" implies an imagined response to a question which is absent. Between the query "Who?" and the word "yes" is a lacunary space where the question of identity opens to an ideal object of desire which would affirm the subject. However, as the "yes" is explicated by "A brief syllable," which is then displaced into a chain of substitutions structured around the word "brief," the sought affirmation is dissipated.

With regard to the reiteration of brevity, an allusion might be made to a scene in *Hamlet* (*Hamlet* is mentioned directly in one of the fragments but Hamlet must also be considered as one of the ghosts haunting the text). While watching the opening of "The Mousetrap," Hamlet remarks, "Is this a prologue, or the posy of a ring?" to which Ophelia replies, "'Tis brief, my lord." Hamlet's bitter response "As a woman's love" accords with the theme of thwarted desire in *Giacomo Joyce* (III.ii).

Moreover, the response mutates into more ambivalent forms; a teasing laugh, a beat of eyelids, which alienate the subject or veil and punctuate the scopic field. The rhythm of blinking eye here may also recall the zootropic mechanism, where the slits in the drum and the spaces between them function both to effect the optical illusion of a moving image, while also to interrupt the act of seeing. Repetition of the word "brief" emphasises the imagined affirmation as temporal and impermanent. The subject, the eye of the subject, seeks, is drawn to, the image of the other and is mapped in the field of the gaze, where the subject imagines itself as the object of the gaze.[21] So, in *Giacomo Joyce* we move from the arrested or suspended question "Who?" to "she" as a series of ellipses in which the subject projects its desire through a substitutive tropic spiral. Thus, her gestures articulate the subject's desire without affirming it: the subject reads "Yes" into these gestures, anticipates "Yes" as affirmation of its desire for identity within the gaze.

From this fragmentary, foreclosed affirmation of identity the subject envisions himself as hero, imparting knowledge to his students:

> I launch forth on an easy wave of tepid speech: Swedenborg, the pseudo-Areopagite, Miguel de Molinos, Joachim Abbas. The wave is spent. Her classmate, retwisting her twisted body, purrs in boneless Viennese Italian: *Che coltura!* [GJ 1]

---

[21] Jacques Lacan, *The Four Fundamental Concepts of Psycho-analysis*, trans. Alan Sheridan (London: Hogarth Press and The Institute of Psycho-analysis, 1977) 106.

The subject as active and knowledgeable, is rendered impotent by the gaze in which he is situated—his "wave" of cultural expertise is greeted ultimately with cultivated indifference. The eyes watching him seem independent of a body, as is signalled by the use of a definite article, "*The* long eyelids beat and lift" (*GJ* 1). What the eyelids reveal is an oblique double—the pupil of his pupil—"a burning needleprick stings and quivers in the velvet iris"—the pupil or aperture in which the subject is himself reflected. The sensuous image of "a burning needleprick" stinging and quivering, like an arrow penetrating the eye of the beholder is a sublimation of a desire to penetrate, to know and, therefore, be affirmed by the object/"she" in the metaphor of the gaze. Ironically, the subject's insecurity is revealed too in the ambivalence of the image chosen; the diminutiveness and vulnerability of the quivering point in the scopic field of the other undercuts its potency. Mapped in the scopic field of the gaze the subject is pictured (determined) and yet is always in question.

Evidently, as the frames cited above suggest, eyes as focal points of otherness are central to the text. The subject seeks a response in the eyes of others to his desire. Eyes serve as metaphors for the contradictory nature of this desire, the subject's quest for identity and affirmation, but also as metonyms for the female genitalia, the opening towards which his sublimated carnality is directed. The eyes of women in the text are thus *full* of meaning. As sexually predatory or threatening, they signify the disruption of the subject's sense of security/control. Repeatedly, he is seized by and in the gaze of the other:

> Under the arches in the dark streets near the river the whores' eyes spy out fornicators. [*GJ* 3]

or

> Belluomo rises from the bed of his wife's lover's wife: the busy
> housewife is astir, sloe-eyed, a saucer of acetic acid in her hand.
> [*GJ* 8]

or

> She greets me wintrily and passes up the staircase darting at me
> for an instant out of her sluggish sidelong eyes a jet of liquorish
> venom. [*GJ* 15]

In each of these encounters, the eye bears a threat which is compounded by the conflation of eye imagery with snake metaphors. These gesture more forcefully towards the subject's anxiety. The eyes of this "she," the mask of the other, are those of a "basilisk," a serpent whose glance is lethal and in whose gaze the subject fears obliteration. As snake, then, "she" represents the greatest threat to subject's identity. The suggestion recurs throughout *Giacomo Joyce* via associations with Eve, scales, the twisting of bodies and the coiling of hair. Snake metaphors allude recursively to Eden and the fall of man, where serpent and woman are blended together as agents of temptation and destruction. In this most phallic form it is she who penetrates him. Therefore, this figure becomes the locus of the power of the other and the subject's fear of annihilation.

Significantly, eyes and seeing are frequently linked with adjectives expressing obscurity. They are reproachful, dark, death-bearing: "I see her full dark suffering eyes, beautiful as the eyes of an antelope,"(*GJ* 11) and, as just mentioned, "Her black basilisk eyes" (*GJ* 15). This darkness impedes the subject's vision, is antonymical to his desire for enlightenment, and, simultaneously, suggests what he cannot see, perceive or master. As the fragment of song he quotes indicates, blindness, failure and even death, loom in the shadows;

> *Mine eyes fail in darkness, mine eyes fail,*
> *Mine eyes fail in darkness, love.* [GJ 3]

The process of seeing/looking gives way not to epiphany, nor to the clichéd resolution, "love," but turns to, or rather, turns by means of frustration, for he can never be at the point from which the gaze emanates.

In the exotic gallery of portraitures intermittently offered by the text, the eyes of "her people" are also envoys of an otherness which excludes him:

> They have owls' eyes and owls' wisdom. Owlish wisdom stares from their eyes brooding upon the lore of their *Summa contra Gentiles*. [GJ 8]

Their "owls' eyes" and owlish wisdom might be correlated not only with night and darkness, but also the beautiful, wise and, above all, asexual figure of the goddess Athena. *Glaukopis Athene*, Athena of the flashing eyes, figures as yet another ghost in the composite otherness of the object of desire. The subject's desire for recognition within the gaze is thwarted by the imperviousness of the mask of the other to him as image of the blank (mirror) stare of birdlike eyes conveys. Yet coexistent with the cold brooding gaze, the pulse of deferred carnal fulfilment, suggested by the mocking prospect of "Long lewdly leering lips: dark blooded molluscs" (*GJ* 5), taunts him.

Desire is, therefore, articulated in the double movement of the gaze which holds the subject within the field of the other and within the "scopic field" in which it situates its objects. Thus the gaze pre-exists the eye and "in the dialectic of the eye and the gaze [...] there is no coincidence, but on the contrary, a lure."[22] The eyes of women, of "her people" in the text pose as lures, as masks of the other, towards which the subject's desire is drawn, in which it is, seemingly, reflected. The mask is "the locus of mediation" between the subject and the other.[23] The notion of the lure is also pertinent to webs and veils in the text which metonymically represent the mask of the other, the

---

22   Lacan, *The Four Fundamental Concepts of Psycho-analysis*, 102.
23   Lacan, *The Four Fundamental Concepts of Psycho-analysis*, 102.

frustration of the subject's visual apprehension. Her "websoft" gown (*GJ* 7), "web of stocking" (*GJ* 9) and "cobweb handwriting" (*GJ* 1) lure him towards further indeterminacy, which the veil typifies and disguises.

The subject is preoccupied with the absences signified by the constant shifting of the veils or masks of the other. Visual satisfaction is deferred and displaced repeatedly in the frames of text. This preoccupation is evidenced textually through sensual and erotic missed encounters with the object of desire. The subject idealises what he can see and yet every image is insufficient. This glissage occurs because what he cannot see always destabilises his idealisation of the object/mask. "She" appears only in fragments that the subject attempts to make his own. The subject's will to knowledge is, therefore, perpetually frustrated in the field of the gaze since he can never perceive a whole, merely endless fragments and divisions. This process is most clearly revealed in the eroticised account of an encounter with the phantom body of the object of desire:

> I hold the websoft edges of her gown and drawing them out to hook them I see through the opening of the black veil her lithe body sheathed in an orange shift. It slips its ribbons of moorings at her shoulders and falls slowly: a lithe smooth naked body shimmering with silvery scales. It slips slowly over the slender buttocks of smooth polished silver and over their furrow, a tarnished silver shadow [...]. [*GJ* 7]

Again the zootropic fantasy of the text is directed towards an invisible or illusory centre glimpsed through various apertures or openings. As the "I" peeps through the funereal veils, the eye is drawn to a succession of coverings/masks. As each slips away, another is perceived; the veil, the shift, the scales, the furrow between the buttocks, the shadow of the furrow—the sentence drifts off in an ellipsis, just as the subject's eye is lured further and further inwards never apprehending a totality. And just as the zootrope requires physical contact, or rather, manipulation, to set its optical illusion in motion so too the "I" of this fragment is desirous of such contact, "Fingers, cold and calm and moving …. A touch, a touch" (*GJ* 7), to propel the apparatus of fantasy and illusion of penetration onward and inward.

The subject's desire to assign meaning to the fragments of "she," the mask of the other, is illustrated through the images used in the text. "She" is a collation of the otherness of all women, who fleetingly appear and recede, from the "pox-fouled wenches" (*GJ* 9) to "virgin most prudent" (*GJ* 9). "She" is the desired enigma, the ideal, a paradigm for the desire of the subject encapsulating multiple, contradictory archetypes, from the fallen figure of Eve to the sublime, in the figure of Dante's Beatrice.[24] The subject renders her metaphorically in images which are diversely sensual, sexual, erotic, ironic and clichéd. These metaphors betray a desire to master, consume, or be consumed by her, and as such they are attempts to objectify her. Thus, "she" is "[r]ounded and ripened: rounded by the lathe of intermarriage and ripened in the forcing house of her race" (*GJ* 2) like a fruit which the subject may hope to eat. Later in the text he sees he as a "filly foal" (*GJ* 3) ungainly yet graceful, who as teacher/master he may potentially train. Similarly, she is configured through irony and cliché in terms of conventional feminine vulnerability or foolish vanity; as an antelope, as a "pampered fowl" (*GJ* 8) or twittering bird, a vulnerability which is sensual and charming, but above all an affirmation of his identity as master as the one who assigns the image.

Other fragmentary images—"the tapping clacking" (*GJ* 1) of her heels, "the short skirt taut from the knobs of knees" (*GJ* 4), her "boots laced in deft crisscross over the flesh-warmed tongue" (*GJ* 4), "a white lace edging of an underskirt lifted unduly" (*GJ* 9), her "leg stretched web of stocking" (*GJ* 9) or the "black veiling" (*GJ* 7) of her gown—are significant doubly, for what is revealed and what is concealed, echoing the fragmentation of the text's typography. Desire resonates in the

---

[24] For an extended exploration of the literary references in *Giacomo Joyce* see Vicki Mahaffey, "Giacomo Joyce," in *A Companion to Joyce Studies.*

sensual, erotic emphasis bequeathed to these fragments which gesture toward an illusory whole which would confirm the subject, as well as towards the subject's desire to penetrate or be penetrated by the body evoked by the fragments.

The apparently interminable round of metonymic substitution, allusion and deferral revolving in the frames of the text encode a tendency towards deviation and deviance through the fetishisation of the masks of the other. In this manner desire for fulfilment, (self) recognition and completeness is sublimated and postponed. In regarding the mask of the other (*objet a*) as fetish the subject attempts to assert possession of "she" as object, and of his desire, which ultimately does not belong to him but to the other. By visualising her metaphorically and metonymically in various forms, he attempts to master the illusion of the other by centring himself in the gaze. However, in the images used "she" fluctuates between signification of the ideal of feminine passivity and the threat of the seductress, mirroring the oscillating desire of the subject. The eroticism of "she," in the eye of the subject, is thus always contingent with images of death or negation. In contrast to the coolness and frailty of her gestures, the "steamy damp" of the theatre where he watches her from a distance, literally from the gods, in her "green broidered gown," melds with "the hue of the illusion of the vegetable glass of nature and of lush grass, the hair of graves"(*GJ* 12).

Following the self-reflexive logic of the gaze, the subject is formulated in the imagined response to his desire. He envisions himself in a contradictory manner, which reflects the shifting impressions of the other; he is thwarted, repulsive yet vulnerable and hesitant, "slobbering James" (*GJ* 9), preyed upon by lustful "pox-fouled wenches" (*GJ* 9), the fiery fangs of a "starry snake" (*GJ* 15). The conflation of "she" with Eve and serpents belies the subject's anxiety regarding his will to knowledge and identity in the field of the gaze. Just as the snake in Eden bears "knowledge" (carnal, intellectual) and hence death, so death haunts the erotic. It is hardly accidental, then, that the subject's focus on the Jewish graveyard, which lies ready to receive her body, slips directly from this mouldy "holy field [...] the tomb of her people" (*GJ* 6) to sensuous eroticised images of this body.

The "mechanism" of desire here, therefore, consists of a double "turning," one towards the identity of the object of desire (the assumption of desire as identity) and the other towards sublimated carnality (the fragment which simultaneously suggests and denies the whole). The subject's desire to transgress this body, the mask of the other, can be witnessed in his melodramatic anxiety and mesmeric fascination in conjunction with her operation:

> Operated. The surgeon's knife has probed in her entrails and withdrawn leaving the raw jagged gash of its passage on her belly. I see her full dark suffering eyes, beautiful as the eyes of an antelope. O cruel wound! Libidinous God! [*GJ* 11]

The passage of the surgeon's knife simulates his desired trajectory, but also the anxiety of the elision of the gaze returning to a play of revelation and concealment. The subject in his careful attention to the "cruel wound," betrays a wish to open up the womb, the entrails of the other which substitutes for a wish to return to a place of origin and hence to identity and truth.

The text climaxes with the subject's fantasy of the other as snake. The "coiling approach of starborn flesh" (*GJ* 15) heralds loss and annihilation but also, perhaps, fulfilment of burgeoning desire. Yet, confronted with the visualised approach of the other, the subject oscillates in hesitation:

> Soft sucking lips kiss my left armpit: a coiling kiss on myriad veins. I burn! I crumple like a burning leaf! From my right armpit a fang of flame leaps out. A starry snake has kissed me: a cold nightsnake. I am lost! [*GJ* 15]

The frustration of the subject's fantasy of apprehension / possession is then turned back upon the act of writing itself: "Write it, damn you, write it! What else are you good for?" (*GJ* 16). Ink and the liquid metaphors which precede, signify the threat of obscurity. The bravado of "Take he now who will!" is already undone by the suggestion that his "abundant seed" is infertile. "[H]is soul" merely dissolves in "the darkness of her womanhood" (*GJ* 14) which he can never apprehend in a seminal way. Writing as a means of representation, substitutes for the veil of the other as "she" and mirrors his desire for signification and his sense of being cut off by the impossibility of possessing, perceiving or reproducing the other. Finally, the thwarted eye of the subject comes to rest upon:

> A bare apartment. Torbid daylight. A long black piano: coffin of music. Poised on its edge a woman's hat, red-flowered, and umbrella, furled. Her arms: a casque, gules, and blunt spear on a field, sable. [*GJ* 16]

This empty scene recalls and, somehow, repeats all those other "empty scenes," the blank spaces which have threatened at almost every point to invade the text, rendering even it invisible. Here, the umbrella, as the final veil of the other, may be considered a symbol of the contradictory, multiple and varied nature of the subject's oscillations between the eye and the gaze. As an image it is both phallic in its "blunt spear" and feminine and dissimulating in its "furls."[25] As a metonym for alterity it encodes within its name both the French *ombre* and Latin *umbra*—shadow, semblance, phantom, ghost.[26] The umbrella as an envoy of the other is both a departing opaque, inconclusive message and a reminder/remainder of the "blind spot" so central to the operations of the gaze. The final sections

---

[25] Jacques Derrida, *Spurs: Nietzsche's Styles/Eperons: Les Styles de Nietzsche*, trans. Barbara Harlow (Chicago: Chicago University Press, 1979) 129; Murray McArthur, "The Example of Joyce: Derrida Reading Joyce," *JJQ* 32 (1995): 238; Louis Armand, "Resistances: Articulating Desire in *Giacomo Joyce*."

[26] Armand, "Resistances: Articulating Desire in *Giacomo Joyce*."

of *Giacomo Joyce* have long been the focus of speculation—the arrangement of umbrella and hat may be visualised as an "a," "p" or "a" and "j"—indeed, perhaps, we should even treat them as a peculiar manifestation of the *objet a*.[27] Whatever the "lettering" of the visual message, Joyce leaves us with a powerfully suggestive final image and a "throwaway" instruction: "Envoy: Love me, love my umbrella" (*GJ* 16), which may be just as perceptive and/or ironically accidental as Bloom's racing tip in *Ulysses* and like that "throwaway" may set yet another course of mis/apprehensions in motion.

[27] Vicki Mahaffey has suggested that the umbrella and hat might form the letter "a" ("Giacomo Joyce" 398), while Joseph Valente makes a case for the letter "p" (*James Joyce and the Problem of Justice*, 130) and Murray McArthur ("The Image of the Artist: *Giacomo Joyce*, Ezra Pound and Jacques Derrida") argues for "a" and "j."

John McCourt

Epiphanies of Language, Longing, Liminality in *Giacomo Joyce*

> *Language like desire disrupts—refuses to be contained within boundaries. It speaks itself against our will, in words and thought, that intrude, violate even, the innermost private spaces of mind and body.*
> (Bell Hooks)[1]

Giacomo Joyce is a marginal text in the Joyce canon but not for that an unimportant one. Disrupted and disruptive, it has proven to be a most difficult work to classify, codify, categorise or even date, perhaps because it was written by an author in transition—caught in a liminal state between the "scrupulous meanness" of the still rejected *Dubliners*, the combination of lyricism and naturalism to be found in the partially completed *A Portrait of the Artist as a Young Man* and the larger, polyphonic structures of a *Ulysses* in the earliest stages of conception. Drawing on a wide and eclectic variety of sources, full of

---

[*] I would like to thank the participants at four successive Trieste Joyce Schools who helped me deepen my knowledge of *Giacomo Joyce* during our week-long seminars on the text there.

[1] Bell Hooks, "'this is the oppressor's language/yet I need it to talk to you': Language, a place of struggle," *Between Languages and Cultures. Translations and Cross-Cultural Texts*, eds. Anuradha Dingwaney and Carol Maier (Pittsburgh and London: University of Pittsburgh Press, 1995) 295.

complex narrative techniques and complicated assemblages of words and images, it is a liminal and often contradictory text, caught among genres, and written by an author still languishing in the no-man's land of non-publication (apart from *Chamber Music*), it was composed chiefly for personal use but also with an eye to being read in the future by a larger public (although Joyce did not attempt to publish it he did choose to preserve it and made a fair copy of it). A multi-modal mixture of several genres—part biography, part poetry, part prose narrative, it is a hybrid, sometimes exasperating, polysystemic text, a collection of tiny *mise-en-abîmes* (stories within stories), which is commonly, for want of a better definition, described as a poem-in-prose.

These sixteen hand-written pages written sometime between 1911 and 1914 on both sides of eight large sheets with uneven gaps between the paragraphs (or perhaps better entries or fragments) are largely written in English with a little interwoven Italian, *Triestino*, Latin, and German by the author who hovers in a rather uncomfortable liminal position both outside and inside the text and is both arbitrator and subject of his own narrative, both author struggling with language and form as well as principal character and focalising consciousness of the narrative.

It achieves cohesion through the fact that all its passages are focalised from Giacomo's perspective, sometimes in an obvious way through the use of deictic cues (as when a snatch of dialogue is heard through free indirect discourse), sometimes more obliquely; through the repeated allusions to the most significant context (Trieste); through a highly patterned arrangement of lexical clusters drawn from a variety of conceptual and semantic fields; and through the constant adoption of phonological, lexical, and syntactical features, linguistic devices which give voice to and at the same time contain the complex ambivalence expressed within the text. Joyce's use of language and form in this transitional textual training-ground is of primary importance and represents for the author a moment of culmination. At the same time, the effects he achieves are important prototypes for the more challenging linguistic enterprises that would follow and which bear much in common stylistically with it.

Much has been written in recent years about the thematic concerns of *Giacomo Joyce*, about its precise Triestine background, about its part Austrian, part Italian, Mitteleuropean and Mediterranean socio-cultural backdrop, and about the relevance of this material for both *Ulysses* and *Finnegans Wake*. Now it is clear that the city of Trieste is powerfully inscribed in the pages of Joyce's text and is not simply a location for this chronicle of a doomed love-story, but an active agent in the development of the narrative, a key source text. In his (albeit shadowy and fleeting) depiction of Trieste, Joyce shows that he is just as alive to the social, political and cultural formations that dominate (and that helped shape him as writer because of his interaction with the city) as he is in his other books towards their equivalents in Dublin. As Carla Marengo Vaglio has shown, *Giacomo Joyce* is Joyce's successful attempt "to illustrate Trieste from within, giving a sort of moral portrait of it (the streets, the harbour, the market, the hospital, the theatre, the house of baron Ralli, the israelitic cemetery, the cloudy Carso mountains, trams, the "huddled browntiled roofs, testudo-form" (*GJ* 8). He achieves this encounter with the predominating discourses of Trieste with an effect which is often highly visual, falling only slightly short of being cinematographic, such as in these descriptions of some distinctive features of Trieste, its streets, its awninged markets, its Carso hills:

> At midnight, after music, all the way up the via San Michele
> [*GJ* 6]

> The sellers offer on their altars the first fruits: greenflecked lemons, jewelled cherries, shameful peaches with torn leaves. The carriage passes through the lane of canvas stalls, its wheel-

spokes spinning in the glare. Make way! Her father and his son sit in the carriage [*GJ* 12]

The lady goes apace, apace, apace ..... Pure air on the upland road. Trieste is waking rawly: raw sunlight over its huddled browntiled roofs, testudoform; a multitude of prostate bugs await a national deliverance. [*GJ* 8]

What seems initially to be detached physical description, through a process of ostension and inference rapidly reveals itself to function on other levels, to be multiply voiced, profoundly and irrevocably inter-textual with the ideological formations (Italian and Austrian, patriotic and economic) battling for the soul and the political control of this city Joyce liked to call "my second country." Knowledge of the political context of Trieste teaches us in an instant that this brief passage can be seen to show a political underside in its masterly evocation of the city's powerful Irredentist movement in the image of the "prostrate bugs" waiting to be emancipated—which represent the Italians awaiting deliverance from the Austro-Hungarian Empire, or as Joyce calls it in *Finnegans Wake* "old Auster and Hungrig" (*FW* 464.27-28). A page later, Joyce states the matter more directly, writing: "They love their country when they are quite sure which country it is" (*GJ* 9)—a signal, this, of the liminal identity of the city, one caught between three worlds—Latin, Germanic, and Slav—and at least partially divided as to which it wished to belong to.

Giacomo Joyce is the author's homage to a very particular city, the "docile Trieste" (*GJ* 10) of the highly-cultured, often Jewish, upper-middle class Middle-European elite it was the author's chore, privilege and pleasure to serve as their "*maestro inglese.*" It is also another example of how Joyce's personal life spills over into and inexorably fuels his insatiable creative needs, because it contains another Joycean self-portrait, one in which a continentalised version of the author (now aged around thirty) becomes fascinated with a mysterious young

Triestine girl.[2] She represents a highly educated type (Joyce would have been one of a procession of private tutors who gave lessons in their homes), that was singularly assured and independent, possessing a range of qualities not always common in other women of their age. Jewish or at least of Jewish extraction, these girls studied music—"A long black piano" (*GJ* 16)—sometimes attended university (in Vienna, Graz, or Florence); they spoke, in addition to the local *lingua franca Triestino*,[3] at least three languages (Italian, German, English or French), and were usually widely read—"A lady of letters" (*GJ* 12); they engaged in rigorous sporting activities, such as cycling, horse-riding, skiing—"Papa and the girls sliding downhill, astride of a toboggan" (*GJ* 4)—gymnastics, and at the same time, were highly fashion conscious—"She is dressing to go to the play" (*GJ* 6).[4] They were (like Nora, but for very different reasons) emancipated and modern young ladies who were aware of the sexual and intellectual attraction they could exercise over a young man such as Joyce.

Beyond an appreciation of these generalised characteristics, the exact identification of the "Who?" is as unimportant to a reader's understanding of the text as a possible identification of the dark lady of Shakespeare's sonnets or as slight as the fact that the woman who inspired Yeats happened to be Maud Gonne (and yet Joyceans, after Ellmann, continue to casually and convincingly name the "culprit" *Giacomo* falls for, as though they knew who it was and as though it really mattered).

---

[2] Three candidates have been identified—Amalia Popper, Annie Schleimer, and Emma Cuzzi—but Joyce's female creation may well be judged to be a composite of all of these and perhaps other students as well.

[3] Joyce never confused *Triestino* with standard Italian, which the Triestines referred to as *regnicolo*, as can be seen in his one hundred odd letters written in a mixture of both to his brother Stanislaus (who joined him in Trieste in 1905 and lived and worked there until his death on 16 June 1955), to his children, Giorgio and Lucia, and to his friends Ettore Schmitz and Alessandro Francini Bruni.

[4] See Raffaella Sgubin, "Between Paris and Vienna: Fashion in Joyce's Trieste," *Le Donne di Giacomo*, eds. Renzo Crivelli and John McCourt (Trieste: Hammerle Editori, 1999) 26-33.

The "Who" question at the opening has led too many of us on a false grail in attempts to solve a puzzle which is as unresolvable as that of the M'intosh mystery in *Ulysses* or the countless linguistic puzzles in *Finnegans Wake*. The fact is that Joyce places a bald rhetorical question—"Who"—simply as the point of departure from which he jolts *Giacomo Joyce* into being written. For this reason, the text is ultimately at least as much about Giacomo himself as it is about the lady or ladies who inspired it and who are brought into being only through the power of the author's distinctly male pen. Like love poetry—it tells us as much about the poet as it does about the object of his affections.[5] If Yeats could construct a body of poetry out of his unrequited love for Maud Gonne, then why should Joyce not allow himself just a few indulgent pages to remember his

---

[5] The Italian-Irish title *Giacomo Joyce* evokes a different vision of the writer to the one to which we are accustomed, suggesting a man comfortably acclimatised to life in Trieste, steeped in Italian culture, literature and language—an Italianised Irishman pleased to stray into the shadows of illustrious Giacomos before him such as Leopardi, Puccini, and Casanova. As various official documents relating to Joyce in Trieste show, the writer was habitually referred to as Giacomo (or sometimes Giac.) and he seems to have enjoyed adopting the name and indulging in the various Triestine nuances it evoked. He signed a letter written in the Triestine dialect to Italo Svevo "Giacometo" and another, dated 8 September 1920 to Francini Bruni, "Jacomo Del Oio, sudito botanico." In this case the "Jacomo" is Giacomo as it would have been spelt in Triestine dialect, the "sudito botanico" a Triestinised version of the Italian "suddito (subject)—it was and is the habit of Triestines never to pronounce double letters and their dialect reflects this—and a pun on Britannico" (British) which Joyce's passport declared he was; the "del Oio" carries a conscious hint of Joyce's financial woes in its echo of a Triestine idiom "Scampar coi bori de l'oio" (to flee from the paying of debts). The writer re-evokes his money troubles in another letter written on 20 February 1924, when he mentions "S. Giacomo in Monte di pietà," referring to the working-class district of Trieste which bore his name and was just up the street from his house in via Bramante (he changed the name slightly from San Giacomo in Monte (Saint James on the hill) to the more apt "San Giacomo in Monte di pietà" (Saint James in the pawnbrokers)—thus evoking a place he was forced to visit as a customer all-too-often during his Triestine years. Finally, in a letter written in the unhappy thirties to Lucia, he ironically translates himself as "Giacomo Giocondo"—James joyful.

Triestine flame or better in which to record his own highly personalised and sometimes erotic feelings about her?

The images of the woman which emerge from the 50 paragraphs of *Giacomo Joyce* are contradictory and clearly mirror Giacomo's own oscillating feelings towards her. While sometimes he imagines her yielding to his advances, drawing him on, other times he clearly attempts to place a gap between himself and this temptress who obsesses him with her gaze, her culture, her style, her education, her physical beauty, her sexuality, her frailness, her youth, her self assurance. For much of the narrative, he remains almost entirely in the shade, like a true voyeur allowing his reader to share a peep with him from the darkness at the unaware object of his desires. In other sections he encounters her in impersonal social, public occasions. Both the public and the private occasions for seeing her reveal that Giacomo's place is uncertain and often he seems at best in a marginal position, hovering about on the edge of her social world, and is totally unsure of his place in her life and of his place in hers.

The class gap which divides them is constantly rendered apparent in the text and it serves to underline Giacomo's liminality, in the sense that it refers to a transitional period during which the participant lacks social status or rank. Giacomo is clearly socially inferior to this "young person of quality" (*GJ* 1); when he calls to her house, and awaits her, he imagines a maid announcing to her in her "upper room" (*GJ* 6): "There is one below would speak with your ladyship" (*GJ* 1). She is so refined that "She never blows her nose" (*GJ* 2), and is someone who "does the simplest acts with distinction" (*GJ* 5). He is often physically distant from her, for example, gazing up at her window "I look upward from night and mud" (*GJ* 6) or seeing her on the Carso hills, "*The lady goes apace apace, apace ......* Pure air on the upland road" (*GJ* 8). The only time he actually manages to look down on her is when he is in the cheap seats in the *loggione* of the Teatro Verdi immersed in "[a] symphony of smells" (*GJ* 12), and she is below is in the expensive and elegant *parterre*, seated, radiantly, among the city's elite.

His ticket to her world, to upper middle class Triestine society is his education and his role as teacher. But even this is something of a poisoned chalice. The *maestro inglese* was tolerated for a couple of hours a week rather than embraced as a family friend, a social equal, and some of Joyce's of haughtier students would have been well capable of reminding him of his place, as what Stelio Crise called a "maestruncolo"—a mere teacher of English.[6] Nora's absence from most of the scenes of this text—including those not directly describing Giacomo's relationship with the mystery lady, has an autobiographical verity—and is no doubt a reflection of Joyce's own embarrassment at bringing a poorly dressed, uneducated wife into the type of society personified by his young female students. There is little doubt that Nora spent at least the early Triestine years almost hidden in one of their many apartments, only occasionally accompanying Joyce to the theatre or to other social occasions—because she had to bear and then look after the children, because she did usually not have the money or the clothes to go out in "society" of any but the lowest sort, and because she lacked the Italian to enjoy most of the company Trieste might have offered. Unlike his partner, Joyce played his educational hand for all it was worth to earn, despite his relative penury, a foothold in the bourgeois Trieste society which is represented in the text by the mystery lady. Thus he had no bones about launching "forth on an airy wave of tepid speech: Swedenborg, the pseudo-Areopagite, Miguel de Molinos, Joachim Abbas" (*GJ* 1)—or about wryly dismissing his student for having dared to express an opinion about his *A Portrait of an Artist as a Young Man*: "She says that, had *The Portrait of the Artist* been frank only for frankness' sake, she would have asked why I had given it to her to read. O you would, would you? A lady of letters" (*GJ* 12).

---

6 Stelio Crise, "Il Triestino James Joyce," *Scritti*, ed. Elvio Guagnini (Trieste: Edizioni Parnaso, 1995) 111-112.

The partial put down contained in his wry comment was poor reward for years of literary labour. As far as most Triestines knew Joyce was just another English language teacher. Yet even if he languished in the no-man's land of non-publication and struggled to make a living, he never let his disappointments block his developing ideas about his own writing. *Giacomo Joyce* represents a crucial moment in the development of those ideas, a key turning point in his creative growth curve. Giorgio Melchiori has identified it as a necessary middle stage in Joyce's career in which the reader can perceive both "his faithfulness to the principles and discoveries of his early youth" and "the effort to reconcile the static character of the epiphany with narrative dynamics."[7] *Giacomo Joyce* is, in fact, Joyce's most concentrated and pure epiphanic work, one which presents a layered succession of transitory moments of revelation and insight constructed around the link between implicit sexuality and an overt attention to language.[8] The text of *Giacomo Joyce* is libidinally driven and the dynamics of its composition and content shows parallels with Friedrich Nietzsche's description of Raphael's *Madonnas* as being the products of an overheated sexual imagination struggling to find literal expression. The *inamorata* of *Giacomo Joyce*, who, as Fritz Senn notes, takes in "almost the whole range of the archetypal manifestations of the female,"[9] is the product—part enchantress, temptress, siren or *femme fatale*, part *Madonna* (*virgo prudentissima*), part muse, part Amazon—of a lively sexual fantasy struggling to be captured in words.

This struggle is bound up in the repeated and varied use of the epiphanic form, Stanislaus Joyce's explanation of which is helpful here:

[7] Giorgio Melchiori, *Joyce: Il Mestiere dello scrittore* (Torino: Einaudi, 1994) 56.

[8] This link fits in rather well with a central dynamic of the later parts of *A Portrait of the Artist as a Young Man* (which were being composed around the same time) as Derek Attridge has shown. Derek Attridge, *Joyce Effects: Transforming Language, History, and Theory* (Cambridge: Cambridge University Press, 2000) 64.

[9] Fritz Senn, "Some Further Notes on *Giacomo Joyce*," *JJQ* 5 (1968): 233.

Another experimental form which his literary urge took while we were living at this address consisted in the noting of what he called "epiphanies"—manifestations or revelations. [...] Epiphanies were always brief sketches, hardly ever more than some dozen lines in length, but always very accurately observed and noted, the matter being so slight. [...] The epiphanies became more frequently subjective and included dreams which he considered in some way revelatory.[10]

In *Stephen Hero*, Joyce himself describes the minor experience that leads Stephen to discover the concept of epiphany and it is one which reveals a parallel with the succession of epiphanic movements all built around a series of rather slight events in *Giacomo Joyce*, most of which are inspired by the mystery lady of the text:

a trivial incident set him composing some ardent verses which he entitled a "Vilanelle of the Temptress." A young lady was standing on the steps of one of those brown brick houses which seem the very incarnation of Irish paralysis. A young gentleman was leaning on the rusty railings of the area. Stephen as he passed on his quest heard the following fragment of colloquy out of which he received an impression keen enough to afflict his sensitiveness very severely.

The Young Lady—(drawling discreetly) ... O, yes ... I was ... at the ... cha ... pel ...
The Young Gentleman—(inaudibly) ... I ... (again inaudibly) ... I
...
The Young Lady—(softly) ... O ... but you're ... ve ... ry ... wick ... ed ...

This triviality made him think of collecting many such moments together in a book of epiphanies. By an epiphany he meant a sudden spiritual manifestation, whether in the vulgarity of speech or of gesture or in a memorable phase of the

10   Stanislaus Joyce, *My Brother's Keeper* (New York: Viking Press, 1958) 124-125.

> mind itself. He believed that it was for the man of letters to
> record these epiphanies with extreme care, seeing that they
> themselves are the most delicate and evanescent of moments.
> [*SH* 211]

Something very similar happens repeatedly in the paragraphs of *Giacomo Joyce* even if the overall epiphanic effect is only realised in the totality of the book's almost web-like structure, in the accumulation of detail and in the undulating intensity of the feelings expressed. The entries of *Giacomo Joyce*, like the epiphany recorded in *Stephen Hero*, are inspired by a beautiful young lady, seen as a temptress; they record a series of "delicate and evanescent" moments "with extreme care" and are replete with examples of "trivial incident," "fragment of colloquy," "vulgarity of speech or of gesture," and "memorable phrase," to such an extent that it seems as though Joyce was attempting to push his use of the epiphanic form to its very limits before abandoning it in *Ulysses* for other, larger and more polyphonic stylistic effects and techniques.

Apart from representing a moment of closure with regard to the epiphanic techniques of the early writing, the stylistic thickening, the heightened linguistic focus, the ever more self-conscious word play and the search for multi-modal effects (for example musical and visual ones), and the generally enigmatic and liminal nature of *Giacomo Joyce* are, collectively, stylistic keys to much of the writing that was to follow and represent the writer passing somewhat uneasily through a threshold which will see him move from Stephen to Bloom, from youth to middle age, from *A Portrait* to *Ulysses*, from being an Irish writer to being a truly continental one, from obscurity to centre stage.

Indeed many telling thematic and textual elements from *Giacomo Joyce* would be transferred by Joyce from the margins of his Triestine prose poem to the centre stage of the Dublin masterpiece *Ulysses*. The text's liminality would be underlined in this plundering of its words, passages and effects used to flesh out Stephen Dedalus's Paris but also, and more significantly, to add substance to Joyce's Mediterranean Dubliner, Molly Bloom. As Neil Davison put it, Joyce created Molly "out of the buried remnants of his dark lady (of *Giacomo Joyce*) coupled with the experience of his true intimacy with Nora Barnacle."[11] And several of his other ladies in *Ulysses* too, for Joyce was far from precious about his materials. If they did not fit in the most obvious place (Molly Bloom) they would not be abandoned but placed elsewhere. Thus our mystery lady and her text would reappear not only in "Penelope" but also in "Calypso" where her "shapely haunches" would be redrawn as the "vigorous hips" (*U* 4.172) and "moving hams" (*U* 4.148) of the "next door girl at the counter" admired by Bloom in Moses Dlugacz's butcher's shop (Dlugacz, a Zionist Jew and friend of Joyce's, is the only Triestine to appear under his own name in *Ulysses*). In "Circe" the mystery girl's "quizzing-glasses" would be worn by Mrs. Bellingham, who recounts that Bloom addressed her "in several handwritings with fulsome compliments as a Venus in furs" (*U* 15.1045), thus recalling the "heavy odorous furs" (*GJ* 1) of *Giacomo Joyce*. Both images aptly recall *Venus im Pelz* by Austrian author, Leopold von Sacher Masoch (1836-1895). The mystery lady turns up again in "Sirens" as Sebastian Knowles has recently shown in his book *The Dublin Helix: The Life of Language in Joyce's Ulysses*:

The dominant narrative voices for *Giacomo Joyce* and "Sirens" are pitched together; witness the parallel descriptions of the hair of the Giacomo girl and Mina Kennedy: "She walks before me along the corridor and as she walks a dark coil of her hair slowly uncoils and falls. Slowly uncoiling, falling hair" (*GJ* 11) and "Miss Kennedy sauntered sadly from bright light, twining a loose hair behind an ear. Sauntering sadly, gold no more, she twisted twine a hair. Sadly she twined in sauntering gold hair behind a curving ear" (*U* 258). The playful, singsong voice in "Sirens" reappears in the opening of *Giacomo Joyce*:

[11] Neil Davison, *James Joyce, Ulysses, and the Construction of Jewish Identity: Culture, Biography and "the Jew" in Modernist Europe* (Cambridge: Cambridge University Press, 1998) 52.

"High heels clack hollow on the resonant stone stairs. [...] Tapping clacking heels, a high and hollow noise" (*GJ* 1). Parallels of word play, musical syntax, and attention to sound, together with the flashes of petticoat, connect the Giacomo girl with the sirens of Joyce's fiction.[12]

Giacomo Joyce became a quarry Joyce would later draw from as well as a polished jewel he felt was finished. Above all else it is evocative of its author being in transition, a fact this, which is symbolised by its being a liminal text, drawing on many genres but belonging to none if not the marginal sub-genre of the epiphany. The textual structure of the work, with its scattered paragraphs divided by surprisingly large and uneven bridges of white space, its words "betwixt and between" significant blank gaps, is itself highly suggestive of liminality. The text repeatedly portrays images of liminal spaces, which are internal and external physical features—the "stairs" of her castle, the "piazza" that he sees her crossing, the window through which he sees her "dressing to go to the play" (*GJ* 6), the "via San Michele" (*GJ* 6) he walks up thinking about her, the "upland road" she travels on horseback, the "vast gargoyled church" (*GJ* 10) in Paris, the "corridor" (*GJ* 10) along which she walks before him, (*GJ* 11) the gap from the *loggione* to the *parterre* of the Teatro Verdi from which he looks down to see her, (*GJ* 12) the doorway of "Ralli's house" (*GJ* 14) where he comes "upon her suddenly," the "yellow shadow of the hall" where she stands (*GJ* 14-15). Liminality is also suggested in the temporal images in the text in which the evocation of the passage between day and night, night and day is a recurring one, to be seen, for example, in the images of the girl crossing the *piazza* in the "twilight," of Trieste "waking rawly" (*GJ* 8) and of "the raw veiled spring morning" (*GJ* 10) of Paris. Further images suggest a transitory state, neither bright nor dark: "summer haze" (*GJ* 2), "moving mists [...] hanging mists" (*GJ* 6), "tawny gloom [...] raw mist-veiled morning" (*GJ* 10), "grey vapour" (*GJ* 14), "the

---

[12] Sebastian D.G. Knowles, *The Dublin Helix: The Life of Language in Joyce's Ulysses* (Florida: University Press of Florida, 2001) 151.

yellow shadow of the hall" (*GJ* 14-15), "vague mist" and "Torbid daylight" (*GJ* 16).

The text also derives much of its liminality from its borrowings from other art forms, for example on visual art techniques and from the sense it produces of being hybrid, not quite fitting into any established categories but occupying an uneasy space somewhere between public and private.[13] The use of artistic techniques is also allied to the fact that the background keeps changing—so completely and totally that it becomes foregrounded in the mind of the reader. I particularly have in mind the second and third pages of the text which move from undefined Trieste to named Vercelli and Padua and then back to unnamed Trieste. In the "ricefield near Vercelli" segment, particular attention is given to colours and hues to the extent that it sometimes verges towards the painterly, palpitating as it does with movement, shadowy light and life:

> A ricefield near Vercelli under creamy summer haze. The wings of her drooping hat shadow her false smile. Shadows streak her falsely smiling face, smitten by the hot creamy light, grey wheyhued shadows under the jawbones, streaks of eggyolk yellow on the moistened brow, rancid yellow humour lurking within the softened pulp of the eyes. [*GJ* 2]

The movement of the shadows is caught in the alliterating sibilants "s" and "sh" of "shadows," "streak," "smiling," "smitten," "shadows," in the repetitions of the substantive "shadow" (an example of anaphora) and of the verb "streak" (polyptoton) and in the closing "s" of "shadows," "streaks," "jawbones," in the assonating internal "s" to be found in "falsely" and "moistened." The iterating hissing of these sibilants connects with images which come later in the text, of a

---

13 For a full discussion of Joyce's complex relationship with the visual arts see Maria Elisabeth Kronegger, *James Joyce and Associated Image Makers* (New Haven: Yale University Press, 1968) and Archie Loss, *Joyce's Visible Art (The Work of Joyce and the Visual Arts 1904-1922)* (Ann Arbor: University of Michigan Research Press, 1984).

temptress who calls to mind Salomé, a coiling, snake-like creature—"a lithe smooth naked body shimmering with silvery scales" who is trying to entrap him with her "cruel eyes" in the sexually charged passage in which the voyeur imagines her taking off her orange shift (*GJ* 7) and which, in just six lines, includes another burst of sibilants in the words "slips, shoulders, slowly, smooth, silvery scales, slips, slowly, slender, smooth, silver shadow."

The colours in the Vercelli passage are not substantive but in-between and their watery, gooey, intermediary nature is underlined by the composite adjectives and nouns Joyce uses to describe them—"wheyhued" and "eggyolk." It seems more than possible that Joyce was learning from his discussions with several of the Triestine artists he knew at first hand, such as the portrait painters, Argio Orell (who had studied with Stuck and Klimt), and Tullio Silvestri (who painted portraits of Nora in 1913 and Joyce in 1914).[14] Francini Bruni remembered that "Silvestri's style of painting was unique—he charged at the painting with darting strokes—impressionistic, with no preliminary drawing" and there seems to be an echo of this technique of "darting strokes" in Joyce's choice of the past participle "smitten" (from "smite") meaning struck, as with a hard blow.

The brief entry which follows: "A flower given by her to my daughter. Frail gift, frail giver, frail blue-veined child" (*GJ* 3), has no sense of time or space but a pragmatic reading of it allows us to connect it with a specific occasion in which the lady gave Lucia a flower. The same event was also the occasion

---

14 Tullio Silvestri was thus remembered by Joyce's best Triestine friend, Alessandro Francini Bruni: "Silvestri was in the group of Francini and Joyce. He was a lively, gay man, the perfect Bohemian, always poor, married to a nice wife. Silvestri used to come to see Joyce all the time. He was a Venetian who had lived in Trieste, played the guitar and sang baritone, Joyce would sing with him. Silvestri's style of painting was unique—he charged at the painting with darting strokes—impressionistic, with no preliminary drawing." In Richard Ellmann's partially unpublished interview with Francini Bruni in July 1954. The notes of this interview are kept in the Richard Ellmann Collection in Tulsa.

of Joyce's almost identical poem, "A Flower Given to my Daughter" which he dated "Trieste 1913." In the *Giacomo Joyce* entry, using the rhetorical device, *conduplicatio*, Joyce insistently repeats the word "frail" in the paratactic second sentence as though forcing the reader to consider its various meanings— easily led into evil, easily destroyed, physically weak. The lack of specific context—time or location—adds to the sensation that woman in general and not just the mystery lady is somehow being defined as frail as though in echo of Shakespeare's "Frailty, thy name is woman" which Joyce would have had fresh in his head from his teaching of *Hamlet* to the Triestines at the *Università Popolare* in 1912. The flower (the gift), a traditional metonym for innocence and youth, is frail in the sense that it is easily destroyed, the giver is frail (a fact further emphasised by the choice of the passive verb form), in the sense that she is physically and morally weak, the child is weak for some or all of these reasons. What renders woman frail is the same flower—her sexuality—passed on from generation to generation as the now mature mystery lady passes it on to Joyce's own daughter.

Which leads neatly into the next passage and a direct sexual encounter. The scene is no longer the liminal, shadowy city of Trieste but a Padua doused in night darkness and populated with whores whose "eyes spy out for fornicators" (which is a nice way of transferring responsibility onto the woman rather than those who avail of their services). It is a nightmare scene (another twist of the image of history as a nightmare from which Stephen Dedalus is trying to awake), in which we are shown the very "darkness of history." If we miss the point, Joyce reiterates the "dark" four times and "darkness," a further four. In all this darkness, his eyes "fail"—not so much "go wrong" as "betray," a failure which is morphologically (through sound association) linked back to "frail" of the previous entry. In yielding in the darkness to prostitutes, he has failed both the mystery lady and his own daughter (not to mention, which he doesn't, Nora). Betrayal is centre stage now as it would be later in *Ulysses* and sex itself has become a dark, shameful act "a dark wave of sense," a personal nightmare.

From the blackness of Padua, the scene returns to the twilight of Trieste. Once again, a Triestine scene is connoted as liminal by the use of dim, in between light, "Twilight," "dusk," which is neither bright nor dark, but at the same time inevitably headed for the decline suggested by another connotation of the world "twilight" (as Trieste undoubtedly was, following the First World War). The location is another space between—the piazza to be crossed—with the sea close by, described in the image of the "wide sagegreen pasturelands," a vision *par excellence* of liminality. The repetition of the word "eve," connotes not just evening but a period before something, another in-between time. This is further complicated by the unavoidable echo of Eve—as Adam's wife, another female temptress figure, another image of women's sexuality leading to man's downfall.

Repeatedly over the following pages, the reader is brought to experience Giacomo's mixture of dread and desire, the psychological confusion which sees him caught between his attraction towards the mystery lady and his sense of duty towards Nora. He resents the power of attraction the mystery girl holds over him and one of his answers to being almost overpowered by her is to render her silent and passive in the text, by depersonalising her into a series of stereotypes—for example in the images that recall a temptress like Salomé and suggest a coiling, snake-like creature—"a lithe smooth naked body shimmering with silvery scales" who is trying to entrap him with her "cruel eyes."[15]

Apart from describing her in sexually charged stereotypical language, his wavering attitudes towards her are suggested by the contrasting images of strength and weakness which he attributes to her. The penultimate paragraph offers a brief re-

---

[15] For a more detailed exploration of the dynamics at work here see John McCourt, "The Importance of Being Giacomo," *Joyce Studies Annual* 11 (2000): 4-26.

run of the battle royal that has been waged between them throughout the book and yet another usage of the visual art techniques that have been apparent throughout.

> Unreadiness. A bare apartment. Torbid daylight. A long black piano: coffin of music. Poised on its edge a woman's hat, red-flowered, and umbrella, furled. Her arms: a casque, gules, and blunt spear on a field, sable. [*GJ* 16]

These combined images convey a still-life quality. In fact there is little movement of any sort but rather an attention to tiny detail, to colour and to light, a sense of harmony. Joyce's description palpitates with potential movement and with life despite the absence of a human subject and the presence of the oxymoronic coffin-like piano. It is a paragraph rich in contradiction as though it somehow summarised all of his ambivalence towards the lady. This is made apparent in the repeated use of oxymorons—the noun "Unreadiness" suggesting a lack of preparation is followed by a detailed description of a carefully prepared scene; "Torbid daylight" (which juxtaposes images of darkness and light); "piano" as "coffin of music" rather than producer of sound; "blunt spear" (a spear by definition is a sharp pointed object). The sense of something about to happen, initially negated by the word "unreadiness" is contained in the "poised" and also suggested by the "furled."

While the earlier "Vercelli" episode had seemed a conscious exercise in impressionism, this bare apartment scene reads almost like an example of the ancient Greek rhetorical exercise of *ekphrasis*—a literary description of a real or an imaginary visual work of art.[16] The *ekphrasis* parallel is given further weight by the fact that one of the classic examples often given of *ekphrasis* is the description of Achilles's shield in the *Iliad*. Interestingly Joyce's vision here also calls to mind heraldry—

---

16 See John Hollander, "The Poetics of ekphrasis," *Word and Image*, 4.1 (1988): 209-219.

the source of one of this segment's key lexical clusters—which is initiated and sanctioned by the fact that she lives in a turreted castle (as we have seen on the book's very first page "Wintry air in the castle, gibbeted coats of mail, rude iron sconces over the windings of the winding turret stairs" (*GJ* 1). Her coat of arms, her blazonry—essentially medieval usages—contains several words to do with heraldry, most of which came into English from Middle French, for example, "casque" (from Middle French) to signify a medieval helmet, "gules" (from Middle French "goules") signifying the heraldic colour red which links with "sable" (black), another one of the heraldic colours. These items of battle-dress (ironic recastings of the hat and umbrella) connect with earlier descriptions of her protective clothing. We see her sliding downhill on a toboggan, "Tightly capped and jacketted, boots laced in deft crisscross [...] the short skirt taut" (*GJ* 4). As is recalled in Shakespeare's *All's Well That Ends Well*, it is "birth and virtue gives you heraldry" (II.iii) and clearly the mystery lady of Joyce's text qualifies on both counts, being both "a young person of quality" (*GJ* 1) and, a "virgin most prudent."

This association of the mystery girl with images of strength is in stark contrast with other depictions of her as a small, weak animal, "small witless helpless" bird, "a sparrow" (*GJ* 7), "a bird twittering after storm, happy that its little foolish life has fluttered out of reach of the clutching fingers of an epileptic lord and giver of life, twittering happily, twittering and chirping happily" (*GJ* 11), a "black pullet"—young hen—(*GJ* 12), a series of specific bird references which form another lexical cluster and can be associatively connected with other words connected with weak animals, such as "filly foal" or with birds. On the very first page we read of "a brief beat" of her eyelids which later "beat and lift," a movement which is suggestive of the flapping of bird wings. Again she is pictured at the top of her "winding turret," a not unlikely place for a bird to nest, but also a place in which both the bird image and the battle dress images can merge if we think of turret not simply as a small tower extending above her castle-like house but as a fortress or weapons platform. These contrasting groups of lexical clusters, calling up images of strength and of fragility alternatively, evoke the larger battle being played out in the text between the mystery lady and her *maestro inglese*.

The final pages of the book represent something of a liberation for the girl and perhaps for Giacomo too. Even if Giacomo has done his utmost to silence this sylph-like figure of desire and dread, the final pages of the text bring something of a reverse. The spell she has cast over him has somehow been broken and with it the artistic stranglehold with which he has constrained her. As Joseph Valente has pointed out: "The poisonous writing of Joyce's antidotal re-reading, which takes some account of her positive otherness, acknowledges, however obscurely, her separate perspective, agency, and value, and in the process, alters the internal design of the work so as to bring out the systematic stifling and gradual emergence of her voice."[17]

If *Giacomo Joyce* shows a silenced lady reluctantly been given a voice, perhaps it also in part dramatises something of Joyce's own trauma at having remained essentially in silence for the better part of a decade in Trieste, his writerly ambitions on hold as he sought to make a living as an English teacher before the publication of *A Portrait* and *Dubliners*. Apart from hinting at his writerly frustrations, the Giacomo of *Giacomo Joyce* leaves an image of Giacomo as an unsettled and liminal figure, not simply caught between lustful longing and guilt and repulsion, but one living with a dramatic sense of not fully fitting in: he no more belongs to the Triestine world of the mystery girl than he does to the Ireland he has long since abandoned. Joyce's two epithets for himself in the book—*Giacomo Joyce* and *maestro inglese*, evoke contrasting images of two distinct in-between figures; on the one hand, a splintered, Italian-Irish hybrid, and secondly, an English teacher, with all the imperialistic backspin

---

[17] Joseph Valente, *James Joyce and the Problem of Justice: Negotiating Sexual and Colonial Difference* (London: Cambridge University Press, 1995) 70.

which that term contains for a semi-colonial Irishman like Joyce. The *maestro inglese*—a master of the English language—image also conjures a view that would have inspired ambivalence in Joyce the writer who often felt the need to break out of the straitjacket of that definition in his later work.

Beyond these epithets, what *Giacomo Joyce* epitomises is a Joyce who has not yet found his place, who is still forced to live unacknowledged in a geographic periphery and in a marginalised public position. This was a situation he had already become familiar with in Dublin having formed himself there as a writer of Hiberno-English trying to impact upon the English speaking world from his own hyphenated culture. His long-term residence in the equally fragmented city of Trieste put a considerable and important new spin on his attitude of non-affiliation however.

All these issues come to a head in the shadowy and multi-liminal text that is *Giacomo Joyce*; in Trieste, a liminal city on the edge of Eastern and Western Europe, a borderland connecting Europe with the East, a sometimes purgatorial workshop through which Joyce must pass before arriving at the promised land of success in Paris. By the end of the book Giacomo has passed through the threshold (from the Latin *limin*) of an important personal epiphany, a rite of passage, a major change, which is in part personal, in part to do with his writing but which has all to do with his coming of age, in every sense of that term. As the final page puts it "Youth has an end: the end is here" (*GJ* 16). The time has come for Joyce to move in from the westernmost and easternmost margins of Europe—Dublin and Trieste—and to position himself at its creative but more neutral centre, Paris, from where he could cease to look inwards with Giacomo and begin to look outwards again with Bloom.

Sheldon Brivic

The Adultery of Wisdom in *Giacomo Joyce*

Joyce's *Giacomo Joyce* practices erotic fantasy as a spiritual exercise in reverse, in which the purpose is not to express devotion to God, but to steal devotion from God. The beauty that is supposed to belong to God is here claimed through art as a subversive parody of divine creation. God's love for the world is turned to voyeurism, and His creative mind, to the contemplation of adulterous lust. By such devilish practice, the conceptual basis of Modernism is laid.

In *A Portrait*, which Joyce was completing around the same time he completed *Giacomo Joyce* in 1914, Stephen Dedalus expands on Aquinas's definition of beauty, which requires three things; wholeness, harmony and radiance (*P* 212). This formula comes from a passage in the *Summa Theologiae* describing Christ (Question 39, article 8), so it describes how God divided himself into the world to produce beauty, and Stephen follows this process through the stages of aesthetic perception.[1] The central sin of Satan was to want to replace God or enact His powers, and Joyce was aware that his artistic imitation of God was always Satanic. When Giacomo is afraid that the woman he mediates on—identified by Richard Ellmann

---

[1] William T. Noon, S.J., explains Stephen's use of Aquinas in *Joyce and Aquinas* (New Haven: Yale University Press, 1957) 105ff.

as Amalia Popper[2]—may not return from a visit to the hospital, he exclaims, "Surely hell's luck will not fail me!" (*GJ* 9). He realises that his attempt to appropriate God's power puts his on the side of the damned.

The object of beauty is always taken from paternal authority, just as language must be taken from tradition. When Giacomo entreats, "Ignatius Loyola, make haste to help me!" (*GJ* 5), he wants to use his skill at recollection through the senses to complete the full depiction of the woman's father. "Papa" occupies the position of Giacomo's potential enemy insofar as the old man wants to protect his daughter. It is necessary for Giacomo to focus on the complexity of the father—who projects not only "benevolence," but "suspicion" and "warning" (*GJ* 5)—for Amalia is dominated by him, inseparable from him, as she is devoted to God (as Joyce's mother was). Giacomo imagines Amalia: "A sparrow under the wheels of Juggernaut, shaking shaker of the earth. Please, mister God, big mister God!" (*GJ* 7). Giacomo associates Amalia with Beatrice Cenci, the heroine of Shelley's *The Cenci*, who is raped by her father and driven to arrange his murder, but remains innocent, "stainless of blood and violation" (*GJ* 11).[3] Giacomo sees the God who causes Amalia to be cut by surgeons (probably an appendectomy)[4] as a sadist like the Sadean father Francesco Cenci: "O cruel wound! Libidinous God!" (*GJ* 11). Giacomo is

[2] John McCourt surveys a number of candidates for the title of the mystery woman in *Giacomo Joyce* and concludes that Popper remains the likeliest. See *The Years of Bloom: James Joyce in Trieste 1904-1920* (Madison: University of Wisconsin Press, 2000) 199-203.

[3] Vicki Mahaffey discusses Joyce's use of *The Cenci*, seeing Orsino, the prelate who lusts after Beatrice, as parallel to Joyce. See "Giacomo Joyce," *A Companion to Joyce Studies*, eds. Zack Bowen and James F. Carens (Westport, CT: Greenwood Press, 1984) 410-11. The political implications of Joyce's use of *The Cenci* are developed by Joseph Valente in *James Joyce and the Problem of Justice: Negotiating Sexual and Colonial Difference* (Cambridge: Cambridge University Press, 1995) 111-114.

[4] McCourt explains that it was another woman whom Joyce might have used as his model, Emma Cuzzi, rather than Popper who had this operation, *The Years of Bloom* (200-201).

glad that her birdlike life "has fluttered out of reach of the clutching fingers of an epileptic lord and giver of life" (*GJ* 11).

In Shelley's extremely anti-patriarchal play, Beatrice finally comes to the conclusion that because God will allow her to be punished for her virtuous parricide, there is no God but her evil father (V.iv.57-73). The brother who participates with her in the plot to kill Count Cenci, but who unlike her is unable to resist torture and so confesses, is named Giacomo.

In rebelling against the Father and desiring an unattainable woman, Giacomo Joyce returns to the oedipal turmoil of adolescence in order to cultivate conflict, remembering earlier anguish (perhaps over Nora or one of the Sheehy sisters [E___ C__]): "Easy now, Jamesy! Did you never walk the streets of Dublin at night sobbing another name?" (*GJ* 6). Because he can see the latest infatuation in perspective, it is a pseudo-adolescence, a fantasy contained by his imaginative or creative aim.

For someone like Joyce, who was trained to see the world as "a theorem of divine power" (*P* 150), to rescue the daughter from the father is to rescue the world from God. The way to do this is to take God's powers and recreate the world as personal vision rather than convention, and the best way to do this is with a woman. The core of the visionary power emphasised by Giacomo is his power to hold Amalia in his mind for as long as seven years, from the time he met her in 1907 or 1908: "All night I have watched her, all night I shall see her" (*GJ* 12). She stays in his mind, and she seems to be the focal point for every part of *Giacomo Joyce*, so that the description of cities, for example, serve as background or contrast to her.

What Giacomo sees all night is Amalia with "olive" face, a "green fillet" in her hair, and a "green-broidered gown: the hue of the illusion of the vegetable glass of nature and of lush grass" (*GJ* 12). What attracts one to the mirror of the world here is its fruitfulness, the creation of nourishment by vegetation. The idea of the world as a green illusion is linked to Berkeley late in *Finnegans Wake*, where the archdruid Balkelly speaks of "too many illusiones through photoprismic velamina of hueful panepiphanal world spectacurum of Lord Joss" (*FW* 611.12-14). On the page following these lines, all of the illusions turn out to be green. But if the idealist sees the world as a veil of illusions, a spectacle or mirror (speculum) of God, the point for Giacomo seems to be that Amalia focuses him on the world. The mirror in which she appears is the material world as distinct from God, as taken from God, and he can only reach this world by focusing on a woman as object of desire. (Historically, the Courtly Love movement shifted literature from the religious to the secular).

One chief device used to show Giacomo's devotion to Amalia is the present tense. As John McCourt says of the text, "it gives the impression of having been written down 'live.'"[5] The text stays in the present through the events of many years, and through flashbacks, such as the vision of Paris, which presumable goes back to 1903, but seems suddenly to switch to the presence of Amalia (*GJ* 10). The extension of a feeling of intense presence through wide areas of time and space insists on the importance of Amalia, or of the fantasy of Amalia. At moments, such as the one where he helps he put on her dress and thinks rather frantically of touching her buttocks (*GJ* 7), there is a feeling that the indulgence in fantasy subtracts from actual ability to make contact. These feelings reach a climax at the end in "Write it [...] What else are you good for?" (*GJ* 16).

The effect of the continuous, immediate present is that the reader cannot locate events in a timeline. This arrangement resembles the opening of *A Portrait*, which contains six or more scenes in not much more than a page, jumping from one to another. One cannot tell whether these scenes are experienced one by one or remembered retroactively at some point, such as the scene of Stephen in bed in the seventh paragraph. As he lies wetting the bed, he may remember his father telling the story and his own invention of the line about "the green wothe

---

[5] McCourt, *The Years of Bloom*, 204.

botheth." Or the fragments of the overture may pass through his mind as he hides under the table at the end (*P* 8).

The distinction between a happening in the present and its recollection by the narrator disappears when one tells a story, for as Freud emphasised, we can only know the past through subsequent reaction. As Slavoj Žižek puts it, "the Cause exercises its influence only as redoubled."[6] This subsequent determination is active in St. Augustine, who says in his *Confessions* that we cannot know what the present means until we know the future, and only God knows the future.[7] So Joyce's recognition that present and future are inseparable, which is linked to Stephen's proclamation that he embraces the future (*P* 251) has perverted theological basis as his assumption of God's power. Stephen's whole life is the telling of a story insofar as he moves toward becoming his own creator.

The evaporation of Giacomo's position and of linear time represents an advanced level of Modernism, connecting with such concepts as spatial form and montage, and leading to the disintegration of *Finnegans Wake*. Derek Attridge hails this overture as one of the most innovative parts of *Portrait*, one that announces "a fresh understanding of the literary potential of language."[8] Attridge says that the overture was probably written as late as 1913, so *Giacomo Joyce* may be seen as developing this technique of the rapid cutting of immediacy.[9]

Giacomo can only reach the living immediacy of the world through devotion to woman as the object of desire. In a parody of God producing the second person to enter the world, Giacomo divides himself through fantasy. He is both in the scene and without it, so he attaches and detaches rapidly, imagining contact with her, but knowing how unlikely such

[6] Slavoj Žižek, *Metastases of Enjoyment: Six Essays on Women and Causality* (London: Verso, 1994) 30.

[7] Saint Augustine, *The Confessions of St. Augustine*, trans. John K. Ryan (Garden City, NY: Doubleday Image, 1960) Book 10, chapter 8.

[8] Derek Attridge, *Joyce Effects: On Language, Theory, and History* (Cambridge: Cambridge University Press, 2000) 73.

[9] Attridge, *Joyce Effects*, 60.

contact is. She wears the green "of lush grass, the hair of graves" (*GJ* 12), because the fecundity of nature is fertilised by death, and every attempt to contact her has to work through sacrifice.

Like all of Joyce's women, Amalia has a dangerous side expressed in fetishes, in this case particularly in the eyes. At the start a, "burning needleprick stings and quivers in the velvet iris" (*GJ* 1), and near the end her eyes dart "a jet of liquorish venom" (*GJ* 15). The image of a woman's eyes as piercingly phallic is extremely attractive to Joyce. The main danger here is that Amalia will not understand Giacomo and will reject him, and this gives her a certain power to resist him and to express herself even before she speaks in the later sections. In the Courtly Love tradition, her danger has to be propitiated by his sacrifice. But her glace also hurts him insofar as he is unable to help her.

His main effort to reach her is through teaching. Here he approaches divinity, but approaches it as an obscene parody: "My voice, dying in the echoes if its words, dies like the wisdom-wearied voice of the Eternal calling on Abraham through echoing hills" (*GJ* 14). His words disseminate themselves in a Derridean sense, spreading into different alternative meanings as they approach her so that his voice is lost in echoes. Yet something effectively reaches her despite this disintegration, or perhaps because of it. It arrives indirectly as synæsthesia, a sound passing through her eyes, her most expressive feature:

> Her eyes have drunk my thoughts: and into the moist warm yielding welcoming darkness of her womanhood my soul, itself dissolving, has streamed and poured and flooded a liquid and abundant seed ...... Take her now who will! [*GJ* 14]

There is no book by Joyce that does not included the idea of giving the beloved to another, but the idea that Giacomo's intercourse with Amalia is so profound that the desired successor will only get leavings is relieved by humour. The weary God who calls Abraham knows that He is asking for a sacrifice that He cannot accept. Isaac, the only son God gives up, prefigures the idea that God creates beauty by sending His son into the world, by losing Himself in matter as His voice is doomed to die in translation, the materiality of language. Joyce gives birth to a new version of himself through devotion to the mystery of Amalia's womanhood, which allows him to extend his perceptions to a perverse divinity.

I think that Giacomo sees his communion with Amalia as an Annunciation, just as Stephen speaks of inspiration as the Angel Gabriel coming to "the virgin womb of the imagination" (*P* 217). As Stephen sees himself as Christ late in *A Portrait* (248), Giacomo starts the second paragraph of his fifteenth page with "They spread under my feet carpets for the son of man." In this Amalia may appear as Mary when he is seen with "a plaid cloak shielding from chills her sinking shoulders" (*GJ* 15).[10] In Simone Martini's famous *Annunciation*, in the Uffizi, Mary holds her cloak around her shrinking shoulders as if chilled by a wind from heaven. A plaid cloak is prominent in this early fourteenth-century painting, but it is worn by the Angel. Martini's Mary seems to greet Gabriel "wintrily" and to dart from "sluggish sidelong eyes a jet of liquorish venom" (*GJ* 15). Her perturbation at the burden she is receiving may be parallel to Amalia's disturbance at the new kinds of knowledge Giacomo is exposing her to.

There is humour in the resentful glances of the Virgin and Amalia, but there is also something terrible. Both Jewish women must suffer to bring about new dispensations, Christ's

---

10 Mahaffey points out a number of images linking Amalia to the Virgin ("Giacomo Joyce," 399). Mahaffey's fine interpretation of *Giacomo Joyce* is very different from mine: she refers to Giacomo and Amalia as Joyce and the lady, and she emphasises his disillusionment and sense of betrayal. Rather than saying that one of us is right and the other wrong, I would say we represent two levels of the text or of Giacomo/Joyce's mind. I will say that Giacomo's sense of betrayal is undercut by the fact that he is married. And if he ended up resenting her as much as Mahaffey claims he does, he would not see her as a "Voice of wisdom" on the fifteenth page.

new vision and Joyce's advancement into a higher level of Modernism through Amalia. The *Stabat Mater* declares that no woman suffers as much as Mary, who beholds her son crucified; but Giacomo sees Amalia as suffering by linking her not only to Mary, but to Beatrice Cenci. This is why the operation is emphasised, and Amalia suffers the dilemma of either being forced to accept Giacomo's new ideas or rejecting him and being lost in conventional womanhood.

The conflict between Giacomo and Amalia is actually symbolised in the arrangement of Martini's *Annunciation*: a line of words, embossed on the gold surface of the painting, goes from Gabriel's mouth to Mary's face. The words are "AVE MARIA GRATIA PLENA DOMINUS TECUM," and they are really headed for her right ear, but they seem to go toward her eyes. This may explain Joyce's image of Amalia's eyes drinking his thoughts. The line between Gabriel and Mary visualises a sort of tug of war in which he is imposing a very heavy patriarchal burden on her and she is resisting insofar as she is only human.

The sense of struggle or contest in the painting raises the possibility that the angel might not have the power to overcome her opposition. This possibility is represented in "The Dead," where Gabriel Conroy is not able to save Gretta from her morbidly sentimental attachment to the past and to another archangel, Michael. So the line between the angel's mouth and the Virgin's eyes suggests her power to change him as he is changing her. In Joyce's use of Amalia we may also recognise the power he gives her.

When Amalia is seen "darting at me for an instant out of her sluggish sidelong eyes a jet of liquorish venom" (*GJ* 15), the image is partly based on Beatrice, whose eyes afflict Marzio, the murderer who confesses that she hired him, informing on her. Marzio says,

O dart

The terrible resentment of those eyes
On the dead earth! Turn them away from me! [V.ii.29-31]

Amalia's glance (while it is certainly sexual, as the word "liquorish" indicates) penetrates Giacomo not only because she resents his ministration, but because he fears that he cannot relieve her suffering. The glare Beatrice levels at Marzio would also apply to her weak brother Giacomo, who confesses under torture. A significant level of Giacomo Joyce's unease is his fear that he may not be brave or perceptive or effective enough to save Amalia, his awareness that his view of women is to a great extent blind. Yet misunderstanding can communicate by the exposure and interaction of differences, and Giacomo's connection with Amalia will reach beyond these conflicts.

Just as Stephen creates his first image, the "green wothe botheth," by making a mistake, so Giacomo can only communicate by being misunderstood. Joyce's works were always aimed primarily at female audiences, starting with his mother. He aimed to deliver women from patriarchal dominance, but his limited understanding of women and his difference from them made it inevitable that he would be greatly misinterpreted. The only level on which Giacomo can conquer Amalia is one in which he disintegrates when he sends himself as words into her body as the world: "my soul, itself dissolving." He must lose his identity to engage hers, to be transformed by hers as he transforms it.

A man cannot possess a woman without losing his ego, and insofar as Giacomo reaches and recreates Amalia, he recreates himself as a being divided into becomings so as to generate new insights. As Joseph Valente argues, Giacomo learns to identify with the subaltern other by giving voice to this Jewish woman, and this leads him to a stylistic freedom of association.[11] The ability to see everything at once springs from his unfolding himself into multiple consciousnesses through her, through recognising that he is implicated in her differences.

The voice he gives her is one that emphasises resistance, but the resistance is conceived of as a defence to protect herself

[11] Valente, *James Joyce and the Problem of Justice*, 125-30.

from the depth of their communion. She says that if *A Portrait* were "frank only for frankness' sake," she would ask why he gave it to her (*GJ* 12). Concerned with the degree to which he is overlapping with her intimacy, she negotiates the border in order to allow then to interact—for him, as he puts it, to expose his "shame" (*GJ* 13) to her in *A Portrait*. Similarly, when she later explains her marriage to him by saying "Because otherwise I could not see you" (*GJ* 16), she means that she could not properly visit him if she did not have a husband pacing outside (*GJ* 15). Yet there is another overtone suggested by Beatrice Justice's use of "Otherwise I could not see you" in *Exiles* (*E* 19). Amalia suggests that a husband allows her to indulge the image of Joyce in her mind. So Amalia's intelligence and activity are finally considerable.

The value of their interchange is confirmed by the final scene of what McCourt calls the novelette,[12] which takes place no earlier than 1914 (it refers to *Ulysses*) in Paris. Here it seems that Amalia visits with Giacomo on a lounge on which he has just engaged in fairly steamy erotic play with a hairdresser (*GJ* 15). Presumably the line "It is the other. She" (*GJ* 15) means that after the hairdresser, Amalia arrives; and this may equate the two women with poles of his fantasy life. Amalia's first statement, "I am not convinced that such activities of the mind or body can be called unhealthy," does not have a clear referent; but it does seem to follow Giacomo's ideas insofar as it apparently allows for latitude in the direction of perversion and it conflates mind and body. In fact it seems to condone the intertwined fantasies that she and he have pursued. It does look as if she has freed herself from patriarchy.

Giacomo greets her words with enthusiasm: "A weak voice from beyond the cold stars. Voice of wisdom. Say on! O, say again, making me wise! This voice I never heard" (*GJ* 15). The voice from beyond the stars suggests the Virgin, who speaks from heaven and is identified with a star in *A Portrait* (*P* 116). The wisdom he derives from her includes the fact that he has

---

[12] McCourt, *The Years of Bloom*, 196.

given her the power to speak. As she grows active at this moment of contact, she grows threatening: "She coils toward me along the crumpled lounge. I cannot move or speak" (*GJ* 15). The word *coil*, repeated three times, conveys the fetishistic image of a "snake" (*GJ* 15).

Confronted by her aggressiveness, Giacomo panics, as he seemed to do when she saucily chose to ask him to help with her dress (*GJ* 7). "No. I will go. I will" (*GJ* 15). Yet the words before these are "Adultery of wisdom," so one thing that frightens him is that he realises that he has achieved an erotic/visionary consummation with her. Their amplitude of revelation depends on their sharing the conflict of breaking the law by sinning together.

At this point, I think it is his wife that Giacomo hears saying "Jim love," for Nora called Joyce *Jim*. The careful pseudo-adulterer Giacomo has not yet mentioned his wife, but after a hysterical paragraph in which a snaky woman kisses his armpit, generating a fang of flame, he mentally cries out, "Nora!" (*GJ* 15). I do not see Amalia kissing his armpit here, so it may have been the dresser or Nora, whom he is now stimulated to remember. More likely, Amalia projects an imaginary aggression or feint that he feels intensely. Presumably Amalia very much enjoys this fetishistic enterprise: she may feel herself shooting off sexiness. As for Giacomo, he seems to realise that he needs his wife and is attached to her.

The action of this long passionate paragraph is one in which Giacomo is assailed by the hairdresser, Amalia, and Nora at once on different levels. So it establishes an important principle for Joyce, that one can mentally embrace several people at once. The major manifestation of this erotic multiplicity is the end of *Ulysses*, when Molly is stimulated by thoughts of Blazes Boylan, Harry Mulvey, Leopold Bloom, Stephen Dedalus, James Joyce, and the reader simultaneously, and says yes to all of them.

Giacomo Joyce presents the cultivation of a wisdom that is crucial to Joyce's career, and that could only be developed through adultery. Indeed the phrase "adultery of wisdom" refers to understanding that is mixed or adulterated, that sustains several different levels at once. By anatomising the birth of creativity through fantasy, Joyce reveals an important aspect of his creative progress. He also shows, as he will in *Ulysses*, how human relations operate continuously on levels below what is permissible or conscious, for it is the exclusion from proper thought that makes these movements so vital.

M.E. Roughley
Apology in an Other's Hand: *Giacomo Joyce*: Who?

> *We have talked of women; about women, he seems a bit disinterested.*
> *Were I vain, I should say he is afraid of them, but I am certain he is*
> *only a little skeptical of their existence.*
> (Djuna Barnes, "James Joyce")[1]

Could this be right? Could Djuna Barnes be right in being "certain" that Joyce was "a little skeptical of [women's] existence"? Joyce, the scriptor of Molly Bloom and Anna Livia Plurabelle? Joyce, the "master" of "writing in the feminine"? Nora's Joyce, *that* Joyce, is a little sceptical of women?

Yet, Djuna Barnes knew Joyce. Knew him well enough to drop in unannounced for a chat; knew him wisely enough to defer indefinitely the introduction promised to/awaited by Gertrude Stein (by showing up, drunk, without him). Was known by him well enough to be the recipient, in 1923, of his annotated copy of *Ulysses* (or so the rumour goes). And, she knew his work well, "consumed" it, was obliterated by it (felt there was no point in writing anything after *Ulysses*) and aroused by it (wrote *Nightwood* after *Ulysses*). Certainly Djuna Barnes knew Joyce and knew him well enough that, despite all

---

[1] Djuna Barnes, "James Joyce" [April 1922], *Djuna Barnes: Interviews*, ed. Alice Barry (Washington, DC: Sun and Moon Press, 1985) 288-96. This quotation, 294.

perfectly beautiful and believable argument to the contrary, I am reluctant to dismiss her *certainty* that he was "a little skeptical of [women's] existence"—only a *little* sceptical, but sceptical nonetheless.

This certain little scepticism, certainly noted by a woman who was a friend and also a writer who shared entire topical pastures with Joyce as well as a place and a time, has troubled me since I first came across it some years ago. Not that I couldn't see the signs of it in, say, Stephen's distancing epiphanies or the "expressions" of his infatuation in the *Portrait*, or in Bloom's epistolary affair or his voyeurism in *Ulysses*: a certain scepticism about the existence(s) of women does mark Joyce's texts (if not all texts, all symbolic signification, to some extent or other). But, I had also succumbed to what appeared to me a literal fleshiness, a certain "pulpy" verisimilitude, in the given words of Joyce's women that read like "existence," and "existence" undoubted. How could a Joyce sceptical of women's existence write "because he never did a thing like that before as ask to get his breakfast in bed with a couple of eggs since the *City Arms* hotel when he used to be pretending to be laid up with a sick voice doing his highness to make himself interesting to that old faggot Mrs Riordan" (*U* 659)? Molly's "voice" is practically irresistible. "[W]ith a sick voice doing his highness to make himself interesting": yes, that's "it": that's the feminine reflection: one gives into it so willingly. At moments like this, it is as if Joyce knows what passes in (or for) a woman's mind. Joyce *knows*. But then, Barnes knows too, and she thinks that he seems a bit disinterested, suspects that he *might* be afraid, is certain that he is a little sceptical ...

Could it be that a little scepticism, or a putative, seeming disinterest, in (or even fear of) the *existence* of the other is a necessary condition of this sort of writing itself? Could it be that one writes thus because the existence of the other is doubtable, cannot be known or even assumed, lying (and lying) as it does on the other side of an unbreachable abyss of experience?

Could it be that one writes in order to pretend (in order to seem interested and interesting), to be pretentious, that one has access to or can understand or command that other "existence"? These are, admittedly, naïve questions which have been superseded or surmounted in critical discourse by questions of a more rigorously systemic (and intellectual) nature. But, at the same time, these apparently redundant questions remain, though it seems that one rarely addresses them anymore, and they remain primarily because Joyce's texts keep bringing them up. It's all a matter of the distance and pretension and scepticism marking the self-definition of the writing, Joyce's work: it's all a fake, a pretend message (envoy) to an addressee with no symbolic postcode, with possibly no existence even beyond the abyss of experience. It, the writing, is also very, palpably, real—an actual body of work—you can hold it in your hands, undeniably. It is a real fake. We can't (Joyce's writing won't let us) get away from this apparent aporia: writing *is* and yet is about, toward, concerning a possible nothing, an unprovable existence or even absolute non-existence: writing is necessary and yet pointless: it necessarily and literally proves nothing, which may well be the "whole point."

As naïve and/or redundant as such (given) assertions about Joyce's writing might seem, here, now, off the cusp of the twenty-first century, I don't think that we have quite finished with them (or the naïve questions either), again because Joyce's work keeps bringing them up and bringing us to them. Perhaps this is because of that work's position at the turning point or crux of (what Freud might call) the "Copernican" revolution of (the understanding of the agency of) the word in which communication was re-forged through the previous century. This is crucial work and radical work and revolutionary work, and, like all crucial radical revolutionary work, it needs must have its apology (its explanation and its defence), which brings me, believe it or not, "by a commodius vicus of recirculation" to *Giacomo Joyce* and the beginning of my argument.

What I want to address here, in this paper, is the possibility of reading *Giacomo Joyce* as an apology of/for a writing that will never reach its mark, an apology of/for a crucially aporetic writing.[2] Why *Giacomo Joyce*? I will defend my topic presently. First, though, I want to devote a little consideration to *"apology,"* a crucial concept in itself and the crucial term, perhaps, of my argument.

According to the *Oxford English Dictionary*, the word "apology" has at least four meanings:

> 1. The pleading off from a charge or imputation, whether expressed, implied, or only conceived as possible [...].
> 2. Less formally: Justification, explanation, or excuse, of an incident or course of action.
> 3. An explanation offered to a person affected by one's action that no offence was intended, coupled with the statement of regret for any that may have been given [...].
> 4. Something which, at it were, merely appears to apologise for the absence of what ought to have been there; a poor substitute.

In each of these four senses, the implication (no matter how it is valorised) is that something (whether in word or deed) has already occurred which has led to a difference of opinion or perception, a contradiction or a *contretemps*, a problem as such, between one and an other. The apology (whether formal, informal or merely cynical) would be that which *might* make possible a resolution of this difference—although it is important

---

[2] The aporia is, literally, an impasse, an impassable or irresolvable contradiction. The aporetic method, in a philosophic context, as defined in the *Cambridge Dictionary of Philosophy*, is: "the raising of puzzles without offering solutions—typical of the elenchus in the early Socratic dialogues of Plato. These consist in the testing of definitions and often end with an *aporia*, e.g. that piety is both what is and what is not loved by the gods. Compare the paradoxes of Zeno, e.g., that motion is both possible and impossible." To say that Joyce's writing is "aporetic" is to suggest that it is predicated essentially on that which cannot be decided or determined rather than on a referent (a subject, a concept, a source) which can be more or less successfully identified, reflected upon, illustrated, interpreted. If you like, it is "aporetic" instead of being "mimetic."

to recognise that "resolution" is not part of any of the four definitions—by offering, by being, a defence or justification or explanation or excuse or substitute of/for an action (or presence?—after all, one offers one's apologies in lieu of one's presence in meetings, at dinners). Apology ([(? a. Fr. *apologie*), ad. L. *apologia*, a. Gr. ἀπολογία defence, a speech in defence, f. ἀπό away, off + λογία speaking]) is what is offered (the pleading, the "speaking") from one side of a difference ("away, off") to the other (the accuser, the offended) in the place of understanding, mutual apprehension, intuition, unmediated presence. Without difference, there would be no (need of) apology. Apology is that which rises out of difference—a speaking off or off-speaking necessitated by difference and the desire to resolve difference—but promises, guarantees, no resolutions. Apology is one thing: acceptance, another.

An apology, moreover, is something "made"—I make my apology—and thus it is supplemented by a notion of fabrication, or fiction. This much is evident in its etymological kinship with the "apologue" ([a. Fr. *apologue*, ad. L. *apologus*, a. Gr. ἀπόλογος account, story, fable, f. ἀπο off + λόγος speech], "An allegorical story, intended to convey a useful lesson; a moral fable"). Of course, an apology is *not* an apologue, but the terms are related in a radical sense and this kinship, a consideration of this kinship, exposes the fictiveness at the heart of the apology (where "speech" and "speaking" are inextricably bound and mutually compromised by "off" and "away"). No matter how "truthful" or sincere one might be in making one's apology, one is still making an "account" of, and in lieu of, what is misunderstood or, in fact, missing. The apology is always a fabrication (no matter its sincerity) and a substitute (for understanding, for presence): ever directed towards absolution or atonement, it will always fail to reach its mark for it is constituted by difference, substitution and fabrication. Perhaps it is this impossibility, or impassability, of resolution that causes us to be so eloquent (at our *most* eloquent), to choose our words with such extreme care, when making our apologies. (Do we not all wrestle with the phrasing in these instances? Is one ever more aware of the otherness of the other than when apologising?)

> In the vague mist of old sounds a faint point of light appears: the speech of the soul is about to be heard. Youth has an end: the end is here. It will never be. You know that well. What then? Write it, damn you, write it? What else are you good for? [*GJ* 16]

Here is a fine apology (justification, explanation, excuse, account, story) or apologia ("esp. A written defence or justification, etc. [...]" [*OED*]) for writing, for the practice of writing in itself: "the end is here. It will never be [...]. What then? Write it, damn you [...]. What else are you good for?" It will never be: then write it (and be damned?). As it will never be, the only good that you can do is to write it. Perhaps it is possible to read this also as an apologia of writing as apology (in the fourth sense), as "a poor substitute." *It* will never be; then write *it*. Replace the it that "ought to have been there," but isn't, with the written it—what else is Giacomo Joyce good for?

(The indeterminate antecedence of that "It" of "It will never be" (what "It"?), complicated or rendered even more ambiguous by the syntax—"the end is here. It will never be"—if we don't simply assume that the "It" is *only* the requital of a love, lends itself to a reading of this writing as aporetic, as the writing of irresolution or impassability or impossibility. The end is here [and/yet] it will never be. The end that is here will never be. Aporia. And, as we have arrived at an aporia, what then? What else is there to do but write "it." I will come, in a little, to the aporetic nature [or method] of this writing: it is enough, for now, to note parenthetically the literal evidence of aporia in the scene, at the instance, of what may also be read as an apology of/for writing.)

This is perhaps the place, near the heart of this essay and for no more than a brief paragraph ("A brief beat of the eyelids"), to suggest that, on an *essential* or "autobiographical" level, at least, *Giacomo Joyce* is an apology of sorts to Nora. *If* Ellmann is right in identifying the young lady and the incident of Joyce's fascination with her as biographical fact, then Joyce did indeed owe Nora an explanation. This would certainly account for the appearance (or the eruption!) of her name "—Nora!—" at the end of the (longest and climactic) paragraph in which "She" ("the other," but not "Nora"?) becomes the serpent-succubus. This "—Nora!—" immediately precedes, opens the way for, the paragraph containing the apology for writing. I am lost: Nora, save me: the end that will never be is here: I must write it. Who was more deserving of such a (qualified) apology? Who could better understand than she who could say (according to Barnes), "It's the great fanaticism is on him, and it is coming to no end"?[3]

One of the beauties of *Giacomo Joyce* is its (mimicry of) autobiographicalness, as if Joyce pauses for a moment, *in media res*, to say (to Nora, to us) this is "it," this is the reason I write, this is what I am good for. It has that confessional quality, the first person voice, the abbreviated references that indicate interiority and inclusion, a beguiling lyricism. It is a text (and an apology) that is difficult to resist: such openness and irony, honesty and self-deprecation (such a rhetorical bag of tricks, such "*ein Schweinerei*"?). It is a rather seductive text: one feels drawn to Joyce, beyond those mediating figures of Stephen and Bloom, in particular. It draws us into what would seem to be the unmediated voice ("like the wisdom-wearied voice" [*GJ* 14]) of the creator, in which are expressed the seminal concerns of statement—the relationship of the one (subject) and the other (object) and the agency of communication. I love her, but between us is only statement, writing, poised on an aporia. It is most tempting to see this eloquent little gem of an apology as a cameo, or an intaglio, of Joyce's *style*.

I don't know how else to describe *Giacomo Joyce*. It escapes precise definition by being properly neither a (prose) poem nor a novelette nor a notebook/diary/epistle: one might say that it is

<hr>

[3] Barnes, *Interviews*, 295.

trans-, even supra-, generic. That it (historically and thematically) occupies the middle position between the *Portrait* and *Ulysses*, between the (apogee, if you like, of the) modernist novel in English and the novel as supra-encyclopaedic form (the-novel-that-encompasses-the-history-of-its-language)   is significant. Between these two texts, a step has been taken (one small step for Joyce, one enormous leap for literature) that will alter forever the way that we think about—at the very, very least—the novel. The nature and effect of this "step," this turn in the revolution of the word, has been so well addressed by the critical community (see almost any directory to Joyce's work) that anything I might add would likely be redundant. It is enough to note the magnitude of this step before turning to my theme, which is the crucial agency of *Giacomo Joyce* as the writing between (and of) these two acknowledged novels, the crucial agency of the step itself—perhaps.

Giacomo Joyce, if we stand back from the Joycean "canon" and observe it as a progression (of artistic development, of publication), is rather like a "brief beat of the eyelids" (*GJ* 1), a blink which both marks and obliterates the formal transition, the passage, from the *Portrait* to *Ulysses*. Joyce apparently had abandoned it in Trieste, left it there (on the midden heap?) when he departed, although he had taken care to write it out "in his best calligraphic hand, without changes" (*GJ* xi) before doing so—a peculiar sort of abandonment. (Was he relying on Stanislaus's jackdaw instincts to "save" it? Did he foresee the agency of the "collector who prefers to remain anonymous" in its preservation? Had he made it attractive to those ends?) Whatever Joyce's intentions for this text, it survived, through the agency of others, to be published posthumously, after his passing—the last book, if you like—and it does seem that this survival may, to a certain extent, have depended on the fact that it was written in Joyce's *best* hand. Not to be kept for publication, yet of sufficient import—in its moment, at least—to be copied out in one's *best* calligraphic hand, to be rendered beautiful, attractive to the eye, legible: all of this suggests a text to be kept in reserve, by others perhaps, by any other (if only as a "kept" text, a mistress). A brief blink of the eye between the end of the *Portrait* and the beginning of *Ulysses* and the reader misses it, but it is "there" nonetheless, although held in reserve until the end, after the end, when it can be called or re-called into play—perhaps, as we are doing now.

What is "missed" in this "brief" blink of the eye (a brief syllable, a brief laugh, the meaning in brief) between Stephen's preparations for migration to Paris (to "forge [...] the uncreated conscience of [his] race") and Buck Mulligan's calling up, invocation of Kinch, the "fearful Jesuit," returned to Ireland? A great deal, in fact: Europe, exile and the death of the mother—the passing into the "other" and of the (m)other—the forge itself, perhaps for Stephen (whose writing is always, in Ireland, deferred) and certainly for Joyce (whose writing "takes place" in exile in Europe beyond the sea, the mother and the motherland). Between the two *published* (and hence "public") texts, *Giacomo Joyce* can perhaps be seen as the setting or the scene of acts of writing (in its exile, its silence) or of the producing of that public writing which obliterates, or at least covers over or displaces, its "source."

From this perspective, *Giacomo Joyce* can be read as if it might be the confession of the silence, exile and cunning which are the only (self-allowed) arms of the artist. If so, it is indeed a very "cunning" confession: not only kept unpublished, "private," but also marked by an apparently inviolable interiority, a perfect prototype or example of the "interior monologue" *style* that *Ulysses* makes such good use of. This is not a writing predicated on utterance—one doesn't utter such "speech"—not unless one wishes to appear mad. What we have, here, is an unutterable confession, an unutterable apology, limited, or saved, by interiority. Such a reading would account for the self-address at the critical moment (of apology): "You know that well. [...] Write it, damn you, write it! What else are you good for?" Giacomo Joyce makes its/his cunning apology in "talking" to it/himself, in silence, in exile from the public, published utterance. It/he needn't be held accountable, if it's all in the mind.

A consideration of the "interiority" of this text necessarily brings us to questions of accountability and of the agency of the "other," in the writing, and of the scepticism of/about the "other." How is the interior or private space of writing constituted in relation to the "exterior," to the not-I? (This question will also bring us, in time, to give some thought to just *what* is being apologised *for*, or confessed.) The other is figured variably in this text, but primarily as that unnamed "young person of quality," the object (for this text) of desire. "She" is quite recognisably the classic object of desire, a right Beatrice, a real poet's object, remote and unrealisable, at least in this life, Italian (and Jewish, a Joycean compounding of a necessary difference) and regal—or at least of a superior class ("quality"). On the other hand, she is quite unlike a (Dantesque or Shelleyan) Beatrice in that she lacks two essential elements which are, interestingly enough, the (public) guarantees of individual "existence": "wholeness" and a name.[4] This would-be "Beatrice" has (beautiful and unbeautiful) parts aplenty—a pale face, movements, laugh, eyelids, handwriting,[5] heels, unblown nose, cheeks, gown, shift, umbrella, and so on—but these are not articulated in a constituency. They remain fragments, in variable settings, articulated by spaces (blanks, gaps, holes) of variable depth and by seemingly random syntax (how *do* we get from "iris" to "High heels" [*GJ* 1]?—neither by sequential logic nor by metaphoric succession nor by contiguity, that's for certain) that render "wholeness" simply impossible. What "body" is here? And the name? "I rush out of the tobacco-shop and call her name" (*GJ* 4), but the name is

---

4 Is it not interesting that the Aquinian qualities of universal beauty *"integritas, consonantia, claritas"* on which Stephen lectures Lynch in the *Portrait*, are denied this Beatrice? Should this, in itself, not encourage us to doubt "her"?

5 This exposure of handwriting as a trace (of an absent or incomplete, fragmented, presence) at this stage, in the opening movement, of this handwritten text is intriguing. Is this, perhaps, an ironic self-reflection, or confession, of the text as trace?

never given, never articulated. There is no title, not even the father's name, under which the parts, from eyelid to the family arms ("a casque, gules, and blunt spear on a field, sable" [*GJ* 16]), might be assembled as an integrated whole. When we get down to it, this object of the subject-I's desire is not properly an object at all. It is no one thing; rather, it is a collection, under the title *Giacomo Joyce*, of textual fragments (some from or for other Joyce texts—*Portrait, Ulysses, Exiles*—some from other writings, other texts, lyrics). The spaces guarantee both the fragmentation and the unalterably *textual* nature of this collection. We cannot escape it—even identifying the historical she who might be the one (de)scribed will not solve the problem.

This unconstituted and unnamed "other" about whom the "interior monologue" stages itself as an articulation of desire— and apology of/for writing—is marked by scepticism. One must doubt its existence, for lack of form or title to clutch at. Of course, we should not perhaps be surprised to find such scepticism in the (modernist and ironic) "interior monologue" of a post-Cartesian subject (I doubt). Yet, there is perhaps something even more profound, here, than the expected scepticism, a problem that even the operations of the dialectic will not solve.[6] On pages 5-6, there is this peculiar sequence of sentences: "Loyola, make haste to help me! [large space] This

---

[6] Underlying this entire paper is the linkage of scepticism, dialectics and the aporia in the history of western philosophy. The definition of "aporetic method" offered by the *Cambridge Dictionary of Philosophy*, part of which I quoted note 2, is usefully illustrative of this linkage: "In Aristotle's dialectic, the resolution of aporia discovered in the views on a subject is an important source of philosophical understanding [...]. The possibility of argument for two inconsistent positions was an important factor in the development of Scepticism. In modern philosophy, the antinomies that Kant claimed reason would arrive at in attempting to prove the existence of objects corresponding to transcendental ideal may by seen as *aporia*." (Joyce, of course, and Barnes, likely enough, would have been aware of this linkage.) But, my use of "aporia" and the "aporetic" is also already after Derrida—after *Psyché* and *Aporias* most particularly—and this will have its effects on my use of "scepticism" and "dialectics," bringing *différance* into play, foregrounding impossibility and undecideability.

heart is sore and sad. Crossed in love? [very large space, the largest in the text, in fact] Long lewdly leering lips: dark-blooded molluscs [no full stop, but end of page] Moving mists on the hill as I look upward from night and mud." This I find a very difficult passage, and not least because of the lack of antecedence or reference (which "heart"? whose "lips"?), and I doubt the possibility of ever producing the definitive, stabilising reading of it. But, it might be possible to suggest that here, on either side of the *largest* gap in the text, one might find the traces of a profound, if "little" or even "disinterested," scepticism that at once exceeds the ministrations of the dialectic and leads us to writing.

What "happens" between the plea for aid, for intercession, "make haste to help me," and the moment of illumination, "I look upward from night and mud," is the presentation of what might be a paralysing (if not for writing?) contradiction, or aporia, in the perception of the (collected) object of desire. (I am taking the liberty, here, of assuming that this heart and these lips are belonging to both the father and the daughter: if to the father, then by extension to the daughter: family heart and family lips, "astride of a toboggan" [*GJ* 4]: an inherited heart and lips, and so part of the collection.)[7] In the middle of the page, we have the heart, "sore and sad," perhaps "Crossed in love." This is a rather romantic heart, a chivalric image even, and it is perhaps not too difficult, if one pauses for a moment, a brief space, to "see" its bearer sitting, remote and chaste, with sorrowful, downcast eyes, in a bower, a castle keep, a nunnery. The Lady of Shallot. The underdetermined sentences allow such latitude: "heart," "sore," "sad," "love," all encourage, even guarantee, such association to the literal and literary host of untouched muses. Ah me! But then, there is this space, the *largest* space, followed by, at the very *bottom* of the page, those "lips": "Long lewdly leering lips," unpunctuated but for that upright colon in the middle of the line, "dark-blooded

---

[7] It might be possible to read the "heart" as that of the I "this, my heart" but what then do we do with the following question?

molluscs," no full stop, without end. So, via the largest gap in the text, we pass from the pitiable heart to the leering lips, from pity to fear, from the romantic to the ironic, from the spirit to the flesh, from love to lust, from the sacred to the profane: in short, we go from the soul to the sex.

It *is* a difficult passage, impossibly contradictory, an impasse, and it seems that the only way to make it—or fake it—is through the largest space between (both constituted by and separating) this heart and those lips. There is an undecidability at work here. The text will not resolve the historical contradiction in the delineation of the (female) other (to the symbolic, to culture, thought, literature); rather, it opts for an articulation of the two, but it is an articulation that cannot resolve or absolve the opposition—the articulation of/by the space, the biggest blank of all. The object of desire, in this text, is undecidably both this and that and the other. Only scepticism about the "other" could permit such continued and continual undecidability as and at the heart of everything. (No wonder he needed Nora to save him.)

If we are still reading *Giacomo Joyce* as an apology for writing, in order for writing to be, there must be the "other" as that (for) which the writing is "about"—the object or purpose or content. This is what *Giacomo Joyce* demonstrates so precisely, so minutely: writing is predicated on an unrealisable desire to articulate, possess, assume, penetrate, couple with the other ("Take her now who will!" [*GJ* 14]), the not-I, death, with that which cannot, *in fact*, be articulated, not *really*. Something that the interiority and scepticism of *Giacomo Joyce* emphasise is the function of the "other" as a projection, if you like, of the writing subject's inevitable impossibility. The end is here [and/yet] it will never be. "Sliding—space—ages—foliage of stars—and waning heaven—stillness—and stillness deeper—stillness of annihilation—and her voice" (*GJ* 16). In this sense, writing will indeed be about no-thing if not the "stillness of annihilation" impossibly, illogically coupled (hyphenated) with "her voice" (presence). Another version of "death and the maiden."

If we are still reading *Giacomo Joyce* as an apology, at least in part, to Nora for "the great fanaticism," in order for the writing to be, there must be that other to whom the writing is addressed, to whom the apology is made. This is what *Giacomo Joyce* suggests, but not so precisely or minutely: writing is supplemental, functioning in lieu of understanding or union or communion. It is a gift, an offering, perhaps the greatest offering—*Non hunc sed Barabbam*[8]—to the other, whether one is a sceptic or not, the gift of life itself, but made in absentia, as it were.

In the end of the text, on the last page, but not quite *at* the end (the mob has only just chosen Barabbas), we have first the apology, then, also, a tableau of absence and of traces of presence, intriguingly opened by the one word sentence, "Unreadiness."

> Unreadiness. A bare apartment. Torbid daylight. A long black piano: coffin of music. Poised on its edge a woman's hat, red-flowered, and umbrella, furled. Her arms: a casque, gules, and blunt spear on a field, sable. [*GJ* 16]

Unreadiness? Unreadiness for what? Death, perhaps? And then the relics: the piano (a coffin), the hat and the umbrella. And then the envoy, the message from "off, away." Is this also an apology of/for writing as the impossible/possible deferral of death, or the impossible/possible substitution in lieu of a death which is here and yet will never be?)

Apologising for and apologising to, the apology itself: but, who/what apologises, who/what makes the apology? The "autobiographicalness" of the piece, the exclamation "Nora!," the self-exhortation of "Jamesy," the references to the *Portrait*

---

[8] See John 18.40. *Not this one but Barabbas*. I haven't commented at all on the intimations of the I's "christliness" in this text, but it might be worth considering the placement of this refusal of Christ, in lieu of or in preference for Barabbas, between the apology and the entrance to the tomb ("coffin of music"). The notion of sacrifice is certainly implicit, as also are the notions of death and, perhaps, iconography.

and to *Ulysses*, the identifiable (according to Ellmann) "best calligraphic hand," all tantalise with the possibility that this is Himself apologising, making apology. But, I have my doubts, for at least two reasons. The first of these is simply the effect of reading, as you do, from left to right, from beginning to end, from title to text: *Giacomo Joyce* [/] "Who? A pale face [...]." Giacomo Joyce. Who? Who, indeed? What a peculiar thing, to begin a text with a sentence composed only of an interrogative pronoun, referent unclear, not altogether decidable. Of course, we will read on, from left to right and from top to bottom, and doing so we will likely come to decide that the who is her of the "movements" and "quizzing-glasses." But, the precedence of Giacomo Joyce is not easily undone. Who *is* Giacomo Joyce? Who/what does this substitution of James with Giacomo—if it is indeed a substitution—signify? Perhaps, it might be that, between the substitution, or translation if you prefer, and the interrogative pronoun, the subject or author or autobiographer makes its escape, has already escaped (this *is* a posthumously published text, after all) before the text begins. If so, this is silence, exile and cunning *par excellence*: here is my apology offered, in my best calligraphic hand, in lieu of my presence which has always already eluded you. Here is my umbrella.

This brings me to my second, and my last, reservation: the actual writing of the words "Giacomo Joyce" and Ellmann's description of the name, written "On the upper left-hand corner of the front cover," as "inscribed in another hand" (*GJ* xii). Which hand is this? Another hand of Joyce's? The hand of someone else? Who wrote this? Who knows?

I could not presume to answer any of these questions: I only know that, here, at the conclusion of this essay, where I might expect to sum up my argument (which, embarrassingly, is at least double the length of the text itself without having "dealt with" more than a tenth of it), I am struck with the impossibility of saying anything definitive about it. It's all too little and too much, this divinely cunning little (un)apology, in an other hand, for a writing that will always tantalisingly miss its mark, this hen-pecked and fork-pocked pretend letter of explanation lost and found somewhere between Giacomo and "—Nora!—," this *intaglio* of a style, this last publicised word, this umbrella. I love it.

Renzo Crivelli

A Portrait of the Artist as an Imaginary Casanova

On 26th June 1914, in a letter written in English to James Joyce, the Italian novelist Ettore Schmidt/Italo Svevo (who was one of Joyce's pupils during the latter's stay in Trieste) expressed a flattering opinion of *Dubliners* and those chapters of *A Portrait of the Artist as a Young Man* which he had read in typescript some years before ("Do you know that I have now discovered that Dedalus is not only an eyeing and looking animal but that he has also a strongly developed sense for smells?"), and he added the plaintive request: "When will you write an Italian work about our town? Why not?"

Seven years had passed, as Svevo's daughter has recalled, since Svevo realised, during an important business meeting at the Admiralty in London, that he did not have sufficient command of the English language, and consequently, he returned to the Berlitz School in Trieste for a series of private lessons. At that time the Triestine writer was still completely unknown. Although he had already published the two important novels *Una vita* and *Senilità* with a small local publishing house, he had made no impact either on the critics

* This paper was originally presented as a lecture at the James Joyce Summer School, University College Dublin, 20 July, 1995.

or on the public. And as is well-known, it was precisely his encounter with Joyce, sent by the Berlitz School to Villa Veneziani at Servola (annexed to the Marine Paint Factory which Svevo managed for his father-in-law, Gioachino) to help Svevo improve his knowledge of English, which led to the launching of the latter in his literary career. This came about thanks to the sincere interest in and respect for Svevo's work felt by Joyce, and that resulted in his introducing Svevo's writings to Parisian literary circles in the mid-twenties.

Hence it was Svevo, well aware of the importance of the advice he had received from Joyce (who, for his part, must have taken due note of letters like the one written on 8th February 1909 in which Svevo explained why he particularly appreciated the third and fourth chapters of *A Portrait*) who suggested the idea of a work set in Trieste, almost certainly without knowing that such a work already existed. Joyce, in that very period, was evaluating the autobiographical relevance of that work with the result that he decided, perhaps on the basis that it was excessive or "compromising," not to confer on that organic material, structured according to narrative sequences that are not always chronological, any official literary standing.

In fact, when the text of *Giacomo Joyce* (which bears no indication of the date on which it was written, but the final version would seem to have been written between *A Portrait* and *Ulysses*) stayed in the drawer for many years, certainly until 1968, when Richard Ellmann came into possession of it— through Stanislaus, who had guarded it jealously after his brother's departure from Trieste—and published it unabridged with Faber and Faber. The manuscript, later bought, as Ellmann records, by a private collector who prefers to remain anonymous, is written in the author's best hand,

> without changes, on both sides of eight large sheets, which are loosely held within the nondescript blue paper covers of a school notebook. The sheets are of heavy paper, oversize, of the sort ordinarily used for pencil sketches rather than for writing assignments. They are vaguely reminiscent of those parchment

sheets on which in 1909 Joyce wrote out the poems of *Chamber Music* for his wife. [*GJ* xi-xii]

On the top left cover of the booklet appears the name Giacomo Joyce (the first word above the second) written in an uncertain hand (the letters are not all joined and the "y" appears to be closed at the top) which with difficulty can be attributed to the author. It is not clear who wrote the title and, although we cannot exclude the hypothesis that it was written by Joyce himself when he was afflicted by disturbed vision, there is no doubt that the use of the Italian name is a very clear indication of the contents. Ellmann, although straining the point, accepted it for the Faber edition giving the following reasons for his decision:

> He was content to keep what he had written under this heading, and it has seemed reasonable to follow his example, since the overtones of self-deflation suit the piece. Joyce allows no doubt that the hero is to be identified with himself, for he calls Giacomo "Jamsey" and "Jim" and once appeals to his wife as "Nora." [*GJ* xii]

"An Italian work about our town": these words of Italo Svevo, who also set his novels in a Trieste that is just as recognisable as Joyce's Dublin, evoke the idea of the "Triestinity" that is certainly well hidden with what can only be called "meticulous attention, if not with constant, obstinate intention, in works like *A Portrait* and *Exiles*, which were written, in large part, in Trieste where Joyce lived from 1904 to 1915 and, after the First World War, from 1919 to 1920. In *Giacomo Joyce*, on the other hand, this barrier falls; the programmatic censorship which forced Joyce to represent an exclusively Irish setting in a total and symbolic rarefaction of the memory (in order to select, perhaps, only a past pregnant with a spirit of revenge and of everyday notations capable of acquiring universality) fails on contact with a strong emotive and autobiographical link in which reality and imagination are mixed. An imagination, however, which emerges directly from an objective reality—sticking to minute, almost minimalist descriptions *ante litteram*—which becomes, at times, a form of hyper-realism.

Critics have discussed at length the definition of the form of *Giacomo Joyce*, oscillating between the idea of a romantic narrative (a proper "short novel" constructed on the basis of a series of epiphanic episodes from which, according to the tenets of imagistic technique, the connecting links have been cut), and the idea of a poetic text or short poem after the manner of Eliot's early fragments, also partly imagistic and rarefied but at the same time realistic and organic in their descriptions of and allusions to the everyday. As we know, Ellmann talks about an "original expressive form," a new imagistic-modernist genre the function of which is to tell a story. But even if the link with the imagist technique seems close, especially considering the fact that it was presumably composed in 1914—which, as Francesco Binni has noted is "the operative hinge, all the more enigmatic in that it is duly submerged by a phenomenology of the epiphanic-imagist image that looks insistently towards a modernist continuum which takes the place of the feasible but impracticable continuum made up of epiphanies only"—it would be too reductive to define the form as "a short poem in prose."[1] If, on the other hand, it is treated as a "romanticised" text, its close collocation to *Ulysses* evokes certain anticipations which, although resting on a basis of regression and, therefore, revealing a merely apparent involution in Joyce's writings, introduce by means of irony (and here the comparison with the early Eliot is even more interesting) both the motif of seduction, and that of fetishism. In the first case, considering the attraction which more than one of his Triestine pupils held for Professor Joyce, it is possible to glimpse a prefiguration of a situation-type such as the one between Leopold Bloom and young Gerty MacDowell on the beach at Sandymount in chapter XII of *Ulysses*, which, as we know, was written in Trieste. Still in

---

[1] Francesco Binni, "Introduction to *Giacomo Joyce*," *James Joyce Poesie e prose* (Milan: Mondadori, 1992) 269.

relation to the influence which Joyce and Svevo exercised on each other, it is certainly also relevant to consider the figure of Angiolina, protagonist of *Senilità*, which came out in 1898 and was given by Svevo to Joyce to read.

Angiolina, exerting all the wiles and seductive charms typical of youth, weaves around the petty clerk, Emilio Brentani, an invisible but insidious web, arousing in him passions which are then barely appeased. She succeeds, by means of a continual alternation between desire and revulsion, titillation and sexual appeasement, in increasing in him the sense of existential disquiet which characterises his grey, everyday existence, precipitating him into the awareness that "his misfortune was caused by the inertia of his destiny." Gerty, in the "Nausicaa" chapter, acts in the same way on the "mature" Bloom. As in the case of Brentani, a thirty-five year old, this "maturity" coincides with an age that is not yet "senile," and symbolises the desire to seduce without conceding anything more than a handful of provocative sensations and opening the way to dreams. Only in this way, in fact, the scene of the fireworks above the bay—a celebratory event common also in Trieste at the beginning of the century— in which the sexual act is projected on to a transfiguring screen, can be interpreted.

In the case of fetishism, the anticipation of certain of Bloom's attitudes is evident and it might be said that the whole of *Giacomo Joyce* is permeated by "fetishistic compensations," which enable the protagonist to sublimate his state of frustration (which could be defined, in Brentani's words, as a state where "the inertia of destiny" is at work). The fetishism in Joyce's work passes through all the canonical Freudian stages; sometimes cloaked as poetry and disguised in the subtle folds of the imagination as detachment and servile devotion, almost as if to symbolise the celebratory function of the female adolescent dear to Provençal literature, only to re-emerge in its true guise of unbridled but unappeased sexual desire. The same frustrated desire which will lead Bloom to the choice of masturbation as a private and liberating fact in response to the instinctive and natural offer of young Gerty which dissolves, in the end, in the ironic charge underlying the text that favours a subsequent relaxing of the physical tension. Suffice it to think of the concluding remark in the love "story," or stories, of Giacomo where, amid a profusion of colours and furnishings, there emerges the symbolic "female" image of the girl's umbrella, "furled" and therefore impenetrable, leaning against the wall in the house; this is associated with the image of Giacomo's umbrella with its clearly masculine connotation: "Envoy: Love me, love my umbrella" (*GJ* 16). If, as Ellmann says, the speaker in *Giacomo Joyce* is certainly the author because of the perfect interchangeability of the names "Giacomo," "Jamesy," and "Jim," and because of the unequivocal reference to Nora, then it is necessary to consider the choice of an Italian name for the protagonist; a choice which confirms the desire to attribute to the Triestine setting a specific relevance that is not only autobiographical but also symbolic, not dissimilar to that which Dublin has in *A Portrait*, a work which saw the light of day in Trieste.

First of all the facts. As we know from Joyce's Registry Office card, which is still preserved in Trieste's town hall and on which figure his various addresses (not all for, oddly enough, there is no mention of his having lived in Via S. Nicolò, although there is, with a correction, the date of birth of Giorgio who was born when the Joyce family lived in that very street).[2] Joyce's name is erroneously indicated, according to the Italian practice of Italianising names in vogue at that time, as Giovanni Giacomo. Also, in the third column of the General Guide to Trieste of 1909, the abbreviation "Giac." to indicate Giacomo

---

[2] The card is rather messy because of the uncertainty in spelling English names (Nora appears as Rosa and Iceland is corrected as Ireland) and we find, along with references to the civic status of the members of the family and the parents of the couple, only their addresses in Via S. Caterina, Scussa, Barriera Vecchia, Bramante, and Sanità with the certification of the presence or absence of the tenants. Their absence was indicated by the abbreviation *slog.* which stands for "moved house."

(the entry reads: "Joyce Giac. prof. d'ingl.") is found. Giacomo is the name by which the writer is known in Trieste, where he is referred to, according to an automatic simplification of his name, as "professor Giacomo Zois." Joyce was aware of this and he himself uses the Italianised version of his name and even the diminutive "Giacometo," with which he signs a letter from Switzerland—still partially unedited—probably dated 1915.[3]

To take another example, in a letter written in Triestine dialect on 8th September, directed to Alessandro Francini Bruni who had been his friend and colleague since the time they both worked at the Bertlitz School in Pola, Joyce signs himself—as he often did—with a play on words in Triestine dialect: "Jacomo del Oio, sudito botanico." The use of the Venetian form "Jacomo" is obvious (Jacomo stands for Giacomo but has a different pronunciation), as is also the play on words of the final phrase. Whenever Joyce had to sign an official form, he was obliged to add his citizenship (in other words, "British Subject" or on Austrian documents: "britischer Untertan") after his signature. In his private correspondence, however, he used the form "sudito botanico" (botanic subject) as though to mock a mother country which he found oppressive (starting from the British Consul in Trieste who, knowing that he was Irish, was reluctant to intervene when Joyce was arrested for "disorderly behaviour" in Piazza Grande in October 1904). As regards the fictitious surname "del Oio," Joyce, who was almost perfectly familiar with Triestine dialect—so much so that he always spoke to his children in it—is alluding to the expression

---

3   The letter, addressed to a "Dear Mr. Zavata" (Dear Mr. Slipper), contains many expressions in Triestine dialect: "Ulysses, you cannot have forgotten him, is still growing older ... sua mare grega (a popular form for "son of a bitch"). Quel m ... atto di suo padre is meanwhile starving ... Dai, dai, esimio sior Papuzza, non la staghi fare il mo...ralista. Bim, bum, bom!" It is quoted by Stelio Crise, who mentions the refusal of the addressee to put it on show at the Lugano Exhibition of April, 1961, in *Academie e biblioteche d'Italia, anno XXIX*, 12th n.s., N.5. (Rome: Palombi Editori, 1961) 10.

"scampar coi bori de l'oio" in vogue in the thirties,[4] which signifies "to sneak off without saying goodbye." This expression refers to a swindle perpetuated in a town in Istria by an administrator of public lighting, who obtained the funds from the town council to buy oil for the braziers and then ran off, leaving everyone high and dry. This is, undoubtedly, an example of Joyce's sense of irony directed against himself and his own tendency to make off without paying his debts.

But alongside the name Giacomo in the representation of himself provided by Joyce in his correspondence, apart from the affable "Jacomo the swindler" hinted at in the name "del Oio," there figure other adjectives such as "Giocondo," from the English word "joyful," which recalls his surname by assonance. It occurs in a letter written in Italian and sent to Lucia on 7 April 1935 (in his letters to his daughter he always signed himself with an affectionate "I embrace you. Daddy" in Italian, while his children spoke to him in "sangiacomino"—a reference to the dialect of the San Giacomo district of the town—which is the "purest dialect of the old part of the city" as Dario De Tuoni recalls).[5] "Giacomo Giacondo," therefore, denotes a mood of merriment but also of rashness; and perhaps in this tender approach to his daughter there may be justification for reading the expression of a desire to regress but also the regret of a lost state of innocence.

Finally, among the possible references to a wholly Italian Giacomo (it was his friend Francini Bruni who reminded him of it: "What do you mean 'James'? You are Giacomo, you are ours by now"), we should insert a reference to Giacomo Casanova, already hinted at in Joyce's narrative in the recourse to the Don Juan syndrome as applied to the "restrained" possessive delirium of the teacher who acts as seducer but who, in fact,

---

4   Mario Doria, *Grande dizionario del dialetto triestino, storico, etimologico, fraseologico* (Trieste: Edizioni Il Meridiano, 1987), and Stelio Crise *È'tornato Joyce* (Milan: Nuova Rivista Europea, 1982).

5   Dario De Tuoni, *Ricordo di Joyce e Trieste* (Milan: All'insegna del Pesce d'oro, 1966) 13.

turns out to be seduced by the charms of his pupils. Here we are in the presence of a character who appears oscillating between the dalliances of Byron's *Don Juan* and those of the adventurer Casanova. Don Juan, exempt, precisely insofar as he is a "hero of spontaneous seduction," from the diabolical perfidiousness of Tirso de Molina's archetype, (don't forget that in *Ulysses*, Bloom gives Molly the complete works of Byron as a gift), and Casanova, a severe judge of "human weakness" who, in *Histoire de ma vie*, willingly resorts to moments of cynicism and perversion, combining vice and astuteness, instinctive behaviour and calculating opportunism. Giacomo "Casanova" Joyce, of course, does not succeed in attaining the stature of the other two, but abandons himself to the much more simple aspiration of re-affirming himself and making use of the seductions affected by others to transform them, in a Byronic sense, into a caricature of the imaginary Casanova, of one who unravels the torment of desire within the protective mesh of irony, in the first place, and then of dreaming, without running the risk of a twofold contamination—physical and moral (in other words "Love me, love my umbrella"). But who are all these *jeune filles en fleurs* who ensnare but are also ensnared by our imaginary Casanova? Far from appearing like the various Bettinas, Giuliettas, Lucias and Nenettas, dear to Casanova in his *Histoire de ma vie*, they belong to the realistic part of *Giacomo Joyce* in which the romanticised text alludes to Joyce's main activity as teacher of English who, to make ends meet, goes daily to the houses of the upper middle class of Trieste to give his lessons. Seeing that in many cases it was not simply an "hourly" visit, we must deduce that his involvement, however transitory, in the lives of his pupils' families, constituted for him a real source of information—cultural as well as emotional—with regards to a social class he did not belong to, such as to arouse in him a fascinated longing more for the *milieu* and for the style of his life of his "hosts" than for the charming girls he had to teach. An education, in other words, that in some ways resembled an *éducation sentimentale*, going far beyond the narrow limits of the room where teacher and pupil played their roles; often, what's more, hampered by the presence of a chaperone as was the practice when a girl was very young and the teacher far from the age when he is above temptation.

During his years in Trieste Joyce taught many pupils. In an episode related by Leon Edel, the English teacher is found in ironic and merry mood (still "Giacomo Giocondo") surrounded by students in a café chantant in Trieste—almost certainly the Caffè Eden in Via Acquedotto (now Via le XX Settembre) which, at that time, was the best one of its kind—while he flirts with young women, some of them his pupils, with sly gallantry. One of them, dressed in an elegant gown set off by a rose is invited by Joyce to dance, but unfortunately during the dance the flower falls to the ground. With admirable elegance mixed with unpardonable effrontery, Joyce picks it up and gives it back to the girl with the freezing comment: "I seem to have deflowered you."[6] His gallantry is also confirmed by Brenda Maddox who comments as follows on his "joyful" disposition to flirt: "He was very popular and woman students continued to be vulnerable to his well-mannered flirtatiousness, so different from the local machismo, although they also found him at times nasty and insolent."[7] Joyce's effrontery always availed itself of the benefit of paradox even though, in a certain sense, he was forced to call his whole intelligence into play in order to be able to see in an ironic light the understandable, obligatory distance—imposed by social norms—between himself and his pupils who were all well-to-do and all destined, at least in theory, to make good matches without running the risk of unnecessary "plebeian" complications. The paradox sometimes found a justification (if not an aid) in alcohol, when Professor Joyce, assiduous visitor of pubs and taverns (as well as houses of "public in-security" as he called the Triestine brothels in a witty play on the words in Italian in a letter

6   Leon Edel, *Stuff of Sleep and Dreams* (London: Chatto and Windus, 1982) 94.
7   Brenda Maddox, *Nora* (London: Minerva, 1993) 113-4.

directed to Svevo from Paris on 5 January 1921), had access to the houses of the upper middle class and infringed the rules of respectability. His passion for wine, especially the wine of Opollo from Lissa, is well-known ("a treacherous white wine which without going to your head cuts the legs from under you" as defined by Dario De Tuoni, Joyce's drinking companion on many occasions)[8] and there are numerous anecdotes in this connection beginning with the refusal of certain fathers, worried about the risks their daughters would run, to let Joyce teach in their family home. An interview conducted by Maddox, for example, quotes the case of the strict paternal veto precluding a young Triestine girl of good family from having the opportunity of studying English with Joyce: "Never with that drunk!"[9] And Vitaliano Brancati, in an article published in *Nuova Stampa Sera* in 1948 on the basis of an interview with a certain Miss G. who evidently wishes to remain anonymous, recalls how Joyce once fell to the floor during an English lesson, causing a great commotion in the family of the house. "Here in Trieste before the war," Miss G. relates,

> I had a teacher of English who taught me very little English. He was called James Joyce [...]. My mother always wondered if it wouldn't have been better to have me learn English from another teacher. He would often talk without stopping. He found things to talk about for two or three hours. He talked about me, about a friend of mine who took lessons with me, about my mother who would come as far as the door and then withdraw immediately, about my father whose voice he heard in another part of the house, about my friends and relatives whose photographs he saw on the walls and tables. Joyce didn't know them but he talked about them just the same.

The lessons, however, never followed the same cliché but went according to the teacher's mood: "Sometimes he would come

---

8   De Tuoni, *Ricordo di Joyce e Trieste*, 57.
9   Maddox, *Nora*, 114.

into the sitting room, light a cigarette and say: 'Listen, talk to me about something!' Since we were too embarrassed to say anything, he would blow in an irritated way on his lit cigarette and away he would go with the corner of his mouth twitching. My friend fell in love with him; she started to write in English and to talk in English. She really lost her head. But her mother cured her." And how did she cure her? Miss G. goes on:

> Joyce would often get drunk. One evening he fell to the floor in our sitting-room. My friend's mother stopped me from giving him a hand to get up; she took a taxi and came back with her daughter who had been visiting friends a mile or so away, Joyce was still on the floor. My friend, on her knees, with a handkerchief in her hand, just like a humble servant cleaning the titles with a rag, observed her teacher's face for a long time, the bubble of saliva on his lips, one gloved hand which seemed more than ever made of cloth, the other half-hidden under his unbuttoned waistcoat, his left eye glittering like a piece of glass under his eyelid [...]. Joyce came to when love had already fled from my friend's heart. It looked as if he had done it on purpose so happy did he seem about what happened. In fact, of course, he hadn't done it on purpose at all.[10]

As Ellmann has pointed out, James and Stanislaus's ways of giving lessons were very different. The latter often had to fill in for his brother during his absences, only to discover that James had been paid in advance and that he would get nothing. "Their styles of teaching reiterated their differences. Stanislaus was punctual and conscientious in his duties. James invariably arrived for his lessons late, and after a brief drill began to converse about all manner of subjects; the lessons would end with teacher and pupil singing an Irish song together, after which James would slide down the banister and leave, also very late."[11] This "free and easy" way of teaching could

---

10 Vitaliano Brancati, "Ricordo del Professor Joyce" *Nuova Stampa Sera*, 30-31 Aug. 1948.

11 Richard Ellmann, Introduction, *My Brother's Keeper*, by Stanislaus Joyce (New York: Viking Press, 1958) xvi.

certainly arouse enthusiasm and, objectively speaking, be more profitable of the immediacy of the approach, but there is no doubt that it was "embarrassing" in the case of a pupil of good family. Adding, however, the problem of social disparity, then episodes like the one of a girl who had pointed to the clock and in a haughty and peremptory tone observed that he had "shortened" the lesson by five minutes, must have been extremely frustrating for Joyce. But things didn't always go badly or turn out unpleasantly. On the contrary, as in the case of the family of Leopoldo Popper whose daughter, Amalia, took lessons with Joyce between 1908 and 1910, Joyce was able to extend his professional horizons to include friendly Sunday "get-togethers." From Michele Risolo, who was to marry Amalia in 1914, we learn that Joyce was an assiduous visitor at the afternoon gatherings in Villa Popper, situated in Via Alice (now 16 Via Don Minzoni, but not, in any case Via San Michele as Ellmann mistakenly affirms) Risolo recalls that,

> Pretty young friends of the Popper sisters would come from the nearby villas. There was the playing of music amid a profusion of monumental cakes and sweetmeats and tea and white coffee according to one's taste. There were also artists present because the lady of the house was a talented painter and one time pupil of Favretto's. Joyce came often alone and then later with his sister Eileen. He would play the piano and they would sing arias (Verdi and a lot of Puccini), love songs and Irish folk songs: both brother and sister had lovely voices.[12]

A carefree atmosphere in which the "English teacher" was quite at ease. There were lots of "jokes and leg-pulling" but it all took place in the "light of day" without more intimate moments portending secret, amorous encounters. Things were different in the private lessons. Risolo goes on to say:

> Among the abundant youthful gathering there was also a Florentine girl of twenty-five—the Poppers' maid. She was tall

---

12 Michele Risolo, "Mia moglie e Joyce," *Il Corriere della sera* 27 Feb. 1969: 11.

and straight and proud, like many Florentine girls. She had an oval face and clear, olive complexion, dark eyes and black hair which she wore knotted at the nape of her neck [...]. She was called Ina Bassano, and she ended up in a Nazi extermination camp. It was always she who would accompany Joyce along the corridor in the villa, preceding him to the front door, at the end of every lesson. During the lesson itself, which was held in the breakfast room, she would sit in the adjoining dining room.[13]

In the same period Joyce frequented other "well-placed" houses in the area (at that time in the area between Via Alice, Via Bellosguardo and Villa Tigor, at the top of Via Promontorio, there were many patrician villas surrounded by extensive parks) and, still according to what Risolo says,

> When Joyce left the house in Via Alice he went on to Via Bellosguardo to give a lesson to an aunt of Amalia's, then he had to come back up Via Alice, which is very steep, and from there he went down to Via Tigor where he stopped at the house of Eva Venezian of the great irredentist and heroic branch of the Venezian family and cousin of Amalia's mother: there he gave a group lesson to four girls.[14]

Is this the ambience, in which Joyce was bringing to a head that "erotic commotion," as Ellmann calls it, which lies at the basis of *Giacomo Joyce*? Certainly such a relaxed atmosphere must have exerted a strong fascination for him, even if, the happy hours spent in the Popper household showed a very different side of the coin while in other cases the distance (also of status) was rigorously maintained.

Ellmann, according to what Stanislaus told him in confidence, insists on the figure of Amalia Popper as the inspiration of Joyce's text, and goes so far as to propose her father Leopoldo (a man with thick handlebar moustache) as the model for Bloom. The year in which Joyce frequented the

---

13   Risolo, "Mia moglie e Joyce," 11.
14   Risolo, "Mia moglie e Joyce," 11.

villa in Via Alice (a solid, white construction of two storeys with an attic, surrounded by a garden and facing the Irneri "castle") can be fixed, according to Ellmann, between 1907 and 1908. But this span of time, considering what Michele Risolo says, has to be slightly modified given the fact that the lessons were held "in three widely-spaced periods" from October 1908 to the beginning of 1910. According to Risolo, Amalia did indeed suspend the lessons from November 1909 and "for almost the whole of the first half of 1910," when she went to Florence to sit in on courses at the Facoltà di Lettere of the Istituto di Studi Superiori Pratici e di Perfezionamento. Her plan was that these additional studies would enable her to sit for the integrative examinations of Greek and Latin obligatory for enrolment in that faculty. Amalia Popper had taken her School Leaving Certificate at the Civico Liceo Femminile in Trieste on 2nd July 1908, and at that school the classical languages were not on the curriculum. Hence, with the permission of the Ministry of Education to sit for the examinations of integration with a view to entering university, Amalia was able to enrol in the Faculty in the academic year 1911-1912 and after four years she took her degree at Florence. Risolo also affirms that from 1910 on, Amalia was not in Trieste and that her lessons with Joyce had ended some months earlier—therefore, Ellmann is mistaken when he talks of 1907 and 1908. However, this statement must also be corrected in the light of what Risolo himself claims to remember:

> Amalia took her last lessons a couple of months after Joyce had moved into a flat in 32 Via Barriera Vecchia. My wife told me that it was a miserable-looking house: the district was the most squalid in Trieste, and also had a bad name; Amalia saw Joyce and Giorgino, Joyce's elder child, for the last time in this house when the child was three and a half or a little more.[15]

---

15 Risolo, "Mia moglie e Joyce," 11.

At this point, however, evidently his memory does not coincide with the facts: first of all, at the end of 1909 Giorgino was already four and a half, having been born in July 1905; secondly, the Joyce family moved to 32 Via Barriera Vecchia only in August 1910. There is proof that they left the flat in 8 Via Scussa (here too Ellmann must be contradicted when he talks of December 1910) before 24 August 1910, because on that date, according to the Registry Office in Trieste, they are described as *sloggiati*, which means they had changed address; this indication is quite clear on the card relating to the Joyce family and still preserved in the town hall. Hence, Risolo in alluding in great detail to Via Barriera Vecchia (he remembers that "Joyce, who had already received, in advance, payment for twelve monthly lessons, talked with amusement to his pupil on the subject of chairs and furniture, concluding that in his new, spacious flat there wasn't enough furniture for everyone"[16]) cannot but refer to the second half of 1910 or, in other words, to a period subsequent to Amalia's first stay in Florence. This goes to show that she took up her lessons again with Joyce, even if for a few months only, in the interval between her two spells in Florence.

As we know from factual references in *Giacomo Joyce*, and taking into account the "internal evidence" in the text, Ellmann maintains that it is possible to date the work between 1911 and 1914. The initial date of the draft is based, among other things, on the reference to "pimply Meissel" who, in the Jewish cemetery in Trieste, weeps on the tomb of his wife, Ada Hirsch, who committed suicide on 20 October 1911:

> Corpses of Jews lie about me rotting in the mould of their holy field. Here is the tomb of her people, black stone, silence without hope ..... Pimply Meissel brought me here. He is beyond those trees standing with covered head at the grave of his suicide wife, wondering how the woman who slept in his bed has come to this end ..... The tomb of her people and hers:

---

[16] Risolo, "Mia moglie e Joyce," 11.

black stone, silence without hope: and all is ready. Do not die!
[*GJ* 6]

And also on the description of how Ettore Albini, critic for the socialist newspaper *L'Avanti* (Joyce is mistaken when he says *Il Secolo*), was ejected from the Scala theatre in Milan for political reasons on 17 December 1911:

> She thinks the Italian gentlemen were right to haul Ettore Albini, the critic of the *Secolo*, from the stalls because he did not stand up when the band played the Royal March. She heard that at supper. Ay. They love their country when they are quite sure which country it is. [*GJ* 9]

Both these indications appear about the middle of the text (on the sixth and the ninth pages of a total of sixteen), and if the existence in *Giacomo Joyce*, at least in relation to the evolution of the story (or stories) narrated is a chronology which goes from the beginning of his infatuation to the moment of repentance and the invocation to his wife Nora, (in a real phase of contrition) as the saviour and ultimate refuge of the "navigator" Giacomo-Odisseo[17] is accepted, the conclusion must be that some of the facts narrated may even go back to before 1911. Certainly, *Giacomo Joyce* is a fragmented text and the recycling of some of the fragments in *A Portrait*, *Exiles* and *Ulysses*, shows clearly that the author considered them distinct from each other. And yet, in the description of an *amore immaginario*, they have strong autobiographical connotations acting as a coagulating force: an interior pattern based on the explosion of an erotic delirium capable of asserting, by means of the possession of a young woman as object of desire, the supremacy of the intellect over social status, of creative instability over the reassuring "normality" of adolescence (that

[17] Why not consider all this as a prefiguration of Penelope in *Ulysses*, a name, besides, which appears in the text on page 15, even though, in fact, that work was conceived in 1914 as stated in the famous postcard to Stanislaus, written in German?

of his high class pupils) totally protected and devoid of worries about the future; in sort, the supremacy of being, over having. In this connection suffice it to quote the scene in the theatre described on page 12, where the contrast between the teacher, relegated to the gallery amid the miasma of the populace (the theatre is the Verdi, much frequented by Joyce),[18] and the pupil in a box, assumes the heartrending and dramatic tone of an illusion:

> All night I have watched her, all night I shall see her: braided and pinnacled hair and olive, oval face and calm and soft eyes. A green fillet upon her hair and about her body a green-broidered gown: the hue of the illusion of the vegetable glass of nature and of lush grass, the hair of graves. [*GJ* 12]

Therefore, the period within which the interior passion revolves may vary, theoretically, from 1905—the year in which Joyce had his first serious emotional crisis with Nora—to November 1914, when the writer took the decision to keep

---

[18] To add weight to the hypothesis that Joyce is referring to the Verdi theatre situated in the centre of the city, not far from the Rive, there is the testimony of Nora Franca Poliaghi, daughter of one of Joyce's pupils: "The gallery was then like it is today, but the people who went there in Joyce's time were different. There was always a crowd that waited for hours to get in, forming a queue that reached from the five flights of steps, along the pavement and even round the corner to the front entrance to the theatre. Evenings full to overflowing. It was normal to wait three or four hours and sometimes even longer, especially for the works of Wagner which impassioned the livelier spirits, always the first to appreciate substantial novelties. It was nothing for them to wait from the early afternoon and then to hurl themselves up the steps. They would then throw themselves on to a bench and keep places for those who had been left behind...And soon the walls would begin to perspire throwing back the vapour they received from the bodies packed on to the benches, on the steps, in the corridors, wherever there was an available space. The atmosphere became heavy, as if by the magic of fire. Vapour and a red colour everywhere. Then the sudden silence and rapt attention. During the intervals kilos of oranges were peeled and consumed and even sandwiches if the wait has been long and dinner had been skipped. Paper and peel were quickly thrown under the benches. Children gorged and soiled themselves. The adults looked, listened and passed comments." (*La Gazetta di Parma* 10 Nov. 1968).

Giacomo Joyce private and completed chapter V of *A Portrait*, inserting into it passages from the work set in Trieste. A span of dates which certainly embraces two important emotional experiences (not to mention, very probably, other difficult situations) which involve two women—two pupils—capable of arousing in the writer a complex and binding sentiment. Of the second, Amalia Popper, we have already spoken; of the first, for whom Joyce's amorous passion can be placed around 1905, we have more to say.

Jim and Nora's matrimonial crisis took place, as we can see from a letter of 4 December 1905 from Joyce to his aunt Josephine, after the birth of Giorgino:

> I have hesitated before telling you that I imagine the present relations between Nora and myself are about to suffer some alteration [...]. It is possible to see that I am partly to blame if such a change as I think I foresee takes place but it will hardly take place through my fault alone. [*L* 128]

It seems to coincide with a strong infatuation for a young pupil: Anna Maria Schleimer. The first person to talk about her was Stelio Crise, a Triestine scholar, who in a lecture given during the celebrations of the Joyce Centenary held in the foyer of the Verdi theatre on 1 February 1982, advanced the hypothesis that the "young unnamed woman" in *Giacomo Joyce*—the unknown "Who" with which the narrative opens—might well not be Amalia Popper at all. "No one," affirmed Crise,

> has ever, in any way, even thought to consider another person who could be identified as the inspiration and model for the protagonist of the Triestine poem: in other words a pupil of his—Annie—whose name can only be mentioned here for the moment. She loved her teacher of English and until her death she preserved a palpitating memory of that love, together with the books and letters she had received from him. The course of love did not run smooth nor could it result in the marriage which Joyce too declared he wanted to enter into, because of the

determined opposition of Annie's father, a successful Triestine businessman who could never have conceded the hand of his daughter to a miserable teacher of English.[19]

"Who? A pale face surrounded by heavy odorous furs. Her movements are shy and nervous. She uses quizzing-glasses. *Yes*: a brief syllable. A brief laugh. A brief beat of the eyelids"(*GJ* 1). The mysterious description with which *Giacomo Joyce* opens, reveals certain details—the paleness of the face, the shyness and nervousness in equal measure, the tones of an imperceptible gaiety, a tendency to laugh (or rather to smile), mitigated by a coy reserve, the coquettishness of the quizzing-glass acting as a frame to the seductive beat of the eyelids, swift as an improvised decorum—which show a rather immature figure, better defined as "a young person of quality." And the allusion to "*Yes*" (a brief syllable) seems to assimilate her very name, marking affirmatively the figure of the woman: Annie, whose name is short and sounds like a "Sì" which in Italian means "Yes."

Annie is, in fact, the short form of the Christian name of one of Joyce's pupils (he gave her lessons between 1905 and 1906) who was called Anna Maria Schleimer and who at that time lived near Piazza di Scorcola, near the sumptuous residence of Baron Ambrogio Ralli, to whom Joyce also gave lessons and who is quoted by name in the text of *Giacomo Joyce*: "As I came out of Ralli's house I come upon her suddenly as we are both giving alms to a blind beggar. She answers my sudden greeting by turning and an averting her black basilisk eyes" (*GJ* 14). Daughter of Andrea Schleimer, who was born at Moswald (the family came from Carintha and owned land in Slovenia) by profession a merchant of citrus fruit and spices, and of Emilia Baumeister, Anna Maria was born in Trieste in 5 Via della Acque (now Via Timeus) on 25 July 1881. According to Crise, who related the episode to Brenda Maddox, "one day

19 Stelio Crise, "Il triestino James Joyce," *Il ritorno di Joyce* proceedings of the Joyce Centenary celebrations, Trieste, 1982, 94-95.

Joyce kissed her and suggested that she marry him. Whether he was serious or not (he was, after all, legally free to marry her), Annie was captivated and told her father. Her English lessons came to an abrupt end. Signor Schleimer was horrified at the thought of his daughter involved with a miserable language teacher."[20] Annie at that time was twenty-four (Joyce was one year younger) and her mother-tongue was German though she also spoke Italian well. Unlike Amalia Popper, she has no Jewish connections. She had a particular inclination for music, loved the piano and had a valuable grand piano at home—"Unreadiness. A bare apartment. Torbid daylight. A long black piano: coffin of music" (*GJ* 16). Lessons with Joyce were previously held, through the Berlitz School, at her home in the Scorcola district of the city (Scorcola 142, not far from Baron Ralli's house in piazza Scorcola 3, now 1), where the family lived until 1915, when they moved to Via da Palestrina, off Via Battisti, where Andrea Schleimer had his firm,[21] and it is here that Annie fell in love with her teacher who was practically the same age as herself—"Whirling wreaths of grey vapour upon the earth. Her face, how grey and grave! Dank matted hair. Her lips press softly, her sighing breath comes through. Kissed" (*GJ* 14). But they also met outside, during excursions to Carso, which Annie loved (especially Monte Taiano, in Istria) in the company of friends and acquaintances. The excursions often ended up in the "Osmizze" (seasonal taverns) for refreshments. Even after the violent reaction of her father (she was to continue living with him after her mother's death) which caused the girl to have a life long period of depression, Annie and Giacomo Joyce continued to keep in touch and at a distance of many years (she died a spinster in the Old People's Home "Villa Verde" in 15 Via Della Bona at Gorizia on 17 September 1972), she showed some letters to her friend Zora Skerk Koren. "I met her for the last time in Gorizia," the latter recalls,

---

[20] Maddox, *Nora*, 90.
[21] Interview with Eddy Schleimer, nephew of Annie, 28 June 1995.

but I had known her since 1954, when I was her guest in Trieste in Via Gatteri, in a five storeyed house without a lift. "I chose it deliberately," she told me, "to keep in shape." She had a heavily marked copy of *Ulysses*. I always saw it well to the fore on a little table. She used to read and reread it, although she complained about her eyesight. The letters were in a packet, tied with red tape, but I don't know what happened to them after her death.[22]

What is more, Annie had a real obsession with umbrellas and, unlike Amalia Popper, she had undergone an operation for appendicitis. These two facts also seem to be reflected in the quotes from *Giacomo Joyce*:

Unreadiness. A bare apartment. Torbid daylight. A long black piano: coffin of music. Poised on its edge a woman's hat, red-flowered, and an umbrella, furled. Her arms: a casque, gules, and blunt spear on a field, sable. [*GJ* 16]

and

The housemaid tells me that they had to take her away at once to the hospital, *povretta*, that she suffered so much, so much, *povretta*, that it is very grave [...]. Operated. The surgeon's knife has probed in her entrails and withdrawn, leaving the raw jagged gash of its passage on her belly. [*GJ* 11]

Hence it is necessary to conclude that the span of time of the narrative runs from 1905 to 1914 (the year of the "definitive" draft) and embraces at least two significant "relationships" of the writer's, not necessarily bearing the mark, as Ellmann maintains, of the "paradigm of unsatisfied love as it takes hold of the no longer young" (*GJ* xix), given the fact that with Annie, the love is between two people of the same age.

---

[22] Interview with Zora Skerk Koren 21 Mar. 1995.

Giacomo Joyce constitutes, not only the trepidating diary of a "violation" of love and of status, but also an organic constellation of epiphanies by means of which physical desire, the real and tangible product of the corporeal closeness between teacher and pupil, becomes spiritualised in the perspective of a dream. It is not a question of "one" woman, but the fusion of two very different women; and, in any case, it represents the symbolic projection of several women, including Nora, united by the common anomalous relationship between a seducer who ends up seduced (Joyce himself) and a pupil who gives lessons rather than receiving them (lessons, obviously, in desire). It is not one specific figure, therefore, but the mental state which regulates, by means of the occult laws of plagiarism—which is itself an underhand form of seduction—the imprecise contours of a complex series of emotions. A diary which draws on facts in order to sublimate them: and this comes out, above all, in the mixture of real and imaginary data. On the one hand, in fact, there is an abundance of everyday "objects," fragmentary physical references; glimpses of the landscape, images of Trieste with its steep streets like Via San Michele, which Joyce went up on his way back from the sea-front to his house in 4 Via Bramante where he lived from September 1912 to June 1915, alongside sinful "glimpses" of female attire; "A skirt caught back by her sudden moving knee; a white lace edging of an underskirt lifted unduly; a leg-stretched web of stocking" (*GJ* 9).[23] On the other hand, the intermittent appearance of "transfiguring" situations. The following are some significant examples: the beat of the eyelids beating out an infinitesimal time—"A brief laugh. A brief beat of the eyelids"(*GJ* 1)— consigned entirely to the spirit; the rhythm of heels, agitated and nervous, reproducing the pulsating emotion in the

---

23 The description is curiously like the one which marks the culminating phase of Gerty MacDowell's "voyeuristic offer" in the "Nausicaa" episode of *Ulysses*. But here, to a completely casual initial fact is to be added the "sin" of insistence of the part of the woman.

breast—"Tapping clacking heels, high and hollow noise" (*GJ* 1); a description of the face "smitten by hot creamy light" (*GJ* 2), which makes use of surrealistic tones; the continual lighting up and going out of lights and the shadowy hues on the features of the woman, with nuances that get lost, as in the case of "kindling opal light" (*GJ* 4) in the pure abstraction of the soul; the recourse to the evanescence of memory capable of dissolving the concrete geometry of the city in a vaporous vagueness—"Moving mists on the hill...Hanging mists over the damp trees" (*GJ* 6); a tendency to scan odour which leads, according to the emotions recollected, to "objective correlatives" of desire (mysterious smells, citrus fruit tickling the nose, images of perfumes connected with the visual selection of various parts of the anatomy or the attire of the woman) or else of frustration and unappeasement—gelid and disquieting ecclesiastical incense, vulgar body smells capable of inhibiting any joyous transport, like those emanating from the gallery in the theatre such as "sour reek of armpits [...] melting breast ointments [...] the breath of suppers of sulphurous garlic, foul phosphorescent farts [...]" (*GJ* 12).

If it is true, as Ellmann maintains, that *Giacomo Joyce* represents Joyce's leave-taking from a part of his life and the prelude to the discovery of a new expressive form, then it also represents the renunciation of a form of addiction—the seducer/seduced syndrome—which he lived as an acute form of suffering (may the scene in the gallery, in which he perceives all the frustration caused by the sense of distance between two beings who are too far apart and too different suffice: he among the populace, she unattainable in her role among the elite). Personal experience is certainly called into play here, especially where Joyce, in an ambiguous alternation between attraction and repulsion as regards betrayal in love, initiates the well-known, contentious correspondence with Nora in August 1909, concerning Cosgrave, and he immerses himself in meditations on the adultery of Bertha/Nora and Robert/Roberto Prezioso (at that time editor of the Triestine newspaper *Il Piccolo della Sera* and supposed lover of Nora) in *Exiles*, a work that was completed at the same time as the final draft of *Giacomo Joyce*.

In the theatrical text, in fact, Joyce seems to feel, by means of the psychology of Robert in love with Nora, the subtle fascination of the ambiguity of seduction, which may imply, at a subconscious level, an "innocent" (but for him disconcerting) complicity on the part of one who, although rejecting it, "dreams" of the consummation of that love. Significantly, in the intimate conversation between Bertha and Robert in which there is an allusion to adultery, which there is no certainty actually took place, the man asks: "Bertha! What happened last night? [...] Were you mine in that sacred night of love? Or have I dreamed it?" To which the reply is: "Remember your dream of me. You dreamed that I was yours last night." And in conclusion Robert says: "In all my life only that dream is real" (*E* 106).

As Anthony Burgess has pointed out, it is precisely in *Exiles* that Joyce makes concrete that operation of destruction of the past which is the prelude to the rational choice, to the final acceptance of the mental state of the "exile" (and it should be added that "exile" is also separation from autobiographical reality), but within the mechanism of the delegitimation of the past, the function of *Giacomo Joyce* cannot be ignored. In this text too, in fact, the reader witnesses a progressive ascertainment of the relativity of language: incapable, in the last analysis, of defining the contours of events, incapable of determining the chronology of facts, reduced to summing up even physical details which never produce—and here lies one of the most recurrent ironies—the totality of the person. Annie and Amalia (like all the other pupils of Joyce's years in Trieste) alternate in a kaleidoscope of fetishistic symbols—ribbons and quizzing-glasses, heels and hats, boots and umbrellas, veils and petticoats barely glimpsed—without ever taking shape as a unified form; without ever achieving, by means of a final adhesion to autobiographical reality, that impulse towards a materialisation of their bodies which, in any case, would only end up by contradicting the growing tension of the writer who wishes "definitively" to sacrifice those palpitating human creatures to his writing.

It may even be claimed that in *Giacomo Joyce* there is a tendency to fragment the physical image of the woman, similar to that which characterised work of the early T. S. Eliot (although with fewer implications of the peculiarly Catholic or Anglo-Catholic sense of guilt). In Eliot, in poems like the "Love Song of J. Alfred Prufrock," it was the equally fetishistic accumulation of physical details (from the woman's *décolleté* to close-ups of her arms covered in jewels but also "spoilt" by pitiless brown hair) that generated in the protagonist a sense of panic and of impotence. In Joyce, it is the glimpses of parts of the female body which constantly emerge and are considered with the analytical exaltation of a literary voyeurism which gradually rejects a real, somewhat pathological, if not altogether autobiographical, voyeurism: "jawbones," "moistened brow," "softened pulp of the eyes," "meek supple tendonous neck," "boots laced in deft crisscross over the flesh-warmed tongue," "long lewdly leering lips," "slender buttocks of smooth polished silver," "fingers, cold and calm and moving." To which may be added the image of the brothel found at the same time in *A Portrait*, and in anticipation of that in *Ulysses*, as an exaltation of that purification of reality by means of dreams and in preparation for the climax of invocation to Nora, a real Dantesque Beatrice, to save him and to absolve him at the moment when temptation has become so "real" that it requires the writer to flee into the dimension of literature.

Only by choosing to be an imaginary Casanova, is it possible for him to confirm the primacy of writing over the interference of the "physical," and to do so, it is necessary to expiate the guilt of desire by passing through a stage of spiritual degradation (a procedure similar to the one expounded in *A Portrait*). From a vision of perdition—"kind gentlewomen wooing from their balconies with sucking mouths, the pox-fouled wenches and young wives that, gaily yielding to their ravishers, clip and clip again" (*GJ* 9)—there is a transition to a vision of Salvation—"She listens: virgin most prudent" (*GJ* 9)—while there comes into play the weapon of irony, capable of reducing the sense of guilt and relieving physical tension: capable, finally, of preparing, by means of a new dialectic relation to reality, the transition to dreams— "those quiet cold fingers have touched the pages, foul and fair, on which my shame shall glow forever" (*GJ* 13). "Pages," in other words, a literary text, which can redeem; a writing that emerges from the formless mass of emotions and memories and for which dreams constitute the only, inescapable, representative form.

The conclusion may be justified by saying that reality, if it is to succeed in reasserting itself, must be diluted in dreams or—and it is here that the extraordinary creative ambiguity of *Giacomo Joyce* lies—that dreams, which is to say the finished literary work, are the true reality—so true as to be tangible. A "page" so physically concrete that it can be touched (and this is the real desire of the artist who was able to transform himself, albeit with great effort, into an imaginary Casanova!) so assertive that it can be consigned definitively to history.

Richard Brown

Eros and Apposition

Too often considered, like *Exiles* and the bulk of the critical writings, an ugly duckling of the Joycean *œuvre*, *Giacomo Joyce* has received less than its due from Joyce criticism. Unpublished during his lifetime (and not intended for separate publication, since choice phrases were harvested from it for key passages in *A Portrait*, for poems, and throughout *Ulysses*) it has sometimes seemed above all to confirm Joyce's genius at knowing when not to publish his work. Lacking the ostentatious narrative scale of the published fiction, it has failed to attract much attention in terms of the increasingly sophisticated theories of narrative that have been applied to Joyce; more surprisingly, even students of Joyce's language have rarely bothered to take it into account.

Despite, or perhaps even because of, the fact that we tend to read it retrospectively, with as strong a sense of the context into which scenes and phrases were eventually transferred as of that in which they appear here, *Giacomo Joyce* is a fascinating work. Since it develops certain obsessive Joycean themes and highlights certain dimensions of his use of literary language, it might serve as a useful testing ground for theories about Joyce: exposing as misconceived any generalisations about what is or what is not properly Joycean that would not apply to this work. Indeed in certain respects—in its use of some linguistic effects;

---

* A version of this essay was published in *Joyce Studies Annual* (1990): 132-141.

in its sophisticated and self-conscious sexuality; and not least in its compact length—*Giacomo Joyce* seems a very available text for some of our critical and theoretical interests into the 1990s and beyond.

The first glimpse of *Giacomo Joyce* was provided in Richard Ellmann's biography, in 1959, where substantial chunks of the whole were quoted and glossed in an appropriately biographical manner (*JJI* 350-60). The complete text appeared in 1968, also under Ellmann's editorial charge. Here the introduction and notes treat the piece more as a finished work in its own right (and some early reviewers were puzzled by the reduced emphasis that was placed on identifying the woman in the work as Joyce's Triestine pupil Amalia Popper). Yet the reading remains one which presents the work as essentially autobiographical in character: noting incidents from Joyce's life which are incorporated into it and which can be given a precise date, and extensively glossing words or phrases that were harvested for *A Portrait*, *Pomes Penyeach* and *Ulysses*.[1]

Not least among the advantages of this kind of presentation was that it enabled us to understand much about the background to the work that may easily otherwise have been irrecoverable. However, there are literary critical disadvantages. In the established reading, the work narrates a reasonably straightforward incident: the infatuation of a teacher for his pupil. The location is Trieste, with dreamlike renderings of other places. It has a simple, chronological plot: beginning with the first sight of the girl, climaxing in an imagined erotic possession, and ending with her rejection of him. A clear line of development of the lover's feelings can be observed. The lover-persona ends by realising that he has failed and opts for writing as a kind of alternative to sex, settling into a resigned middle-aged belief that "youth has an end."

---

[1] A useful review of this material is contained in Vicki Mahaffey's "Giacomo Joyce," *A Companion to Joyce Studies*, eds. Zack Bowen and James F. Carens (Westport, CT: Greenwood Press, 1984).

I would not argue that none of these things are there, or that there is another secret plot that has hitherto been missed, but such accounts tend to obscure what is essential to the experience of reading the work. As a narrative *Giacomo Joyce* is oblique, opaque, and disconcerting. The reader is rarely sure of the dividing line between vividly particularised dream and fantasised real experience. Locations shift, with or without direct identification: from the house of the teacher to that of the pupil, around exterior city scenes, from Trieste to Paris and back, and to other more fantastic locations, in a way that is not always easy to follow or to explain. Narrative sequence is markedly discontinuous and chronology subverted.

Identities are destabilised by the use of pronouns rather than proper names for the lover and beloved. The first word is an interrogative "Who?" and the pronouns of the enigmatic final "Envoy: Love me, love my umbrella" may refer either to the woman (whose umbrella we have just seen), or to Giacomo (as a Prufrockian symbolic stage property), or (since the *envoi* of a *ballade* is traditionally a further recommendation or gloss given in the first person of the poet) to Joyce himself. The "I" of the poem is no more stable: Joyce's persona mixes confessional intimacy with the most extravagant posturing; unleashed unconscious fantasy with cool, rational detachment; unmediated autobiographical detail with his tentative, fragile, ironic self-translation into the Casanova of the title, that is itself only one of the intertextual filiations that can be unwoven from the text.[2] Identity is further destabilised through the transformatory language of images that is adopted throughout.

Most readers would agree that there seems to be or has been a rejection of the lover at the end (some suggest that there may

---

[2] Besides Giacomo Casanova, intertextual identifications include the four heretical theologians mentioned, the Lövborg of *Hedda Gabler*, Hamlet, Christ, "slobbering" James I of England, John Dowland, Shakespeare, Dante, and the count Orsino or brother Giacomo in Shelley's *The Cenci*. Jacques Derrida played on such self-translation in *La Carte postale* (Paris: Aubier-Flammarion, 1980), 255: "James (les deux, les trois), Jacques, Giacomo Joyce—ta contrefacture fait merveille, ce pendant a l'invoice: 'Envoy: love me love my umbrella.'"

have been an inverted anticipation of Molly's first and last words in *Ulysses*, since this woman begins with a "Yes" and ends with a "No") (*JJII* 348, *GJ* xx). But even such apparent certainties are fragile. This interpretation rests heavily on the moment when the woman greets the lover "wintrily" at the end and yet, right at the beginning of the piece (and apparently forming an essential part of the atmosphere of erotic anticipation and attraction), she is described in terms of the "wintry air" of a gothic castle that is suddenly conjured up by the clacking hollow sound of her high-heeled shoes (*GJ* 1). Indifference may be an attractive quality in her throughout and her umbrella as much an invitation as a denial.

Frankly sensual and semi-hallucinatory transformations are the characteristic features of a work whose poetry plays with surface appearances and their changeability. Rather than being a work which develops towards an end, *Giacomo Joyce* seems to be a work which is profoundly static. It is not static, though, in Stephen's sense in *A Portrait*, when he talks of an aesthetic stasis which is "above desire and loathing" (*P* 205). The stasis of *Giacomo Joyce* is one where the lack of clear progress toward a goal serves to keep desire and loathing very much in view as they writhe together in an explosive and irresolvable tension.

One feature of *Giacomo Joyce* which sums up this static but transformatory quality and is essential to its unique and powerful poetry is the consistent and characteristic use of the startling poetic "image" or "visual pun" as it has more recently become known in such English poets of the younger so-called "Martian" generation as Craig Raine and Christopher Reid. We may also, to be sure, be struck by the synæsthetic play with musical and other sounds, with tastes, touch ("A touch, a touch"), and above all, with the smells and the odours of the streets and of the woman herself, yet the visual (as the term "image" sometimes implies) seems to predominate.

It is no surprise that *Giacomo Joyce* should be so made up of images, since it was at the time of the request from Pound for new work in December 1913 (when Pound was at the height of his "imagist" propagandism) that Joyce seems to have been gathering images for the work (*JJI* 360-2). Images or imagistic elements in the prose-poem include the profusion of concrete visual details and the use of briefly evoked locations for whatever symbolic resonance they may create, without resorting to intrusive or directive comment. Not least, brooding images are the food of morose delectation: the voyeuristic eroticism that fixes its attention on the female object enough to turn a "Martian" poet towards Venus.

The woman herself is transformed in a phantasmagoria of successive verbal images. By synecdoche she becomes parts of her body or qualities of her manner. Repeatedly dressed in shadows, she is purring cat, princess, "filly foal," evening (or Eve), blushing innocent or incestuous harem courtesan, a sparrow, "a pampered fowl," an owl or daughter and sister of owls, Dante's Beatrice, the Beatrice of *The Cenci*, a surgical patient, an antelope, a bird again, a black pullet, a quagmire (albeit one with pure fingers), an odourless flower, an odalisque, a basilisk, a gay Parisienne, a "starry snake" or "cold nightsnake,"[3] and ultimately, a hat and an umbrella, that are themselves heraldically transformed into helmet and spear.

This list makes up an astonishing bestiary of shifting and sometimes contradictory perceptions. Far from offering any portrait of the woman in which she could be expected to or might want to recognise herself, it offers an *eidolon* whose surfaces, whose outlines, and even whose identity are invaded and traduced by the observer's desire. Sexual politicians have discussed and will discuss whether and the extent to which such invasions and traductions represent an entrapment or a liberation for a woman imaginatively subjected to them, or whether they may, in fact, represent both. These are complex

---

[3] It seems not to have been noticed that this "starry snake" may be read astronomically as a reference to the constellation Serpens: a strange constellation inasmuch as it is composed of two separate parts, one each side of the constellation Ophiuchus. There may clearly be some relevance here to the psychology of the division of the female object.

questions and ones made still more complex in this text by the elements of subjection and traduction that are presented as essential to the lover's state of mind. It is, at any rate, the proliferation and predominance of these images (as well as the significance of each one) that demand attention.

A pattern repeated in three of the four-dozen widely spaced paragraphs (and echoed within several others) stands out as offering the semantic experience of this prose-poem in its purest, simplest form:

Long lewdly leering lips: dark-blooded molluscs. [*GJ* 5]

Great bows on her slim bronze shoes: spurs of a pampered fowl. [*GJ* 8]

My words in her mind: cold polished stones sinking through a quagmire. [*GJ* 13]

Each statement contains the naked apposition of object and images that is the privileged form of congressional semantic behaviour in this type of poetry. In the first two the apposition is between the visual object as directly perceived and the same object transformed into something it may be thought to resemble. The third, equally familiar in poetic writing and especially so in justifications for imagistic writing, is between the abstract "thought" and a concrete image for it. In each the analogies are not familiar or clichéd but surprise by the heterogeneity of the elements joined in the Renaissance "Metaphysical" manner. In each the unglossed analogy demands a powerful feeling, as well as disturbing and contradictory connections between delight and disgust. In each, the action of analogy is reinforced, above all, through the grammatical relation of the two phrases to another, which is one of apposition: syntactic or syntagmatic parallelism or reduplication. Furthermore, in each, this appositional status is marked by means of punctuation: with a colon.

Apposition or grammatical parallelisms and the related use of the colon as a punctuation mark seem even more pervasive and characterising features of *Giacomo Joyce* than images themselves. Items in the portrait accumulate or agglomerate rather than progress from cause to result: observations, transformations, and interpretations heaping on one another in a way that is still further emphasised by the purely appositional device of repetition that so colours the opening passages: "A brief syllable. A brief laugh. A brief beat of the eyelids" (*GJ* 1); "shadow her false smile, [...] Shadows streak [...] grey wheyhued shadows" (*GJ* 2); and "Frail gift, frail giver, frail blue-veined child" (*GJ* 3).

Joyce uses colons a remarkable fifty times in these few pages. Such arithmetic is fairly pointless but that makes just over three per page, one per paragraph or one every five sentences. (This last statistic sounds far less exceptional, defining sentences as units bounded by a full stop. But when we remember how few of these "sentences" are syntactically complete and how many are themselves single words, exclamations and so on, the full picture becomes clear.)

In discursive English usage the colon can have a number of different functions. According to the *OED* it serves merely to mark a discontinuity of syntactical construction greater that that of a semi-colon but less than that of a full stop.[4] Other authorities are more specific. It may be used when the preceding part of the sentence is complete in sense and construction and the following part arises from it in sense though not in construction. It may mark a step forward from clause to main theme or from premise to conclusion. Or it may introduce an example, a list of items, direct speech, or a quotation.[5]

Joyce's "colonialism" functions in a poetic rather than discursive context and should remind us of the origin of the

---

4 *The Oxford English Dictionary* (Oxford: Oxford University Press, 1971), 469a.
5 Slightly adapted from *The Oxford Dictionary for Writers and Editors* (Oxford: Clarendon Press, 1981).

word colon in Greek prosody where it meant a division or part of a sentence or strophe in poetry. In *Giacomo Joyce* a colon may gloss or expand upon an opaque phrase like the reference to her "rounded and ripened" breeding (*GJ* 2). It may introduce direct speech or a quotation, or a list like that of the "symphony of smells" at the opera: "sour reek of armpits, nozzled oranges, melting breast ointments, mastick water, the breath of suppers of sulphurous garlic, foul phosphorescent farts, opoponax, the frank sweat of marriageable and married womankind, the soapy stink of men [...]" (*GJ* 12). Typically, though, the colon is used to separate a symptomatic observation from a gloss that diagnoses or interprets it: "Cobweb handwriting [...]: a young person of quality" (*GJ* 1); or again: "She listens: virgin most prudent" (*GJ* 9). Or else it may retrospectively gloss rather than introduce a piece of direct speech: "*Yes*: a brief syllable" (*GJ* 1); or "*Mio padre*: she does the simplest acts with distinction" (*GJ* 5), creating an effect of translation which is heightened by the mixture of languages used here and elsewhere in the text.

More typically still, like the instances quoted above, colons are used to introduce striking images: "The long eyelids beat and lift: a burning needleprick stings and quivers in the velvet iris" (*GJ* 1); or (an image Joyce liked so much he re-worked for "Scylla and Charybdis," "Sirens," and "Circe"): "A long black piano: coffin of music" (*GJ* 16).[6]

Appositions allow a break in the necessary sequence, the teleological insistence, of the syntactic chain and open up the opportunity for a whole range of alternative semantic possibilities: for fascinating considerations of the grounds of relationship between lips and snails, women's shoes and cockfighting, ideas and how they feel, blinking and acupuncture, music and death, and so on. Literal reference

---

[6] In "Scylla and Charybdis" books are "coffined thoughts" (*U* 159.19); in "Sirens" a baby grand piano appears as a crocodile (*U* 233.39); and in "Circe" Father Dolan emerges from the "coffin" of the pianola (*U* 458.2-4). In general so much of the linguistic play of *Giacomo Joyce* is re-used and, for that matter, so many of its scenes may be said to have been reworked that a full list of such re-writings is well beyond the scope of such a short article as this.

becomes harder and more challenging to establish; metaphorical and symbolic references abound. Liberated from the iron syntax of the text, items resonate in the intertext.

What we can see here is Joyce experimenting with new possibilities in syntax and it is interesting to see how frequent use of colons resurfaces in the naïve style of Stephen in the early chapters of *A Portrait* and in the brooding interior monologues of Stephen in "Proteus" and Bloom in "Lotus Eaters" and "Lestrygonians." Joyce is neither markedly correct nor consistent in his use of colons. He occasionally uses commas, semi-colons, and full stops for just such appositions as these.[7] But that itself seems right for a piece in which the colon serves primarily as a licentious device that permits all kinds of things to lie next to each other and intermingle suggestively with each other in the text without formal syntactical introduction, let alone binding syntactical marriage.

Such yokings are, in their very nature, free from conventional grammatical ties and able to enjoy degrees of polysemy, an "adultery of wisdom" (*GJ* 15), that more structured or legitimate liaisons could not allow. Pairs of dots form a kind of double negative: straining to enforce a separation between semantic items that, like Pyramus and Thisbe, have a natural attraction for each other which is so strong that it finds a chink in the wall through which transgressive and even perverse minglings can take place. No doubt there are semantic equivalents for the dangerous liaisons, the palpitations and osculations, the veilings and unveilings, the masochistic adorations, foot, hair, and clothing fetishisms, the humiliations, the inquisitions, the sacrilegious eroticisation of Notre Dame, the prostitutions, the adulteries, polygamies, and miscegenations, the voyeurisms, the bestialities, the Sadean lacerations, the necrophiliae, incestuous executions, and surgical sex murders that subliminally decorate this text. And if it all makes Kathy Acker look like Enid Blyton, it does so not at least because polysemy permits such polymorphous perversity

---

[7] Compare, for instance, "Frail gift, frail giver, frail blue-veined child" (*GJ* 3).

to be shown here as a threatening undercurrent of the everyday.[8]

What characterises *Giacomo Joyce* may then be this device of apposition. The related term "juxtaposition" was once familiar to literature students as a quick way to impress an examiner but has more recently gathered dust. It is an important and relevant concept, though, and looking through places where it arose before it became so clichéd, one comes upon the work of the poet Arthur Hugh Clough. In Canto II of his epistolary poem the "Amours de Voyage" (published in 1858), the traveller/hero Claude finds himself in tempting proximity to Miss Georgina Trevellyan. In the vertiginous nineteenth-century atmosphere of detheologisation, Claude dilates on the distinct and respective powers of juxtaposition and affinity in affairs of the heart.[9] It is, of course, a crucial distinction and a sharply phrased one: the term affinity implying a historical or sometimes even mystical community of origins or of ultimate goals, whilst juxtaposition or apposition need imply no further connection beyond the physical contiguity of the present moment. We may like to believe that true love marriages are made in heaven and last forever, but then how is it that they seem to spark off between two people sitting next to each other on railway cars?

Linguistically and erotically *Giacomo Joyce* is a text where the balance is tipped toward apposition rather than endogamous attractions, by temporary connections that Joyce felt no compunction in converting to other ends. The classroom setting

---

[8] Again an exploration of this "semantic perversity" is well beyond my scope here but one could, perhaps, start with the almost bottomless range of intertextual echoes that the language seems to generate, or. for instance, the tendency of certain decontextualised phrases to attain a kind of self-referential quality, or special prophetic resonance for the textual interpreter. "It is the other. Shc"; "A lady of letters"; "The unseen reader"; and "Adultery of wisdom" all seem to be such phrases.

[9] For a recent annotated selection of Clough that includes the whole of "Amours de Voyage" and the poem "Natura Naturans" in which Clough also deals with "juxtaposition," see *Arthur Hugh Clough: Selected Poems*, ed. Samuel Chew (Manchester: Carcanet, 1985).

is, no doubt on one level, autobiographical or confessional. It also has the heightening effect of turning language from medium to object, drawing attention to the synecdoche that recurs in the text: "She never blows her nose. A form of speech: the lesser for the greater" (*GJ* 2). Still further, though, it draws on the tensions of a social occasion where intimate proximity and the mutual interpenetration of ideas between strangers familiarly takes place whilst full physical intimacy is usually precluded.

A truant, as Richard Ellmann pointed out, from the recently opened aesthetic school of the Stephen Dedalus of *A Portrait*, but an attentive pupil of the new academy he opens in the Trieste lectures and reviews and in the library episode of *Ulysses*, the Joyce of *Giacomo Joyce* seeks out an art that is based, like Wilde's art, according to Joyce's view, on a kind of sexual "sin" (*CW* 7-10).

"That age is here and now" (*GJ* 9). Does *Giacomo Joyce* only make a consoling overture to a period of resigned middle age? In this phrase we are referred not to personal ageing but to the historical age of Shakespeare's Dowland, *Hamlet*, and the "court of slobbering James": a disturbingly contradictory period of a musical and poetic beauty that seems "quaint and far" but also a period of violently emerging national politics and of "pox-fouled wenches," disease and death. Uneasy, in love as in language, with the confinements of conventional romantic feeling and the restrictions of the orthodox church conceptualisation of legitimate affinity, the poetry and sensuality of *Giacomo Joyce* recreate such a Renaissance moment of total erotic, poetic, and indeed political possibility that Joyce found in the chance appositions of Trieste on the eve of the First World War.

Louis Armand

Resistances: Symptom and Desire in *Giacomo Joyce*

From its very first word *Giacomo Joyce* is involved in the play of
an analytical will to knowledge. The question *Who?* will have
opened the text at the outset to a philosophical or analytic
grammar; a grammar preoccupied with the "inspection,
appropriation, identification and verification of identity."[1]
However, it is precisely such a grammar that is most radically
resisted in Joyce's text. The logic of identity is suspended at
every turn, suspending analysis in the interval of deferred
signification, held there in suspense of the enigmatic phantasm
of its referent:

> Who? A pale face surrounded by heavy odorous furs. Her
> movements are shy and nervous. She uses quizzing glasses.
> [*GJ* 1]

* A version of this paper was presented at the XIVth International James Joyce
Symposium, 12-18 June, 1994, University of Seville, Spain.

1 Jacques Derrida, *Spurs: Nietzsche's Styles/Eperons: Les Styles de Nietzsche*, trans.
Barbara Harlow (Chicago: Chicago University Press, 1979) 103. N.B. It is not my
intention here to attempt an explication of Joyce's posthumous text. Instead I
propose to situate my discourse in a topological relation to it, according to what
I will call the *resistance* of fantasy; of the phantasm or ghost; between the eye
and the gaze; in order to remark certain ways in which *Giacomo Joyce* operates
within this articulated opening of desire.

A question, with neither object nor predicate, opens the text in a gesture of interrogative dis-location and dis-placement. This ambivalent colophon points us on the way of indefinite articulation: a fragmentary play whose ocular metaphor is immediately encoded in a signifier of identity "effaced" in gendered, or rather genital, difference: *A pale face surrounded by heavy odorous furs.* The implied transposition from feminine identity to female sex is suggestive of a whole tradition of like symbolism, from *Venus im Pelz* to Freud's "Medusa's Head." Cliché, or archetype, this libidinised visage nevertheless "gives" the only consequent response to the question of identity posed at the outset of *Giacomo Joyce,* and subsequently assumes a negative formation in the "quizzing" of a visual prosthesis. Its force and form as an *exemplum* of a certain subversion of the subject (*Who?*) likewise orientates a disavowal of the analytic inertia which underwrites the above schematisation of desire.[2] Operating in what Jacques Lacan elsewhere describes as a "punctiform, evanescent function":

> it leaves the subject in ignorance as to that which lies beyond [it], an ignorance characteristic of all progress in thought that occurs in the way constituted by philosophical research.[3]

The question marks a general displacement in the mode of reference: it arrests, in advance, the grammatical and analytic subject in its "desire" towards/for identity, but it does not substitute itself as a stable referent in place of identity. No sooner does the question *Who?* present itself than it fades, diffused with other significations; it immediately shifts its ground through a play of substitution: "A pale face," which is in turn displaced as the visual locus by "heavy odorous furs," "Her movements," and so on. Identity is indefinitely suspended

² Cf. Sigmund Freud, "Medusa's Head," *The Standard Edition of the Complete Psychological Works of Sigmund Freud,* vol. XVIII, trans. J. Strachey (London: Hogarth Press and The Institute of Psycho-analysis, 1955).

³ Jacques Lacan, *The Four Fundamental Concepts of Psycho-analysis,* ed. Jacques-Alain Miller, trans. Alan Sheridon (London: The Hogarth Press, 1977) 77.

in the text's forethrow of signifying possibility and the desire toward affirming, "definite" articulation. In the shadow of the translational proper name, "Giacomo Joyce," *we will not know from whence, or to whom, the question is addressed.*

The open-endedness of this question can be seen to engender an entire tropology of *Giacomo Joyce,* without allowing it to refer to any *point de corps* or determinate identity. It marks simultaneously the lifting of the referent and the remains of reference,[4] re-marking the text's lack of "purposive unity."[5] At each turn it says: "the end is here. It will never be. You know that well. What then?" (*GJ* 16). Beginning with the question *Who?* Joyce's text marks a perpetual hesitation in the determination of the subject: of the assumption of a desired "self" beyond a mere prosthesis of signification (as the *assent* of Cartesianism). Hélène Cixous has suggested that we can account for this hesitation by considering Joyce's text to be "crossed right through by a subject-waiting-for-itself" which would assume the "formal appearance of a quest,"[6] what we might otherwise call a will to knowledge as interrogative self-conceptualisation (*cogitare me cogitare*).

This hesitancy is characterised in *Giacomo Joyce* by the *shy* and *nervous* movement of *she;* the question towards the always other; the perpetual differing-deferral of a subject-desire; so that this subject as "subject-waiting-for-itself" will effectively come to symbolise, in Lacan's words, "its own vanishing and punctiform bar in the illusion of the consciousness of *seeing oneself seeing oneself,* in which the gaze is elided":

4 Jacques Derrida, *Dissemination,* trans. Barbara Johnson (London: The Athlone Press, 1981) 211; and *Of Grammatology,* trans. Gayatri Spivak (Baltimore: Johns Hopkins University Press, 1976) 44.

5 Immanuel Kant, *Critique of Pure Reason,* trans. Norman Kemp Smith (London: Macmillan, 1952) A694/B722.

6 Hélène Cixous, "Joyce: the (r)use of writing," trans. Judith Still, *Post-structuralist Joyce: Essays from the French,* eds. Derek Attridge and Daniel Ferrer (Cambridge: Cambridge University Press, 1984) 15.

> I look upward from night and mud [...]. A light in the upper
> room. She is dressing to go to the play. There are ghosts in the
> mirror ..... [*GJ* 6]

For Lacan, the gaze that the subject encounters "is, not a seen
gaze, but a gaze imagined in the field of the other"; a bi-
partition between the other and its semblance or verisimilitude
of self-ideality (*je-idéal*).[7] In the elision of the gaze the other
gives of itself a mirror, a mask, a fetish, a double or ghost; *lettre*
or *l'être, envoy* or *envoi*; a sending "on the way" (or *en voie*), at or
from a distance, of this specular double.

Captivated in the illusion of the "quizzing" gaze, the subject
is unable to abstract itself from the apparent reflexivity of this
"dialectic of desire" as it manifests itself in the undecidability of
the question and in the prosthesis of (indefinite) articulation.
This is perhaps the point Nietzsche is making when he asks of
the will to truth:

> *Who* is it that here questions us? *What* really is it that wants "the
> truth"? [...] Which of us here is Oedipus? Which of us sphinx?[8]

The question *Who?* will have already responded, in advance of
itself; another voice; a ventriloquistic call that returns to us in
the way of a frail *gift*, which is also a symbolic debt, an invoice,
as Jacques Derrida says, "without the least memory of itself"; at
once questioning us, drawing us into its question, into the
question that it is, giving its question in place of itself as a
question addressed *to* itself; miming the subject who must
nevertheless respond to it or for it.[9] Which is to say, the desire
of the subject is the desire *of* the other.[10] In *Giacomo Joyce* the

---

[7] Lacan, *The Four Fundamental Concepts of Psycho-analysis*, 84.

[8] Friedrich Nietzsche, *Beyond Good and Evil: Prelude to a Philosophy of the Future*,
     trans. R.J. Hollingdale (London: Penguin, 1990) 33.

[9] Jacques Derrida, *Cinders*, trans. Ned Lukacher (Lincoln: Nebraska University
     Press, 1992) 77.

[10] Jacques Lacan, *Écrits*, trans. Alan Sheridan (New York: Norton, 1977) 312.

otherness, or similar prosthetic function of this other-subject's "desire," is emphasised:

> My words in her mind: cold polished stones sinking through a quagmire. [*GJ* 13]

And later:

> She speaks. A weak voice from beyond the stars. Voice of wisdom. Say on! O, say again, making me wise! This voice I never heard. [*GJ* 15]

And again:

> She coils toward me [...]. I cannot move or speak. Coiling approach of starborn flesh. Adultery of wisdom. No. I will go. I will. [*GJ* 15]

She, this pronominal other, marks at once the promise of knowledge, wisdom (of that type of transcendent inner-truth characterised by Plato as writing on the soul or *alētheia*)[11] and the impossibility of dialectising or sublating the "distance" of this *coiling approach*. Her celestial, "starborn" voice (*en voix*), barely perceptible to the point of never having been heard, calls to the inner ear of this other-subject's "desire" with a Circean allure; the adulteration of wisdom or "untruth of truth"[12] which Derrida situates in the "ever veiled promise of her provocative transcendence":[13]

> Distance—woman—averts truth—the philosopher. She bestows the idea. And the idea becomes transcendent, inaccessible, seductive. It beckons from afar [...]. Its veils float in the distance. The dream of death begins.[14]

---

11 See Plato, *Phaedrus*, 276a-b; cited in Derrida, *Dissemination*, 148.
12 Derrida, *Spurs*, 51.
13 Derrida, *Spurs*, 89.
14 Derrida, *Spurs*, 87-89.

In *Giacomo Joyce* it is possible to detect certain resonances of this veiled transcendence in the affective desire of phenomenological revealing, whose "indefinite articulation" in Joyce echoes Mallarmé's *L'Après-midi d'un faune*: "Trop d'hymen souhaité de qui cherche le *la*."[15] The defile of aporia or the aporia of defilement? Like the intoxicated Stephen in "Circe" (closed eye to eye-socket with the other-spectre [*U* 579]), this imaginary subject reels blindly in a dream or dance of death, entangled in the fantasised *jouissance* of the other's black veils:

> Whirling wreaths of grey vapour upon the heath. Her face, how grey and grave! Dank matted hair. [*GJ* 14]

> She raises her arms in an effort to hook at the nape of her neck a gown of black veiling. She cannot: no, she cannot. She moves backwards towards me mutely [...]. I hold the websoft edges of her gown and drawing them out to hook them I see through the opening of the black veil her lithe body sheathed in an orange shift. It slips its ribbons of moorings at her shoulders and falls slowly: a lithe smooth naked body shimmering [...]. [*GJ* 7]

Our attention is continually drawn, in *Giacomo Joyce*, to the manifold figure of woman; its constant shifting between virgin, prostitute, mother, daughter, wife, phantasm, all of which seem to coalesce in the paradigm of "the other," as desired object, which nevertheless remains "multiple, variegated, contradictory even."[16]

> She walks before me along the corridor [...] simple and proud. So did she walk by Dante. [*GJ* 11]

---

15 Stéphane Mallarmé, 'L'après-midi d'un faun,' *Poésies* (Paris: Classiques Français, 1993) 49.
16 Derrida, *Spurs*, 103.

She, as desired other, describes a movement between archetypal sublime and original sin: the Beatrice of Dante's *Commedia*, the Eve of *Genesis*, but also the figure of Lilith, of Sacher-Masoch's "lady of fables," and perhaps even of Nietzsche, Rilke and Freud's intellectual *succubus*, Lou Andreas Salomé. She marks at once the virginal, "immaculate," *hortus conclusus* of transcendent truth in beauty (Plato's *Agathon epekeina tes ousias*) and the "sodden walls" (*GJ* 12) of "The tomb of her people and hers: black stone, silence without hope" (*GJ* 6). *She* traces out a path for the transgression of taboo; adultery, masochism, onanism, incest, necrophilia; and yet remains as a kind of symptom, a perversion (or *père-version* as Lacan says);[17] the "threat of castration," posed at or as the nexus of eroticism and death:

> Her face, how grey and grave! Dank matted hair. Her lips press softly, her sighing breath comes through. Kissed. [*GJ* 14]

By following a detour here from the opening question, "Who? A pale face [...]," through to "Her face, how grey and grave!" it can be seen how the question *Who?* is sustained in its association, via a will to knowledge and the paradigm of "woman," to a metaphorics of castration and death encoded in the machinations of the gaze. As with Nietzsche's sphinx, the feminised other poses (as) the question, and within the question lies the possibility both of annihilation and forbidden *jouissance*, the *glissage* effect of desire's representation and the prohibitory interstice of impossible transcendence:

> Sliding—space—ages—foliage of stars—a waning heaven—and stillness—and stillness deeper—stillness of annihilation—and her voice. [*GJ* 16]

---

17 Jacques Lacan, *Joyce avec Lacan*, ed. Jacques Aubert (Paris: Navarin Éditeur, 1987).

The other, *she*, like the sphinx, "in as much as truth, is scepticism and veiling dissimulation."[18] In Sophocles's tragedy it is so easily forgotten that the staff of Oedipus, which symbolically links patricide and the son's exile, also marks the lie of the sphinx's riddle, and ultimately the fictionality of the analytic truth posed against it. As in Stephen's disquisition on *Hamlet* in *Ulysses*, the son is always already the recurrence of the father's ghost; translated signifier of the paternal phallus and its inevitable usurpation (*père-version*); such that this phantasm that he carries at his side (a staff or "ashplant"— *Nothung!*—as signifier of castration's lack) will mark what paradoxically *remains*, in the form of a supplement, outside the totalising force of the riddle's "truth," structuring it and circumventing it in the same gesture. The Sophoclean echo in Nietzsche (*Ecce Homo* and elsewhere) hence describes a symbolic displacement wherein (for Lacan) the subject "itself" takes on the value of this "lack," as symptom or *sinthome* which, in the person of Giacomo-Oedipus, *remains* uniquely outside the sphinx's riddle, but also at its locus.

This subject, however, is never resolved in its relation to and as the ghost of the signifier. It vacillates always in the between of signification, between the eye and the gaze, in the *resistance* of fantasy, where "The 'model' is always the dreamt-of ghost."[19] This resistance marks the paradoxical economy of an "I" that speaks "in the very lacunae of that in which, at first sight, it presents itself as speaking."[20] The subject, marked already by indeterminacy, is constantly deferred in its desire from one fantasised object to an-other through the lure and elision of the gaze; just as it does in "Araby," where the scopic drama of the "I" is played out within a seemingly blank field of desire (Araby Bazaar, Mangan's nameless sister), which nevertheless also describes and determines it through the machinations of a

---

18 Derrida, *Spurs*, 57.

19 Jacques Derrida, *The Truth in Painting*, trans. Geoffrey Bennington and Ian McLeod (Chicago: Chicago University Press, 1987) 217.

20 Lacan, *The Four Fundamental Concepts of Psycho-analysis*, 83.

gaze concealed behind the anonymous "neutrality" of the desired object. In *Giacomo Joyce* the lure of the gaze will also have marked out in advance the *en-voyage* of desiring subjectivity, firstly through the deferred agency of the question and the suspension of identity:

Who? A pale face surrounded by heavy odorous furs.

From the initial posing of the question, and its relation here to a Freudian psychoanalytic deciphering of the symbolic function of the female genitalia, the subject's desire is crossed through by a radical experience of the "uncanny."[21] Identification is suspended, a subject-object cut off from itself, dissected at the hyphen, and in its place is inscribed a dialectised affirmation (*syllable, laugh* ...) whose form is nevertheless disavowed; both projection and articulated opening of the subject's desire in the scopic field of the gaze:

Yes: a brief syllable. A brief laugh. A brief beat of the eyelids. [*GJ* 1]

This "yes-laughter of a gift without a debt, light affirmation, almost amnesiac,"[22] marks the play of a strange contingency at work in Joyce's text. In the blink of an eye "a rhythmic blindness takes place in the text,"[23] an indefinite mode of articulation which intervenes at the point of reference, where the gaze is elided, and the promise of the subject's self-conceptualisation fades into the perpetual affirmation of a desire which is equally a promise, a premise and a symptom.

In place of an identity, in the deferral of the subject, it is, it will be, the *Yes* that signs. The subject, precisely at that point at which it would situate itself in its being-present, encounters

---

[21] Sigmund Freud, "The 'Uncanny,'" *SE* II.

[22] Jacques Derrida, "Ulysses Gramophone: Hear Say Yes in Joyce," *Acts of Literature*, ed. Derek Attridge (London: Routledge, 1992) 294.

[23] Derrida, *Spurs*, 101.

only the recurrent phantasm of its desire: the returned envoy, *Yes*. But if it is the question *Who?* which initially frames the subject according to the "quizzing" gaze of the other, sustained in the illusion of identity's immanence, then it is equally the *Yes* which casts the barely-formed subject back into the unguarded anxiety of castration and blindness; a disavowal (*Verneinung, Verwerfung, Verleugnung*) marking the repetition of a cut or partition that returns the subject to the irresolvable dilemma of a *return* of the repressed:

> Operated. The surgeon's knife has probed in her entrails and withdrawn, leaving the raw jagged gash of its passage in the belly. I see her full dark suffering eyes, beautiful as the eyes of an antelope. O, cruel wound! Libidinous God! [*GJ* 11]

There is, as Gilles Deleuze says, "a desire for scientific observation, and subsequently a state of mystical contemplation. [...] pleasure is postponed for as long as possible and is thus disavowed."[24] At the same time, the subject's desire takes on an hysterical formulation, spiralling in a pornotropic frenzy which at once exposes to view what is "interior" to the other, and glimpses, in an instance of "dread desire," the "O" (the circle, annulus, abyss) of the "wound" described in the other's invaginated eye.

As the speculative double of castration, the operation of the subject's panoptical desire likewise orientates itself according to a myth of origin (transference or translation of the lack as symptom within a libidinal economy of otherness in the self, through a type of *maculated* conception) binding it to an implicitly "anatomical" desire of analysis; to rend the veil, to inseminate, to *subject* the other to the probing eye of analytic reason; or equally to name, to identify, to "know" in a particularly carnal sense its hidden part as metonym for the unknowable whole. Consequently, the "prior possibility" of the

---

[24] Gilles Deleuze, *Coldness and Cruelty*, trans. Jean McNeil (New York: Zone Books, 1991) 33.

subject as *incarnation* of the other-locus, as Lacan says, "is presented only in the form of a strange contingency, symbolic of what we find on the horizon of our experience, namely, the lack that constitutes castration anxiety."[25]

Following Derrida's critique of ideality in the Husserlean concept of the sign, we could say that "The present of self-presence" is here "as invisible as *the blink of an eye*."[26] This blindness (which is also the significatory blind of the Saussurean algorithm signifier/signified; S/s in Lacan's reformulation) also marks the way in which the text is punctuated through the traces of an averting gaze:

> Her long eyelids beat and lift: a burning needleprick stings and quivers in the velvet iris. [*GJ* 1]

This lancinating aversion pre-empts the subject to the point where every approach to the other, as an averred "presentation" of itself (in the illusion of a *cogitare me cogitare*), will be characterised as a form of repetition-revenance:

> Her eyes have drunk my thoughts: and into the moist warm yielding welcoming darkness of her womanhood my soul, itself dissolving, has streamed and poured and flooded a liquid and abundant seed [...]. [*GJ* 14]

The projective illusion of the "I"—injecting itself into the eyes' "yielding welcoming darkness," which returns (to) it, and in so doing says "yes," as the receipt of the other's veiling dissimulation; a dark, web-like scription; writing itself, inscribing itself in its frustrated hermeneutic:

> Write it, damn you, write it! What else are you good for? [*GJ* 16]

---

25 Lacan, *The Four Fundamental Concepts of Psycho-analysis*, 72-73.

26 Jacques Derrida, *Speech and Phenomena: and other Essays on Husserl's Theory of Signs*, trans. David Allison (Evanston: Northwestern University Press, 1973) 59.

In this way, *Giacomo Joyce* stages its own production (*auto-poiēsis*), writing itself in the topological fold between the consumptive eye of the thwarted subject and the scopic field of the other; but only in the sense, however, that the "between" of this *auto-poiēsis* simultaneously describes an emplacement in advance. The ironic pose of this catachresis. Invention *of* the other, in the dilated opening of the "I" of the author-subject:

> Here, opening from the darkness of desire, are eyes [...] their shimmer the shimmer of the scum that mantles the court of slobbering James. [*GJ* 9]

A defilement of the eyes, marking the "I" in its base reflexivity: exiled, pretended (James, Giacomo); slobbering, abject-ejaculatory. The *auto-poiēsis* of onanistic torpitude, entropy of a pronominal spiral. Writing down into the decadence of the sign "sinking" into the quagmire of itself. The "I" both disingenuous and dis-engendered, according to which one might say *I write myself* or *I send myself*, transitively or intransitively (a form of "anality" which anticipates Shem's excremental "double dye" in *Finnegans Wake* [185.32]), as the "slobbering James" who is also a figure of arcane transmutation, transference or translation of an absent, dead or hypostatised other-scriptor; of the one who signs *Giacomo*). "In the latter sense, one might say that if one sends oneself, then one's envoy (or *envoi*) [...] has to be one's double or ghost."[27] This other-subject writes itself, writes to itself, to the other (in itself), in this posthumous text's "penultimate," elusive dispatch:

> Envoy: Love me, love my umbrella. [*GJ* 16]

In the *Envois* section of *La Carte postale*, Derrida exploits the paronomasian effect in French of the English word "umbrella" and its Italian echo, *ombrello*, to read in Joyce's "Envoy" its own

---

27 Alan Bass, Glossary, *The Post Card: from Socrates to Freud and Beyond* by Jacques Derrida, trans. Alan Bass (Chicago: Chicago University Press, 1987) xxi.

shadow or double: "Love my *ombre, elle*—not me."[28] The subject as object-pronoun dispatches itself, sends its envoy in place of itself, immediately giving itself over to the dissimulating play of the French *ombre* and Latin *umbra*: shadow, semblance, phantom, ghost. I, not I. The word "umbrella" sustains the subject at a distance from itself; at a distance from *she, elle,* as the pronominal relation of the desired "other." As Derrida writes elsewhere:

> The umbrella's symbolic figure is well-known, or supposedly so. Take, for example, the hermaphroditic spur of a phallus which is modestly enfolded in its veils, an organ which is at once aggressive and apotropaic, threatening and/or threatened.[29]

Moreover, it symbolises the repetition of the "frail gift," or filial trace of the other as a form of *invoice*; a symbolic debt encoded in what barely remains; what *of* the other has been left, "forgotten," calculated or by chance:

> Unreadiness. A bare apartment. Torbid daylight. A long black piano: coffin of music. Poised on its edge a woman's hat, red-flowered, and umbrella, furled. [*GJ* 16]

These vestiges of desire (a woman's hat and umbrella, flowered and furled) mark what remains of this fantasy of the other. In the vacancy of this naked *apart-ment*, these vestiges continue to mark the evanescent function of an elided gaze in the scripting of a desire "in language." A metonymic reduction, of what separates the bareness of the apartment from what it nevertheless "encloses"; the anomalous emblems of a "love" deferred, or détourned, *seriatim*. A glissage effect, measured across the resistance of the fantasy or phantasm which stands always in place of the other; the surface on which the "eye" is constantly poised in a morbid state of "Unreadiness"; as

---

28 Derrida, *The Post Card*, 238-239.
29 Derrida, *Spurs*, 129.

symptom, spectre, ghost, *ombre*; the furled signifier of an ambivalent desire, between an objective and possessive pronoun: love me, love my "I."

Hélène Cixous
Giacomo Joyce: The Ironic Sobs of Eros

In Trieste, in 1914, while he was teaching English to various bourgeois in the town in order to survive, finishing *A Portrait of the Artist as a Young Man* and conceiving *Ulysses*, James Joyce came to feel, with a degree of poignancy, that the artist was no longer so young. He was thirty-two, almost the age of Leopold Bloom (thirty-eight), and imagination allowed him to look back in reverse, to listen, as it were, to his hair growing grey. The artist's game with death is always translated, for Joyce, in a tragic-comic fashion. Love and writing, the letter and the pen, are the natural weapons of this admirable simulator who was able to perceive the least tremor in the lives of others without ever placing himself "in contact" with reality. "Oh! Touch me," begs Bloom when he is whipped. Between the two, Joyce evokes the encounters of others with the art of the voyeur who knows well what he is. Hence the double existence of Giacomo Joyce—minor in terms of what Joyce wrote, but nevertheless overwhelming in its verity—a type of Cassanova, just as Bloom

---

* Originally published as "Giacomo Joyce: Les sanglots ironiques d'Éros," *Le Monde*, 17 Aug. 1968: iv. Supplément au numéro 7338 ivc ["Le Monde des Livres"].

is a type of Don Juan, fleshed out with fervour, terror and ridicule.

Who is the love object? A notebook of sixteen pages of careful calligraphy in Joyce's hand opens upon a question: who? Her name was Amalia Popper; a student with *"una grandissima ammirazione per il suo maestro inglese,"* as her father—patriarch among the favoured, one of the prosperous Jews of the Triestine community, from whom the most illustrious of Joyce's pupils, Italo Svevo, was descended—confides. Cold, myopic, fierce, beautiful, inaccessible, fragile, distinguished, slim, wise virgin, simple and proud, daughter of Zion with antelope eyes, she is not named in this *roman de la rose*, but she traverses the effervescent days of the dreams of Giacomo, and from every meeting surges a poem in prose, "an emotion draped in words," which inscribes itself in the imagination of the artist, not only in words but also in images. In effect, on each page, drawn two or three times, is a music for all the senses in which one recognises, through tears of desire, fear, adoration, the artist crouching behind the man.

The story is archetypal: it is the eternal Joycean myth of flirting with the cold Virgin, attractive because cold, since only the woman cautiously held at a distance is lovable. He courts her by seeking to dazzle her with his culture and learning. She in turn dazzles him, in hundreds of instances real and dreamt, as the embodiment of a baroque yet innocent sensuality; a primarily visual object, contemplated in humility or humiliation, like that evening at the opera when, ironically, he is in the gods, she in the orchestra—and yet it is she who is above and he beneath, in the hell of human stench, the sour odour of armpits, sulphurous garlic breath, the frank sweat of the female tribe—where he contemplates her the entire evening; the entire evening seeing her, hair braided and pinnacled, her face oval, eyes soft and calm, her body enveloped in a green embroidered tunic.

All the erotic themes of the work weave together here into an evanescent fugue. She is pure, he is dirty, like Bloom: "Those quiet cold fingers have touched the pages, foul and fair, on which my shame shall glow forever. Quiet and cold and pure fingers. Have they never erred?"

Joycean eroticism is not merely satisfied with a one-sided sin: therefore, in spite of her, he sins à la Joyce, first in dreams and, as with Stephen Dedalus, sexuality is confused with death: "Her face, grey and grave! Dank matted hair. Her lips press softly, her sighing breath comes through. Kissed." Is it she who has had him? He will have her, in reality, through the gaze: "She leans back against the pillowed wall: odalisque-featured in the luxurious obscurity. Her eyes have drunk my thoughts: and into the moist obscurity of her womanhood my soul, itself dissolving, has streamed and poured and flooded a liquid and abundant seed ...... Take her now who will! ..."

It must be said that for Joyce the process of fertilisation is reversible: masculine-feminine, the artist is fertilised himself by the channel of the imaginary. The actual act is not of interest because the only act is writing; but if writing substitutes for the act, it is also because Joyce was incapable of any other relationship with the real. And not the least among the charms of *Giacomo Joyce* is its confession, mixed with defiance, of a desired and inevitable failure: "Youth has an end: the end is here. It will never be. You know that well. What then? Write it, damn you, write it! What else are you good for?" It is in this "there," in which the end-of-life is situated, that this man of thirty-two years broaches the "here" of his art.

Translated by Louis Armand and Clare Wallace

APPENDIX II

Fritz Senn

Some Further Notes on *Giacomo Joyce*

The following notes are meant to supplement those that
Richard Ellmann has appended to the facsimile edition of
Giacomo Joyce (New York: Viking Press, 1968) xxiii-xxvii. Joyce
evidently used some more words or phrases from *Giacomo Joyce*
in the *Portrait* and, especially, in *Ulysses*, but some of my entries
here do not have the status of verbal echoes and might best be
termed just similarities, in some cases accidental ones perhaps,
but nevertheless worth pointing out.

Page and line numbers refer to the definite text of *A
Portrait*, ed. Chester G. Anderson (New York: Viking Press,
1964), and to, first, the new Random House edition of *Ulysses*
and, afterwards, to the old one (New York: Modern Library,
Random House, 1961 and 1934, respectively).

Page	Line	
1	13, 10	A brief beat of the eyelids—"and his thin quick eyelids beat often over his sad eyes." (*P* 228.13).

---

* First published in the *JJQ* 5 (1968) 233-236.

	6ff	speech [...]. The wave is spent.—"[...] wavespeech [...]. And spent, itsspeech ceases" (*U* 49.29-32 / 50.20-23).
2	4	the lathe of intermarriage [...] of her race.— "Jews [...] are of all races the most given to intermarriage" (*U* 205.36 / 203.17).
	6-11	The whole paragraph, interlarded with food terms, anticipates the technique and the vocabulary of the Lestrygonians chapter.
	7	Shadows streak her falsely smiling face.— "streaked by sunlight" (*U* 545.08 / 532.28), "Cranly's face, [...] lit up by a false smile of false patience" (*P* 232.02).
	8	smitten by hot creamy light.—"smitten by sunlight" (*U* 268.07 / 95.3f).
	9	grey wheyhued shadows under the jawbones.—"whey-pale face" (*P* 193.34).
	9-10	streaks of eggyolk yellow.—"like yellow streaks on his face" (*U* 9f.06 / 95.3f).
3		Some of the motifs ("middle age," line 3, "Mine eyes fail in darkness," 8-9, "Twighlight," 11) may have gone into the poem, "Bahnhofstrasse," written in Zürich 1918.
	11	grey eve—"at eve of day, / Grey way [...]" ("Bahnhofstrasse").
4	2	the Grand Turk.—"Even the grand Turk sent us his piastres" (*U* 329.42 / 324.07). A White flash.—"Watch! Watch! Silk flash rich stockings white. Watch!" (*U* 74.27 / 73.25). The woman that Bloom is watching also has "high brown boots with laces" and appears to be rich.
	8	I rush out of the tobacco-shop [...]— Similarly Bloom, on seeing Boylan drive by,

		rushes out of Daly's tobacconist shop (*U* 264 / 153.42).
	10	and slowly her pale cheeks are flushed with a kindling opal light.—"[...]a telltale flush [...] crept into her cheeks" (*U* 349.17 / 343.11).
5	10	This heart is sore and sad. Crossed in love?—"I am sure she was crossed in love [...]. My heart's broke" (*U* 155.05-13 / 153.42).
6	4	ghosts in the mirror [...]. Candles! Candles!—"ghost-candle" (*U* 10.20 / 12.10), "ghostcandled" (*U* 48.01 / 48.34).
	6	Easy now Jamsey!—"Easy now" (*U* 50.10 / 50.42).
7	7f	[...] shift [...] at her shoulders [...] over the slender buttocks [...] over their furrow.— "Shoulders. Hips [...]. Night of the dance dressing. Shift stuck between the cheeks behind" (*U* 92.32 / 91.26).
8	1	spurs of a pampered fowl.—The Honourable Mrs Mervyn Talboys "stamps her jingling spurs" (*U* 467.28 / 459.10). Molly, also cruel and "in disdain," is "plump as a pampered pouter pigeon" (*U* 441.09 / 434.03).
	3	*The lady goes apace, apace, apace.*—"Bello Cohen, riding Bloom, utters the same line: "The lady goes a pace, a pace" (*U* 534.24 / 522.28). "a pace a pace" (50.08 / 50.40).
	13	its wheel-spokes spinning in the glare.— "wheelspokes spinning in the glare" (*U* 253.27 / 249.40).
9	6	virgin most prudent: from the Litany of the Blessed Virgin.
10	1-2	morning Paris: aniseed, damp sawdust, hot dough of bread.—"Paris [...]. Moist pith of

		farls of bread, the froggreen wormwood" (*U* 42.28 / 43.26).
	5	in the vast gargoyled church [...] (line 6-11 refer to the mass on Good Friday).—"Harsh gargoyle face [...]. *C'est vendredi saint!*" (*U* 200.10-13 / 197.34-37).
	15	Her soul is sorrowful.—The "sorrowful" mysteries of the Blessed Virgin are contemplated in the second chaplet of the Rosary, they include the Crucifixion. See *P* 148.23.
	16	Weep not for me, O daughter of Jerusalem!—Luke 23:28.
11	1	a dark coil of her hair slowly uncoils.—"Lank coils of seeweed hair" (*U* 243.28 / 240.06).
	26	lord and giver of life.—From the *Book of Common Prayer*, "Lord and Giver of Life" (*U* 389.25 / 383.15).
12	6	Come! chook! chook! come! The black pullet is frightened.—"Afraid of the chookchooks" (*U* 55.32).
	10	sour reek of armpits.—"the odour of her armpits [...] the lion reek of all the male brutes (*U* 501.13-15 / 490.30—491.02).
	11	melting breast ointments.—"Melting breast ointments [...]. Armpits' oniony sweat!" (*U* 236.24 / 233.07).
	11	sulphurous.—"Sulphurous dung of lions" (*U* 236.26 / 233.09).
12	11-20	There is a similarity to the situation of the gentleman who looks down at Molly Bloom in the theatre: "Chap in dresscircle, staring down into her with his operaglass" (*U* 284.38 / 280.15).

	16	braided and pinnacled hair.—"Gold pinnacled hair" (*U* 256.07 / 252.07), "braided and pinnacled" (260.28 / 256.26), "Hair braided over" (281.25 / 277.04).
13	6	Her body has no smell: an odourless flower.—"He tore the flower gravely from its pinhold smelt its almost no smell" (*U* 78.14 / 77.09).
14	2	Dank matted hair.—"hearthrug of matted hair" (*U* 502.23 / 492.02).
	2	Her lips press softly.—"the dark pressure of her softly parting lips. They pressed upon his brain as upon his lips [...]" (*P* 101.19).
	7	odalisque-featured in the luxurious obscurity.—"[...] in luxury [...] her odalisk lips lusciously smeared [...]" (*U* 477.07, 12 / 468.07, 12).
15	4	her black basilisk eyes.—"basiliskeyed" (*U* 40.04 / 41.04), "miscreant eyes [...]. A basilisk" (*U* 194.20-1 / 192.09-10).
	7	They spread under my feet carpets [...]. She stands in the yellow shadow of the hall.—"Open hallway. Street of harlots [...]. Red carpet spread" (*U* 47.05-9 / 47.40-48.02), "red carpet spread" (571.21 / 557.06).
	14	a jet of liquorish venom.—"her jet of venom" (*U* 431.24 / 424.24).
	15	peagreen.—*U* 350.41 / 344.34.
	19	Symbol of the intellectual conscience [...]. Intellectual symbol of my race.—"conscience of my race" (*P* 253.02).
	31	Coiling approach of starborn flesh.—"[...] it flows about her starborn flesh [...] winding, coiling [...] myriad metamorphoses" (*U* 414.35-9 / 407.35-8). "myriad" is in line 35.

	35	I crumple like a burning leaf! From my left armpit a fang of flame leaps out.—"made his trembling hand crumple together like a leaf" (*P* 50.26), "squeezing his hands under his armpits" (*P* 49.12).
	37	A starry snake has kissed me.—"A snake coils her, fang in's kiss" (*U* 199.09 / 196.34).
16	7	What else are you good for?—"What else are they invented for?" (*U* 40.27 / 41.26).

The unnamed girl of *Giacomo Joyce* is evoked not only in various moods and styles, but also in a series of analogies, taking in almost the whole range of the archetypical manifestations of the Female. The literary parallels—Dante's Beatrice and Beatrice Cenci—are the most explicit ones (*GJ* 11). Liturgical echoes (*GJ* 9, 10) represent her, in common with most major and some minor figures in the Joyce canon, as the Virgin Mary. One phrase devoted to her (*GJ* 5) in *Ulysses* refers to a nun. At the other end of the spectrum, she combines the various aspects of the Temptress, having traits of the temptress in Stephen's villanelle or else blushing (*GJ* 4) or being exhibitionistically provoking (*GJ* 9) like Gerty MacDowell. Her proud demeanour and some of her apparel also characterise the rich, attractive, haughty and cruel society women in "Circe." The girl becomes a siren whose body is "shimmering with silvery scales" (*GJ* 7), and she lends her "braided and pinnacled hair" (*GJ* 12) to the barmaids who do duty as sirens in *Ulysses*. She is likened to the whore in A Portrait (GJ 14) and many of her attributes are dispersed among multiple inhabitants of "Nighttown" in Ulysses. On her own small scale, she is comprehensive as Molly Bloom, who *Yes* is attached to (*GJ* 1), and yet she also remains elusive, which may be one reason why Giacomo Joyce opens with the question "Who?"

APPENDIX III

Gayatri Chakravorty Spivak
Love Me, Love My Ombre, Elle

1

When a man writes, he is in a structure that needs his absence as its necessary condition (writing is defined as that which can necessarily be read in the writer's absence), and entails his pluralisation (when the poet is absent, he *becomes his admirers*).[1] Writers resist the troubling necessity and desire to record the living act of a sole self—an auto-bio-graphy. Whatever the argument of a document, the marks and staging of this resistance are its "scene of writing." When a person reads, the scene of writing is usually ignored and the argument is taken as the product of a self with a proper name. Writers and readers are thus accomplices in the ignoring of the scene of writing. The accounts given of texts are informed by this complicity.

La carte postale foregrounds this "scene of reading and writing" in three different ways in its first three essays.

The book has a double ending, one describing the status of Derrida's own writing in terms of a scene resembling Jacques Lacan's reading of the "Purloined Letter," which is the subject

---

[1] Cf. W.H. Auden, "In Memory of W.B. Yeats," 1.17.

of the third essay of the book[2]; another (the back cover) written like the last page of the first piece (*Envois*), which is a collection of letters to an undisclosed person. Strictly speaking, there is yet another ending: one in the endpapers is a foldout of a reproduction of the *carte postale* which gives the book its title and cover illustration, a picture of Plato behind the seated Socrates at his writing desk.

These inter-enclosing endings make the book as a whole a part of its parts: an effect that Derrida has called "invagination."[3]

It is possible to read the invagination effect a little further. In the first piece, one of the many reading Derrida gives to this postcard of S *et* [and] p is to read it as S *est* [is] p—the formula for the proposition: Subject is predicate. The scene of writing of the second essay can also be read in terms of the initials of the principals. The latter is largely about the game of *fort:da* ["gone—here"] played by Freud's grandson and recounted by Freud in *Beyond the Pleasure Principle*. Thus one might say that S is p (the postcard) is rewritten in the second essay as *fort:da* which proffers the play of absence and presence that we cover under the copula "is." One could thus read *fort:da* (carrying the shadow of the French Socrate: Platon in its assonance)—f:d—as freud:derrida, with the erased copula marking the place of the problem of inheritance.

Yet another "part" exceeds *Envois* outside the cover of *La carte postale*, in the form of an article entitled "Télépathie" published in *Furor* 2. It is described by Derrida as a collection of four letters written between 9 and 14 July 1979. It would fit between the pages 219 and 223 of *La carte postale*, where we are given nine letters marked as "between the 9th and 19th of July, 1979." Ignoring all numerological fantasies, let us note what Derrida says in the first footnote to the article:

---

2 Jacques Derrida, *La carte postale: de Socrate à Freud et au-delà* (Paris: Flammarion, 1980) 549.
3 Jacques Derrida, "The Law of Genre," trans. Avital Ronell, *Glyph* 7 (1980).

> These cards and letters became inaccessible to me, at least
> materially, by unapparent accident, at a precise moment. They
> should have figured, as fragments and according to a system
> already adopted, in *Envois* (Part One of *La carte postale*) ... In an
> equally fortuitous way, I found them near at hand but too late,
> for the proofsheets had already gone back for a second time.
> Perhaps one will speak of omission by "resistance." ... To be
> sure, but resistance to what? to whom? Dictated by whom, to
> whom, how, in that way? From this tangle of daily messages
> which date from the same week, I do not have the space to
> extract more than a part for the moment. No time either, for the
> treatment—sorting out, fragmentation, destruction etc., to
> which I had to subject this exchange.[4]

Given that the accounts and accountings of historical "verity"
are being put into question here, the details of this "un-
verifiable" footnote seem of interest. In this supplement to the
(w)hole in/of the book, which is a consideration of Freud's
curious suspended disbelief in telepathy, Derrida uses a
stylistic device that also questions the limits of "inside" and
"outside." There is a long section where Derrida speaks of
telepathy "in Freud's voice" as Socrates speaks "in the Sophist's
voice" in *Phaedrus*. All the arguments made in "Plato's
Pharmacy"[5] about the status of the good simulacrum—as that
which disproves its own validity and thus defies the
boundaries of model and image—come to mind. This too
would fit within the open-ended taxonomy of "invagination" in
Derrida's language.

Let us suppose the initial resistance to overcome: why we
should read an elabouration of such a problematics given the
urgency of "the rest of the world?"[6] In the first essay, Derrida

---

[4] Derrida, *La carte postale*, 5.

[5] Jacques Derrida, "Plato's Pharmacy," *Dissemination*, trans. Barbara Johnson
(Chicago: Univ. of Chicago Press, 1981).

[6] I borrow the phrase from Derrida's incisive consideration of the politics of
institutional psychoanalysis in "Geopsychanalyse: and the rest of the world,"
Confrontations, February (1981). In the project of the Constitution of 1977, as it
was accepted at the 30th Congress of the API in Jerusalem, a parenthetical

does not think love letters are too frivolous to be put in with serious studies of Freud, Lacan, and the French psychoanalytic movement, and is not embarrassed by the writer as lover, as in the figure of Joyce in the *Envois*. In the second essay Freud's itinerary in *Beyond the Pleasure Principle* is discussed as a search for autobiography (as autothanatography) using his daughter/mother Sophie. In the third essay, Lacan's reading of "The Purloined Letter" is critiqued as phallogocentric. Although I will comment on these gestures in what follows, my chief interest is in the place of "woman" in the development of Derrida's vocabulary; the possibility, for instance, that the structural project of this book can itself be called *invagination*.

The pragmatic style of North American and English criticism (feminist or masculinist) might find in such appellations "a kind of word play ... detached from what we have to struggle with."[7] This presupposes a three-part description of reality: practical complexity (what we have to struggle with)—responsible theory (in touch with that complexity)—irresponsibly word-playing theory. In this view, good theory is seen to abstract the principles of the concrete struggle, leading to efficient understanding. By contrast, I understand Derrida's project as an undoing of such oppositions, a suggestion that even the most abstract-seeming judgements are arrived at by way of, even constituted by, unwittingly value-laden story lines. These narratives are so practiced that they seem self-evident logical propositions. When Derrida offers a counter-narrative through counter-

sentence defines in a way the divisions of the psychoanalytic world: "(The association's main geographical areas are defined at this time as America north of the United States-Mexican border: all America south of that border, and the rest of the world [sentence in English original] ... [the last phrase] names at bottom Europe, place of origin and the old metropolis of psychoanalysis ... and, in the same "rest of the world," all the still virgin territory, all the places in the world where psychoanalysis has not yet, so to speak, set foot)" (12). Something in the politics of a discourse is disclosed when one computes "the rest of the world" that the discourse defines monolithically.

7 Colette Gaudin et al., "Introduction, " *Yale French Studies* 62 (1981): 10.

naming, it is, first, to undo the abstract-concrete ranking in judgements and, secondly, to change the shifting grounds of judgements and decisions. The general argument of this essay is that the naming of woman is such a counter-narrative, and that the naming has slowly moved into the scene of Derrida's own writing.

I shall attempt to show in the body of this essay how it is the implications of this counter-narrative that provoke the moral outrage against Derrida, which ranges from the conservative to the radical in literary criticism. For it is indeed a moral outrage rather than disinterested refutation (whatever that may be) that we encounter from the opponents of deconstruction. What do M.H. Abrams, Dennis Donaghue, and Terry Eagleton have in common, apart from their distaste for Derrida?[8] They are all academic critics and as such they share a belief, in the last instance, in the adequate subject of the critic and his company, in the adequacy of theory (that will allow the critic to have the privilege over "mere practice" and guarantee him the sense of a controlling role in culture or politics, in cultural politics), a faith in the availability of an analyzable reality purged of its relationship with the sexed subject. As is abundantly evident to any careful reader of Derrida, he does not claim that there is *no* intention, *no* reference, *no* practice, *no* world. He attempts to "situate" them and claims that they are never self-adequate, never (except strategically) altogether distinct from their political opposites, and any practice will have to account (necessarily inadequately) for this. It is this uncertainty that

[8] M.H. Abrams, "The Deconstructive Angel," *Critical Inquiry* 3.3 (1977); Edward A. Said, "The Problem of Textuality: Two Exemplary Positions," *Critical Inquiry* 4.4 (1978) and "Opponents, Audiences, Constituencies and Community," *Critical Enquiry* 9 (1982); Dennis Donaghue, "Deconstructing Deconstruction, *New York Review of Books* 27.10 (1980); Terry Eagleton, "The Idealism of American Criticism," *New Left Review* 127 (May-June 1981). Eagleton has since then produced a guarded apology for Derrida as a "post-structuralist" in *Literary Theory: an Introduction* (Minneapolis: University of Minnesota Press, 1983). The powerful continuist misreading of Derrida produced by Perry Anderson, *In the Track of Historical Materialism* (Berkeley: University of California Press, 1983), is a different case and worth more careful scrutiny.

troubles the critical establishment across the political spectrum. This essay will suggest that, in however rarefied a way, Derrida has seen the name of woman inscribed as the curious subject of the practice that would take these lessons of deconstruction into account, never once and for all, since it *is* (we shall see what a practical responsibility the positioning of a copula entails) a practice. In other words, although Derrida's detractors and followers have paid little attention to it, I will suggest that it is possible to say that "woman" on the scene of Derrida's writing, from being a figure of "special interest," occupies the place of a general critique of the history of Western thought.

To chart the movement of woman in Derrida's vocabulary, I will take *Spurs* as my starting point.[9] Here woman is taken, via Nietzsche, as a name for citationality.[10]

Briefly: the so-called appropriate enunciation of a truth can only be defined over against that *in*-appropriate enunciation which wrenches the truth into a context other than its own and uses it as a mere citation. "Truths" used within "fiction" or "theatrical frames" are, by this argument, examples of citing. Citation can thus be seen as a condition of possibility of self-adequate truth, indeed even to contain the case of truth as one of its effects. Nietzsche writes in the *Gay Science* "[women] 'give themselves,' even when they—give themselves."[11] Women "acting out" their pleasure in the orgasmic moment, can cite themselves in their very self-presence. It is as if the woman *is* quotation marks and vice versa. If men think they have or possess women in sexual mastery, they should be reminded that, by this logic, women can destroy the proper roles of

9 Jacques Derrida, *Spurs: Nietzsche's Styles*, trans. Barbara Harlow (Chicago: University of Chicago Press, 1979).

10 The figure of woman agitates Derrida's work at least as early as *Of Grammatology*. For a desexualised (although presented in the context of an intellectual tradition seen as homoerotic) account of citationality see Derrida, "Limited Inc: abc," trans. Samuel Weber, *Glyph* 2 (1977).

11 Friedrich Nietzsche, *Gay Science*, trans. Walter J. Kaufmann (New York: Vintage Books, 1974) 317

master and slave. Men cannot know when they are properly in possession of them as masters (knowing them carnally in their pleasure) and when in their possession as slaves (duped by their self-citation in a fake orgasm). Woman makes propriation—the establishment of a thing in its appropriate property—undecidable.

Another version of this, by way of Mallarmé, is given in "The Double Session." The theme that the dancing woman seems to mime, to act out, or dance is the rendering to the male spectator, "the nudity of [his] own concepts" but only "through the last veil that remains forever, ... writ[ing his] vision in the manner of a Sign, which she is"—indicating the absence of that vision even as it is presented. The proper outlines of the vision are thus distanced or "cited" into the divided structure of a sign. The veil that stands in for citing the vision is related by a certain metaphoric logic, to the "gold" of the hymen, where "presence-in-sexual pleasure" is dislocated as neither in soul nor in body, for the hymen is that lining of the "insides" of the body which is also its "outside" skin. "Now, if we can begin to see that the 'blank' and the 'fold' cannot be mastered as themes or as meanings, if it is within the fold and the blank of a certain hymen that the textuality of the text [as citation rather than transparent simulacrum of speech as presence] is re-marked, then we will have outlined the very limits of thematic criticism."[12]

Of course these deductions are based on a curious view of woman and an implicit identification of (male) pleasure ["sem(e)-ination"] as the signified, however besieged. To see indeterminacy in the figure of women might be the effect of an ethicolegal narrative whose oppressive hegemony still remains largely unquestioned. Yet it must be recognised that the deduction allows Derrida's reading of Nietzsche and Mallarmé to make woman the mark of the critique of the proper. If in the best-known Derrida texts it is Being that is taken as pre-

---

[12] Derrida, *Dissemination*, 243; 246-47. N.B. I have modified translations wherever necessary.

comprehended and therefore inaccessible to the ontotheological question, in *Spurs* and "The Double Session" propriation is taken to be pre-comprehended even before the question of Being is posed. That something can "be" takes for granted that something can "be proper to itself": "The question of the sense or the truth of being is not *capable* of the question of the proper … The abyss of truth as non-truth, of propriation as appropriation/a-propriation, of declaration as parodic dissimulation, one wonders if this is not what Nietzsche calls the form of style and the non-place of woman."[13]

If the word "woman" can thus be associated with the narrative of this set of problems, it can take place upon the Derridean chain which contains "difference," "parergon," "writing." It is by no means one among many Derridean themes. It is perhaps the most tenacious name for the limit that situates and undermines the vanguard of every theory seeking to be adequate to its theme. The limit is where the proper becomes undecidable, is put within the double (or indefinite) mirror-structure of the *abyme*: any invocation of the "abyssal limit" in Derrida (whenever, for example, a proper name undermines its propriety and breaks into common words in the "mother-tongue"—"connect, I cut") entails the "name" of woman—a "name" itself undecidable.[14] When in "To Speculate—On Freud," Derrida uses the concept of semi-mourning (demi-deuil) to describe the conduct of the text, once again the abyss structure that can be named "woman" is invoked.[15] For Freud suggests in *Mourning and Melancholia* that

[13] Derrida, *Spurs* 111-13; 119-21.

[14] Derrida's critique of legitimation through the patriarchal proper name can be appreciated in the most commonsensical way. The Western metaphysics of everyday life does indeed make a woman's name undecidable. It is either her father's or her husband's. What is her "own" name? She might take her mother's father's or create a fictive name which does not effectively threaten the circuit of legitimacy.

[15] Published in English translation as "Speculations—On Freud," *Oxford Literary Review* 3 (1978). The translated title seems to miss the point of the infinitive and of giving Freud as a citation.

successful mourning accepts the lost objects as lost. According to the abyssal structure named woman, who is also the lost object par excellence, there can be no proper and self-identical acceptance of loss. We achieve only an asymmetrical economy of mourning and melancholia—a semi-mourning—which feeds our desire for establishing ourselves as an autobiographical self. Derrida charts this "feminine operation" in his reading of *Beyond the Pleasure Principle.*

Spurs begins with the declaration: "But—woman will be my subject." One must always remember that the word "subject" can mean both subject matter (object) and the self. Halfway into the piece, however, Derrida writes: "therefore woman will not have been my subject."[16] This is because no determined essence of woman can be located objectively.

Of all the names that Derrida has given to originary undecidability, woman possesses this special quality: she can occupy both positions in the subject-object oscillation, be cathected as both, something that *différance, écriture, parergon, supplément,* and the like—other names of undecidability— cannot do without special pleading. Derrida's arrival at the name of woman seems to be a slow assumption of the consequences of a critique of humanism as phallogocentrism. But at least since *Glas,* the graphic of sexual difference is never far from Derrida's work.

In his earliest published book, Derrida suggests that Edmund Husserl, unable to give a phenomenological account of the moment or space before the institution of geometry, assumes it is already accomplished, and concentrates instead on the historical reactivation of that institutionality. This allows Husserl to analyse the privileged concept of Language as the condition of possibility of such a history. I am suggesting here that woman in Derrida is such a privileged figure. Her place is different from that of names such as *différance, trace, parergon* and the like—attempts at giving a name to the pre-institutional origin of institution. Woman is the name of the absolute limit of

---

[16] Derrida, *Spurs,* 37; 120.

undecidability that such attempts must encounter. My suggestion takes on plausibility when we consider that Derrida describes Husserl's project of historical reactivation in terms that, nearly twenty years before its publication might well describe *Envois*:

> Husserl ... speaks of *Rückfrage*. We have translated it by return inquiry ... Return inquiry ... is marked by the postal and epistolary reference or resonance of a communication from a distance ... [It] is asked on the basis of a first posting [*envois*]. From a received and already readable document, the possibility is offered me of asking again, and in return, about the originary and final intention of what had been given me by tradition. The latter, which is only mediacy itself and openness to a telecommunication in general, is then, as Husserl says "open ... to continual inquiry."[17]

Are Plato and Socrates, then, standing in for the institution of the metaphysical tradition, and *Envois* a legend of the thought that any return inquiry to grasp the pre-institutional origin can do no more than stall at the absolute limit—undecidability as woman?

Although it is not a clear demarcation, deconstruction can be seen as two different projects. First, as the "deconstitution of the founding concepts of philosophy" and second, as "affirmative deconstruction." The former project is carried out in the many meticulous analyses of the texts of phallogocentrism—the only texts we have. The latter project is more mysterious, leads to orphic utterances, is concerned with forging a practice that recognises its condition of possibility in the impossibility of theoretical rigor, and that must remain apocalyptic in scope and tone, "render delirious the interior voice which is the voice of

---

[17] Jacques Derrida, *Edmund Husserl's The Origin of Geometry: An Introduction*, trans. John P. Leavey, Jr. (Stony Brook, N.Y.: Nicolas Nays, 1978) 50.

the other in us."[18] This project is almost invariably associated with woman. Here explicating Nietzsche: "she plays dissimulation, ornamentation, the lie, art, artistic philosophy, she is a power of affirmation. If one still condemned her, it would be to the extent that she would deny that affirmative power from the man's point of view would come to lie in a belief in truth to reflect in a specular way the foolish dogmatism that it provokes" [*Spurs* 67]. In a text as early as "Structure, Sign and Play" the well-known final figure accompanies a call for affirmative deconstruction:

> I employ these words, I admit, with a glance towards the operations of childbearing—but also with a glance toward those who, in a society from which I do not exclude myself turn their eyes away when faced with the as yet unnameable which is proclaiming itself and which can do so, as is necessary whenever a birth is in the offing only under, only under the species of the nonspecies, in the formless, mute, infant and terrifying form of monstrosity.[19]

Here we see one of the first subliminal articulations of the longing for the name of the mother. The critic belongs to a group of men who watch, yet would not watch. The emphasis is still on the apocalyptic practice, the monstrous infant. But the father is noticeably absent, and the operation of birthing fills the stage.

In "Plato's Pharmacy," the mother's son is directly related to another name for undecidability: writing. Logos or speech is the father's legitimate son, whose parent is authoritatively present. Writing is the mother's illegitimate son, who can be claimed by anyone. The phallocentric philosopher systematically resists the possibility that all the discourse is dependent upon the

---

18 Jacques Derrida, "Of an Apocalyptic Tone Recently Adopted in Philosophy," trans. John. P. Leavey, Jr. *Semeia* 23 (1982): 71, translation modified.

19 Derrida, "Structure, Sign and Play in the Discourse of the Human Sciences," *Writing and Difference*, trans. Alan Bass (London: Routledge, 1978) 293.

producer's absence, and thus irreducibly illegitimate—a mother's son. (The daughter is not in sight.)

2

It is of course risky to generalise about the work of someone who calls the possibility of adequate generalisation into question. Let us risk one of those shifting grounds: When Derrida analyzes philosophical or theoretical texts, however canny they might be, "the scene of writing" is seen to be betrayed rather than declared. When he reads literary or visual texts on the other hand, the scene of writing seems more directly "thematised" in what is being read. Such a difference in treatment is due perhaps to the combination of a stringent subdivision of disciplinary labour by the French Ministry of Education and the corresponding pedagogic system, on the one hand (thus a separation from the ideology of literary production), and the Parisian tradition of non-academic high-journalistic writing on the occasion of literature, on the other. Whatever the case may be, we are not surprised to find Derridean statements such as: "It was not normal that the [dislocation of the founding categories of the language and the grammar of the *epistēmē*] was more secure and more penetrating on the side of literature and poetic writing"[20]; and, "when a writing marks and re-marks this undecidability, its formalising power is greater, even if it is 'literary' in appearance, or apparently the tributary of a natural language, than that of a proposition, logico-mathematical in from, which would not go as far as the former type of mark."[21]

Thus when Derrida wishes to *mime* as he does in *Glas*, the scene of reading and writing, he produces a type of discourse that seems, to the "common experience" which allowed

---

[20] Derrida, *Of Grammatology*, trans. Gayatri Spivak (Baltimore: John Hopkins University Press, 1976) 92.

[21] Derrida, *Dissemination*, 222.

Socrates and Freud to assume the phenomenon of pleasure, like literary discourse. This I think is the case of *Envois*, the first piece in *Le carte postale.*

In the light of Derrida's work, and of Derridean criticism, it is not difficult to understand that traditional phallocentric discourse is marked by, even as it produced, "the name of man." The disclosure of the denegated scene of writing-reading, the acknowledgement that propriation is indeterminate, as undertaken by Derrida, can be seen to articulate a certain "(non)name of woman." I have made the argument in some detail in the previous pages and I think it is a point worth making. At certain moments in this essay, where I comment on the operative importance, in Derrida, of the critique of propriation through the disclosure of the scene of writing-reading, I will simply refer to this (non)naming of woman, in the expectation that the argument will be recalled.

It is already within this expectation, then, that I give below an outline of the scene of writing-reading as deployed by *Envois*:

I. The sender is (always) undecidable. This is paradoxically thematised (I think Derrida would prefer the word "stenographed" or "legended") through the proliferation of plausible biographical detail—Derrida's visit to Yale, Oxford, any many other university towns.[22] The book's "origin" is given in an incident involving Cynthia Chase and Jonathan Culler. Yet since the book may well be written in a code known only to Derrida himself, a singular crypt, those data might be "cited" as part of a game. Derrida invokes this possibility in *Spurs* and elsewhere and many times in this book.[23] I quote an example from the letter-in-excess on the back cover which supplements *Envois*: "This satire of epistolary literature had to be stuffed:

[22] I discuss the implications of "legend" in "Glas-Piece: A Compte Rendu," *Diacritics* 7.3 (1977). "Stenography" would, presumably, yield "a writing in little" a "miniaturisation," even a "metonymic contraction" rather than metaphorisation or symbolisation. Ulmer interestingly suggests that Derrida's trips and returns are a fon:da-ing of the subject, "Post-Age," 43.

[23] Derrida, *Spurs*, 135-39.

with addresses, postal codes, crypted missives, anonymous letters, all seeped in many modes, genres, and tones. I also give false dates, signatures, titles or references, the language "itself." Thus the "postcard, an open letter," is "where the secret appears but undecipherably." It cannot be overemphasised that this stenography mimes the structure of all messages through exaggerated foregrounding, as indeed the word "satire" implies.

II. The receiver is also undecidable. The point is made many a time that the sender does not really know who the receiver really is, if (s)he exists. It is indicated that it might be wrong to think of *Envois* only as a heterosexual exchange.[24] After all, the picture on the many copies of the "same" postcard that the sender sends the receiver (the plurality of the "same" is probably stenographed here) may be of a famous homosexual couple *a tergo*. Yet the "normal" aura of the male-female couple (which can also inhabit a certain sort of homosexual coupling) is very strong in *Envois*. The second person allows a partial cover for "sexual identity." But there are enough adjectives with feminine endings to support the "normative" expectations. (Just as you need satiric exaggeration to stenograph the scene of reading-writing, so do you need a greater effort at dislocation to counteract the sexual "norm" of epistle literature. Plato and Socrates's homosexual aura is supported after all by an abundantly expressed classical Greek cultural "norm." Derrida says of Rousseau—"Rousseau does not doubt that imitation and formal outline are the property of art, and he inherits, as a matter of course, the traditional concept of mimesis" [*Grammatology* 208]; so would I hesitantly advance: the concept of love that Derrida seems to be working with is "the traditional concept of love, which takes for granted that an irrational fixation upon the unique is a property of love." It underscores another feature of the epistolary tradition: he speaks *for* her, she remains mute, reported; written to; Diotima to his Socrates

---

[24] Derrida, *La carte postale*, 57; 60, and passim.

more than Socrates to his Plato.[25] Some of the letters in this collection, have, apparently, been burned. In the matter of burning letters, women cannot be "as subtle" as the philosopher.

> I made a fire: being tired
> Of the white fists of old
> Letters and their death rattle
> When I came too close to the wastebasket.
> What did they know that I didn't?
> Grain by grain, they unrolled
> Sands where a dream of clear water
> Grinned like a getaway car.
> I am not subtle
> Love, love, and well. I was tired
> Of cardboard cartons the colour of cement or a dog pack
> Holding in its hate
> Dully, under a pack of men in red jackets,
> And the eyes and times of the postmarks.
> —Sylvia Plath, "Burning the Letters"

A traditional concept of love seems also to be implicit in the handling of the child as justification or sublation of a relationship. It is the "impossible message" that cannot be a sign. It is the most vivid phantasm. Derrida speaks of the child growing in him but also of "my sorrow I love it as a child of yours" as he walks in and out of Oxford colleges. Although he writes of suckling the child and feeling it breathe in his belly, the banal metaphor of "the philosophic heritage" is too strong

---

[25] The fact that "Derrida" is aware of this problem does not change the reading: "and if because I love them too much I don't publish your letters (which by rights belong to me). They will accuse me of effacing you, silencing you, of making no mention of you. If I publish them, they will accuse me of appropriating myself, of stealing, of raping, of keeping the initiative, of exploiting woman's body, always the prick [*toujours le mec, quoi*]. *Ah, Bettina, mon amour ...*" *La carte postale*, 247. Is this Bettina von Arnim, whose childhood letters to Goethe, collected and published by herself in maturity as *Briefwechsel mit einem Kinde*, are of course always carefully cross-indexed to Goethe, the overshadowing receiver? I am grateful to Sandra Shattuck for this suggestion.

to be ignored, especially when Derrida himself gives it support.[26] When he writes: "without delay we would make ourselves a child, and then come back to sit in that compartment as if nothing had happened,"[27] although I know that Derrida *might* be *parodying* that Platonism which, identifying orgasm with semination—as in the male—declares in the *Laws* that the law of nature is coupling destined for reproduction.[28] I cannot not think that, like Norman Mailer and his thousand ancestors, he might also be *repeating* it; and, repeating his own critique of Freud, I would withhold the benefit of doubt: "description takes sides when it induces a practice, an ethics, and an institution, therefore a politics assuring the tradition of its truth."[29]

This tradition can accommodate the rich specificity of the discourse of erection and countererection which, through the French colloquial verb "bander" (to get a hard on) is made, as usual, to communicate with contraband, the binding of *Bindewort* (copula), the binding of "bound energy" in Freud, and leads to an "économie bindinale" as distinct from an "économie libidinale." Vagina and hymen remain as "supply-side" as the child. I would recommend a more down-to-earth critique to binary oppositions:

> Perhaps masculinist thinking divides life into dualities and dichotomies so that men can get the half that suits them. Children per se have been divided into the concept and the reality. Men are in charge of the concept of the child (they decide when life begins, or which child is "illegitimate," for example), while women are in charge of the reality (morning sickness, toxemia, breech births, cracked nipples, three meals a day, fevers, snowsuits, bathtimes, nightmares, and diapers).[30]

[26] Derrida, *La carte postale*, 29-30; 45; 49; 236; 144, the basic argument in "To Speculate—On 'Freud'"

[27] Derrida, *La carte postale*, 208.

[28] Derrida, *Dissemination*, 152-53.

[29] Derrida, *La carte postale*, 509.

[30] Letty Cottin Pogrebin, "Big Changes in Parenting," *Ms* 10.8 (1982): 46.

There is, so to speak, a rich ore of narrative ingredients to be minded here.

One feels similarly uneasy about the pervasive use of certain words in an over-determined way: "generation" as in computers of succeeding generations, or "reproduction" as in the mechanical reproduction of postcards. One might have expected a deconstitution of the sedimentation of these metaphors, as Derrida recommends in the case of the word "literature": "Literature is annulled [*s'annule*] in its limitlessness … This should not prevent us—on the contrary—to labour [*travailler*] to find out what has been represented and determined under that name—literature—and why."[31] In the same spirit one might suggest that one must labour to find out why technological or mechanical systems that understand themselves at least partially as co-opting human functions have chosen to name themselves from the field of human sexuality, most specifically from human continuity through coupling.

I am not necessarily faulting Derrida here. I am restraining the enthusiasm of readers like the two (women) intellectuals in France who maintained pedagogic discussion that Derrida "wrote like a woman."

> I have also thought that they might consider, reading the scattered mail, that I send myself these letters, all by myself: no sooner dispatched than they arrive (I remain the first and the last to read them) by the trajectory of a receiver-sender "hook-up" ["*combiné*"]. By the banal device, I would be the listener of what I tell myself. And, if you follow, that arrives a priori to its destination … Or perhaps, what amounts to the same thing, in the process of waiting for myself or attaining myself, it arrives everywhere, always here and there at the same time, *fort* and *da* … Then it always arrives at its destination. Eh! That's a good definition of the "ego" ["*moi*"] and the phantasm, at bottom. But I speak of other things, of you and of Necessity.[32]

---

[31] Derrida, *Dissemination*, 223

[32] Derrida, *La carte postale*, 214.

Although the implication in these lines is that "they" would be wrong if they thought these were self-addressed letters, we cannot ignore that possibility either, for it is a good definition of the "ego," an ensemble of a *carte postale* [postal map] where all sorts of things arriving here and there combine to produce an ego-effect. The associations are of Nietzsche hinting at the subject's irreducible plurality when he calls women "his truths."[33] The beloved of *La carte* is then the truth(s) of the subject. One might also think of Mallarmé's "Prose (pour Des Esseintes)"—a poem celebrating Huysman's hero, who put reality "under glass,"[34] where the divided self entertains itself as itself and its sister: "We led our faces (I maintain that we were two) over many charms of the landscape, O sister, comparing yours to them … But this sensible, tender sister carried her glance no further than to smile, how to understand her is an old care of mine."[35] The links between "Mallarmé's" project and "Derrida's" are multiple and abyssal, including of course, the other's existence only as mutism and citation. Here I will comment merely on the last sentence from the passage from *La carte* that I quote above: "But I speak of other things, of you and of Necessity."

If a good definition of the "I" (ego) is a staggered contingent self of postal relays arriving at multiple points at the same time, to say "you," to speak of Necessity, is to contravene that definition by transforming it into a "metaphysical" situation of distinct subjects and objects bound by law. This deliberate contravention is the peculiar position of the philosopher who knowingly mimes a scene that puts the value of knowing in question. He is obliged actively to forget the lesson he has learned, wittingly to attempt to perpetrate autobiography: he is obliged to make "an offer on the scene where attempts multiply

---

33 Cited in Derrida, *Spurs*, 105.
34 Derrida, *Dissemination*, 263.
35 Stéphane Mallarmé's "Prose (pour Des Esseintes)," trans. Anthony Hartley, *Mallarmé* (Harmondsworth: Penguin, 1965) 62-64.

to occupy the place of the *Sa* (understand absolute knowledge [Savior absolu: but of course also the possessed female thing and the Signified—the purloined letter in Lacan's analysis] stenographed in *Glas*), all the places at once, of the seller, the buyer, and the auctioneer": just as "the old man dreams of the complete electro-cardio-encephalo-LOGO-icono-cinemato-biogram."[36] Thus there is a repeated insistence on many metaphysical themes questioned by deconstructive method: the uniqueness and proper-ness of the beloved as addressee, the reference point behind everything that the addresser presents in public (Derrida specifically mentions "The Law of Genre," a lecture given first in Strasbourg in 1979). Such insistence goes against the fractured alterity of the scene, of reading and writing and against the notion that the signature earns its effect because it is irreducibly citable. *La carte postale* is "personalised" for each recipient of a complimentary copy with the handwritten first name of that recipient under "Envois" and Derrida's handwritten signature at the end of the prefatory note. (To anticipate, this also contradicts the propriety of the deconstruction of firsthand and secondhand readings set up on "The factor of truth," and thus once again renders undecidable—"feminises" the very credibility, of Derrida's own argument. And to generalise, it is this irreducible asymmetry and complicity between discourse and example that, moment by moment, seems to tip the narrative toward a mere reversal of the opposition man/woman, rather than present an accomplished displacement, whatever that might be.)

III. Let us resume our description of the deployment of the scene of writing in *Envois*. Not only the sender and the receiver, but the message is too undecidable. The burnt-out blanks of this collection have been arranged according to a code of 52 (twice the number of letters in the Latin alphabet, the number of playing cards [*cartes*] in a pack, does that *mean* anything?)[37] The

---

[36] Derrida, *La carte postale*, 549; 76.

[37] I am grateful to John Willett-Shoptaw for reminding me of the deck of cards. I look forward to the appearance of his work on Joyce in *La carte postale*.

blanks do indeed come at important moments, when a crucial secret seems just about to be revealed. Further, the addressee is repeatedly asked to "guess" important details. The letters are peppered with gestures of deferment (the most common being *"Bon, laissons"*) that remain dead ends. The writer remarks upon the many marks (words and strokes) that he makes upon the actual postcards. Yet we have nothing but the generalised copy on the cover (not identical with the one he projects in a letter, where all the customary information would be inscribed upon Socrates's phallus)[38]; the endpaper: and the coloured reproduction in the corner of page 268. (Again one must insist: this is *not* to say that specifically *writing* cannot capture reality: but to stenograph that *all* discourse is constituted by thus missing the mark.) All discourse must structurally recall "the generality of writing ... hymen, reference set apart [*écartée*] by difference ... And this generality of writing is nothing other than the production, by writing, of generality: the weaving, according to the setting aside of the referent, of that 'veil of generality' which is of no woman in particular."[39] Each particular postcard is different from itself. As such all postcards share the general predication of writing. Derrida's representative postcards *mime* this condition. The undecidability of the message is emphasised by means of a topos: the "author" would like us to think of *Envois* as "preface to a book that I did not write."[40]

IV. In *Envois*, Derrida/sender is not only a writer of letters, but also a reader of the picture postcard. As such, he constructs interpretations of what's going on in the picture that would seem wildly fantastic by the rules of reason. If one consults Freud's account of the dream-work, however, one can surmise that Derrida is foregrounding the notion that the work of the dream resembles and operates *all* reading, however we might want to disavow it in our quest for the proper. We notice in his

[38] Derrida, *La carte postale*, 268-69.
[39] Derrida, *Dissemination*, 242.
[40] Derrida, *La carte postale*, 7.

reading of the postcard the multiple and displaced determinations that Freud calls the "overdetermination" of the dream-text. Words are treated as things and vice versa, as in the case of the dream-rebus. If a "connection" can be made, it is made, and "logical" ones are not privileged. Suffice it here to say that this "im-proper" use of language and utterance acts out a critique of the propriation of meaning. I remind the reader of my opening argument that such a critique might be the woman's mark in the Derridean text.

History is seen here as a series of chain letters written on postcards. This is a version of saying that "truth" is a chain of substitutions, or history a series of displacements within a restrained economy (a lopsided binary system not producing sublated third terms), or the concept (of the) metaphor (and vice versa) is an autobus or a boat that cannot be stopped.[41] The chain is constituted by the possibility of non-arrival, first because the idea of arrival cannot otherwise emerge, and secondly (and more "radically") because all arrivals are irreducibly askew. Such a chain of substitutions and displacements (of senders-receivers-messages and so on) takes place because the origin and the end of anything be they only of an "act" of signification, or of the theory and practice of revolution, cannot be identical. If origin and end were or could be identical, as idealists or socio-political engineers of all types believe (allowing for calculable compensations falls within this belief), there would be no chink out of which history could emerge. History is the difference between origin (*archē*) and end (*telos*), each the postponement and holding-in-reserve of the idealised other. Even the idealisation stops short when it suspects that each end is an abyssal limit, where the proper identity of "propriation" of each and other becomes undecidable. The chain is used to declare that those two "women" at the limit do not exist, that the project remains the (adequate recovery of the) indivisible self-identity of the phallus.

---

[41] Jacques Derrida, "The *Retrait* of Metaphor," *Enclitic* 2.2 (1978): 7.

3

What happens when we read theoretical texts as itineraries of desire? Not a "rejection" of theory, but a recognition that it is subject to production and that therefore its use-value is not *simply* theoretical, explicatory, curative, a rule from above. The author is caught in and enabled by the same net as other men. The net is always that of resistances to abyssal limits.

Freud is in this predicament in *Beyond the Pleasure Principle*, a text that has caused most Freudians some embarrassment, since the master seems to be playing here on the borders of mysticism and biologism. Derrida fixes his glance on the scene of writing betrayed by the text. On the one hand, in each of its seven sections, the essay seems to propose one breakthrough after another from pleasure principle as the last instance to repetition compulsion, thence to the death instinct, next to sex as the drive to life, and finally to the biologism of the last brief chapter, via Aristophanes's myth of the originary unisexual egg. This progression is achieved by postponing difficulties at every step and deciding to move on to a bolder doctrine, a method that can be described as the very *fort:da* game that, Freud concludes, allowed his grandson Ernst to cope with the absence of his mother, Freud's daughter Sophie. It is Freud's contention that Ernst received more pleasure from the *fort* than from the *da*. The un-pleasure of the *fort*, in other words, is, for the sake of the assurance of the pleasure of the *da*, more pleasing than the pleasure "itself." This renders the phenomenal identity of pleasure undecidable: and keeps the game forever in-complete, although Freud insists on the contrary. As Freud recounts the normality of Ernst's game (chosen by Freud in his text after the quick dismissal of the enigma of traumatic behaviour in Section II of *Beyond*), he "identifies" with him as grandfather of the subject. Every move in the game, however, is interpreted with the reported agreement of the mute daughter Sophie. Thus Freud also plays out his role of father of the object (Sophie). He would rather that Ernst had played at railways trains with his bobbin, for then it would have remained securely in his hand and he would not have had to look back. By throwing his reel over the bed and under its skirt Ernst copes with his desire for his mother, brings the bed into his game: by playing at trains with controlling string and back turned, Freud transforms himself from mother's son to psychoanalyst, turns the bed into a couch. (This is akin to the power play over the woman that Derrida notices in Lacan's "Seminar on 'The Purloined Letter.'") Even this inadequate summary shows that the founding of psychoanalysis in Freud's proper name is related by Derrida to the desire for the woman as daughter/mother.

Derrida's reading weaves in and out of *Beyond the Pleasure Principle* with consummate skill. I shall outline three of his conclusions, because they relate to the "name of woman." First, each inconvenient difficulty that Freud bypasses as he pushes his argument by yet another step beyond, is the possibility of an incursion of undecidability in his argument. Each of these steps is an attempt to take a "pas au-delà." By calling his own book "De Socrate à Freud et au-delà," Derrida might be indicating his own inability to step across undecidability and give a proper name to the woman, name his book. (He might, in other words, remain stuck "aux deux-là," beyond.) Each "pas", literally a "step" in French, is also the negative supplement in the compound French negative "ne pas." Thus each step beyond the abyssal limit is itself marked by undecidability.[42] The game remains incomplete.

Indeed, the general method that Freud must employ is also similarly marked by undecidability. Derrida calls it a-thetical, quoting Freud again and again to show Freud's "speculation" is avowedly neither philosophy nor empirical observation. The father of psychoanalysis speculates because he has an "interest": to bring death within the grasp of the proper. Death

---

[42] For an elaboration of this, see Derrida, "Pas I," *Gramma* 3/4 (1976).

is postponed (sent *forth*) by the repetition compulsion so that each individual can articulate his own proper death rather than yield to the impersonality of nature, can write autobiography as autothanatography. But even thus appropriated, death cannot be allowed to win. Freud turns to the *Symposium* and quotes Aristophanes's fable: the unifying sex drive is treated as the final determinant.

Freud seems constrained to overlook the fact that the fable has a conditioning frame in the *Symposium*. It is spoken by Aristophanes, elsewhere described as Socrates's worst detractor. Within the scene of writing of the *Symposium*, the value of the fable is not at all clear. Aristophanes cannot speak when his turn comes because he has the hiccoughs. He is obliged to yield his place and can only speak when he has cured his hiccoughs by sneezing. This is hardly the proper production of a self-adequate truth. Within the dialogue, it seems likely that Aristophanes tells this curious fable because he wishes to be different from the other speakers around the table—the discourse of difference, then, and not of identity. Most importantly, in Socrates's own speech, Diotima seems to contradict Aristophanes's fable. When Aristophanes attempts to answer Socrates, Alcibiades enters and the *Symposium* takes a new turn. At the very end of the dialogue, we see the still sober Socrates convincing the drunken Aristophanes.

In other words, by extracting Aristophanes's account without the multiple frame, Freud is ignoring Socrates.[43] As Derrida writes:

[43] This emphasis on the frame might seem in one way to contradict citationality. Since every utterance is citable the appropriate context seems not to need emphasis. In fact, however, the insistence upon context or frame might mark the displacement of the binary opposition between citationality and contextuality, suggesting that the "appropriate context" itself is no more than one condition of citation. The frame is also what stages a seemingly transparent argument within the scene of writing, thus undoing the opposition between argument and scene. Just as "theory" is always normatised by its "practice," the frame can always be shown to be framed by part of its content (*La carte postale*, 513 n.27). The relationship between this graphic and the positivistic project of Erving Goffman's *Frame Analysis* (New York: Harper Collophon, 1947) is

to omit Socrates when one writes, is not to omit anything or anyone, especially when one writes on the subject of Plato. Especially when one writes on the subject of a dialogue of Plato where Socrates, a Socrates, and the Socrates, is not simply a figure. Of course this omission is not a murder, let us not dramatise. It effaces a singular personage whom Plato writes and describes as a character in the *Symposium* but also as someone who will have made him or allowed him to write without writing himself, the scene of an infinitely complex signature where inscription arrives only to efface itself.[44]

Effacing Socrates, Freud inscribes him all the more. For the ostensible purpose might be to step beyond the Socratic heritage of Plato. Freud speculates upon the view that Plato is the heir of something as mysterious as the biological domain, namely, the Brihadaranyaka Upanishad: "For Plato would not have adopted a story of this kind which had somehow reached him through some oriental tradition—to say nothing of giving it so important a place—unless it had struck him as containing an element of truth."[45]

As surely as Ernst, however, Freud cannot risk an absolute *fort*, the open horizons of biology and "the East." He resists a complete solution [*Lösung*] as surely as, according to his own speculation, the patient might resist analysis by falling back within the repetition compulsion. He conserves the *da* by repeating yet another gesture of the "feminine operation" of undecidability. In the limping short section that serves almost as a postscript to the rest of his book, he makes a declaration of the suspension of belief in all that he has said in *Beyond the Pleasure Principle*. He ends with the supplementary prosthesis of

comparable to the relationship between grammatology and I. J. Gelb's *A Study of Writing: The Foundation of Grammatology* (Chicago: Chicago University Press, 1952), cited in *Of Grammatology*, 323 n.4. I am grateful to Professor Michael Ryan for bringing Goffman's book to my attention.

[44] Derrida, *La carte postale*, 398.

[45] Sigmund Freud, *Standard Edition of the Complete Psychological Works*, trans. James Strachey et al. (London: Hogarth Press, 1964) 18.58.

a repeated citation—*citing* Goethe *citing* the Scriptures recommending a limping gait when a firm tread (beyond?) is made impossible by the nature of the terrain.

Derrida is thus careful to point out that *Beyond the Pleasure Principle* ends in the undecidable folds of "citationality," which, as I have pointed out earlier, is one of the chief arguments in Derrida's "situating" of the propriation of truth. The fold of citationality is marked by the concept-metaphor. I remind the reader of my opening suggestion: such a description here, of the end *Beyond the Pleasure Principle*, might be the description of a text that is operated by the (non)name of woman.

(It is a reminder of the "reality principle" that only in the middle of the next century—after Derrida's death and if the "free market place of ideas" still considers him sufficiently important in the postal relay of the Great homoerotic Tradition from Socrates to Freud and beyond—can a similar reading of the Derridean scene of writing—with the text of "life" crosshatched into the text of "arguments"—of the *fort* of Freud with the *da* of Derrida, be undertaken).

4

"The Factor of Truth," the third essay in *La carte postale*, is well known to most students of Derrida. It was first published in *Poétique* in 1975, and published in English translation in *Yale French Studies* in the same year.[46] As I have already mentioned, the essay is a critique of Jacques Lacan's "Seminar on [Poe's] 'The Purloined Letter.'" Derrida's critique of Lacan can be summarised as follows:

By ignoring the open-ended frame of Poe's story (within the narrative as well as within the trilogy of Poe's tales of

---

[46] The authorised translation of the title is "The Purveyor of Truth." "Purveyor" seems to me to lack the notion that truth can be "situated" as merely a "factor," rather than the end of "signification." On the other hand, the sense of "facteur" as mailman is one of the archaic senses of the English "factor."

detection), Lacan is able to preserve the transcendental status of the phallus. The letter travels from hand to hand in the story. Thus in an intersubjective situation must the signifier be displaced until its true status is revealed: it is the phallus as signifier of the truth that every (male) subject must accede to in order to be inserted into the symbolic order where the signifier always "means" the absence of the signified; the mother (as truth) unveiled shows that she is castrated. Although the phallus as signifier does not symbolise either the penis or the clitoris, in effect, as Derrida argues, it symbolises (the lack of) the penis (in the mother). Thus the phallus, which must arrive at this destination, has a trajectory *proper* to it. And, as Lacan argues, it must also be "indivisible"—the letter even if cut up must remain the *same* letter. This bestowal of propriety and indivisibility idealises the phallus; curiously enough, Lacan names it the "materiality"—the letter as thing—of the signifier.[47] If Lacan had attended to the multiplicity of Poe's frames, he would have seen that rather than the proper trajectory of truth, it is rather the undecidability of the signifier that gives the story its plot: for the letter is constituted in its putative identity by the fact that it can be different from, *improper* to, itself, that it might always not arrive at its destination. In the curious vocabulary of women in the scene of writing, it is indeed the victory of the hymen (which makes defeat or victory undecidable) over the phallus. [48]

[47] A sustained analysis in this direction would certainly question Rosalind Coward's and John Ellis's insistence that "the dialectic of desire as it appears in Lacan is in no way comparable to Hegelian idealism." *Language and Materialism: Development in Semiology and the Theory of the Subject* (London: Routledge, 1977) 108.

[48] Derrida also defends Marie Bonaparte's reading of "The Purloined Letter." Bonaparte did indeed see the significance of the letter as the mother's castration, but she averred that the explanation of truth as castration seemed appropriate only for men. With Ernest Jones and Melanie Klein, whom Lacan also disparages, Bonaparte sees the phallus as "part object" rather than indivisible whole. She sees the button above the chimneypiece where the letter is hung as a clitoris where the phallic signifier is imposed. Lacan follows Baudelaire in misplacing the letter—no mention of the displaced clitoris—

In the end Lacan must read Poe's detective Dupin in two ways: as a dupe and as a super analyst. He implicitly identifies Dupin when he writes, of the Queen's monetary reward to Dupin: "Do we not in fact feel concerned with good reason when for Dupin it is perhaps a matter of withdrawing himself from the symbolic circuit of the letter—we who make ourselves the emissaries of all the purloined letters which at least for a time will be in sufferance with us in the transference. And is it not the responsibility their transference entails, which we neutralise by equating it with the signifier that is the most annihilating of all signification, namely money."[49] Derrida endorses Bonaparte's reading: that Dupin is on the circuit because he desires the (Queen) mother, and the mother rewards him with money in exchange for the penis. According to Derrida, as Freud on the scene of writing of *Beyond the Pleasure Principle*, so Lacan demotes the Queen from mother to patient.

The most interesting addition in this new version of "The Factor of Truth" deals with the relationship between Lacan and Heidegger. Derrida distinguishes between two Heideggers, generally in terms of Heidegger's reading of Nietzsche. In *On Grammatology* the distinction is made without reference to sexual difference.[50] On the other hand, sexual difference becomes the determining factor in establishing this distinction in *Spurs*. It is not surprising that, in these additions to the "Factor," Derrida shows that Lacan relates to the other Heidegger, who "missed the woman in truth's affabulation,

between the two legs of the chimney piece and declaring it to be the phallic signifier disclosing the mother's lack. Cf. Marie Bonaparte, *Life and Works of Edgar Allan Poe*, trans. John Rodker (London: Image Pub. Co., 1949); cited in *La carte postale*, 487. Re "partial objects": type of object towards which the component instincts are directed without this implying that a person as a whole is taken as love-object. Cf. J. Laplanche and J.-B. Pontalis, *The Language of Psycho-Analysis*, trans. Donald Nicholson-Smith (New York: Norton, 1973) 301.

49 Derrida, *La carte postale*, 68.

50 Derrida, *Of Grammatology*, 19-21.

[who] did not ask the sexual question or at least submitted it to the general question of the truth of being."[51]

5

I have suggested a possibly insufficient differentiation in Derrida's handling of child, reproduction, generation. A similar possibility could be charged against Derrida's treatment of the quotation from Crébillon that ends Poe's tale:

—Un dessein si funeste,
S'il n'est digne d'Atrée, est digne de Thyeste.

Derrida does indeed point out that "The Purloined Letter" begins with the indeterminacy of open textuality—in a library—and ends with a citation. If my sustained reminders are plausible,[52] this describes the story as a "feminine operation," in the (non)name of *woman*, an operation which frames the Lacanian account of it as a disclosure of the mother's castration, the realisation of which operates the accession to the name of *man*.

Yet Crébillon's text is itself "citational" of the classical narrative of Atreus and Thyestes. They were brothers, as, on the circuit of the signifier, are the Minister and Dupin. Thyestes is the lover of Atreus's wife and is punished for it. Since one cannot know if Dupin is donning Atreus's or Thyestes's mask in the citation, the duo fill up undecidably the places of the King and the unknown letter-writer—another Atreus-Thyestes pair.

It should be remarked that there is one detail of the mythic narrative that does not fit into the symbology of Poe's story. Atreus punished Thyestes by making him eat his children. The siblings in "The Purloined Letter," fighting over mother's

---

[51] Derrida, *Spurs*, 109.
[52] Derrida, *La carte postale*, see pages 21-25, 27, 33.

phallus and the father's place, do not make Oedipus's mistake but rather learn from it, as on the oedipal scene. They do not breed actual children by the mother. This negative detail would not be perceptible if the Atreus-Thyestes story had not been invoked. I think Derrida is right when he says that Oedipus is complicated in Poe's scene of writing.[53] This particular complication, the manipulation of the Atreus-Thyestes story, dramatises the phallocentric initiation scenario which Freud calls the passage through the Oedipal scene. It acts as a displaced representation of the situation of "the actual" Oedipus, symbolically purged of the violence of crime and punishment. Even if one undertook a deconstruction of the theory of representation by demonstrating that the origin is irreducibly a text, the mechanics of working the phallocentric Oedipal scene *through* (the appropriation of the feminine operation of) citation remains noteworthy.[54]

The scope of this essay will not permit extended consideration of "Du Tout," the interview with René Major that closes *La carte postale*. Here as elsewhere, when Derrida speaks of collaborative or institutional work, it is from a precarious "singular" position. "Affirmative deconstruction" seems not to suggest a micrological inscription as regards collective work.

The "du" in the title carries the ambiguity of the French genitive. The conversation may be part of, or be about, the entire psychoanalytic scene. On the other hand, since "du tout" in French comes after "pas" to emphasise a negation, it might indicate that, like the mothers' sons he discusses here, Derrida too has been attempting to take *pas* after *pas*—step after step— beyond the abyssal limits of theoretical production where reading and writing, fact and fiction, become undecidable. And

---

[53] Derrida, *La carte postale*, 461.

[54] What does it mean to make such an analysis? Dupin corrects the Minister vis-à-vis the Queen. Lacan updates Freud vis-à-vis the Queen's story and Marie Bonaparte. Derrida re-inscribes the Queen, Poe, and Marie Bonaparte on the occasion of Lacan's reading.

this postcard shows either that he could not do it at all, or how those steps relate to the "all" of psychoanalysis. But the relationship is still expressed in terms of the excluded individual (also "plural," of course) who can be neither swallowed nor thrown up, who is inevitable—since you cannot, at the limit, escape avoiding him—and must be "inevited" into psychoanalysts' meetings. Apart from the splendid last sentence about wanting all the places on the circuit that I have already quoted, it seems a bit of a letdown as an endpiece. But then, Derrida might always say it matches Freud's limping clubfoot of a last section in *Beyond* …

6

What we have in *La carte postale*, then, is a spectacle of how a male philosopher trained in the school of Plato and Hegel and Nietzsche and Heidegger acknowledges the importance of sexual difference and tries to articulate the name of woman. He does not deny that he is tied to the tradition. He cannot show his readers womankind made heterogeneous by many worlds and many classes. Although such a philosopher can wish to deconstruct the methodological opposition between empiricism and structuralism, in fact it is a binary opposition he often seems to honour, with the privilege going to structure. One example among many: "The interest of this recurrence [of certain motifs], and of its spacing is not, for us, that of an *empirical* enrichment, of an experimental verification, the illustration of a repetitive insistence. It is *structural*."[55]

Thus it would be unwise to look in Derrida for a deconstruction of the history of the concept "it-woman"—as opposed to "we-men"—where the line between empiricism and structuralism would shift and waver. Yet we might want to attend to him because the tradition that he is thus "feminising" or opening up has been the most prestigious articulation of the

[55] Derrida, *Grammatology*, 162; *La carte postale*, 487.

privileging of man. He thus shows us the dangers of borrowing the methodological imperatives of that tradition uncritically.

It is surely significant that, even today, the men who take to him take everything from him but his project of re-naming the operation of philosophy with the "name" of woman. Although sexual relations of reproduction are still crucial in every arena of politics and economics—and the tradition of love letters has been the most powerful ideological dissimulation of those relations, such letters continue to be considered merely frivolous in a world of bullets and starvation. Although Derrida is using them as texts for interpretation and suggesting their complicity with the objective tradition of intellectual discourse, they can still be dismissed as a mark of bourgeois individualism. It would be absurd to claim that Derrida (like Joyce or Lacan) "writes for the working class." If, however, academic women of the First World observe Derrida's minuet with the epistles of love, we might learn that sexuality, "the woman's role," is not in simple opposition to "real politics," and that a vision that dismisses a man's conduct in love as immaterial to his "practical" stands would not be able to see the generally warping legacy of masculism implicit in the following polarisations:

> Who, among my numerous calumniator and venomous enemies, has ever reproached me of having the vocation of playing the leading rôles of the lover in a second class theatre? And yet, it is true. If those scoundrels were astute, they would have painted on the one side "the conditions of production and circulation (of commodities)" and on the other, me at your feet … Love, not for the being of Feuerbach, not for the transmutation of Molechott, not for the proletariat, but love for the beloved, and particularly for you, makes a man a man.[56]

This, I think, is why Derrida reads great men's letters and writes about them as he writes about their "serious" work. The

---

[56] Marx to Jenny, 21 June, 1856, in Pierre Durand, *La vie amoureuse de Karl Marx* (Paris: Juliard, 1970) 60, 62.

project for *Envois* might have begun in a reading of Plato's Epistles. I have commented on the feminine operation of the simulacrum with reference to "Télépathie," where Derrida speaks "as Freud." It is possible that in *Envois* Derrida speaks "as Plato," exhorting the correspondent to burn the letters, an exhortation only imperfectly obeyed. Perhaps *La carte postale* shows the "true author" of Plato's scene of writing in more than one sense.[57] Let us re-read a bit of the end of "Plato's Pharmacy," where Derrida finishes rereading Plato's "Second Letter," a dispraise of writing, which was not burnt despite the sender's injunction to the receiver, who, after many postal relays, retrieves it from phallogocentrism for the undecidable limit of grammatology:

> And to finish that Second Letter ... Reflect upon this and make care lest at some time in the future you may have to repent of having divulged your views in an unworthy form. The best safeguard is to avoid writing and learn by heart. For it is impossible that what is written not fall into the public domain. That is the reason why I have never written anything these things. There is not, and there never will be a written treatise of Plato's. What are now called his are the work of a Socrates restored to youth and beauty. Farewell; be guided by my advice, and begin now by burning this letter when you have read it through several times ... —I hope this one won't get lost. Quick, a double ... graphite...carbon ... have reread this letter [technology and the psychic machine] ... burn it. There are ashes there. And now one must distinguish, between two repetitions ...[58]

---

[57] There is a distant prefiguration in "Freud and the Scene of Writing," written at least a decade before *Envois*: "And the 'sociology of literature' perceives nothing of the war and ruses where the origin of the work is thus at stake, between the author who reads and the first reader who dictates. The sociality of writing as drama [the scene of writing] requires an entirely different discipline." Derrida, *Writing and Difference*, 227.

[58] Derrida, *Dissemination*, 170-71.

Selected Bibliography
Works on *Giacomo Joyce*

"A Fragment and Four Furrows." *Times Literary Supplement* 23 May 1968: 526.

"La femme d'Ulysse." *Le Figaro Littéraire* 26 février-3 mars 1968: 18.

"Notes on Current Books: Literary Studies." *Virginia Quarterly Review* 44 (Spring 1968): lvii.

"Sinking Stones." *Time* 19 Jan. 1968: 93-94.

Adams, Robert M. "A Very Pretty Piece of Protocol, Mr. Ellmann." *JJQ* 5.1 (1968): 229-31.

Bacigalupo, Massimo. Review of *James Joyce's Italian Connection: The Poetics of the World* by Corinna del Greco Lobner, and *Joyce Studies in Italy (volume 2)* edited by Carla de Petris. *Modern Languuges Review* 86 (Oct. 1991): 988-990.

Barolini, Helen. "The Curious Case of Amalia Popper." *New York Review of Books* 20 Nov. 1969: 44-48.

Benstock, Bernard. "Paname-Turricum and Tarry Easty: James Joyce's *Città Immediata*." *James Joyce 3: Joyce et l'Italie*, eds. Claude Jacquet and Jean-Michel Rabaté. Paris: Lettres Modernes, 1994. 29-38.

Best, Marshall A. "Giacomo Joyce." *Times Literary Supplement* 11 July 1968: 737.

Bilinski, Krzysztof. "Struktura lirycznego mikrofactu *Giacomo Joyce* Jamesa Joyce'a [w Przekladzie Macieja Slomczynskiego]." *Wokol Jamesa Joyce'a: szkice monograficzne.* Ed. Katarzyny

Bazarnik and Finna Fordhama. Kraków: Universitas, 1998. 55-61.

Binni, Francesco. "Introduction to *Giacomo Joyce.*" *James Joyce Poesie e prose*. Milan: Monadori, 1992.

Brancati, Vitaliano. "Ricordo del Professor Joyce." *Nuova Stampa Sera* 30-31 Aug. 1948.

Brown, Richard. "Eros and Apposition: *Giacomo Joyce.*" *Joyce Studies Annual* (1990): 132-141.

Brunazzi, Elizabeth. "'The Voice of an Unseen Reader' in *Giacomo Joyce.*" *The Languages of Joyce: Selected Papers from the 11th International James Joyce Symposium, Venice, 12-18 June 1988*. Eds. Rosa Maria Bosinelli, Carla Marengo Vaglio and Christine van Boheemen. Philadelphia: Benjamins, 1992: 121-6.

Burgess, Anthony. "Portrait of the Artist in Middle Age." *Nation* 4 Mar. 1968: 309-10.

Cherslica, Bruno. *È'tornato Joyce: iconografia triestina per Zois*. Milan: Nuova Rivista Europea, 1992.

Chiabrando, Simonetta. "Tra realità e sogno: un'icona femminile / Between Dream and Reality: A Female Icon." *Le Donne di Giacomo: Il mondo femminile nella Trieste di James Joyce; The Female World in James Joyce's Trieste: Palazzo Costanzi, Trieste, 4 giugno - 15 luglio 1999*. Trieste: Hammerle Editori, 1999. 14-23.

Cixous, Hélène. "Giacomo Joyce: Les sanglots ironiques d'Éros." Rev. of *Giacomo Joyce* by James Joyce. *Le Monde* 17 Aug. 1968: IV. Supplément au numéro 7338 ivc ["Le Monde des Livres"].

Costello, Peter. *James Joyce: The Years of Growth, 1882-1915*. New York: Pantheon Books, 1992.

Crise, Stelio. "Il Triestino James Joyce." *Scritti*. Ed. Elvio Guagnini. Trieste: Einaudi, 1994.

Crise, Stelio. Commentary. *È'tornato Joyce: iconografia triestina per Zois*. By Bruno Cherslica. Milan: Nuova Rivista Europea, 1992.

Crivelli, Renzo and John McCourt, eds. *Le Donne di Giacomo: Il mondo femminile nella Trieste di James Joyce; The Female World in James Joyce's Trieste: Palazzo Costanzi, Trieste, 4 giugno - 15 luglio 1999*. Trieste: Hammerle Editori, 1999.

Crivelli, Renzo. "Annie, la prima ispiratrice di *Giacomo Joyce* / Annie, the First Inspiration behind *Giacomo Joyce*." *Le Donne di Giacomo: Il mondo femminile nella Trieste di James Joyce; The Female World in James Joyce's Trieste: Palazzo Costanzi, Trieste, 4 giugno - 15 luglio 1999*. Trieste: Hammerle Editori, 1999. 49-54.

Crivelli, Renzo. *Itinerari Triestini James Joyce Triestine Itineraries*, trans. John McCourt. Trieste: MGS Press, 1996.

Curci, Roberto. "Chi? Quella 'fiamma' triestina." *Il Piccolo di Trieste* 13 Jan. 1991.

Curci, Roberto. "Emma, quasi un romanzo (d'appendice) / Emma, Almost a (Serial) Novel." *Le Donne di Giacomo: Il mondo femminile nella Trieste di James Joyce; The Female World in James Joyce's Trieste: Palazzo Costanzi, Trieste, 4 giugno - 15 luglio 1999*. Trieste: Hammerle Editori, 1999. 55-59.

Curci, Roberto. *Tutto è sciolto: L'Amore triestino di Giacomo Joyce*. Trieste: Edizioni Lint, 1996.

De Petris, Carla, ed. *Joyce Studies in Italy*, 2. Rome: Bulzoni Editore, 1988.

De Petris, Carla. "Giacomo e i suoi fratelli: le voci del bog." *MondOperaio: Rivista mensile del Partito socialista italiano* 44.3 (Mar. 1991): 94-97.

De Tuoni, Dario. *Ricordo di Joyce e Trieste*. Milan: All'insegna del Pesce d'oro, 1966.

Delville, Michel. "'At the center, what?' *Giacomo Joyce*, Roland Barthes, and the Novelistic Fragment." *JJQ* 36.4 (Summer 1999): 765-80.

Delville, Michel. *The American Prose Poem: Poetic Form and the Boundaries of Genre*. Gainesville: University Press of Florida, 1998.

Derrida, Jacques. "Envois." *The Post Card: From Socrates to Freud and Beyond*, trans. Alan Bass. Chicago: University of Chicago Press, 1987.

Ellmann, Richard. Introduction. *Giacomo Joyce* by James Joyce. New York: Viking, 1968: xi-xxvi.

Ellmann, Richard. *James Joyce*. New York: Oxford University Press, 1959; revised, 1982.

Ellmann, Richard. Response to Helen Barolini, "The Curious Case of Amalia Popper." *New York Review of Books* 20 Nov. 1969: 48-51.

Fremont-Smith, Eliot. "New Year's Day—And a New James Joyce." *New York Times* 1 Jan. 1968: 13.

Geissman, Erwin W. "James Joyce." *Catholic World* June 1968: 139-40.

Gillespie, Michael Patrick. "A Critique of Ellmann's List of Joyce's Trieste Library." *JJQ* 19.1 (1981): 27-36.

Gillespie, Michael Patrick. "Joyce's Trieste Library and His Intellectual Backgrounds, 1904-1920." *Dissertation Abstracts International* 41.9 (Mar. 1981): 4030A.

Gillespie, Michael Patrick. Rev. of *James Joyce: Poems and Shorter Fiction: Including Epiphanies, Giacomo Joyce and A Portrait of the Artist,* eds. Richard Ellmann, A. Walton Litz and John Whittier-Ferguson. *JJQ* 29.2 (1992): 432-6.

Glasheen, Adaline. Review Article. *A Wake Newsletter* 5 (June 1968): 35-47.

Guidoni, Elise. "A proposito de: Giacomo: El texto secreto de Joyce: Prologo y version anotada de Liliana Heer y J.C. Martini Real." *Tokonoma: Traduccion y Literatura* 5 (1997): 102-5.

Hartshorn, Peter. *James Joyce and Trieste.* Westport CT: Greenwood Press, 1997.

Hodgart, Matthew. "Portrait of the Artist as a Middle-Aged Adulterer." *New York Review of Books* 29 Feb. 1968: 3.

Hollander, John. "The Dark Lady." *Partisan Review* 35 (Summer 1968): 459-62.

Hughes, Eileen Lanouette. "The Mystery Lady of *Giacomo Joyce.*" *Life* 2 Feb. 1968: 36.

Jacquet, Claude and Jean-Michel Rabaté, eds. *James Joyce 3: Joyce et l'Italie.* Paris: Lettres Modernes, 1994.

Joyce, James. *Araby,* traduzione e biografia essenziale di Amalia Popper, nota di Stelio Crise. Rome: Ibiskos editrice, 1935; 1991.

Kenner, Hugh. "The English Teacher Who Wrote *Ulysses.*" *Book World* 11 Feb. 1968: 8.

Kitazawa, Shigehisa. "Giacomo Joyce: Jigyakuteki Ai no Etsuraku." *Joyce kara Joyce e*, ed. Yukio Suzuki. Tokyo: Tokyodo Shuppan, 1982: 197-203.

Kresh, Paul. "A Gulliver Exposed to Lilliputian Arrows." *Saturday Review* 25 May 1968: 23-24.

Laporte, Neurine W. "A Word Index to Giacomo Joyce." *The Analyst* 26 (Sept. 1971): 1-21.

Levin, Harry. "Love Letter." *New York Times Book Review* 21 Jan. 1968: 22.

Maddocks, Melvin. "Joyce's Poem Unspoken." *Christian Science Monitor* 18 Jan. 1968: 11.

Mahaffey, Vicki. "Fascism and Silence: The Coded History of Amalia Popper." *JJQ* 32.3-4 (1995): 501-22.

Mahaffey, Vicki. "Giacomo Joyce," *A Companion to Joyce Studies*, eds. Zack Bowen and James F. Carens. Westport CT: Greenwood, 1984: 387-420.

Mahaffey, Vicki. "James Joyce in Transition: A Study of *A Portrait of the Artist as a Young Man, Giacomo Joyce, Exiles* and *Ulysses.*" *Dissertation Abstracts International* 41:7 (Jan. 1981): 3102A-3103A.

Mahaffey, Vicki. "Joyce's Shorter Works." *The Cambridge Companion to James Joyce*, ed. Derek Attridge. Cambridge: Cambridge University Press, 1990: 185-211.

Mahaffey, Vicki. "The Case Against Art: Wunderlich on Joyce," *Critical Inquiry*, 17 (1991), 667-692.

Mahaffey, Vicki. *States of Desire: Wilde, Yeats, Joyce and the Irish Experiment*. Oxford: Oxford University Press, 1998.

Marengo Vaglio, Carla. "*Giacomo Joyce* or the *Vita Nuova.*" *Fin de Siècle and Italy*. Ed. Franca Ruggieri. Joyce Studies in Italy, 5. Rome: Bulzoni Editore, 1998. 91-106.

Marengo Vaglio, Carla. "Trieste as a Linguistic Melting-Pot." *James Joyce 3: Joyce et l'Italie,* eds. Claude Jacquet and Jean-Michel Rabaté. Paris: Lettres Modernes, 1994. 55-74.

Martella, Giuseppe. "*Giacomo Joyce*: Hypertext and Wisdom Literature." *Classic Joyce*. Eds. Franca Ruggieri et al. Joyce Studies in Italy, 6. Rome: Bulzoni Editore, 1999. 319-37.

Matteo, Sante. "How Giacomo Taught James to Become Joyce." *RLA: Romance Languages Annual* 8 (1996): 232-37.

McArthur, Murray. "The Example of Joyce: Derrida Reading Joyce." *JJQ* 32.2 (1995): 227-41.

McCourt, John. "Amalia Popper: 'Il fantasma nello specchio' / Amalia Popper: 'The Ghost in the Mirror'." *Le Donne di Giacomo: Il mondo femminile nella Trieste di James Joyce; The Female World in James Joyce's Trieste: Palazzo Costanzi, Trieste, 4 giugno - 15 luglio 1999*. Trieste: Hammerle Editori, 1999. 60-65.

McCourt, John. "The Importance of Being Giacomo." *Joyce Studies Annual* 11 (2000): 4-26.

McCourt, John. *James Joyce: A Passionate Exile*. London: Orion, 1999.

McCourt, John. *The Years of Bloom: James Joyce in Trieste 1904-1920*. Dublin: The Lilliput Press, 1999.

Melchiori, Giorgio. "Mr. Bloom in Venice." *JJQ* 27.1 (1989): 121-4.

Nichols, Lewis. "American Notebook." *New York Times Book Review* 8 Oct. 1967: 66.

Nickson, Richard. "Joyce's *Giacomo Joyce*." *Explicator* 28 (1969): Item 38.

Owen, Rodney. "James Joyce and the Beginning of *Ulysses*: 1912 to 1917." Ph.D. dissertation, University of Kansas, 1980.

Pallotti, Donatella. "'An order in every way appropriate': The Spacial Arrangement of *Giacomo Joyce*." *Mnema. Per Lino Falzon Santucci*. Ed. Paola Pugliatti. Messina: Armando Siciliano, 1997. 293-316.

Pallotti, Donatella. "'everintermutuomergent': The 'cobweb (hand)writing' of *Giacomo Joyce*." *Classic Joyce*. Eds. Franca Ruggieri et al. Joyce Studies in Italy, 6. Rome: Bulzoni Editore, 1999. 339-52.

Pissarello, Giulia. "'Who?' *Giacomo Joyce* di James Joyce." *La performance del testo*. Eds. Franco Marucci and Adriano Bruttini. Siena: Ticci, 1986: 51-58.

Pissarello, Giulia. "'Who?' Giacomo Joyce di James Joyce; Atti del VII Cong. Nazionale dell'Assn. It. di Anglistica, Siena, 2-4 Nov. 1984." *La performance del testo*. Ed. Franco Marucci and Adriano Bruttini. Siena: Ticci, 1986. 51-58.

Power, Henriette Lazaridis. "Incorporating *Giacomo Joyce*" *JJQ* 28 (1991): 623-30.

Pugliatti, Paola. "'Nookshotten': The Text Known as *Giacomo Joyce*." *Classic Joyce*. Eds. Franca Ruggieri et al. Joyce Studies in Italy, 6. Rome: Bulzoni Editore, 1999. 293-301.

Raymont, Henry. "MS. of a Joyce Autobiographical Love Story Found." *New York Times* 28 Sept. 1967: 1.

Risolo, Michele. "Mia moglie e Joyce." *Il Corriere della sera* 27 Feb. 1969: 11.

Risolo, Michele. Response to "Casanova senza qualità." *L'Espresso* 24 Nov. 1968: 3.

Ruggieri, Franca et al., eds. *Classic Joyce*. Joyce Studies in Italy, 6. Rome: Bulzoni Editore, 1999.

Scholes, Robert. "*Giacomo* once again." *JJQ* 5.1 (1968): 234-35.

Seed, David. Rev. of *James Joyce: Poems and Shorter Fiction: Including Epiphanies, Giacomo Joyce and A Portrait of the Artist*, eds. Richard Ellmann, A. Walton Litz and John Whittier-Ferguson. *Notes and Queries* 38.4 (1991): 553-4.

Senn, Fritz. "Some Further Notes on *Giacomo Joyce*." *JJQ* 5 (1968) 233-6.

Sokolov, Raymond A. "Joyce's Toccata." *Newsweek* 22 Jan. 1968: 90.

Sonne, Jørgen. "Joyce dukker op: Til *Giacomo Joyce* 1914/1968." *Horisonter: Introduktioner of essays*, ed. Jørgen Sonne. Copenhagen: Munksgaard, 1973: 139-43.

Spivak, Gayatri. "Love Me, Love My Ombre, Elle." *Diacritics* 14.4 (1984): 19-36.

Thompson, R.J. Review of *James Joyce and Trieste* by Peter Hartshorn. *Choice* 35.9 (1998): 1534.

Updike, John. "Questions Concerning *Giacomo*." *New Yorker* 6 Apr. 1968: 167-74.

Valente, Joseph. "Dread Desire: Imperialist Abjection in *Giacomo Joyce*." *James Joyce and the Problem of Justice: Negotiating Sexual and Colonial Difference*. Cambridge: Cambridge University Press, 1995: 67-131.

Wallace, Clare. "Desire and the Machinations of the Gaze in *Giacomo Joyce*." *Litteraria Pragensia* 9.17 (1999): 50-9.

Notes on Contributors

Louis Armand directs the Intercultural Studies programme in the Philosophy Faculty of Charles University, Prague. His books include *Technē: James Joyce, Hypertext and Technology* (2003) and *Incendiary Devices: Discourses of the Other* (2006). He is the editor of *Hypermedia Joyce Studies*.

Sheldon Brivic teaches at Temple University. His books include *Joyce between Freud and Jung* (1980), *Joyce the Creator* (1985), *The Veil of Signs: Joyce, Lacan, and Perception* (1991), and *Joyce's Waking Women: An Introduction to Finnegans Wake* (1995).

Richard Brown is Chair of English at the University of Leeds. He is the author of *James Joyce and Sexuality* and *James Joyce: A Post-Culturalist Perspective*. He is the co-editor of the *James Joyce Broadsheet*.

Renzo Crivelli is Professor of English at Trieste University. His books include *Itinerari Triestini James Joyce Triestine Itineraries* (1996). He is the director of the literary periodical *Prospero*.

Hélène Cixous is Professor of English at the University of Paris VIII. She is the author of *The Exile of James Joyce* (1972) and *Prénoms de personne* (1974), as well as numerous books on literary and feminist theory and many novels, plays and other literary works.

Michel Delville directs the Centre Interdisciplinaire de Poétique Appliquée at the University of Liège, Belgium. His books include *The American Prose Poem: Poetic Form and the Boundaries of Genre* and *Postwar American Poetry: The Mechanics of the Mirage*.

Murray McArthur is Associate Professor and Chair of English at the University of Waterloo, Canada. He is the author of *Stolen Writings: Blake's Milton, Joyce's Ulysses, and the Nature of Influence*.

John McCourt teaches at Trieste University and is the co-ordinator of the Trieste James Joyce Summer School. His books include *James Joyce: A Passionate Exile* and *The Years of Bloom: James Joyce in Trieste 1904-1920*.

Vicki Mahaffey is Associate Professor of English at the University of Pennsylvania. Her books include *Reauthorizing Joyce* and *States of Desire: Wilde, Yeats, Joyce and the Irish Experiment*.

Kevin Nolan co-directs the Cambridge Conference of Contemporary Poetry and edits its translation series. His books include translations of Pierre Alferi and Philippe Beck, and *The Translations of Frank O'Hara* (ed.).

M.E. Roughley is a lecturer in literature and cultural studies in the Norwegian Studies Centre at the University of York. She has published on Djuna Barnes, Virginia Woolf, James Joyce and Julia Kristeva.

Fritz Senn is Director of the Zürich James Joyce Foundation and a founding member and former president of the International James Joyce Foundation. His books include *A Conceptual Guide to Finnegans Wake* (ed. with Michael Begnal) and *Inductive Scrutinies: Focus on Joyce* (ed. with Christine O'Neill). He is a former editor of *A Wake Newslitter* and the *JJQ*.

Gayatri Chakravorty Spivak is Professor of English and Comparative Literature at Columbia University. Her books include the translation of Jacques Derrida's *Of Grammatology* (1974) and *In Other Worlds: Essays in Cultural Politics* (1987)

Joseph Valente teaches at the University of Illinois at Urbana-Champaign. His books include *James Joyce and the Problem of Justice: Negotiating Sexual and Colonial Difference* (1995). He is the editor of *Quare Joyce* and co-editor of *Disciplinarity at the Fin de Siècle*.

Clare Wallace is a senior lecturer at Charles University and the University of New York, Prague. Her books include *Suspect Cultures* (2006), *Global Ireland* (ed. with Ondřej Pilný; 2005) and *Monologues* (ed., 2006).

Index